Deep South

Paul Theroux is the author of many highly acclaimed books. His novels include *The Lower River* and *The Mosquito Coast*. His travel books include *Ghost Train to the Eastern Star* and *Dark Star Safari*. He lives in Hawaii and on Cape Cod.

PAUL THEROUX

Deep South

FOUR SEASONS
ON BACK ROADS

HAMISH HAMILTON
an imprint of
PENGUIN BOOKS

HAMISH HAMILTON

UK | USA | Canada | Ireland | Australia
India | New Zealand | South Africa

Hamish Hamilton is part of the Penguin Random House group of companies
whose addresses can be found at global.penguinrandomhouse.com.

Penguin
Random House
UK

First published in the United States of America by Houghton Mifflin Harcourt 2015
First published in Great Britain by Hamish Hamilton 2015
This edition published by Penguin Group (Australia) 2015

1 3 5 7 9 10 8 6 4 2

Portions of this book appeared in *Smithsonian* magazine.
Some names in the text have been changed in the interest of privacy.

Printed and bound in Australia by Griffin Press

A CIP catalogue record for this book is available from the British Library

ISBN: 978–0–241–14673–6

penguin.com.au

To the memory of George Davis (1941–2013) of Medford, Massachusetts—athlete, traveler, teacher, civil rights stalwart, unsung hero of Selma's Bloody Sunday—in gratitude for fifty years of friendship

"We felt like we were alone and couldn't make a difference. But what happened with the movement? People grouped together. It was a beautiful thing."

On the red clay roads of the African bush among poor and overlooked people, I often thought of the poor in America, living in just the same way, precariously, on the red roads of the Deep South, on low farms, poor pelting villages, sheepcotes, and mills — people I knew only from books, as I'd first known Africans — and I felt beckoned home.

— *The Last Train to Zona Verde:*
My Ultimate African Safari (2013)

In this preposterous, unclassifiable book of my *Travels,* the thread of the stories and observations does not so much break as become intertwined, and in such a manner that, I am fully aware, much patience is needed to unravel and trace it in such an untangled skein.

—Almeida Garrett
(João Baptista da Silva Leitão),
Travels in My Homeland
(*Viagens na Minha Terra*, 1846)

Contents

· PART ONE ·

___

Fall: "You Gotta Be Going There to Get There"

The stranger filleth the eye.

— Arab proverb, quoted by Richard Burton,
First Footsteps in East Africa (1856)

Be Blessed: "Ain't No Strangers Here"

In Tuscaloosa, Alabama, on a hot Sunday morning in early October, I sat in my car in the parking lot of a motel studying a map, trying to locate a certain church. I was not looking for more religion or to be voyeuristically stimulated by travel. I was hoping for music and uplift, sacred steel and celebration, and maybe a friend.

I slapped the map with the back of my hand. I must have looked befuddled.

"You lost, baby?"

I had driven from my home in New England, a three-day road trip to another world, the warm green states of the Deep South I had longed to visit, where "the past is never dead," so the man famously said. "It's not even past." Later that month, a black barber snipping my hair in Greensboro, speaking of its racial turmoil today, laughed and said to me, in a sort of paraphrase of that writer whom he'd not heard of and never read, "History is alive and well here."

A church in the South is the beating heart of the community, the social center, the anchor of faith, the beacon of light, the arena of music, the gathering place, offering hope, counsel, welfare, warmth, fellowship, melody, harmony, and snacks. In some churches, snake handling, foot washing, and glossolalia too, the babbling in tongues like someone spitting and gargling in a shower stall under jets of water.

Poverty is well dressed in churches, and everyone is approachable. As a powerful and revealing cultural event, a Southern church service is on a par with a college football game or a gun show, and there are many of them. People say, "There's a church on every corner." That is also why, when a church is bombed—and this was the fiftieth anniversary of the bombing of the sixteenth Street Baptist Church in Birmingham, where four little girls were murdered—the heart is torn out of a congregation, and a community plunges into pure anguish.

"You lost?"

Her voice had been so soft I had not realized she'd been talking to me. It was the woman in the car beside me, a sun-faded sedan with a crushed and cracked rear bumper. She was sipping coffee from a carryout paper cup, her car door swung open for the breeze. She was in her late forties, perhaps, with blue-gray eyes, and in contrast to the poor car she was dressed beautifully in black silk with lacy sleeves, a big flower pinned to her shoulder, wearing a white hat with a veil that she lifted with the back of her hand when she raised the coffee cup to her pretty lips, leaving a puckered kiss-daub of purple lipstick on the rim.

I said I was a stranger here.

"Ain't no strangers here, baby," she said, and gave me a merry smile. The South, I was to find, was one of the few places I'd been in the world where I could use the word "merry" without sarcasm. "I'm Lucille."

I told her my name and where I wanted to go, the Cornerstone Full Gospel Baptist Church, on Brooksdale Drive.

She was quick to say that it was not her church, but that she knew the one. She said the name of the pastor, Bishop Earnest Palmer, began to give me directions, and then said, "Tell you what."

One hand tipping her veil, she stared intently at the rim of her cup. She paused and drank the last of her coffee while I waited for another word.

"Shoot, it's easier for me to take you there," she said, then used the tip of her tongue to work a fleck of foam from her upper lip. "I don't have to meet my daughter for another hour. Just follow me, Mr. Paul."

I dogged the crushed rear bumper of her small car for about three miles, making unexpected turns, into and out of subdivisions of small bungalows that had been so hollowed out by a devastating tornado the previous year, they could accurately be described as fistulated and tortured. In the midst of this scoured landscape, on a suburban street, I saw the church steeple, and Lucille slowed down and pointed, and waved me on.

As I passed her to enter the parking lot, I thanked her, and she gave me a wonderful smile, and just before she drove on she said, "Be blessed."

That seemed to be the theme in the Deep South: kindness, generosity, a welcome. I had found it often in my traveling life in the wider world, but I found so much more of it here that I kept going, because the good will was like an embrace. Yes, there is a haunted substratum of darkness in Southern life, and though it pulses through many interactions, it takes a long while to perceive it, and even longer to understand.

I sometimes had long days, but encounters like the one with Lucille always lifted my spirits and sent me deeper into the South, to out-of-the-way churches like the Cornerstone Full Gospel, and to places so obscure, such flyspecks on the map, they were described in the rural way as "you gotta be going there to get there."

After circulating awhile in the Deep South I grew fond of the greetings, the hello of the passerby on the sidewalk, and the casual endearments, being called baby, honey, babe, buddy, dear, boss, and often, sir. I liked "What's going on, bubba?" and "How y'all doin'?" The good cheer and greetings in the post office or the store. It was the reflex of some blacks to call me "Mr. Paul" after I introduced myself with my full name ("a habit from slavery" was one explanation). This was utterly unlike the North, or anywhere in the world I'd traveled. "Raging politeness," this extreme friendliness is sometimes termed, but even if that is true, it is better than the cold stare or the averted eyes or the calculated snub I was used to in New England.

"One's supreme relation," Henry James once remarked about traveling in America, "was one's relation to one's country." With this in mind, after having seen the rest of the world, I had planned to take one long trip through the South in the autumn, before the presidential election of 2012, and write about it. But when that trip was over I wanted to go back, and I did so, leisurely in the winter, renewing acquaintances. That was not enough. I returned in the spring, and again in the summer, and by then I knew that the South had me, sometimes in a comforting embrace, occasionally in its frenzied and unrelenting grip.

Wendell Turley

A week or more before I'd met Lucille, past ten o'clock on a dark night, I had pulled up outside a minimart and gas station near the town of Gadsden in northeastern Alabama.

"Kin Ah he'p you," a man said from the window of his pickup truck. He had that tipsy querying Deep South manner of speaking that was so ponderous, fuddled beyond reason, I half expected him to plop forward drunk after he'd asked the question. But he was being friendly. Stepping out of his darkened, oddly painted pickup and gaining his footing, he swallowed a little, his lower lip drooping and damp. He finished his sentence, "In inny way?"

I said I was looking for a place to stay.

He held a can of beer but it was unopened. He had oyster eyes and was jowly and, though sober, looked unsteady. He ignored my appeal. I was thinking how now and then the gods of travel seem to deliver you into the hands of an apparently oversimple stereotype, which means you have to look very closely to make sure this is not the case—the comic, drawling Southerner, loving talk for its own sake.

"Ah mo explain something to you," he said.

"Yes?"

"Ah mo explain the South to you."

In my life as a traveler this was a first. From a great blurring distance, people sometimes say, "This is how things are in Africa," or "China's on the move," and similar generalizations, but close-up never something so ambitious as, "I'm going to explain this entire region to you," promising particulars.

"I'm just passing through. Never been here before. I'm a Yankee, heh-heh."

"Ah knew that from your way of talking," he said, "and from the plates on your vehicle."

I told him my name and he extended his free hand.

"Ahm Wendell Turley. Ah have a business here in Gadsden. This vehicle is mah beater. Ah done that mahself."

He was referring to the body of his old olive-colored pickup truck, stenciled all over with brown and green maple leaves.

"Camo," he said. "This here I use for hunting deer."

"Many deer around here?"

"Minny."

And now I noticed that the pocket of his shirt was embroidered *Roll*

Tide Roll, the slogan of the University of Alabama football team, passionately supported by Alabamians, some of whom I'd seen with the scarlet letter *A* tattooed on their neck, in homage. This seemed a way of reclaiming the true meaning of the word "fan," which is short for "fanatic."

"What were you going to explain to me about the South, Wendell?"

"Ah mo tell you."

To a traveler, a stranger in this landscape, and especially one who is hoping to write about the trip, a man like Wendell is welcome and well met — patient, friendly, expansive, hospitable, and humorous in his manner. The man was a goober and a gift, especially late at night on a back road.

"What the hail . . ."

Before he could say more, a low-slung and rusted Chevrolet drew up beside us, loud hip-hop blaring from the open windows, and I caught the line "Have these niggas just waiting for a favor . . ."

A man in a greasy hat with its visor turned sideways swung his legs out and stood, leaving the engine running and the door open, so the music was amplified by the gaping doorway. Coarse tufts of stuffing were visible in the burst-open upholstery of the driver's seat.

Wendell widened his oyster eyes and said softly, as though to reassure me, "Ah know that there man."

The man was red-eyed and unshaven and looked menacing, but seeing Wendell, he saluted clumsily and showed the gaps in his teeth.

"What's going on?" the man said, but kept walking.

"How y'all doin'?" Wendell said, and went silent.

"It's all good, brother."

"I hear ya."

We waited, the noise from the car washing over us, echoing in the night-black trees around the parking lot, and waited more until the man in the twisted cap left the minimart with a six-pack of beer, heaved himself into his car, reversed into the darkness, and took the howling with him.

"You were saying, Wendell?"

"Ah'll tell you," he said, "'bout the South." He leaned toward me, speaking close to my face and very slowly. "We good people. We not educated people like you people up north. But we good people. We God-fearing people." He squinted and seemed to search his memory for an example, then said, "It takes some education to ask questions like, Do God really exist?"

"I suppose so." And I thought, He did not say *edjumacation*.

"Nemmine! We don't ask no questions like that in the South. But we good people." He braced himself and stood a bit taller to deliver another thought, which he did with deliberation. "Not one person in the South, black or white, will allow y'all to leave they home without offering y'all something to eat—a meal, or a sandwich, or peanuts, or anything." In a slow and certain voice he said, "They will feed you, sir."

"Tell me why."

"'Cause it's the only right thing to do."

"That's hospitality," I said.

"That's hospitality! And when y'all come back to Gadsden, you stop on over and see me and Sandy, and we'll eat something." He put his free hand on my shoulder. "Ah only just met you, but Ah can tell y'all an educated man. You are good folks. Ah mo head on home right now and tell Sandy."

And then he warned me against staying the night in Gadsden, but to drive on to Fort Payne, where I'd find a better-quality motel, but that when I came back, he and Sandy would be happy to host me.

"Which direction is Fort Payne?"

Wendell raised his head, faced the darkness and the obscured on-ramp, and pointed with his lips.

"*Tell about the South. What's it like there. What do they do there. Why do they live there. Why do they live at all.*"

What Wendell had said, and even the way he had clamped his hand on my shoulder, had made an impression, put me in mind of the much-quoted lines (it's a Canadian, Shreve, who's speaking) from Faulkner's *Absalom, Absalom!*—to which Faulkner, the master of decorous obliquity in a whole long shelf of books, attempts various replies. But I felt Wendell had an answer, and I drove into the night happier.

The poor, having little else, keep their culture intact as part of their vitality, long after the well-off have dumped it. This was one of the many encounters that showed me how a traveler may arrive and slip into the rhythm of life in the South, the immersive power of its simple welcome amounting to a spell.

Road Candy: Traveling in America

Most travel narratives, perhaps all of them, even the classics, describe the miseries and splendors of going from one remote place to another. The quest, the getting there, the difficulty of the road, is the story; the journey not the arrival matters, and most of the time the traveler — the traveler's mood, especially — is the subject of the whole business. I have made a career out of this sort of slogging and self-portraiture, and so have many others in the old laborious look-at-me way that informs travel writing. As V. S. Naipaul shrewdly explained in *A Turn in the South,* the traveler is "a man defining himself against a foreign background."

But traveling in America is unlike traveling anywhere else on earth. Early on in my trip to the Deep South I stopped at a convenience store in a small Alabama town, aiming to buy a soft drink. But I had really stopped because the store sat on its own small slab of cement, on a side road, and was made of weathered boards, a rusted Coca-Cola sign nailed to the wall. On the front porch — a roof over it — was a bench where I could sit and drink and make notes. A store with a homely, enduring look like that had to be run by someone who'd talk.

A man of sixty or so, standing behind the counter wearing a baseball hat, greeted me when I entered. I took a bottle of soda from the cooler, and paying for it, I saw that the counter was crowded with glass bowls — like goldfish bowls — filled with small loose pieces of wrapped candy. It was a glimpse of my youth: Sam's Store, on the corner of Webster and Fountain streets in Medford (circa 1949), the countertop of jars brimming with penny candy.

"When I was a boy . . . ," I said, and the man listened politely to my memory. I finished saying, "We used to call it penny candy."

"Road candy," he said. "Eat it while you're driving."

Road candy seemed to me a perfect summing up of the pleasures of driving through the Deep South. What I saw, what I experienced, the freedom of the trip, the people I met, the things I learned: my days were filled with road candy.

Breezing from place to place on wonderful roads seemed so sweet, so simple. Such travel is full of deceptions, though — especially that one, that the great roads are proof of prosperity and make America easily knowable. The paradox is that many roads in America lead to dead ends. The arrival is the object and the challenge, often in unexpected ways, in a country with an improvisational culture that makes a fetish of despising regulation. I was to discover that America is accessible, but Americans in general are not; they are harder to know than any people I've traveled among.

The ease of travel in America is so complete that any conventional narrative cannot be about the journey at all, not about locomotion, the ordeal of getting from one place to another, which is often the heart of the travel narrative. The American road is so well made and lacking in obstacles that it disappears from the traveler's tale, except when it is thanked as a benefit, with the same gratitude as that of Prince Husayn, of his magic carpet: "mean to look at, but such are its properties that should any sit thereon and wish in mind to visit country or city, he will at once be carried thither in ease and safety" (Richard Burton, *Supplemental Nights*).

A dangerous or difficult road can be the subject of a journey; the magic carpet isn't. The classic travel story is a tale of risk, often a quest, a retelling in trekker's gear of the *Odyssey,* and concerned with enduring the vicissitudes of a quest, and then getting home safely. Such a book becomes a mimicry of many legends, but particularly of the traveler beset by obstacles — demons, witches, bandits, whirlpools, the temptations of sirens, a chronicle of delays. "We walk through ourselves," Stephen Dedalus says in *Ulysses,* summing up the travel experience, "meeting robbers, ghosts, giants, old men, young men, wives, widows, brothers-in-love. But always meeting ourselves." The torments of the road are the tale, and the getting there is the subject of most travel books, from the seventeenth-century Bashō's *Narrow Road to the Deep North* and Parkman's *The Oregon Trail* (1849) to the great travel books of our own day: the vomiting camels of Thesiger's *Arabian Sands,* the muddy Congo paths of Redmond O'Hanlon's *No Mercy,* the flitting and plodding of Bruce Chatwin in Patagonia — and, I

should add, to a lesser degree, nearly everything in travel that I have written. The travel book is, typically, about struggling to a destination.

But in America the journey is a picnic: traveling anywhere, particularly in the empire of the open road, is so easy as to be superfluous to
write about. The challenging fact is that, because of our superior con-
nectedness, one cannot write about the United States in the way one does
any other country — certainly it is cheating to pretend that it is any sort of
logistical ordeal.

"The land was big and varied, in parts wild. But it had nearly everywhere been made uniform and easy for the traveler," V. S. Naipaul writes
in his book of Southern travels. "One result was that no travel book (unless the writer were writing about himself) could be only about the roads
and the hotels." He goes on to say that America is not alien enough, which
is questionable: in his trip through the South Naipaul concentrated on
the larger cities, and his stated theme was the lingering effects of slavery
(*Slave States* was a provisional title for his book). In a helpful insight he
adds, "[America] is too well known, too photographed, too written about;
and, being more organized and less informal, it is not so open to casual
inspection."

That is, unless you're deliberately creating obstacles or indulging in
mock heroics, in a narrative based on a Victorian model of what travel
writers are supposed to do — suffer, be afraid, overcome hardships, endure
privations and bizarre rituals, find the Heart of Darkness, meet the Jum-
blies, converse with God-botherers and Mudmen, observe the Anthro-
pophagi and the Men Whose Heads Do Grow Beneath Their Shoulders,
be heroic, and survive to tell the tale. Many do, even in this happy land. I
think of their books as mock ordeals.

The Mock Ordeal

Some narratives of travel in America succeed in a small way because they
purport to be frightening, dangerous, risky, life-or-death adventures — a
domestic version of the struggle against the odds that is a commonplace
in books of foreign travel. This posturing, Walter Mittyish tendency might

have begun with Henry David Thoreau, who, literary genius though he proved to be, lived a jostling existence with his parents, like many so-called cellar dwellers today, after he graduated from Harvard, rarely venturing far from the family home. He suffered from ill health for most of his short life (he died at the age of forty-four). He was not attempting hyperbole when he wrote in his journal, "I am a diseased bundle of nerves standing between time and eternity like a withered leaf."

He was twenty-six at the time, plagued by chronic bronchitis, mood swings, and recurrent narcolepsy. He celebrated the outdoors, he extolled hiking, yet he was anything but robust. In his experiment with independence at the age of twenty-eight, building a small cabin on the shore of Walden Pond, he is often depicted as a lone witness, living a hermit-like existence in the wild. Yet he was a mere mile and a half from his mother, who baked him pies and washed his clothes. Huckleberry parties occupied his Walden summers when he wasn't writing or reading.

One of the books Thoreau read at Walden was Melville's just-published *Typee,* subtitled *A Peep at Polynesian Life.* This highly colored account of Hawaii and a Pacific whaling voyage describes Melville's jumping ship with another crew member at the remote Marquesas Islands and his idyllic romance with the sylph-like island beauty Fayaway: "Fayaway and I reclined in the stern of the canoe, on the very best terms possible with one another; the gentle nymph occasionally placing her pipe to her lip, and exhaling the mild fumes of the tobacco, to which her rosy breath added a fresh perfume."

Henry, who was two years older than Herman, could not have known that Melville prettified his island experience and exaggerated his time in the Marquesas, where he'd spent one month—he claimed it was four months. He made his reputation with this book, and its notoriety and its exuberant adventures in this distant, unspoiled, and unknown portion of the world (cannibals, water nymphs, nakedness) made a powerful impression on the celibate, bronchitic man at Walden (rejected some years before by the only woman he'd ever loved), who, after a year on his own, felt the pressing intimations of cabin fever.

Partly as a response to *Typee,* and out of an ardent desire to achieve a wilderness adventure of his own, something original to write about and lecture upon, Thoreau went on a shuttling journey to Maine: took a train to Boston, another train to Portland, a steamboat up the Penobscot River to Bangor, and there he met his cousin and two lumber dealers. The four went by jolting stagecoach to inland Mattawamkeag. From there, by canoe for about twenty-five miles, where they arrived at North Twin Lake. The abounding forest thrilled Thoreau, who found it "savage and impassable," the way it must have looked to "the first adventurers." The region had "a smack of wildness about it as I had never tasted before."

Overwhelmed in authentic wilderness, he had at last discovered something wild, primitive, and dangerous to rival Melville's Marquesas. The group hiked through the woods to the lower slopes of Mount Katahdin. Thoreau climbed the mountain alone, feeling (he said) like Prometheus. The Katahdin climb inspired him to brilliant description: "Nature was here something savage and awful, though beautiful. I looked with awe at the ground I trod on, to see what the Powers had made there, the form and fashion and material of their work. This was that Earth of which we have heard, made out of Chaos and Old Night. Here was no man's garden, but the unhandselled [unpenetrated] globe. It was not lawn, nor pasture, nor mead, nor woodland, nor lea, nor arable, nor waste-land. It was the fresh and natural surface of the planet Earth, as it was made forever and ever."

This was a jolly two-week jaunt, four men on a mere woodland walk. Thoreau made it into an epic journey, a voyage of discovery. Later he claimed that the wilderness he had found in Maine was more primitive, more difficult of access, than anything Melville had experienced in the remote Marquesas, and he went on deludedly believing that it had been an ordeal.

THIS OCCURRENCE OF the mock ordeal became a feature of travel narratives in America that has persisted to our own time. To his credit, Henry James, who wrote about taking lengthy train journeys from Boston to San Diego, never complained of hardship but only of New York's "pin-cushion profile," the "visual ugliness" of some cities, and the "confined & cooped-up continuity" of the Pullman car. He was glad to return to London.

"I think it impossible, utterly impossible, for any Englishman to live here, and be happy," Charles Dickens wrote after the trip he recalled in *American Notes* (1842). As proof of Dickens's judgment, here are four English travelers who took bus rides in America:

"New York City's vast Port Authority Terminal is a terrifying place in which suddenly to find oneself coping on one's own," the prolific and otherwise imperturbable Ethel Mannin laments in *American Journey* (1967), about the start of her bus ride. She goes on, "It is important to resist the temptation to sit down and weep."

Mary Day Winn, in *The Macadam Trail: Ten Thousand Miles by Motor Coach* (1931), describes her suffering the ordeal in Arizona of an armed man stopping her luxury coach. "At the first sight of the drawn pistol the girl behind the driver — she of the over-worked make-up — screamed shrilly." Instead of robbing them, the gunman turns this holdup into farce, insists on kissing six of the women on the bus and, before he takes leave of the anxious twenty-seven passengers, says, "I couldn't go another day without I kissed a pretty gal."

A hardship for the English writer Ernest Young, in San Antonio, Texas, is having to wake up early to catch a bus, for his *North American Excursion* (1947): "My first day's journey, of 430 miles, about the distance from Berwick to Land's End, necessitated another of those early risings, which I always make with reluctance. A hasty breakfast in a roadside hut, with rain and foggy gloom outside, was not the best beginning to a lengthy bus ride."

"People of a score of races who came to America to be rich . . . have stayed on to live like unpampered animals," James Morris writes in *Coast to Coast* (1956). He goes on, "In such a climate of existence, racial prejudices thrive, and you can often catch a faint menacing rumble in a bus or on a street corner — a drunken Negro cursing the white people as he slumps in his seat, a white man arrogantly pushing his way through a group of Negro women."

Though Morris's book is otherwise good-hearted and generous, it is also a chronicle of timid reflection. "Violence is an ever-present element in American life," he writes. And later, recounting storms, floods, the Rio Grande in spate, and a high wind (he calls it a "typhoon") in Vicksburg, Mississippi, "You are never far from brutality."

"You can sense the underlying savagery, restrained of course, but present, at many gatherings of respectable business people, [even] among the Elks or the Kiwanis" is another of Morris's assessments. His trip itself is dainty; certainly no savagery is visited upon him, though he remarks,

"At other times, gentlemen would buttonhole me with dark questions." A sex change a dozen years later turned James into Jan, and she bought an apartment in New York, a city she came to praise. "British journalists named Clive, Colin, or Fiona," Charles Portis comments, "scribbling notes and getting things wrong for their journey books about the real America, that old and elusive theme."

It must be said that none of these travelers is climbing a mountain or bushwhacking through a forest or crossing a desert on foot. They are fiddle-faddling on good roads in comfy buses or cars. But they are not alone in their dramatic exaggerations. Many American writers have succumbed to the mock ordeal, re-creating the struggle of traveling on American roads. "The Mojave is a big desert and a frightening one," John Steinbeck writes in *Travels with Charley* (1962). And here is an example of this danger: "About fifty yards away two coyotes stood watching me . . . 'Kill them,' my training said." An investigative journalist, Bill Steigerwald, followed Steinbeck's journey and proved, in *Dogging Steinbeck* (2012), that the soon-to-be Nobel Prize winner did not actually travel to half the places he described, that much of the time he was swanking with his wife in excellent hotels, and that a great deal of what he wrote was flapdoodle, fudged and fictionalized, and perhaps there was no coyote.

In *The Air-Conditioned Nightmare* (1944) Henry Miller writes about his road trip (late 1940 into 1941) from New York to Los Angeles. "I felt the need to affect a reconciliation with my native land," he writes at the start, but later calls it "this lugubrious trip across America." His book is filled with complaints, the tedium of driving, the terrible food (an entire indignant chapter is devoted to the poor quality of American bread), and the dreadful cities.

For Miller, St. Louis is a particular horror: "The houses seem to have been decorated with rust, blood, tears, sweat, bile, rheum and elephant dung. Nothing can terrify me more than the thought of being doomed to spend the rest of my days in such a place." California is just as bad: "The real California began to make itself felt. I wanted to puke. But you have to get a permit to vomit in public." One year after this ordeal, Miller took up residence in California, first in Big Sur; he ended his days in Los Angeles, a happy man, as he said, "always merry and bright."

Arduous America, alone in the elements, is the subject of Edward Abbey's *Desert Solitaire: A Season in the Wilderness* — facing the bleak elements alone. "A man on foot, on horseback or on a bicycle will see more, feel more, enjoy more in one mile than the motorized tourists can in a hundred miles," but he failed to disclose that he had a car, and, "Wilderness. The word itself is music," he wrote. In his celebration of solitude and his lonely communing with nature in southern Utah, Abbey does not mention that for one five-month period he was living in a trailer with his third wife, Rita, and their young son, not far from his drinking buddies and a town with a saloon.

In *Old Glory: An American Voyage* (1981), my good friend Jonathan Raban describes his trip in a small powerboat down the Mississippi River. One of the great descriptive writers of travel, a shrewd analyst of manners, he is insightful and witty in the book and, as an outsider, sees much of this country that Americans miss. Though there is minimal mock ordeal in his wonderful book, at one point he becomes fearful of a flock of birds. "On the Illinois side there was a dead tree which seemed to function as a skid-row hotel for a gang of large ne'er-do-well birds." He is terrified of the birds. "I dug my dark glasses out of my grip, possessed by the thought that the first thing they'd try to peck out would be my eyes."

Menacing though they seem, the birds do not peck out the English traveler's eyes. He endures periods of bad weather, a failed love affair, and a near-drowning, but arrives in New Orleans unscathed. Another, more recent — but lazier, less ambitious — traveler sailing down the Mississippi, Mary Morris, in *The River Queen*, makes a meal of the mock ordeal. The boat is not to her liking, the cocaptains, Tom and Jerry, irritate her. The food disgusts her. Her ordeal can be summed up in one of her rants: "I hate pizza. I hate all that doughy stuff. I want a meal, shower, amenities."

Hiking the Appalachian Trail one would have thought to be a bracing and satisfying experience for a healthy pedestrian. Many have accomplished it. Bill Bryson, who traipsed it with a friend for his book *A Walk in the Woods* (1998), includes a classic mock ordeal, his encounter with a bear while camped one night near a spring in Virginia. A bear — possibly two, all he sees are the eyes — wanders near for a drink. "I sat bolt upright. Instantly every neuron in my brain was awake and dashing around frantically, like ants when you disturb their nest. I reached instinctively for my knife." He has no knife, he has fingernail clippers — the deflating beauty of this episode lies in its self-mockery. "Black bears rarely attack," he goes on. "But here's the thing. Sometimes they do . . . If they want to kill you and eat you, they can, and pretty much whenever they want."

"Finally, this being America," Bryson says at another point, "there is the constant possibility of murder."

The bears leave him alone, he is not murdered, and apart from sore feet, he is hardly inconvenienced in what is, for all its mock ordeals, a likable book.

"Call me crazy," Elijah Wald writes at the beginning of *Riding with Strangers* (2006). "I'm standing at a highway rest area outside Boston, in the rain, trying to get the first ride in yet another cross-country trek." But this hitchhiking book is surpassed in both self-mockery and hilarity by John Waters, who, on a whim, bummed rides from Baltimore to San Francisco, resulting in *Carsick* (2014), which is filled with mock ordeals, most of them (as he freely admits) the delusions of the fearful and fevered brain of a wealthy gay movie director who can easily afford to fly first class, but who longs for an ordeal, to endow his laborious trip with some squalid glamour.

There are many other similar books, hundreds, perhaps thousands, but each in its peculiar, even revelatory way is an approximation of travel in far-off places, reimagining the United States as a foreign, hostile landscape, making travel into a risky exertion, a deadly sport, or a dangerous stunt.

Their exaggerations aside, some of these are worthy books, but what is missing is the plain fact that the United States puts very few delays in the path of the traveler. In walking, boating, hitchhiking, and camping these travel writers set out to make the business harder and to call attention to themselves, but nothing is easier than traversing this country by road. The car journey is celebrated in Larry McMurtry's *Roads: Driving America's Great Highways* (2000), a meditation on motoring: "What I want to do is treat the great roads as a river, floating down this one, struggling up that one." This satisfying essay on driving across the country recounts the idiot joy of talking to oneself at the wheel, the reverie of the road, recalling books, old movies, reflections on the past: "blank driving, accompanied by minimal thought."

"My old friend the 90," McMurtry writes of one highway. On another ride, "Then I'm in Alabama for an hour," and he seems airborne. He speaks of a 770-mile drive, Duluth to Wichita, remarking how "I never had to go more than one hundred yards off the highway for food, gasoline, or a restroom," and, he might have added, a motel. His book accurately reflects what I feel in traveling in America—the solitary road trip that is in many respects a Zen experience, scattered with road candy, unavailable to motorists in any other country on earth.

BUT THERE ARE obstacles to travel in the United States, or at least obstacles to penetrating the country. We are a naturally welcoming people, but with too strenuous a response from the stranger, the welcome wears off, it shreds, it cools, it vanishes and becomes wary and reluctant. We are full of opinions, but we are temperamentally inhospitable to opposition or to searching questions—and the best traveler has nothing but questions. Americans will talk all day, but they are terrible listeners and have an aversion to probing or any persistent inquisitiveness by a stranger.

Americans share with the simple furrow-browed villagers in the folk societies of the world a deep suspicion of personal questions. We say we tolerate dissent, but the expression of a strongly held contrary view can render you undesirable, or even an enemy. A difference of opinion is often construed as defiance. You would not know that from our obsessive self-congratulation and our boasts of liberty and freedom. New Americans, refugees, people fleeing the horrors and tyrannies of their homelands, who have come to the United States for its freedoms, are often the most narrow-minded and censorious. We tolerate difference only when we don't have to look at it or listen to it, as long as it doesn't impact our lives.

Our great gift as a country is its size and its relative emptiness, its elbow room. That space allows for difference and is often mistaken for tolerance. The person who dares to violate that space is the real traveler.

Becoming a Traveler Again

Driving south, I became a traveler again in ways I'd forgotten. Because of the effortless release from my home to the road, the sense of being sprung, I rediscovered the joy in travel that I knew in the days before the halts, the checks, the affronts at airports — the invasions and violations of privacy that beset every air traveler. The discouragement and indignity of this querying casts a pall over the whole experience of travel — and this is before any forward progress can be made. All air travel today involves interrogation, often by someone in a uniform who is your inferior.

Once, you slipped away unseen, showed your ticket, boarded the plane, your luggage and peace of mind intact; you set off undisturbed. Earlier in my traveling life, this was my happy lot.

There is so much disturbance in travel itself, it is intolerable that it begins so quickly, even before you leave. These days the airport experience is not only a disagreeable foretaste of all the insults to come on the trip, but also an annoying way of reminding the prospective traveler that he or she is an alien at home, and not just a stranger but someone perhaps to be feared, a possible danger, a troublemaker if not a terrorist — the hooha, shoes off, belt off, no jacket, denuded and simplified and subjected to screening while tapping your feet, eager to get away; all this while still in a mode of predeparture, scrutinized, needing to pass inspection before you can even think of the trip ahead.

An airport is an obstacle course, and because of that it can sour you on the whole notion of travel. By degrees, over the years, the airport experience has become an extreme example of a totalitarian regime at work, making you small and suspect, depriving you of control. Such is the clumsy questioning of motives that one's usual response is the sort of suppressed rage that was the traveler's emotion in Soviet-era Eastern Europe with its bullying policemen. Travel was once a liberation; now it is the opposite — air travel, that is. Younger travelers have no idea what has been lost.

The sense that you're agreeing to this intrusion, that you're collaborating ("It's for my own good"), is worse than demeaning; it combines all the excuses and evasions that helped to create the oppressive dictatorships and tyrannies of the past. The stripping, at all airports, of the traveler's dignity, forcing the traveler to submit, is the antithesis of what one seeks in travel. Yes, we live in dangerous times, but if that means surrendering all our rights to privacy, then it is hardly worth the misery of leaving home.

There is a remedy, but it is for the lucky few, those who live in a vast country like ours who have the option of avoiding all airports: those who stick to the open road. Even the lowest jalopy is better than a first-class seat on a plane, because to get to that seat you are forced to submit to the indignities of official scrutiny and a body search. But no one has the right to question your slipping into a car and driving away at high speed. There is no prologue, only the bliss of a sudden exit.

The dubious achievement in travel these days is enduring the persistent nuisance of a succession of airports in order to arrive at a distant place for a brief interlude of the exotic, maintaining the delusion that it is travel. This is the equivalent of being measured like a projectile and being shot out of a cannon, and that's how most of us feel in such a state, like a human cannonball, dazed and confused, in the company of other cannonballs.

There is a better way, a truer way, the old way—the proud highway, the rolling road.

Going South

Traveling without a specific destination, I had left home on Cape Cod, early on a morning autumnal and damp, steering my car south, dropped down past New York City and skirted Washington, D.C., keeping on until way past sunset, and drove into Front Royal, Virginia, in the dark. It was October. I was headed for the Deep South, so I still had a way to go. But already I knew the pleasant trance-like state of long-distance driving, the onset of highway hypnosis and white line fever in the long empty stretches: the satori of the open road, the ordinary experience of driving transformed into a higher spiritual path.

Normally I felt a tremor of anxiety before I set off on a long trip. This time I felt only joy, an eagerness to start, no passport, no security check, no plane to catch, no crowds. I felt a thrill throwing a jackknife into my bag. I loaded up with books; I had a tent and a sleeping bag just in case. I emptied out the refrigerator and had a bag of food too—juice and hard-boiled eggs, a container of homemade chili, cheese, fruit, and bottles of wine.

I was in the Deep South because I hardly knew it, and for the sheer pleasure of driving my own car, for the freedom of not having to make onward plans, because only in America can you travel in confidence without a destination: the humblest town has a place to stay, probably on its outskirts, probably a beat-up motel; and a place to eat, at best a soul food diner, but probably a Hardee's, an Arby's, a Zaxby's, a Lizard's Thicket, or a disenfranchised chicken place reeking of hot oil, but friendly. Typically it was a small eatery with a counter that displayed an anthology of fried food—catfish, chicken, burgers, corrugated French fries, even fried pie—peasant food eaten by everyone. A deep tray of okra, as viscous as frog spawn, next to a kettle of sodden collard greens looking like stewed dollar bills. You were always offered a wet biscuit, and often a blessing. I stayed away from the big cities and the coastal communities. I kept to the Lowcountry, the Black Belt, the Delta, the backwoods, the flyspeck towns.

In the presidential debates during the election campaign of 2012 the candidates made constant reference to America's middle class—how it was under siege, overtaxed, burdened by debt and uncertainty, and how each candidate was going to save the middle class—and appealed for their votes. On the way down, in New Jersey, I heard on the radio that fifty million Americans lived in poverty, not many where I was coming from, a great number where I was headed. Sixteen percent of Americans were classified as poor—and it was twenty percent in the South, in places where the income gap was growing wider than at any time in history. The presidential candidates did not allude to saving the poor.

"They avoid using the word 'poor,'" a social worker in Alabama told me early on in my trip, and explained, "'Poor' is shorthand for 'black.'"

I was curious about the poor in the South. It is impossible to travel the country roads of the South and not be in regular contact with America's underclass. I was traveling for my usual reasons, out of restlessness and curiosity, to look at places that were new to me. We travel for pleasure, for a door-slamming sense of "I'm outta here," for a change of air, for edification, for the big vulgar boast of being distant, for the possibility of being transformed, for the voyeuristic romance of gawping at the exotic.

"You've been everywhere," people said to me, but that's a laugh. My wish list of places is not only long, but in many cases blindingly obvious. Yes, I had been to Patagonia and the Congo and Sikkim, but I—an American—hadn't been to the most scenic American states, never to Alaska, Montana, Idaho, or the Dakotas, and I'd had only the merest glimpse of Kansas and Iowa. I had not traveled in the Deep South. I wanted to see these states, not flying in but traveling slowly on the ground, keeping to back roads, and defying the general rule of "Never eat at a place called Mom's, never play cards with a man called Doc."

Nothing to me has more excitement than the experience of rising early in the morning in my own house and getting into my car and driving away on a long, meandering trip through North America. Not much can beat it for a sense of freedom—no pat-down, no passport, no airport muddle, just revving an engine and then "Eat my dust." The long, improvisational road trip by car is quintessentially American, beginning with reliable autos, early in the last century.

The first cross-country road, the Lincoln Highway, was inaugurated in 1913. Linking New York and San Francisco, this notional thoroughfare, pieced together from an assortment of east-west–trending roads, was not a US government project but rather an idea seen through to completion by private businessmen. These men, all of whom were associated with the automobile industry, were supervised by Carl G. Fisher, who manufactured car headlights in Indianapolis. (He also built the Indianapolis Speedway.) An accepted north-south route was established at around the same time. Scott and Zelda Fitzgerald took a celebrated trip on it in a 1918 Marmon Roadster, from Connecticut to Alabama in 1920, three months after their marriage. Scott wrote a jaunty account of it in *The Cruise of the Rolling Junk,* one of the earliest American car journey narratives.

Many other road books followed: Henry Miller's, Kerouac's, Steinbeck's, and William Least Heat-Moon's *Blue Highways* being the notable ones. The road trips Nabokov took all over America with his wife at the wheel, seeking butterflies, resulted in *Lolita,* a novel that is also incidentally a road trip. Charles Portis's *The Dog of the South* is one of the great road trip novels, starting in Arkansas and ending in Honduras, a wild ride, played for laughs, and wise too: "The car ran well and I glowed in the joy of solitary flight. It was almost a blessed state."

EVER SINCE THE advent of the motorcar people have turned road trips into narratives, both in America and in Europe. Rudyard Kipling was an early motorist, and bought a Rolls-Royce in 1910 in which his chauffeur drove him around England while he made notes. Edith Wharton was an enthusiastic car owner; she took her first ride in 1902, bought a Panhard-Levassor in 1904, and later a black Pope-Hartford. Wharton wrote *A Motor-Flight Through France* (1908), its first sentence, "The motor car has restored the romance of travel." Like Kipling she had a chauffeur, and her bachelor friend Henry James was often her passenger. James loved her cars and called her new one the "Vehicle of Passion."

"James grew to admire her and wonder at her energy," Colm Tóibín wrote in *Vogue* of "the Master." "During a heat wave on one of his stays at The Mount"—Wharton's estate in Massachusetts—"the only relief James found was in 'incessant motoring.' They motored, Wharton wrote, 'daily, incessantly, over miles and miles of lustrous landscape lying motionless under the still glaze of heat. While we were moving he was refreshed and happy, his spirits rose.'"

WHILE ALL ROADS in America are pretty much the same, and predictably smooth, American places and its people are distinctly different and pose other problems. The roads in general represent effortless and standardized pleasure, even with the traffic, which no one wants to hear about. This makes the abrupt arrivals, and encounters, somewhat surrealistic—in one day, driving from my house on Cape Cod, an abode of familiarity, and on that same road, at nightfall, finding myself in an utterly different landscape, among people who, while polite enough, did not want to be known.

In Africa and China and India and Patagonia, the locals seem grateful to be visited by a stranger. This is the drama, the color, the encounter in the familiar travel book. But in the United States, a visit by another citizen is not an occasion to rehearse traditional hospitality, or to utter the Arabic formula "*Salam aleikum ya dayf al-Rahman!* Peace upon you, guest of the Merciful One!" or the Hindi version, "Welcome! *Atithi devo Bhava!* The guest is God!"

One is more often greeted with suspicion, hostility, or indifference. In this way Americans could be more challenging, more difficult to get acquainted with, more secretive and suspicious and in many respects more foreign, than any people I have ever met.

The Submerged Twentieth

Traveling in a spirit of inquiry, I was in the South because I had hardly been there and knew so little about it. Everyone knows that in the smugger pockets of the South there is wealth and stylishness and ease — estates, horse farms, fine dining, salubrious cities, upscale suburbs, some of the finest real estate in America.

But that is the Old Magnolia South, and away from it, though not far away, there is hunger and squalor and great poverty. The poorest parts of America can also be found in these sunny states, in the most beautiful parts of the South, the rural areas: the Lowcountry of South Carolina, the Black Belt of Alabama, the Mississippi Delta, the Ozarks of Arkansas. These poor folk are poorer in their way (as I was to find) and less able to manage and more hopeless than many people I had traveled among in distressed parts of Africa and Asia. Living in the buried hinterland, in fractured communities and dying towns and on the sidelines, they exist in obscurity.

Poor Americans, who have very little, still have their privacy — in many ways it is their last possession, and they resist losing it. That is a challenge for a traveler who is curious to know: What do people do when they don't appear to do anything?

The traveler, by selecting a singular route, invents the country, but the truthful traveler cannot invent experiences, and these experiences are the stuff of the narrative. Many books have been written about the conspicuous excitements of the South, but I made it my habit to drive past the buoyant cities and obvious pleasures in favor of smaller places and huddled towns, to meet the submerged twenty percent.

Dot Indians

On the road out of Front Royal ("Ain't got but one") and a detour ("Cain't miss it") along Skyline Drive through Shenandoah National Park, spectacularly beautiful on this sunny autumn day, the brittle curled leaves aflame in russets and yellows, blowing and twisting like shredded rags across the narrow winding road along the ridge, the valley below seen from three thousand feet, I thought of Africa's Great Rift Valley.

An American cannot travel the world without returning home and making comparisons. East African imagery ran through my mind all day as I dawdled past New Market and Harrisonburg and Wytheville, thinking of thorn trees and the highlands and villages and shops and Indians who'd inserted themselves all over East Africa as shopkeepers and traders known as *dukawallahs*. The Great Rift Valley, blighted by recent tribal massacres and filled with refugee villages, was puny compared to this majestic landscape.

I drove all day in a mood of bliss through these golden hills and sifting-down leaves and the tufted-mulch odors at the window.

At nightfall in Bristol, in the southeast corner of Virginia, the edge of Appalachia, I stepped into the lobby of an inexpensive motel and was hit with the sharp aroma of incense partially cloaking the odor of curry, the smell of every interior of India, every Indian *duka* in Africa.

"Yes?"

A small, frowning man brushed through the beaded curtain hung across the door to the back, another Indian touch, bringing more aromas with him, the smells suggesting the particularities of a whole narrative, sticks of incense smoldering to the gods behind the curtain, also masking other odors, the perfume that makes your eyes itch.

In a landscape of whites and blacks, the most conspicuous person I saw was this man, my first Indian in the South, the owner-manager of a motel, a dot Indian with a caste mark on his forehead rather than a feather Indian. Motels, gas stations, convenience stores: they had a lock on them, and the first one stood for so many I was to find. One of the whispers in the South is that whites sold these businesses to Indians as an act of defiance, in order to keep them out of the hands of blacks. I met hundreds more Indians, nearly all of them from the state of Gujarat in western India, many of them recent immigrants.

HIS NAME WAS Mr. Hardeep Patel, from Surat, in Gujarat. Gujaratis, looked down upon by Punjabis, are Indians plain and simple: the shopkeepers of East and Central Africa, the store owners and operators of subpost offices on the high streets of Britain, the motel owners of the South.

Mr. Patel had immigrated to Canada, stayed a few years, then crossed the border to settle in the States. You first think: This poor man laboring alone in his business! But they are the first to reveal that they are related to all the other Gujaratis in the town or district, the Patels and Desais and Shahs.

"I knew some people — other Indians, running motels. They helped me."

"Are there other Indians in Bristol?"

"Fifteen families." Interesting: he spoke of families, the Indian social unit, and not of individuals.

In the morning, after the seven or eight Budget Inn rooms had been vacated, it was Mr. Hardeep Patel whom I saw pushing a laundry cart from room to room, piling it with bed linens and used towels. After almost forty years, it seemed he still cleaned the rooms and, this morning at least, had no menials or housekeepers to help him. Did this indicate that business was poor and Mr. Patel hard-pressed? No, it perhaps explained the new Lexus parked in front.

There is another category of Indian immigrant in the South. For a number of years Indian doctors could access the fast track to a US visa by agreeing to work in the poorer parts (designated "underserved areas") of America. Now this program is called the National Interest Waiver.

Beginning in the 1990s, thousands of visas were handed out under this preferential program. But the subsequent history of the successful visa applicant was never checked. Many of these visas were issued from the US consulate in Madras to doctors in Tamil Nadu State, and also to ones in Hyderabad in adjacent Andhra Pradesh, with the understanding that the recipient would serve for a period of years in certain designated needy areas, Appalachia in particular.

Not long after this program was begun, a specialized form of visa fraud developed: many of these Indian doctors filed, through the Immigration and Naturalization Service, for "physician's assistants" to come to the United States on temporary worker (H-1B) visas to work in their offices. These alleged assistants were invariably doctors themselves who wished to gain US citizenship. Authorities noticed patterns of deception in the filing process, which led to the discovery of a fraud ring.

Neither the workload nor the income of the doctors in Appalachia justified the need for these "assistants." It was obviously a means for the doctors to get to the States and then seek ways to adjust their residency status while they were here. Many of the Indian doctors (largely Hyderabadi, a number of them involved in a visa fraud scam) did end up in Appalachia, at least for several years, and then they moved on to more lucrative practices in urban areas, either legally or when they could slip under the radar.

Though he was well educated, Mr. Patel was not one of those doctors. His wish all along was to rid himself of India and settle in America. As we talked, I heard an older woman giggling into the phone behind the beaded curtain, Mrs. Patel perhaps. This man and wife lived in the motel in the same way East African Indian families lived at the back of their shops. The Patels had three daughters, all married.

"You arranged the marriages?"

"Love match," he said, wobbling his head. "American way."

There were no pictures of his daughters on the wall of family photographs—that would have been slightly indecent. Grandchildren were shown, the largest photo his sixteen-year-old son, whom Mr. Hardeep Patel described proudly in three words: "He plays golf."

Big Stone Gap

I first heard the name Big Stone Gap forty-odd years ago, in Charlottesville, Virginia.

The first time I was eleven years old, staying for a summer with my uncle, a military doctor, at Fort Lee, Virginia, adjacent to Hopewell, on the Appomattox River. The nearby town of Petersburg was famous for the Battle of the Crater, a Union defeat, and the ensuing eight-month siege of the town by Union soldiers, ending in its surrender. Of the summer of 1952, I remember visits to the battlefield, the small signs on the doorjambs of restaurants lettered WHITE (explained to me by my whispering uncle), the red clay roads, a ride on a handcart on a rural railway, and a sight that has never left my mind: an enormous tooting calliope on a wagon, a gilded organ with red-painted scrollwork, a tall smoking chimney and steam-spouting pipes wobbling as it rolled, being played by a white man ostentatiously seated before it in a top hat and frock coat. And when the colorful front of the calliope passed by, a view of the back: a black man in ragged overalls, his wide-apart legs braced on a platform, his face gleaming with sweat, shoveling coal into the fiery furnace of the boiler. Even then, just a boy, I saw this calliope as a powerful social metaphor.

In Charlottesville, twenty years later, my second time in the South, I taught writing for one semester. I was filling in for the vacationing writer-in-residence, Peter Taylor. Taylor was an accomplished short story writer, a friendly man, and a sympathetic teacher. His roots were in Tennessee, where his grandfather had served both as a governor and later as a US senator. Peter Taylor was respectable and, as he was quick to point out, a member of the Southern gentry, and with this elevated ancestry came a defiant backward-looking provincialism that made me smile. In conversation, this otherwise nice and subtle man had all the conventional conceits of the South: a canting view of the Civil War, a sly mockery of Yankees, a defensive position on obscure Southern crotchets, a deep suspicion of the disruptions of the civil rights movement, and an innocent or credulous notion (commonly held in the South) that white Southerners understood blacks in a highly subtle way that Yankees never could. I was unable to account for him except as a self-conscious Southerner, suspicious of outsiders.

The difference in our ages might also have been a factor. I was a rebellious young man whose books were selling; he was twenty years older than me, an appendage to academia, out of print and enjoying a professor's salary. He seemed to view me, with wry amusement, as some Southerners did then, as an upstart from another country, the cold, iron-dark North.

To my utter bewilderment, a number of faculty members were slyly mocking of William Faulkner, another outsider, who had been a writer-in-residence in Charlottesville ten years before and whose late-life passion in Virginia (he had only a few more years to live) was horsemanship — hacking and fox hunting. His portrait was painted, Faulkner looking like a posh Englishman, in the riding habit of the Farmington Hunt Club. But the mockery was envious, the sort that is brought to a bitter pitch by academics, and was noted by one of my colleagues, Joe Blotner, who later mentioned it in his biography of Faulkner. Blotner wrote, "Some in Charlottesville, aesthetes and intellectuals, sneered at what were to them affectations unworthy of a great writer."

By chance, in a hospital lobby in Charlottesville, I met a disconsolate couple, very poor, who had come there to seek treatment for their afflicted child. They lived, they said, in Big Stone Gap. I forgot their name, but I remembered the name of their town, and it became one of those evocative place names that I kept in my head and vowed to seek out someday – an alluring name, like Zanzibar and Patagonia, the sort that beckons to a traveler.

Big Stone Gap is in Virginia, the edge of it, lying at the mountainous convergence of Kentucky and Tennessee, and North Carolina is only twenty-five miles away. I drove there from Bristol on a road that circled around steep hills and cut through a river valley – the wooded slopes so pretty, the towns along the way so mean, many of them trailer settlements and scruffy roadside bungalows and the poorest shops: "Thrift Store," "Discount Store," "Family Dollar Store," "Budget Store," "Affordable Stone Monuments." Here and there among the trailers and the scattering of old wood-frame farmhouses were a few solitary mansions of red sandstone and granite, most of them the pompous residences of coal barons. Coal is the industry here, and neatly lettered signs nailed to telephone poles announced: SUPPORT COAL.

Big Stone Gap appeared at the end of the flattening road, a few cross streets set in a sudden valley, wrapped by two forks of the Powell River, most of its stores defunct or sitting moribund in the noon sunshine.

One storefront advertised itself as a craft shop, pottery and homemade jewelry and paintings for sale. I stopped in because I could not see any other shops. It was staffed by Mrs. Moore, who made jewelry. I asked her about the coal mines.

Mrs. Moore, who had lived in Big Stone Gap for twenty-four years, said, "I don't know where they are – they're all private."

In the bright and empty town, the brick storefronts were shuttered, though Mrs. Moore said that on the coming weekend Mountain Empire Community College would be holding a Craft Day. "There'll be storytelling and bluegrass music."

The center of social activity in Big Stone Gap was the Mutual Drugstore on East Wood Street, a place that was not only a pharmacy and convenience store but also a cafeteria, with a menu chalked on a board. *Lunch Special — Chicken strips — Mashed Potatoes, Green beans, Apple Pie, Cream Pie.* It was a meeting place too, people in work clothes ducking in and out of booths, "How y'all doin'?" and "If I knew you were coming I'd let you buy me lunch. Heh."

In spite of the apparent emptiness of the town, there was an air of contentment, mingled with resignation, a slow and certain way of walking, leaning forward as stout people do, burdened by the swollen belly, or skinny and loping, throwing one leg ahead of the other.

I asked about Indian doctors.

"There's a couple of Hindu doctors here."

Two in Big Stone Gap, Dr. Karakattu (a Kerala name) and Dr. Gupta, and one in the town of Appalachia, Dr. Tarandeep Kaur. Of the thousands who had received visas under the National Interest Waiver, for most it seemed their interest had waned.

I did not see a black face in Big Stone Gap, none in the town, none on the way, nor any in Weber City, on the Tennessee state line, which I passed through. I did not know then what I learned later, the racial geography of the South: the towns and villages in the mountains and hills are mainly white, and in the Lowcountry, the great sprawl of flat agricultural land where cotton and tobacco were grown, they are mainly black — the persistence of history.

Gun Store

I stopped at a gun store on my way into nearby North Carolina. It was, like most of the other gun stores I saw, also a pawnshop, since the most costly and pawnable item in a hill country household is a firearm. Pawnshops revealed a great deal about possessions in the rural economy — I could verify the things that people pawned or sold, guns mainly, but also TV sets, VCRs, computers, obscure car parts, wristwatches, but not much jewelry. In many pawnshops there was a tray of Civil War memorabilia, or arrowheads dug up locally, or knives. A large, rusty, and greasy category was building equipment—drills, block and tackles, sickles, wrenches, hammers, pressure gauges, pipefitting contraptions, nail guns, and band saws, all of them well used, the tools of the trade of men who were no longer employed.

Because they were buyers as well as sellers, gun shop/pawnshop owners were usually chatty, which was helpful to me. Whenever I stopped at such a place, I inquired about buying a gun, explaining that I was a Yankee, far from home, with no local residence.

The clerk inevitably looked pained at the idea of someone like me traveling through the South without a weapon.

"I can't sell you a handgun," the man at this gun shop said. "I can sell you a long gun, though—any long gun you see, ammo too. An AK-47, if I had one."

This seemed preposterous to me then, but a few months later, in Mississippi, I saw two Romanian-made AK-47s for sale at a gun show.

Pressing him, I said, "I was hoping to buy a handgun, maybe a Glock?"

"Cain't do it. Anyway, only the jigaboos have them."

Do I challenge him in his racial abuse? No, let him talk. I said, "It's strange, I haven't seen many black people around these parts."

"Yep. Nice, huh?"

Hearing this, at a nearby counter, a young salesclerk—a fat white woman—and a just as fat policeman hee-hawed and covered their mouths, wheezing laughter into their hands.

Encouraged by their reaction, the man said, "I was in Columbus, Ohio. Place is full of jigaboos. But up in Ohio they said to me, 'You're a hillbilly. You got one leg shorter than the other from stepping around the side of the hills.'"

He demonstrated this by raising one leg and canting his body sideways and hopping a little, as though negotiating a steep slope.

"Took it as long as I could—just put up with it," he said, of the term "hillbilly," which is not the conventional jokey aside of television humor but contemptuous and bitter in the hill communities of Appalachia, implying poverty and ignorance. "Finally I couldn't take no more. I says to these Ohio boys, 'You got one leg shorter than the other too, from stepping off the sidewalk into the gutter'"—and he demonstrated this with his legs—"'to let the niggers go on by.'"

Asheville: "This We Call the Block"

I left Big Stone Gap and drove via the gun shop into North Carolina, slipping from road to road, heading for Asheville, where I wanted to verify something that had been preying on my mind. My friend the late, well-known American painter Kenneth Noland was born in Asheville, and lived there from 1924 until 1942, when he enlisted in the US Army. After his discharge, he returned to attend freewheeling and experiment-obsessed Black Mountain College, fifteen miles up the road from his home.

In time, Noland became part of the vanguard of the 1960s Color Field movement, painters of pure color in blobby, random, or geometric shapes — many of Noland's paintings, the size of a garage door, resemble archery targets, or chevron badges for the epaulets of giants. Color Field painters regarded figurative artists as old hat. "Picasso is shit," Ken Noland used to mutter to me with a smile, and he fully believed that the mission of modern painting was to drench the canvas in bright color, to eliminate meaning and emotion by drowning them in dumb and untelling paint. For much of his work Noland used a long-handled foot-wide paint roller, and he worked it on a canvas laid flat on the floor, like a man waterproofing a deck. I never saw him hold a brush. He told me that he could not draw a rabbit. Not surprisingly, Noland became the darling of interior decorators, who spruced up rooms for wealthy clients using his paintings as accents, to tone with the color schemes of their chintzes; in their fussy parlance, the primary colors of his simple staring canvases "drew a room together."

Many of Noland's paintings and most of his theories seemed to me a crock, but the man himself was a lovable grump, and we often went fishing together in Maine, where he lived. In tranquil moments he reminisced about the South. One day over a drink, speaking to me of his youth in Asheville, he said, "Know what? I had a paper route. I went all over, even delivered papers in Niggertown."

To tease him, I said, "Who lived there, Ken?"

"Who do you think lived there? Niggers."

"What did *they* call that part of town?"

He frowned in bafflement and began gabbling. He had no idea, but quickly saw the absurdity of a black person in Asheville identifying this district that way. He used the word now and then, but he was not a racist. He had grown up in segregated Asheville. He called himself a hillbilly, but even so, he was indignant when he told me stories of how blacks in Asheville were condemned to sit in the balcony of the downtown movie theater. "And you'd never see one in a restaurant or even walking down the sidewalk of the main street — they wouldn't dare."

He was speaking of the 1930s and '40s, and by 1950 (when race relations were just as bad and backed up by laws requiring racial segregation) he had left Asheville for good, and spent the rest of his life in the North. But when he referred to the place, speaking of his youth, he sometimes lapsed into the language of the past, and over that distance he did not see blacks, he saw "niggers," living in "Niggertown."

Asheville, which prospered as a spa town, sited in the healthful air of the Blue Ridge Mountains, is home to ten colleges and even more hospitals and sushi bars. For people living within hundreds of miles it is a cultural center. The town is of course the obsessive subject of Thomas Wolfe, who was born there and is buried there. In my travels it was, or so it seemed to me, one of the happiest, most habitable and well-heeled towns I saw in the South.

I was headed to the Deep South, but I had something on my mind that I wished to settle when I got to Asheville. I fell into conversation with a man at the town's museum and asked him where the black population historically lived — where Ken Noland had delivered newspapers as a teenager in the 1930s.

"Take a right," he said, pointing out of the front of the museum, "and another right. Keep going."

I followed his directions, heading through the main square, then downhill, in what was after ten minutes' walk clearly the black part of Asheville. "He came slowly over past the fire department and the city hall. On Gant's corner, the Square dipped sharply down toward Niggertown, as if it had been bent at the edge," Wolfe writes in *Look Homeward, Angel*. "Niggertown," a forbidden and sultry aspect of Asheville's underworld, figures often in the narrative. One of the dramas in the novel concerns Eugene Gant's paper route in Niggertown, which was also Thomas Wolfe's paper route. What a coincidence! It occurred to me that in claiming to have delivered papers in this part of Asheville, Ken Noland — habitual teller of tall tales, casual assumer of other artists' experiences — might have been appropriating a bit of Wolfe's personal history.

Strolling downward, I plunged from a precinct of granite buildings in a sunlit plaza to narrow, leafy streets and humble wooden houses, walking in the shade. And seeing me approach, a man waved hello to me as he stepped back from a picture he was painting on a city wall, a large portrait of a basketball player in the stars-and-stripes uniform of the Harlem Globetrotters. His name was Ernie Mapp.

"Nice picture," I said.

"Bennie Lake," Ernie Mapp said, and indicating the athlete's uniform he added, "Born in Asheville. He was a Globetrotter. And he was a good soul."

Seeing us talking, a man wandered over to join us. This was Tim Burdine, stout and bearish in a heavy coat and wool hat, his arm in a sling. "I busted it," he explained. Tim was about sixty, Ernie much younger.

"I'm a stranger here, and a little lost," I said after we'd chatted a bit. "What do you call this part of town?"

"This we call the Block," Tim said.

"Or the East End," Ernie put in. "Everything below Eagle Street and over to Valley Street."

Ernie's picture on the wall of the abutment below Market Street was part of an urban art project, the Triangle Park Mural Project, memorializing local people, most of them black, and historical events in seven-foot-high panels. The Triangle Park Mural Project's website described it as "a collaborative community mural commemorating the history of the Block, Asheville's historic black business district." The painters and organizers were all local too, both black and white, bursting with civic pride.

"That's Nina Simone in that picture," Tim said, leading me to another part of the wall. The singer was depicted with her hair drawn back in her iconic Nefertiti profile, and she was surrounded by musicians.

"Those guys playing are from the group Bite, Chew and Spit," Tim said. "You must have heard of them. House band of the Orange Peel. The Kit-Kat Club was just up there, Market Street."

On this chilly late afternoon, other painters were absorbed in working on separate panels of the mural.

"Who you suppose that guy is?" Tim Burdine asked me, pointing to a slender young black man in stylish dark glasses, a jaunty tam-o'-shanter on his head, striking a pose, life-sized, in one of the murals. Tim walked over and leaned against the painted figure. "Me! Big glasses — I was skinny, I was cool! Eighteen years old. High school kid."

A car swung by, music blaring — James Brown's "Get Up Offa That Thing" — and, parking it, a heavyset woman got out, leaving the music playing.

"This is Bubbles," Tim said, giving her a hug with his good arm. "She's one of the artists too."

"I try," Bubbles said, and bopped to James Brown. She was smiling, a motherly presence, about Tim's age, and walking through Triangle Park, this large woman, bulking in her heavy winter coat, seemed to possess it.

"She's president of our club, ain't you, girl?" Tim said, following her.

"What club is that?"

"We call it the Just Folks Club."

We sat down at a picnic table, Tim and Bubbles and I, as Ernie went back to dabbing at his mural with a long-handled brush.

"Yes, uh-unh, we watched movies from upstairs in the theater," Tim said, answering one of my questions, "and it lasted a long time. Segregation didn't end in 1964 with the Civil Rights Act. It kept on into the 1970s."

"And later," Bubbles said.

"It's over," Tim said. "No one's angry. No hard feelings. Everyone gets along."

When I got up to leave, Tim said, "You come back in a few months, this project's going to be finished. We're fixing to have a ceremony. You're welcome."

"Who Am Ah?"

On my way out of Asheville the next day, on the back roads of camphor groves, where in the dooryards of some houses the scuppernong vines dangled clusters of fruit, and through Flat Rock (where Carl Sandburg lived for the last twenty-two years of his life on his goat farm, Connemara) and the hamlet of Zirconia, and over the state line into South Carolina and Greenville, I had the radio on: the Allman Brothers' "Ramblin' Man."

I began to ruminate on how you might attempt to ramble in the rest of the world, but there are always obstacles, and sometimes serious risks, and many dead ends. In America you are free to travel without a destination, simply circulating. This suited my mood of restlessness and my love of the road and was a relief from the uncertainty and suspense I had felt on trips elsewhere — my last in Africa, for one. And even in the poorest places in America, where there are shacks and rotting house trailers, the roads are wonderful.

I spent the night in Greenville, South Carolina, youthful and buzzing with activity on this Saturday evening, its downtown thronged with restaurants and bars. Less than fifty years ago it was heavily policed and reserved for whites, the main streets off-limits to blacks, who were forbidden to use the public library or eat in any of the restaurants or stay in any of the hotels. In my lifetime, and the lifetimes of many in Greenville, the racial restrictions have been lifted and the laws overturned. I was traveling on the fiftieth anniversary of the civil rights movement, usually referred to as a struggle, but it seemed to me — and to some blacks I spoke to — more like a war, with many battles and many bombings and many deaths. But you would not know that from the festive streets of Greenville today.

In the morning, I drove to Columbia, circling the city, looking for a place to have lunch. I settled on a Southern option, Lizard's Thicket. Its motto was "Real Country Cooking," and on the menu chicken and dumplings, fried chicken livers, liver and onions, pulled barbecue pork, meatloaf, biscuits and gravy.

As I was getting out of my car, a stout man approached the car next to mine from the direction of the restaurant. He had the sleepy, satisfied, slightly winded look of someone who had just eaten a huge meal.

"Hi there. How you doing?"

"I'm fine," I said. "Hungry, though."

"Have the liver and onions," he said. "It's delicious. It's on special today."

"Thanks for the suggestion. I'm passing through. I'm from Massachusetts."

"What church are you affiliated with?"

I had never been asked this before by a stranger, in the United States or anywhere else in the world. I got it so often in the South I became curious about the mystical beliefs of the people there. The question was often phrased as, "What church do you fellowship with?" People asked it out of the blue, and because I did not have a simple answer, they would fill the silence with "I'm Hope Chapel" or "We're AME"—the African Methodist Episcopal, a church founded more than two hundred years ago by free blacks in Pennsylvania. Or "Shubach Deliverance World Ministries." Or someone would preface his introduction with "We're fellowshiping with Heaven on Hah."

The question made me look closely at the man. He was pale and fat and short of breath, with thinning hair, lightly freckled, wearing a short-sleeved shirt and a striped tie. He was perspiring and postprandial, squinting at me in the bright sun. He had an unhealthy, somewhat clerkly look, three pens in his breast pocket, but a mild, hospitable manner. I think he was surprised by my hesitation at his question about my religion.

"I am an unaffiliated Baptist," he said, as though to encourage me. "You look like a teacher, something to do with books or teaching. I'm Al Mc-Candless, nice to meet you. I was in insurance, still deal with it a bit, but it's funny, I always wrote poetry. I'd get a thought and turn it into a poem. When I was forty years old I found out I was adopted. My grandmother told me accidentally. We were talking about something one day, something to do with my brother, who was misbehaving, I think, and the old woman said, 'Well, you know you're adopted, like your brother.' I knew he was adopted, but I thought I was a natural child. I asked my folks about it, but all they said was 'Who in hell told you that?' That wasn't really an answer, so I asked them again, and they said, 'You're ours, you're all ours, you'll always be ours.' But I knew what they meant, and after they passed away I found my birth mother. She was eighty, living just a few miles away from where I grew up. She had but a second-grade education. She had a few more children—so I had a real sister and two half-sisters. I had three years with her until she died. But I also thought about my other mother, and my brother the adopted one, and where I grew up. I didn't know what-all to do, so I wrote a poem about it."

Through this he had been gasping, mopping his sweat-beaded face, blinking at me—his damp eyes and pale eyelashes. He had a big square mouth and a lazy tongue, but his suffering expression might have been an effect of the sun, the glare and the heat.

"I called the poem 'Who Am Ah?'"

"A big question," I said.

He opened wide again and his mouth went square. "'Who Am Ah?'" And then he said, "You'll like the liver and onions."

Inside Lizard's Thicket, a gray-haired black man in a baseball cap was just leaving, saying, "Ah mo just leave mah money heah fo y'all," and he tipped his hat and said, "I came to see y'all, say hello to y'all, make mahself feel better."

"Nu Man, Yanna Weep-Dee We Dan-Ya"

I was learning that throughout the South it was possible to meet many people casually, and the merest hello might provoke a torrent of reminiscence, like Al McCandless's lament. But some folks were hard to find and reluctant to confide their business, especially if their business was survival and they were living below the poverty line, in silence and shadows.

What inspired my trip through the Deep South was the notion that as a traveler the people I had been meeting in Africa and India and elsewhere were more and more familiar to me. I am not speaking about their common humanity but their circumstances. Many Americans were just as poor as many Africans, or as confined in rural communities as many Indians; they were as remote from anyone caring about them, too, without access to decent housing or medical care; and there were portions of America, especially in the rural South, that resembled what is often thought of as the Third World.

The name Bernie Mazyck was given to me as that of a man who might provide an introduction. Bernie was the founding president and CEO of the South Carolina Association of Community Development Corporations, about which I was curious, but I was also curious about his name. Bernie Mazyck was the friend of a friend. I had driven to Columbia to meet him and seek his help.

The South Carolina Association of Community Development Corporations describes itself as "a state-wide trade association of non-profit, community-based development corporations within the state's economically distressed communities," adding, "The SCACDC places particular emphasis on promoting development in communities that have been left out of the economic mainstream, especially minority communities."

Its mission was "to raise the quality of life for low-wealth families," of which there were many in South Carolina. In one of the poorest parts of the United States the word "poor" was never used by bureaucrats, perhaps because it seemed demeaning or stigmatizing. But it seemed to me a powerful word that was studiously avoided. The organization helped the "low-wealth families" by loaning money, offering advice, and guiding people through the paperwork. It also encouraged the passive poor to educate themselves and to become leaders. In a previous interview Bernie Mazyck had said, "For South Carolina, leadership is often viewed as the property of a certain select group of folk," and he hoped to change that. "Select group," when spoken in the South, is shorthand for "white."

Bernie, dressed formally in a white shirt and silk tie, was waiting for me at one end of a gleaming, twenty-foot-long boardroom table. He looked up from a stack of papers, and if he was surprised by my street clothes — blue jeans and a long-sleeved polo shirt — he did not betray it. He seemed right at home in the boardroom; I looked like a janitor. I took him to be in his fifties, an intense, serious, compact man who spent his life going from board meeting to board meeting. He handled his papers with an economy of gesture, and had the restrained, almost clerical manner of someone who was often in the position of having to explain his work to people who had no idea of what his sort of development entailed. I was not surprised when he told me later that he was pursuing a master of divinity degree ("with an emphasis in urban development").

"We take a community-based approach, to create permanent economy," he said to me. "In this new model of development, there are assets to be leveraged . . ."

He went on in this abstract vein, describing economic uplift, emphasizing the importance of housing in giving people a sense that they had equity and a stake in the community. Old houses could be "rehabbed and retrofitted" and made energy efficient. He talked about "economic justice" and "partnerships" and "resource development."

This was the sort of bureaucratic jargon about policy and development I had heard in Africa, often at similarly well-appointed boardroom tables, in well-carpeted rooms, in comfortable chairs, while outside—out there somewhere—low-wealth people needing help were houseless and scavenging.

I admired Bernie Mazyck's earnestness, his serious manner, and even the opaque language of his mission fascinated me, because I could understand so little of it. Most of all I was intrigued by something else, and after we talked for a while I told him this.

"May I ask you about your name?"

He smiled, he relaxed, he took off his glasses, he smoothed his mustache with the back of one finger, and he pushed his chair away for comfort. For the next forty-five minutes he talked about his name, his family history, his relatives, his mother, his church.

It was a Southern manner of introduction, the assertion of rootedness and local experience. Though we met as strangers, we had a friend in common. He had been persuasive when talking about development plans, and he was an optimistic man, full of ideas; but what truly animated him and gave him authority was his telling me about his family, his life in South Carolina—he was a native of Charleston—and his unusual name.

Pronounced "mah-zeek," it was a Huguenot name, he said. One of the earliest settlers in Charleston had been Isaac Mazyck, who'd arrived and founded the first Huguenot church in the port city in the late seventeenth century. I later checked and found that the name Mazyck originated in Belgium, in the town of Maeseyck or Maaseyek or Maaseik, in which case his was a *nom de terre* and probably—though Bernie did not say so—the name of a slaveholder, since slaves usually took the name of their owner.

We talked about his extended family, his roots, about his sense of African identity, his strong feeling of being a descendant of the Akan people of what is now Ghana but historically one of the great empires of coastal West Africa, the Kingdom of Ashanti. Bernie saw Akan resemblances in family relationships, in the matrilineal way he'd been raised, even in certain religious practices that had persisted in Christian churches in the South. And he said with feeling, "You need God on your side. The church is the center of my life."

And I began to understand in a little more detail how in the South the past still mattered, partly because it cast a long shadow, but also because there was so much frustration in the present. The past was easier to understand, more coherent, and it helped to explain the present.

Gullah, for example. Many people in South Carolina alluded to this black culture that retained its Creole language and traditions on the coast. But Bernie could quote the language. "Kumbayah" — as in the song — was a Gullah expression, meaning "Come by here." He told me how his mother would use Gullah expressions to teach him. Gullah penetrated everywhere, as a private language, as an enduring culture.

"My mother used to say, 'Nu man, yanna weep-dee we dan-ya!'"

Meaning: "No, man, you're up there and I'm down here," a way of emphasizing class distinctions, high and low.

His mother's name was Seypio, which was a version of her grandfather's name, and his was Scipio, as in Scipio Africanus, the great Roman general, conqueror of Hannibal in the Battle of Zama (thus his title, Africanus).

Talk of slavery and sacrifice led Bernie to explain the conflicting views of the past. As an example, he told me about the African-American History Monument near here in Columbia, on the grounds of the state capitol — how it was years in the planning, and that in all the preliminary discussions it seemed impossible for anyone to agree on how the South Carolina black experience should be depicted on the bronze panels. A proposed panel showing the Ku Klux Klan lynching blacks was shelved. A great fight ensued about images of the Confederate flag. And there was the question of what to do about the stirring figure of Denmark Vesey, a slave who, having won a lottery, had bought his own freedom and in 1822 led a slave revolt in the state. It was the largest insurrection ever organized on behalf of slaves in the United States, involving thousands of plotters, much larger than Nat Turner's in Virginia. But the plan was betrayed, and Vesey was hanged, along with many others in Charleston. To South Carolina blacks, and to historians generally, Vesey was a man ahead of his time, in the mold of Haiti's revolutionary Toussaint L'Ouverture (whom Vesey admired): an enduring image of rebellion, a hero, and an inspiration.

"That was almost two hundred years ago," Bernie said. "But they wouldn't show his face on the monument." He smiled and said, "See, we got a ways to go."

We talked about the coming presidential election, the vexed question of the hated voter ID law. This restrictive law, which posed serious obstacles to voters, was advocated by the South Carolina governor, Nikki Haley, who was the daughter of immigrant Sikh parents. Having immigrated to Canada, the Randhawas had percolated over the border from Vancouver and had worked as schoolteachers in the tiny hamlet of Bamberg (pop. 3,604), the same size as Pandori Ran Singh Village (pop. 3,624), outside Amritsar in the Punjab, where the Randhawas were raised. In Bamberg they had started a successful clothing company, Exotica International, which ceased doing business in 2008. Less than two years later, Nikki (by then married to a white Southerner and converted to Methodism) was governor and her parents were living in luxury in Hilton Head.

"Odd," I said, "a second-generation Indian American elected governor of this state."

"An awful lot of people didn't know she was a person of color," Bernie said. "She looked white in her political posters. She doesn't have an Indian name. She's a Christian. She's a right-wing Tea Party Republican. She hates the unions. And she kept her folks way in the back. Her daddy's turban would have been a problem for a lot of white voters here."

"That's funny."

"It's really sad," Bernie said. "How can I help you?"

I said, "I'd like to see some of the places you're working to help develop".

"Anything special?"

"The poorest."

He nodded and poked some numbers into his phone.

Route 301: "No One Ever Goes There"

Go to Allendale via Orangeburg, Bernie had said. But I got a late start, because I wanted to see the African-American History Monument at the statehouse that Bernie had mentioned – and the Confederate flag still flying on the grounds (it had been moved from the capitol dome after decades of objections). On meandering roads past twiggy fields of tufted white, the blown-open cotton bolls brightening the spindly bushes, I came to the town of Walterboro and saw a booth with a signboard that read INFORMATION. Though I now had a map to Allendale, I asked directions, merely so that I could talk to the old woman who supervised the booth and handed out pamphlets to local points of interest: the Verdler House, Bonnie Doone Plantation, the museums and galleries, Frankie's Fun Park. Or Wally's Tow Service:

BLACK OR WHITE

DAY OR NIGHT

YOU CALL

WE HAUL

"I have worked here for twelve years and no one has ever asked me how to get to Allendale," she said.

"That seems unusual."

"No," she said. "No one ever goes there."

And once I'd found the right road, Route 301, what she said seemed true. It was a ghost road of astonishing decrepitude — weird to look at, shocking to reflect upon.

In a lifetime of travel, I had seen very few places to compare with Allendale in its oddity, and approaching the town was just as bizarre. The road, much of it, was a divided highway, two broad side-by-side roads amounting to an old-fashioned turnpike, split by a grassy median, a central reservation much wider than I was used to — wider than many sections of the great north-south interstate, Route 95, which is more like a tunnel than a road for the way it sluices cars in both directions at great speed.

But this proud highway I was on, a substantial dual carriageway cut through low empty hills, was devoid of traffic: a royal road amid the green landscape and farms so fallen and abandoned they seemed like mere sketches of former habitation. The great rolling road was like a road to nowhere. No other cars on it today, no towns that I could see, no gas stations, no motels, no stores, like a road leading to the end of the world.

From the 1930s into the late 1960s this highway was the most important road through the South. A well-traveled thoroughfare, Route 301 was once the way from Delaware to Florida, the highway that the earliest Northern drivers took to find sunshine and ease, and that Southerners took to seek work, and a life, in the North.

It is usual in traveling through the developing world to find roads under construction—wide roads, narrow roads, highways, toll roads, and the clattering machinery, tracked excavators and bulldozers, clawing at the soil and disfiguring the land. It is rare in those places (I am thinking of Africa and India) to find finished roads, in good shape, totally neglected or unused. But throughout the rural South there were such roads, great gleaming highways that seemed to lead nowhere, and this one, Route 301, in this poor midsection of South Carolina, was one of them—startling in its strangeness.

Approaching the outskirts of Allendale, I had a sight of Doomsday, one of those visions that make the effort of travel worthwhile and proved to me that my setting out for the South had been an inspired decision. I had no idea that I would find what I saw that day of blue sky and sunshine, a mild breeze in the pines.

It was a vision of ruin, of decay, of utter emptiness, and it was obvious in the simplest, most recognizable structures—motels, gas stations, restaurants, stores, even a movie theater, all of them abandoned to rot, some of them so thoroughly decayed that all that was left was the great cement slab of the foundation, stained with oil or paint, littered with the splinters of the collapsed building, its rusted sign leaning. Some were brick-faced, others made of cinderblocks, but none of them was well made, and so the impression I had was of devastation, as though a recent war had ravaged the place and destroyed the buildings and killed all the people.

Here was the corpse of a motel, the Elite—the sign still legible—broken buildings in a wilderness of weeds; and farther down the road, the Sands and the Presidential Inn, collapsed, empty; and the restaurants empty too, one unmistakably the curved roof and distinctive cupola of a Howard Johnson's restaurant, another just a wreck but with a gigantic sign, its peeling paint promising LOBSTER. And another fractured place with a cracked swimming pool and broken windows, its rusted sign, CRESENT MOTEL, the more pathetic for being misspelled.

Most of the shops were closed, the only functioning ones owned by

Indians. The Art Deco single-screen movie house, once the Carolina Theater, was boarded up. The wide main road was littered. The side streets,
lined by shacks and abandoned houses, looked haunted. I had never seen
anything quite like it, the ghost town on the ghost highway. I was glad I
had come.

The presence of Indian shopkeepers, the heat, the tall dusty trees, the
sight of plowed fields, the ruined motels and abandoned restaurants,
the inactivity, a somnolence hanging over the town like a blight — even
the intense sunshine was like a sinister aspect of that same blight — all
these features made it seem like a town in Zimbabwe. It looked as though
the colonizers had come and gone, the settlers had bolted, most of the local people had fled, and the place had fallen on evil days. Lingering at Mr.
Patel's shop, I saw a succession of black customers buying cans of beer and
going outside to sit under a tree and drink.

All this was a first impression, but it was a powerful one. Later, just
outside Allendale proper, I saw the campus of the University of South
Carolina at Salkehatchie, with eight hundred students, and the old main
street, and the handsome courthouse, and a small subdivision of well-
kept bungalows. But mostly, and importantly, Allendale, judging from
Route 301, was a ruin — poor, neglected, hopeless-looking, a vivid failure.

Allendale County Alive

On a back road of sunny, bleak Allendale, in an office tucked inside a
mobile unit, resembling a static house trailer and signposted ALLENDALE
COUNTY ALIVE, I found Wilbur Cave. Bernie Mazyck had given me his
name as someone who was involved in county revitalization, general
counseling, and housing improvement.

After we shook hands, I mentioned the extraordinary weirdness of
Route 301.

"This was a famous road once, the halfway point from up north to
Florida or back," Wilbur said. "Everyone stopped here. And this was one
of the busiest towns ever. When I was growing up we could hardly cross
the road. I remember we couldn't cross the road without an adult. All the

motels had No Vacancy signs. There were lots of stores—people driving through needed to shop for food or clothes. Lots of garages and repair shops. The town was booming!"

But there were no cars today, or just a handful. "What happened?"

"Route Ninety-five happened."

And Wilbur explained that in the late 1960s, when the interstate route was plotted, it bypassed Allendale forty miles to the east, and like many other towns on Route 301, Allendale fell into ruin. But just as the great new city rising in the wilderness is an image of American prosperity, a ghost town like Allendale is also a feature of our landscape. Perhaps the most American urban transformation is that very sight—that all ghost towns were once boomtowns.

"Nowadays, this is as country as it gets," Wilbur said.

"Country" was one way of putting it. Another might have been "This is what the world will look like when it ends."

Poor Allendale's nearness to wealthy towns was another surrealistic feature (but that too was an American trait). In South Carolina's smallest county (also called Allendale, with a population of 12,000), on the Savannah River and the Georgia state line, the town was less than two hours from the mansions and gourmet restaurants of Charleston; it was about the same distance to salubrious Augusta, Georgia, and no more than an hour and a half to Hilton Head, where for more than thirty years the wonks, the wise, the well-heeled, and the sententious gathered every year on Renaissance Weekend to declaim uplifting messages and debate the future of the world. All these luminaries and sages really needed to do was to spend a few days in Allendale County and they would perhaps understand that the theories of Hilton Head denied the realities here: every development problem I have ever witnessed in fifty years of traveling the world existed in Allendale as a persistent agony.

But as the woman in the information booth had told me, no one goes to Allendale. And this was why Wilbur Cave, seeing his hometown falling to ruin—its very foundations devolving to dust—decided to do something to improve it. Wilbur had been a record-breaking runner in his high school, and after graduation from the University of South Carolina at Columbia, he worked locally and then ran for the state representative's seat in this district. He was elected and served for six years. He became a strategic planner, and with this experience he joined and reenergized the nonprofit Allendale County Alive, which was committed to helping provide decent housing to local people. The town itself had a population of 4,500, three-quarters of them black, like the county.

"It's not just this town that needs help," Wilbur said. "The whole county is in bad shape. In the 2010 census we are the tenth-poorest county in the United States. And, you know, a lot of the others are Indian reservations."

The funding was minimal, an initial budget of $250,000 annually at the outset, but had been decreasing over the years because of cuts and economies and lack of donors. Compared to US-funded housing programs I had seen in Africa and South America, this was a piffling amount. It was, by any measure, a small-scale operation that depended more on ingenuity, innovation, and good will than on money.

"In 2003, I was the new sheriff in town," Wilbur said. "I thought this might be a cruise to retirement. How wrong I was!" Then he smiled. "But we persevere."

Wilbur Cave was sixty-one but looked ten years younger than that, compact, muscular, still with the build of a running back, and energetic, full of plans. He dressed informally in an open-necked shirt and blue jeans. On the walls of his tiny office in the small unit that served as his headquarters were family photos, upbeat slogans, and graphs showing a steady increase in home ownership in the county.

Wilbur's family had lived in the area for many generations. His mother had been a schoolteacher at Allendale County Training School. "The black school," Wilbur explained. "The white one was Allendale Elementary."

The Allendale schools were finally fully integrated in 1972. Whenever someone in the South mentioned a date, I tried to recall where I'd been at the time. Invariably I'd seen myself in a distant place, marveling at the exoticism of it all. In 1972, when Allendale was struggling to emerge from nineteenth-century notions of segregation and separate development, I was in England, planning my *Great Railway Bazaar* trip, in search of more colorful differences.

I remarked on how recently social change had come to the South.

"You have to know where we come from," Wilbur said. "It's hard for anyone to understand the South unless they understand history—and by history I mean slavery. History has had more impact here."

Without realizing it, only smiling and tapping a ballpoint on the desktop blotter, he sounded like one of the wise admonitory Southern voices in Faulkner, reminding the Northerner of the complex past.

"Take my mother's family. They were cotton farmers for generations, right here in Allendale County. They had a hundred acres or so. It was a family activity to pick cotton. The children did it, the grandchildren. It was a normal after-school job. I did it, I sure did—we all did it."

The small cotton farms, like those belonging to Wilbur's family, were sold eventually to bigger growers, who introduced mechanical harvesters. That was another reason for the unemployment and the decline in population. But farming was still the mainstay of Allendale County, where forty percent of its people lived below the poverty line.

"What are the problems?" he said, in answer to my obvious next question. "Drugs—crack cocaine mostly—health, crime, guns, and the school dropout rate, almost fifty percent."

There was hardly any work. There were no visitors, as in years past. Once there had been textile factories in Allendale, making cloth and carpets. They'd closed, the manufacturing outsourced to China, though a new textile factory was scheduled to open in a year or so, he said. The local industry was timber, but the lumber mills—there were two in Allendale, turning out planks and utility poles—did not employ many people.

I was to hear this story all over the rural South, in the ruined towns that had been manufacturing centers, sustained by the making of furniture, or appliances, or roofing materials, or plastic products, the labor-intensive jobs that kept a town ticking over. Companies had come to the South because the labor force was available and willing, wages were low, land was inexpensive, and unions were nonexistent. And so a measure of progress held out the promise of better things, perhaps prosperity. Nowhere in the United States could manufacturing be carried on so cheaply. And that was the case until these manufacturers discovered that however cheap it was to make things in the right-to-work states of the South, it was even cheaper in sweatshop China. The contraction and impoverishment of the South has a great deal to do with the outsourcing of work to China and

India, Even the catfish farms — an important income-producing industry all over the rural South — have been put out of business by the exports of fish farmers in Vietnam.

The current debate fiercely fought in the state legislature was not about jobs or outsourcing, but voting rights: the South Carolina voter ID bill, a restrictive law that would make it impossible for a person to vote unless he showed a photo ID, even though his name was listed on the voter roll. In the absence of a driver's license, it would be necessary to obtain a birth certificate to apply for an ID — not an easy matter if you happened to have been born in another county or state.

"This makes it feel like the sixties all over again," Wilbur said. "I mean, proving who you are is an obstacle, a way to prevent a person from voting. The excuse is 'preserving the integrity of the system,' eh? But I have an aunt who's ninety-six who's having trouble getting a copy of her birth certificate, and she was born right here in Allendale."

Wilbur went on to say that one of the keys to development (and I'd heard this from Bernie Mazyck too) was home ownership. Having a house was a way of grounding people, obligating them in positive ways and imposing responsibilities that helped them to grow; it produced visible changes and sometimes attracted outside funding.

"Public education is underfunded," he said. "But you can't make money improving education, or health care — they're not income-producing. Come on, let's look around."

He drove me through the back streets of Allendale, saying, "Housing is important," as we passed along the side roads, the lanes, the dirt paths on which stood two-room houses, some of them fixed up and painted, others no more than wooden shanties of the sort you might see in any Third World country, and some shotgun shacks that were the emblematic architecture of Southern poverty.

"That's one of ours," Wilbur said of a tidy white wood-frame bungalow on a corner. "It was a derelict property that we rehabbed, and now it's part of our inventory of rentals. That's income for us to rehab other houses."

People qualified for a rehab if their income was eighty percent below South Carolina's median income. A one-person household with an income of less than $27,000 was designated as poor; a three-person household with less than $34,000 income; a four-person household with less than $38,000. Not only was this a small amount of money to live on; half the people subsisted on much less. But with an improved house came a better life and brighter prospects.

"We also have a homeowners' education program," Wilbur said. "We teach the intricacies of buying and owning a home. After that we may give some down-payment assistance, and the house might cost anywhere from twenty-five to seventy-five thousand."

To attract businesses and create a climate for investment, the look of the town and the county had to be improved, which was another reason for the intensive drive to fix up the shacks.

"My feeling is, if South Carolina is to change, we have to change the worst," Wilbur said as we passed a small weathered house of sun-blackened planks and curling shingles, an antique that was beyond repair. But a man had lived in it until just six months before, without electricity or heat or piped water.

I asked if I could see inside that one, or perhaps the next one, which was a shack with a hole in the roof, a family of eight (four generations) living inside.

"We'll need permission," Wilbur said. "It might take time. You'll have to come back another day."

I said I wanted to come back.

"You hungry?" Wilbur asked.

I said I was, and he took me on a short drive to the edge of town, the Barnwell Highway, to a local diner, O Taste and See, sought out for its soul food, fried chicken and catfish, biscuits, rice and gravy, fruit pies, and friendliness. The owner, Mrs. Cathy Nixon, with a child on her lap, explained, "It's from the Bible." And she quoted: "'O taste and see that the Lord is good. Blessed is the man that trusteth in him.'" The very existence of good food in this poor town seemed strange, but I found it to be a feature of the South: even the most distressed town usually had a soul food restaurant, a family place, often one small room on a back road, simple cooking and a warm welcome. Mrs. Nixon was seventy-three and had seven great-grandchildren.

"You're a traveler," Wilbur said, after he said grace — another ritual, strictly observed in the soul food diner.

"Oh, yes."

He had not read anything I'd written. If my name rang a bell at all, I was taken to be Henry David Thoreau — he was a Yankee too, wasn't he? Most of the Southerners I encountered had no more than a nodding acquaintance with books, and that gave them either an exaggerated respect for authorship or an utter indifference to it. When there was an exception, and I came across a handful, often in the unlikeliest places, the reader was passionate, with a house full of books, like an isolated bookworm in a Chekhov story.

Being unrecognized as a writer was a distinct advantage. I was more easily summed up as an older man from the North, probably retired, who had driven here with a lot of questions. I had no history, no reputation, no aura, no persona, no news, nothing attached to me. And I enjoyed being the foreigner, Mr. Paul with the hard-to-spell last name — the stranger — because that was how I viewed these people I was traveling among in this unusual place, some parts of the South as odd and remarkable as any I had seen in my traveling life.

When Wilbur alluded to my traveling, I took it as an opportunity to say that I had been in Africa not long before, and that in Namibia I had discovered that the US government had granted $360 million to improve Namibia's education, energy, and tourism sectors. Around $67 million had been earmarked for tourism alone, though it was mainly European tourists, not Americans, who visited Namibia. I mentioned this because parts of rural, underdeveloped Allendale County resembled parts of rural, underdeveloped Africa. And Allendale itself — sleepy, decaying, unemployed, with defunct motels, Indian shops — was reminiscent of an upcountry farming town in Kenya that had gone to the dogs. And Kenya, too, got hundreds of millions in US development aid.

"Money is not the whole picture, but it's the straw that stirs the drink," Wilbur said. "I don't want hundreds of millions. Give me one thousandth of it and I could dramatically change public education in Allendale County."

His operating budget was $100,000, and his organization was self-sustaining thanks to the income from the rented houses they'd rehabbed.

Wilbur said that he didn't begrudge aid to Africa, but he added, "If my organization had access to that kind of money, we could really make a difference."

"What would you do?"

"We could focus our energy and not worry about funding. We could be more creative and get things done." He smiled. "We wouldn't have to worry about the light bill."

Orangeburg and the Massacre

With nowhere to stay in sunny, desolate Allendale – all the motels abandoned or destroyed – I drove up Route 301, the empty, once-glorious thoroughfare, for forty-five miles to Orangeburg. It was a small town, its main street a collection of sorry shops, boarded-up stores, and gloomy churches, but its outskirts were near enough to the interstate (the highway to Charleston) to have motels and diners. The poorer motels and beat-up restaurants were in town, a threadbare remnant here, but still alive.

The town was kept buoyant by its schools and colleges, well-known ones, among them Claflin University (founded in 1869) and South Carolina State University, both of them historically black (and still with mainly black student bodies). And there were some others: a Methodist college, a technical school, private academies, and public schools.

Walking along the main street the day after I arrived in Orangeburg, I fell into step with a man and said hello. And I received the glowing Southern welcome. He wore a dark suit and carried a briefcase. He said he was a lawyer and gave me his card, *Virgin Johnson Jr. Attorney at Law.* I inquired about the town, just a general question, and received a surprising answer.

He said, "Well, there was the massacre."

"Massacre" is a word that commands attention. This bloody event was news to me, so I asked for details. Virgin Johnson told me that in spite of the fact that the Civil Rights Act had been in force for four years in 1968, Orangeburg was still segregated. A bowling alley on the main road (All Star Bowling Lanes) refused to allow black students inside – and it was the only bowling alley in Orangeburg.

On a day in February '68, objecting to being discriminated against in the bowling alley and elsewhere, several hundred students held a demonstration at the campus of South Carolina State across town. The event was noisy but the students were unarmed, facing officers from the South Carolina Highway Patrol, who carried pistols and carbines and shotguns. Alarmed by the jostling students, one policeman fired his gun into the air — warning shots, he later said. Hearing those gunshots, other policemen began firing directly at the protesters, who turned and ran. Because the students were fleeing, they were shot in the back. Three young men were killed, Samuel Hammond, Delano Middleton, and Henry Smith; twenty-eight were injured, some of them seriously; all of them students, riddled with buckshot.

"What did you think?" I asked Virgin Johnson.

"I was twelve years old," he said in the country way, *twel'*. "I didn't think much. Later on, people talked about it."

"What do people say nowadays?"

"It's not a big subject," he said. "There's a memorial service every year, but as for the issue itself, I don't know how far it extends beyond the campus."

Most Americans know of the killings at Kent State in Ohio, which took place in 1970 — four students murdered during an antiwar demonstration. "Kent State" is an expression loaded with implication: innocent protesters gunned down by panicked National Guardsmen. The Boston Massacre of 1770 is well known — five colonists killed by British troops on King Street; my father used to show us the massacre memorial on Boston Common. We knew the curious name of one of the victims, Crispus Attucks, a mixed-race black and Wampanoag resident of Boston, a sailor perhaps. The murder of the men helped stir revolutionary passion; almost 250 years later, their graves in the Granary Burying Ground are garlanded and solemnly contemplated, the men regarded as martyrs and heroes.

For anyone outside Orangeburg, the town's name summons up no images of repression or the shedding of innocent blood. The eight policemen who fired on the crowd were tried for causing the deaths but acquitted, and the only person who found himself in prison was one of the demonstrators, Cleveland L. Sellers, who was convicted on a charge of riotous assembly. Sentenced to a year, he served seven months, with time off for good behavior. Some of these facts I learned not from Virgin Johnson but later from a detailed account of the incident, *The Orangeburg Massacre*, by Jack Bass and Jack Nelson, published in 2003. Though he was African

American and an Orangeburg resident, Johnson could not offer many details, saying he'd been too young to understand, and "it was a long time ago." Another explanation for his amnesia was that the Orangeburg Massacre had been overshadowed by greater atrocities of 1968, a year of violent incidents — the assassinations of Dr. Martin Luther King and Robert F. Kennedy, the Tet Offensive in Vietnam, riots in Washington, Baltimore, Chicago, and elsewhere — a year of death and mayhem.

I mentioned Kent State to Johnson, how everyone knew the name.

He smiled. He said, "But you know those kids that died were white."

Virgin Johnson's profession as an attorney surprised me, because he seemed so vague about the massacre. I'd expected a lawyer, especially a local man, to have more facts, and yet he was forthcoming and helpful about this forgotten episode.

"I can introduce you to some people who were there," he said. And he recommended the book by Bass and Nelson, which I later read.

I thanked him for his assistance, and before I went on my way, I said how odd it was to me to be holding this conversation with someone I'd met by chance, simply asking directions on a public street. I added that where I came from, such a casual encounter would have lacked both warmth and information. I was grateful for his taking the time with a stranger who had so many questions.

"People here understand how it is to need help," he said. He meant black people; he meant himself. He added, "To be neglected." And he went on, "It's the whole environment — it's not easy to get away from it. They go through it all the time. That's why they can sympathize and relate."

"Do you feel that way?"

"Sure do," he said, and tapped the business card I'd been holding. "You let me know if you want to meet some people who know more than I do. Why not stop in to my church this Sunday. I'll be preaching."

"Your card says you're an attorney."

"I'm a preacher too. Revelation Ministries over in Fairfax. Well, Sycamore, actually. This is the South, there's a church on every corner. Come on down see us."

"Where's Sycamore?"

"Nearby Allendale. You familiar with Allendale, Mr. Paul?"

Charleston: Gun Show

With a few days to kill, I went to Charleston. Compressed in its narrowing spit of land, lapped by its placid harbor, tumbled into its tiny islands, Charleston is a city of rich cultural history and architectural marvels — old ornate mansions, churches, and forts — its downtown lined with gourmet restaurants, all the metropolitan attributes that held no interest at all for me.

Tourists visit Charleston to go sightseeing (Fort Sumter, plantations), to eat, and to listen to anecdotes of the Civil War and tales of Gullah and Geechee lore. I found the city, like most tourist cities, pleasant enough, but glittering and impenetrable, class-conscious and house-proud, perhaps justifiably smug. I was there to go to a gun show.

One of a handful of good gourmet meals I ate during my travels in the South I had in Charleston, but really it was not much better than many I'd had in the soul food diners or barbecue joints I found in nearly every small town, nothing to compare for friendliness and good food with tiny O Taste and See in Allendale or Dukes in Orangeburg or Lottie's in Marion, Alabama; not with Doe's Eat Place in Greenville, Mississippi, or the fried chicken and catfish buffet at Granny's Family Restaurant in West Monroe, Louisiana, where a sign cautioned, "Take all you want, but eat all you take." As for the Charleston museums, churches, mansions, and gift shops: nothing for me.

The cultural event that got my attention was the Gun and Knife Expo I'd seen advertised the previous week, to be held at the Charleston Area Convention Center, in North Charleston. I drove there from Orangeburg on a rainy weekend — gun shows are generally two-day affairs — and was surprised to see the size of the arena, half as big as a football field, with a long line of people waiting to go in and the enormous parking lot crammed with cars. From the moment I arrived I was struck by the order and politeness of everyone — staff, traders, gun-show-goers, hot dog and popcorn sellers — and a vibration, too, a sense of anticipation, eagerness, pleasure.

Entering was a slow process of paying an admission of eight dollars and, if you had a firearm, showing it. Many of those entering were armed—pistol on a belt holster, rifle slung on a shoulder—but personal weapons had to be unloaded and tagged at the entry desk. At the end of these checks and inspections, entrants were issued with the sort of plastic identity bracelet you get at an emergency ward and finally shuffled past the greeters and food carts, staying in line, just a few mutters, everything orderly.

After that lobby business, the huge arena was filled with tables and booths and stalls, most selling guns, some selling knives, others stacked with piles of ammo. Just the sight of it seemed to make the attendees smile and swallow, jittery with joy, as though the array of all these naked weapons, pistols and rifles, amounted to gun porn. I had never seen so many guns, big and small, heaped in one place, and I suppose the notion that they were all for sale, just lying there waiting to be picked up and handled, sniffed, and aimed, provided a thrill.

"Pardon me, sir."

"No problem, scoot on bah."

"Thank you much."

No one on earth—none I had ever seen—is more polite than a person at a gun show; more eager to smile, more accommodating, less likely to step on your toe. Among so many weapons there are no insults; there is only patience, sweetness, and occasional joshing. In a place where everyone is armed, good manners are helpful, perhaps essential. But that demeanor didn't seem forced: everyone was glad to be there. Happiness amounting to rapture was the prevailing mood of the gun-show-goers—good humor and exquisite manners.

Muffled cries of "Look at that" and many educated questions. That was something else that struck me: the plainspoken and roughly dressed but very knowledgeable crowd. These men were living proof of Christ's words in Luke 22:36, a verse many could probably quote: "He that hath no sword, let him sell his garment and buy one." A man who seemed adrift and lost, scruffy camo cap, bearded, in a greasy jacket and worn-down boots, asked a stallholder with a table of vintage assault rifles, "That underfold-stock AK-47, is that the Zastava variant?"

"No, this the WASR, pre-ban. Flash suppressor. All the standard features."

"What kind of mag?"

"I got an assortment I could show you. And it comes with a bayonet. See the lug?"

The inquiring man rubbed at his frizzy beard with the back of his fist. "I heard loose mag wells are a problem."

"Not with this one. I've shot it plenty."

"How much is that AK?" I asked, chiming in.

"Fifteen hundred."

"I could buy that?"

"If you got the money. Cash. Private sale."

In spite of this knowledge of the weaponry that bordered on connoisseurship, most of the gun-show-goers were just looking, hands in pockets, sauntering, nudging each other — admiring, dazzled by the size and rarity of the guns, as though they had gone there to gape, swap stories, meet old friends, drink coffee, and walk among the tables the way people do at flea markets. And this greatly resembled a flea market, but one smelling of cleaning oil and wood polish and a dustiness of scorched steel and gunpowder. They were at the show, man and boy, less to buy than to be reassured by the firepower.

Yet there was something else in the atmosphere, a quality of mood I could not define as I walked among the weapons; it was an attitude, a vibration, a buzz. As I strolled and listened, and registered the pulses of the air and the postures of the men, the feeling became more apparent. I could not at first understand what it was that I felt.

"Thank you much."

"You're very welcome."

"Go right ahead, sir, pick that bad boy up."

The long tables of knives were the least visited, but they showed every sort of blade, from exquisite penknives to machetes to iron hackers, some of them engraved, with bone and ivory handles — and swords and bayonets too. At other tables, military memorabilia, Nazi blades. "That's an Ernst Röhm dagger," one side of the broad blade etched *Alles für Deutschland,* the motto of the Sturmabteilung (SA) that Röhm cofounded with Hitler, as the seller explained to me. After Röhm was arrested for treason by Hitler on the Night of the Long Knives, in 1934, he was executed. As for these daggers that he had distributed to his Brownshirts, the inscription

In Herzlicher Kameradschaft Ernst Röhm was obliterated from the blade with a stone grinder.

"See? They got rid of the Röhm business. If your knife had it showing, you'd be in trouble. This is highly collectible."

Gas masks, helmets, belts, harnesses, badges, flags, all with swastikas, and many 9-millimeter Lugers.

"That's a working gun. You could fire that. But don't dry-fire it here."

Civil War paraphernalia—powder flasks, Harpers Ferry rifles, peaked caps, insignia, Confederate money, and pistols—a number of tables were piled with these battered pieces of history. Nearly all of them were from the Confederate side. Bumper stickers too, one reading *The Civil War—America's Holocaust*. Another, *Hey Liberal, You're the Reason We Have the 2nd Amendment*, and many denouncing President Obama: *NObama, Obummer, Obamanation*, and *Advocates of Gun Control: Hitler, Stalin, Castro, Idi Amin, Pol Pot, Obama*.

"My uncle has one of them powder flasks."

"If it's got the apportioning spigot spout in working order, your uncle's a lucky guy."

Many of the rifles and pistols at other tables were old muzzle-loaders, percussion varieties, or big, mean revolvers that shot black powder ammo. Because they were antiques, and theoretically unworkable, they could be sold to anyone. But black powder ammo, though rare, was obtainable, and any one of these old weapons could still open a fatal hole in a man or a beast.

"That there's museum quality," a seller said of a musket with an engraved barrel and a beautifully carved stock. I had the impression that many of these gun guys had brought their best weapons as boasts, in the boyish, proud, show-and-tell manner of collectors, and would not have parted with them for anything.

But a greater number of the stallholders looked hard-up and desperate to sell the stack of battered guns and tarnished magazines and parts lined up in front of them. At one of these tables, alongside a plastic Glock and a .22 plinking rifle, I saw a German World War Two–era .32-caliber Mauser pistol. I picked it up and hefted it.

"Three hundred fifty bucks and it's yours. I got extra mags that go with it."

"I'm from out of state."

"Don't matter. Private sale. Okay, three hundred even."

Not every sale was private. Half a dozen sectioned-off areas were authorized dealers, and inside the enclosure scowling men sat at smaller tables, filling out applications for background checks, while staff members swiped credit cards through machines. These were registered guns, better quality, more of them. A background check would not take more than thirty minutes, I was told.

Some were reenactors: one man in a Confederate uniform, another dressed in period cowboy costume, looking like a vindictive sheriff, black hat and tall boots and pearl-handled pistols. He saw me staring.

"Howdy, partner."

One of the tables was set up like a museum display of World War One weapons and uniforms, as well as maps, books, postcards, and framed black-and-white photos of muddy battlefields. This was a commemorative exhibit put up by Dane Coffman, who had driven down from Leesburg, a hundred miles away, and rented eight tables to mount a memorial to his soldier grandfather, Ralph Coffman, who had served in the Great War. Dane, who was about sixty or so, wore an old infantryman's uniform, a wide-brimmed hat, and leather puttees, the getup of a doughboy. Nothing was for sale. Dane was a collector, a military historian, and a reenactor; his aim was to show his collection of belts and holsters, mess kits, canteens, wire cutters, trenching tools, and what he called his pride and joy, a machine gun propped on a tripod.

"I'm here for my grandfather," he said. "I'm here to give a history lesson."

Throughout the gun show, I saw a mixture of private and commercial, mostly poor or out-of-work-looking men in cracked boots and faded hats, but there were a few well-heeled buyers, some obvious cranks, and loiterers. A few people were selling flags and patriotic items and comical signs: *Warning—I'm a Bitter Gun Owner Clinging to My Religion,* which was an echo of what Barack Obama had said when campaigning for president; *No Trespassing—Violators Will Be Shot—Survivors Will Be Shot Again;* and *Gun Control Is Being Able to Hit Your Target.*

"And I'll tell you something else," a man leaning on a fat black assault rifle expostulated. "If that damn vote goes through, we're finished."

"Oh, yeah. They're fixing to change this whole bidniss," another man added. "You can kiss your AR goodbye."

This made the first man indignant. "I would like to see someone try and take this away from me. I surely would."

Others were ranting quietly, but not many, because there was no disagreement in the hall. These were all gun guys, gun owners, gun rights people—men and women, whole families—all on the same side. It was my first glimpse of a large gathering of white Southerners, and some observers have commented that white Southerners are like an ethnic group, similar to Irish or Italians—"a culturally distinct group."

Reverend Johnson's Story

"I'm just a country boy from bottom-line caste, born and raised in Estill, Hampton County," Virgin Johnson told me a week later, over the daily special at Ruby Tuesday, up the road in Orangeburg, where he lived. Estill was the sticks, he said, deep country, cotton fields. Never mind. He smiled; he had a way of showing two prominent front teeth when he smiled, as if to demonstrate he was being ironic. Then, with a mock-resigned sigh, he said, "Po' black."

Still in his dark suit, he sipped at his iced tea and told me about his life. This was another man speaking, not the Sycamore preacher, not the shrewd Orangeburg trial lawyer, but a quiet, reflective private citizen in a roadside restaurant, reminiscing about his life as a loner. I told him I'd been to a gun show in Charleston.

"I got guns," he said eagerly. "I got all sorts. I got an AK-47, I got so many. The legitimate gun owners don't cause the deaths—it's the illegal guns that are the problem, the criminals. Tell ya, I want some protection. This can be a dangerous place."

"Give me an example," I said.

"My father ran for a county council seat in Hampton in 1968. Virgin Johnson Senior—he was a stonemason, and later a teacher and a county councilor. My grandfather picked the name, it seemed special—Virgin Mary, virgin soil, virgin anything. My son is Virgin the Third." Virgin

Johnson leaned toward me and tapped the table. "'Sixty-eight was not a good year for a black man to run for anything. He got a message in the mailbox. It said, 'If you win, we will kill you.'"

"Did he drop out of the race?"

"Didn't stop him," Virgin Johnson said. "But know why he lost? Because people knew about the message, and the ones who liked him — and there were many — voted against him. Didn't want him to dah. He ran again, years later, and won. My daddy was at my service today. He's ailing, but he always comes. He's a popular man in these parts.

"I was born in 1954. In 1966, the year of what they called 'voluntary integration,' I was the only black student at Estill Elementary School. Happened this way. There were two buses went by our place every morning. I had said to my daddy, 'I want to get the first bus.' That was the white bus. He said, 'You sure, boy?' I said, 'I'm sure.'"

It was so odd to be here, in a busy restaurant — whites and blacks together at booths and tables — almost fifty years later, as Virgin Johnson recalled this episode that left such a mark on his life, the matter of a black student on a white bus.

"The day I hit that bus, everything changed. Sixth grade — it changed my life. I lost all my friends, black and white. No one talked to me, no one at all. Even my white friends from home. I knew they wanted to talk to me, but they were under pressure, and so was I. I sat in the back of the bus. When I went to the long table for lunch, thirty boys would get up and leave."

He sipped his tea, nodded, and smiled ruefully. The Ruby Tuesday waiter led prospective diners to a booth beyond, and the three glanced at the well-dressed man — the only man in the restaurant wearing a suit and tie.

"I was twelve," he said. "The funny thing is, we were all friendly, black and white. My grandfather was beloved by all. Oncle Henry, they called him — Henry Frazier. We played together in and around Estill. We picked cotton. My daddy and uncle had a hundred acres of cotton. Uncle Clayton still farms cotton, corn, watermelon. I picked a hundred or a hundred twenty-five pounds a day with my family and my friends. But when I got on the bus, it was over. I was alone, on my own.

"When I got to school I knew there was a difference. There was not another African American there—no black teachers, no black students, none at all in the elementary school. Except the janitors. The janitors were something, like guardian angels to me. They were black, and they didn't say anything to me—didn't need to. They nodded at me as if to say, 'Hold on, son. Hold on.'

"So I lost all my friends, and I learned at an early age you have to stand by yourself. That gave me a fighting spirit. I've had it since I was a child. It's destiny. What happens when you let other people make your decisions? You become incapable of making your own decisions. They were not all bad days. In those days you had to earn respect. Nowadays no one cares about respect. It's more of a political show."

We continued to eat our meal, and he went on talking, reminiscing. He was a reflective man, pausing between thoughts, punctuating sentences with silences, so it was easy for me to take notes and go on eating.

"When I was thirteen I had a job pulling string for a surveyor. He was white. I liked the job. This was the summertime, the sixties. We were surveying a farm, the man and me. We pulled up on a property and started our work.

"Then I hear a voice: 'I don't want that boy on the property!'

"The owner of the property, see. He took out his shotgun and shot it in the air. I was thirteen! So we left, the white surveyor and me. That was in Hampton County, and this man's daddy was in the Klan. But they all had that mentality because of him.

"I was the first African American to go to law school from my side of the county. University of South Carolina at Columbia. I was in a class of one hundred—this was in the eighties. I was the only black person. Passed the bar in 1988. Got a license to preach.

"There's no contradiction for me. I'm happy doing both. I just wish the economy was better. This area is so poor. They got nothin'—they need hope. If I can give it to them, that's a good thing. Jesus said, 'We have to go back and care about the other person.'"

In the silences that followed I asked about Orangeburg and Sycamore and Fairfax, and especially about Allendale, which seemed to me so woebegone.

"These are friendly places—nice people. Good values. Decent folks.

Next time you come down here, pay us a visit at our church, Revelation Ministries. Promise you will."

"I promise," I said, and the notion of returning made me happy.

"We have issues—kids having kids, for one, sometimes four generations of kids having kids. But there's so little advance. That does perplex me, the condition of this place. Something's missing. What is it?"

And then he made a passionate gesture, flinging up his hand, and he raised his voice in a tone that recalled a preaching voice.

"Take the kids away from this area and they shine!"

Atomic Road

The narrow country road through the fragrant yellow pinewoods I saw on my map was named Atomic Road. A back road, it branched as Route 125 from dear, dilapidated Allendale and doom-laden Route 301 with its ruinous motels, and it followed the course of the Savannah River, which was the South Carolina–Georgia state line, to Augusta. "Atomic Road" was just too tempting a name to pass by. Seeing a big fence and a sentry box, I stopped to ask what was behind the fence.

"Turn your car around, sir, and keep going."

"I just wanted to ask a few questions."

"Did you hear me, sir?"

It was too late to stop at the nearest town, Aiken, to make inquiries, but I thought: The next time I come this way—when I visit Revelation Ministries—I'll look closer. But I knew that the fence enclosed the Savannah River Site, a nuclear facility known locally as the Bomb Factory.

That was another thing that distinguished this trip from others I'd made in my life. In Africa or China I never said, I'll come back in a few months and continue. Instead, I pushed on to a destination and then went home and wrote about it. But in the South I traveled in eccentric circles, in and out of the fourth dimension, always hopeful, making plans to return, and saying to myself, as I did that day on Atomic Road: I'll be back.

Believers on Bikes

On the way through Georgia to Tuscaloosa, I met Kelly Wiggly at an Alabama rest stop. He was with his wife, taking a breather. I saw he was towing a beautiful Harley-Davidson three-wheeler on his flatbed trailer, and asked him about it. A stout, white-haired man in his mid-sixties, in bib overalls and boots, he was a biker, but a kindly one, so mild-tempered as to be beatific.

"We're on our way home from Hatfield, Arkansas, on the Oklahoma state line, where we had a meeting of the Christian Motorcyclists Association," he said. "We ride for the Son — Son of God. We had three thousand bikers there from all over the country, other places in the world too. One biker from South Africa. We get together every year to witness, bless bikes, and to pray."

"You see any Hells Angels?"

He laughed and said, "We welcome the Hells Angels, the Banditos, anyone. It doesn't matter that they're dirty or violent — we have bikes in common. We say, 'Come on over for coffee. Four in the morning? That's okay. Any time is fine, you're welcome. Then we talk to them about Jesus, and maybe we share a little about the Bible, pray some, fellowship a little, no pressure."

"Do you make many converts?"

"They're pretty rough but they can be saved. Hey, some of them just got out of prison. All they have to do is listen and witness. I know we can bring them around. All you need is a Ride Plan. Step one: Pick your road. Step two: Consider your destination — we've all taken wrong turns. Step three is: Realize your dilemma — everyone's spiritual ride ends at the Canyon of Sin and Death. But God made a bridge over it, and that's Step four: Cross the bridge today — make a decision to cross that bridge, with the help of God."

"How was your weekend?"

"It was beautiful. All of us were camping there in Hatfield. Camping and witnessing. And you know what? This movement of Believers on Bikes started with one man, some years ago. It has grown tremendously. Listen, I'm about to retire, and when I do, my wife and I are going to ride this Harley all over the country, camping and witnessing." He thought a moment. "Maybe out of the country too. Know the fastest-growing Christian country in the whole world? It's China."

"I wonder why."

"'Cause they want to be saved. Gotta go now, off to Scottsboro. Bless you, brother."

Tuscaloosa: Football Matters

I drove to Tuscaloosa, Alabama, to get my bearings, to go deeper south, into Hale County and Greene County.

Tuscaloosa is a college town—more than half the town is the campus of the University of Alabama, celebrated as having the best football team in the country and the highest-paid coaches. It is the home of the Crimson Tide, the scarlet letter, the enlarged italic of the Alabama *A* on cars and clothes and often showing as a bold red tattoo.

I arrived on a Friday night, and the next day Tuscaloosa was in the grip of something more intense than a carnival. A riotous hooting tribal rite possessed the whole town, because of the University of Alabama football game that day in a stadium that held more than 100,000 people. I remarked on this and on the fans—everyone in Tuscaloosa was a fan. A man said to me, "This is a drinking town with a football problem," and winked to show he was joshing.

That idle quip has been made of many college towns, but is football a problem in Tuscaloosa? It seemed to me a chronic condition, and perhaps not a problem but a solution. The town is consumed by the sport. It is funded by football, and it prospers. Football is the town's identity, and the game makes its citizens happy—resolves their conflicts, unifies them, helps them forget their pain, gives them membership in a cult of winners—and it makes them colossal, monologuing, and rivalrous bores.

"Football's a religion here," some Tuscaloosans also say, and smile in apology, but they are closer to a complete definition in that cliché than they perhaps realize. Even the most basic of psychological analysis can explain why that neat formula is so fitting. Not any old religion, certainly not the mild, private, prayer-muttering, God-is-love creed that informs decisions and gives us peace. The Crimson Tide football religion is one that is awash in fury, something like Crusader Christianity reared on bloodthirstiness, with its saber charges and its conquests, or like Islam in its most jihadi form, the blazing, red-eyed, uncompromising, and martyr-ing faith; an in-group cohering around the sport to demonize and van-quish an out-group. In Tuscaloosa it is a public passion, a ritualized belief system, a complete persona. It is why in Alabama some men have the *A* tattooed on their neck, and some women on their shoulder: a public state-ment, a commitment for life, body modification as proof of loyalty and cultural differentiation, like a Hindu's caste mark or a Maori's tattoo or the facial scarring of a Sudanese Dinka.

Most towns are justifiably proud of their sports teams—a winning team always improves the mood of a place—but the Saturday crowd in Tuscaloosa, the processions of cars flying battle flags, the whooping and the costumes (and every seat in the enormous stadium spoken for) con-vinced me that this in-group mattered in a much more complex way than in other places I'd been. Its nearest equivalent in terms of tattoos, finery, and chanting was a traditional ceremony enacted by a defiant people who had once been colonized, asserting their tribal identity.

In Alabama football, fan loyalty bolstered self-esteem, not just of stu-dents but of almost the entire state. This group behavior is explained in "social identity theory," an encompassing proposal of the British psychol-ogist Henri Tajfel, who described the sympathies and reactions of persons choosing to attach themselves to a social class or a family or a club—or a football team—and become a member of an in-group. The groups to which people belong are, Tajfel writes, "an important source of pride and self-esteem. Groups give us a sense of social identity: a sense of belonging to the social world."

The sports fan is an example of someone engaged in group member-ship, for whom association and affiliation matter so greatly you could say it gives him or her a purpose in life. You develop a group membership by identifying yourself with a team and participating in "in-group favorit-ism." Such membership builds self-confidence and self-worth; you're in-vested in cheering for the team and raising its status. You're more than a passive member; you're an active booster, helping to make the team bigger and stronger. And it's good for your esteem, too. In Tajfel's view, "In order to increase our self-image we enhance the status of the group to which we belong."

To say that when your team wins you feel you're a champion is a pretty straightforward definition of the appeal of fandom. People often laugh self-consciously when they talk about their loyalty to a team, their pride in its success, but in Alabama, where fandom fervor is multiplied a thousandfold, no one laughs. There's nothing funny about chanting "Roll Tide, roll!"—the devotion is dead serious, and at times (so it seemed to me) defiant, hostile, verging on the pathological.

The power figure on any team is the coach. In Alabama folklore it is Paul Bryant, nicknamed "Bear" because as a youth in Arkansas he reputedly accepted the challenge of wrestling a captive, muzzled bear (and was mauled).

The three biggest funerals in Alabama history define the state's contending loyalties, I was told: George Wallace's, Martin Luther King's, and Bear Bryant's.

As a coach, Bear Bryant was a towering figure, statistically the most successful in the history of college football, who guided Alabama for twenty-five years and whose beaky profile and funny checkered snap-brim hat are emblems. His name is emblazoned on Tuscaloosa streets and buildings and on the vast stadium. Charismatic, noted for his heavy drinking and his toughness (he played on a broken leg in a college game in Tennessee), he was renowned as a motivator. He avoided recruiting black players for years, but in 1971 he brought in his first one, Wilbur Jackson, offering him a football scholarship. Thereafter the team became a career path for black athletes and a rallying point for the races.

Among his achievements, Bryant won six national championships for Alabama. But the present coach, Nick Saban, in just four seasons has won three national championships, and his contract runs until 2018. Saban, who is beloved for his victories and his rapport with players, presently earns $6.9 million a season, the highest-paid college football coach in the nation.

It is natural for a nonbeliever to cluck about the money, but college sports is a business—colleges need this national attention as a way of creating a cash flow. Donors, alumni, and booster clubs provide money to augment salaries; ticket sales are a strong source of revenue. And there is the licensed merchandise. Much of the logo paraphernalia is traditional — the numerous styles of caps, T-shirts, banners, and flags. But a great deal of it is culturally Alabama-specific: Crimson Tide trailer hitch covers, valve stem caps, a sexy lady's satin garter with lace picked out in "Roll Tide," baby slippers, garden chairs, "pillow pets," "child's hero capes," wall-sized "man cave flags," Crimson Tide car chargers, dog jerseys, puzzle cubes, games, watches, clothes, luggage, garden gnomes, table lamps, bedding, drinking glasses, gas grill covers, golf gear, car accessories, toothbrushes, and vinyl boat fenders, each carrying the Roll Tide logo or an enlarged and unambiguous *A*.

All this contributes to substantial football-related revenue, which in 2012 was $124 million, and $45 million of that was profit. Added to this is the improved status of the university itself, resulting in increased enroll-ment, higher teachers' salaries, and an expanded campus. Alabama's emi-nence as a university of football champions attracts nonresident students: more than half the students are from out of state, paying three times the in-state tuition.

The financial return is indisputable. The benefit in self-esteem is harder to gauge, but it is palpable. And perhaps it is predictable — the simple feel-good inevitability of identifying with the team and the elaborate costum-ing and imagery to go along with that identification — that it amounts to a complete lifestyle. This sort of social behavior has its counterpart in the enclosed in-groups of the world, especially the folk cultures, epitomized by the glorious and assertive "sing-sing" you'd see in the western high-lands of Papua New Guinea: the Goroka Show, the convergence of Asaro Mudmen and jungle-dwelling warriors fitted out with pig tusks and nose bones, with its extravagant finery, headdresses, weapons, beads, feathers, face painting, jitterbugging, spear shaking, mock charges, drumming, and hollering.

Reflecting on the Crimson Tide, I ceased to think of it as football at all, except in a superficial way; it seemed much more like another Southern reaction to a feeling of defeat, with some of the half-buried emotion I'd noticed at gun shows. In a state that is so hard-pressed, with one of the highest poverty rates in the nation, with its history of racial conflict, and with so little to boast about yet wishing to matter, it is natural that a winning team — a national champion — would attract people in need of meaning and self-esteem in their lives, and would become the basis of a classic in-group, The Tide was robust proof of social identity theory.

Sister Cynthia

"Please sign in," said the woman in the bright yellow dress, and then she looked closer at me and gave me the warmest smile. "I know you. You're Mr. Paul."

"How do you know that, sister?"

"You was at our service yesterday."

That was true. I was the sinner sitting among the publicans, well behind the Philistines, in a back pew. I was not normally a churchgoer, but what made a Sunday in the South complete was a church service, a gun show, or a football game.

"How kin Ah he'p you?"

"I'm here to see Miss Burton."

"I'll tell her you're here. Please sign the visitors' book."

Next to the names in the visitors' book, in a column headed *Reason for Visit*, I saw "Food" and "Clothes" and "Water" and "Light bill"—people seeking help in desperate inky scrawls. I signed my name and wrote, "Miss Cynthia Burton."

She greeted me a moment later, an imposing but wounded-looking woman of about sixty, walking unsteadily but determinedly on bad knees, supporting herself with a walker. She was the executive director of Community Service Programs of West Alabama. Moving slowly, shoving the walker ahead of her, she showed me to a large room with bare walls where a bare table dominated the space.

We began by talking about the football game that had enlivened the Tuscaloosa weekend.

"It's all football here—football mad, football disease," she said. "I understand that football is an economic engine, but absolutely everything is built around it. There's far more important things in life than winning a football championship."

"I think it's about more than football," I said, but resisted explaining how I felt it created a social identity.

"Some of the athletes profit from it," she said. "From a coach's attention especially. Because of the lack of a male head of household, we've lost two generations. Drugs — your mother's got two jobs and she's dog-tired. You see that someone makes money selling drugs, so you do it and you become addicted. A lot of these kids need a coach." Then she smiled and asked, "How did you find me?"

I said that a mutual friend had given me her name when I'd mentioned that I was planning to travel in the South. Cynthia Burton was involved in community development, he'd said, and added, "She knows everyone."

"Your receptionist recognized me," I said. "That made my day. She'd seen me at her church service at Cornerstone Baptist."

"That's nice, but I'm a Catholic," Miss Burton said. She was settling herself, making notations in a thick appointment book. "It's kind of an interesting story why I'm a Catholic."

"Please tell me."

"I was born in Gadsden," she said. "My parents were poor but very hardworking people. And decent people. My father worked for Goodyear Tire Company. My mother was a nurse. She had little education, but she got experience from the hospital, and learned nursing on the job."

Miss Burton sighed and hitched herself forward, and seeing that I was writing in a notebook, she tapped her finger near the notebook and spoke emphatically.

"My mother didn't want me to go to segregated schools, as she had to, so she and my father saved their money to find me a better school. They asked around, what to do. The local nuns, Daughters of the Holy Ghost, suggested that she send me north, to Connecticut, to attend Putnam Catholic Academy. This was 1961. Segregation."

She let this sink in. I said, "Your parents sound amazing."

"Listen, my parents were so far-thinking for their generation. My father only got to the fourth grade, my mother to the sixth grade. But they wanted the best for their kids and they were willing to make sacrifices. My high school, Gadsden High, was not integrated until 1968."

And I thought: Four foot-dragging years after the Civil Rights Act.

"They got their money together and I went up north to Putnam. I was the only black student at the academy. But there were five black families in the town of Putnam. They adopted me, sort of. They looked after me. It was not a normal education. Those little rich girls taught me. One day, in assembly, the top ten students were shown to the others. I was one of them — I was second, very proud."

Miss Burton began to chuckle softly, remembering, and she tapped her finger again near my notebook.

"The mother of the girl who came third called the nuns and challenged my grades. I was very upset. I called my mother. She said, 'Stand your ground — I can't come up there, so you'll have to do it. But remember to work and study. Cynthia, you must always be ahead of that girl.' And I did study, and stayed on top."

"This sounds like an exclusive private school," I said. "How did you get along with the girls?"

"Very well. Those girls were so rich. They were picked up in Rolls-Royces and Bentleys to take them home. And they were very nice and friendly to me, nothing they wouldn't do for me. I was the only black student. I was like a pet to them! They invited me to their homes — huge homes, mansions. I recall the time we went to Philadelphia. Five of us girls went in the limousine. We were all hungry when we got there, and the girl whose home it was called to the kitchen for food. 'Got something for us?' We went down, by and by, and there were three servants making our meal."

"Were you tempted to stay in the North? Lots of Southerners find more opportunities there."

"I loved the North," she said. "I became a Catholic there. I went to Loyola in Chicago, but I had to come back to Alabama. My mother needed me. And more than that, I felt I was blessed with so much that I had to share. I decided to be impactful with a large group of people. I've been with this agency for nine years. We have an $18 million budget for eight counties — maybe a million people. Most are federal funds, some are grants. We have five hundred units — affordable housing, both rentals and home ownership. And we help people in other ways."

"How is it working?" I asked.

"There's a lot of social conservatism here. I am a firm believer in self-sufficiency. Some people need help more than others, but people also need to help themselves."

"How does your agency help?"

"With housing, home ownership, rentals, all sorts of ways," she said. "Want to hear a strange thing? Some of our people have large holdings — lots of acreage. They don't want to subdivide. They're land rich and property poor. It's not unusual for someone with a large amount of land to live in a shack and go to food pantries and get energy assistance."

"You see them?"

"We get them here," she said, her voice rising. "They might come for food. Or help with their heat or electricity bill. That allocation is Low-Income Heating Energy Assistance, what we call LIHEAP. You need to be income-eligible. They get assistance for the heating-cooling cycle. There's also a weatherization program, for sealing the house. The largest parcel I know is about two hundred acres, and the people are poor. Not a lot of people in that situation, but some."

"Poor, with lots of land?"

"Yes, sir. They won't sell their land. In the African-American community the goal is to own rather than be owned. And because farming has become an organized business, it's hard for these people to compete. Some grow cash crops. But some grow corn or vegetables — peppers, cabbages, squash — and hay. They keep cattle. The land is passed on through the generations. Or they might just leave it there, lying idle, choosing not to grow food."

Or, because the land had been handed down in the family, it devolved into fractionated ownership (to use the legal term), with so many names on the deed the land was unsalable. So-called Indian land suffers the same consequences; in six generations a parcel might be owned or shared by more than two hundred people.

"It's an odd dilemma, like you say."

"So many folks here are behind the eight ball."

"I'd like to meet some."

"I'll put you in touch with them," she said. "And with people who are trying to improve things."

The Cornerstone Full Gospel Baptist Church

The church has always been the centerpiece of the rural South," Bishop Palmer said. He was someone Sister Cynthia said I ought to see. "I'm from Birmingham, but I went to school here at Stillman College, historically black, but now it has some white students."

He was a big man, impressively built, barrel-chested, white-haired, with a white beard trimmed into a Vandyke, a power figure, a patriarch with kindly eyes and a booming laugh. That was when he was in his pinstripe suit, before I saw him in his purple bishop's robes; at his lectern, tapping the text with his bear paw of an authoritative hand, he looked like an Old Testament prophet.

We drove in his car to Stillman and around the walled-off campus, weaving among the tidy buildings and the sports fields.

"There's one. There's another."

White students, hurrying past. Bishop Palmer smoothed his beard against his great jaw and tapped his chin. His features made his profile judge-like, and I was thinking how some men, physically, look born to lead.

"You have the perfect name for a preacher. Earnest Palmer."

"A man of faith, carrying a palm," he said.

"I think of a palmer as a pilgrim, bringing a palm from the Holy Land. Like the line in Chaucer."

He slowed the car and glanced over at me.

I said, "*Canterbury Tales.* 'Palmers for to seken straunge strondes.'"

He smiled as people sometimes do when hearing an unintelligible language brazenly spoken, or a dog with an odd bark.

"'To ferne halwes, couthe in sondry londes,' I recited. "Palmers—pilgrims searching."

He laughed. It seemed like news. He drove out of the campus and changed the subject. "When I was here we had a sit-in at Ed's, a restaurant over there. Up that street. They wouldn't let blacks eat there. Man, those white boys beat us up."

"Was it worse here than in other places?"

"Tuscaloosa was the headquarters of the Alabama Klan," he said. "The leader, Robert Shelton, had an office on Union Boulevard. He was also a printer. While I was a student, I went there to get some things printed once. My friends said, 'You went *where?*'"

Robert Shelton, judged "a truly evil man," also a factory worker and tire dealer and the Imperial Wizard of the Alabama Knights of the Ku Klux Klan when Earnest Palmer was a student at Stillman, eventually was bankrupted and put out of business by a lawsuit that arose from a Klan lynching in Mobile. Shelton died of a heart attack in 2003 at the age of seventy-three.

Meeting Bishop Palmer made me want to visit his church, and so I did the following Sunday. That was the morning I met Lucille, who drove ahead of me to the church to show me the way. Lucille, who had said to me sweetly, "Be blessed."

THE CORNERSTONE FULL Gospel Baptist Church was larger than it seemed when I approached. It lay in a hollow of a low, poorish neighborhood of small houses near a narrow creek, Cribbs Mill Creek.

"Black Southerners find in their churches a unifying focus and respite from a hostile (or strange) majority culture," John Shelton Reed writes in *The Enduring South* (1972), adding, "as immigrant ethnic groups do." Bishop Palmer's congregation resembled just such an ethnic group, like-minded, looking for solace. The warm-up prayers were impassioned and delivered by a deep-voiced woman greeting the faithful, who were filing in, formally dressed, women in hats and gloves, men in suits. Two women took seats in front of me, so beautiful that my gaze kept drifting toward them, and even when I was looking away the fragrance of their perfume warmed my face and made me smile, as though I was breathing their beauty.

"The devil is a liar this morning!" the preaching woman said from her podium at the front of the hall, reminding me that I was sinning in my heart. "Say the name of Jesus! He is great! He is the great 'I am'! Behold the triumph of Zion . . . !" She was singing, she was chanting, she filled the church with her voice.

Twenty minutes of this exhortation and then the choir ranged along the stage, fifteen men and women and a seven-piece band, rocking a hymn.

> *Our God reigns!*
> *He reigns!*

More music, stirring the congregation, which now occupied every seat in the church. But they were all standing, swaying, smiling, now into a third hymn.

> *You are the help*
> *Of the hopeless and broken . . .*

And then we sat and listened to announcements of events. This order became familiar to me from other churches I was to attend: the warm-up, the hymns, the announcements: news of schools, of classes, the "Women's Retreat—Restoring Body, Mind, and Spirit," and the seminar called "How You Livin'?"

A man came forward, smooth-voiced, reassuring, a deacon in a pin-stripe suit. "There were two men on a desert island," he said, and raised his hand, indicating that we must listen carefully. "One of the men was frantic. 'We lost, brother! What we gon' do?' He was beside himself, he was a mess." The cautioning hand went up again. "The other man was very calm—just settin', just smilin', not a care—though the island was far away and it all seemed there was no hope. The first man, the worried man, he say, 'Whah?' 'Tell you whah,' the calm man said. 'I'm a tither. I earn ten thousand dollars a week. I ain't worried. My pastor will find me.'"

There was laughter and the soaring notes of an organ—most of the preaching was accompanied by theme music. A procession of ushers appeared at the side of the church, and they hoisted buckets.

"What time is it? It's givin' time!"

The buckets were filled, with crumpled bills, with stiff white envelopes, and they were passed back to the ushers.

And then the music stopped, and in this hush Bishop Palmer entered from the side, in a purple and gold robe, holding his Bible. A big man, he was even bigger in his robe, and though he moved slowly and statesman-like, and I expected his voice to boom, his first words were soft and reas-suring.

"Good morning, brothers and sisters," he began. And then, after a lengthy pause, "God wants you back."

That was his theme, a return to faith, a renewal of belief in the love and compassion of God, and from the moment he began he held the attention of everyone.

"In the slave period here, one of the things that was prominent was the song—how the songs extolled the glory of God," he said. "You know that. They needed it. Some people were so low they had to look up to see the ground. Where were they living? On the other side of the tracks. But what will God do? God will build a bridge over the tracks for me to get across!"

It was a sermon with the theme that times are hard, but don't despair. Have faith—things will get better. If you're wavering, remember that God wants you back. The bishop was preaching hope and forgiveness and the acknowledgment that everyone is having a hard time. The Bible is full of hard times, and blessed with salvation.

"Just because your billfold is empty doesn't mean you won't have a blessing. And remember, it's not only raining on you—it's raining on everyone. Look at Isaiah forty-three, verse one to six. 'When you walk through the fire you will not be scorched. Do not fear.'"

He again harked back to slavery for consolation, to compare, to dem-onstrate that hard times always end. He appealed to us to remember that.

"The plan of God is never been that you will remain in bondage to anyone, or anything," he said in his reassuring voice, sounding like a doc-tor telling a patient she'd get better. "You will be freed."

Someone called out a halloo of thanks, and others chimed in.

"My friends, my fellow saints," Bishop Palmer said, "God wants me back—and God wants you back." And now he pointed, the sleeve of his robe sweeping the air like bunting. "God knows where you are. He knows what you're going through. Consider Psalm Thirty-seven, verse twenty-five. 'I had been young and now I am old, yet I have not seen the righteous forsaken, nor his seed begging bread.' Meaning?"

He took a step back and straightened his bulk, his robe rippling across his arms, a thick finger plumping his Bible.

"Meaning this," and he shouted: "You might eat baloney now, but you'll have rib eye later!" There was laughter. "In the meantime, Hebrews thirteen, verse five. 'Make sure that your character is free from the love of money—being content with what you have.'"

He went on in this vein, urging moderation, belief, and patience, and delivering a message of hope, nearly always in his reasonable voice, but from time to time in his voice of booming reassurance.

"'Close it down, Palmer,'" he said at last, speaking to himself softly. And replied, "Yes, Lord."

We stood and sang, and the two lovely women in front of me were beaming, their heads thrown back, singing into their veils, their bodies twitching with pleasure beneath their silken dresses, and I had to remind myself that I was in church.

At the end, after more hymns, Bishop Palmer invited everyone to come forward and drink some juice, and to take a piece of fruit from the pile of oranges and apples and grapes on the table.

"The Lord commanded, 'Fruit of the vine.'"

Bishop Palmer seemed exhausted when I said goodbye, but—it was no illusion on my part—the congregation seemed fortified, encouraged, in good humor, embracing, reassured, going back to their lives with a little more hope. It was touching to see how some serious tinkering with Scripture could lift people's spirits.

The Black Belt

Tuscaloosa is a cluttered urban island in a great soft rural sea: the misleadingly serene surfaces of the South—low hills, grassy swales, cotton and bean fields, swamps humming with flies, dejected woods. But the city is not unusual in that way. It exemplifies the Southern pattern of settlement, where most towns and cities are islands. Asheville and Greenville, Columbia and Charleston, Augusta and Atlanta, Birmingham and Tuscaloosa—all are insular, with a certain level of prosperity, an agreed-upon identity, a well-heeled area and a poor section, places where "the other side of the tracks" is not an abstract metaphor but a specific place as well as a condition and a social class.

Yet the cities do not relate to each other and do not in the least resemble anything in the surrounding countryside. It has been argued (by, among others, John Shelton Reed in *The Enduring South*) that the cities of the contemporary South have "nothing distinctly Southern about them." You have to leave them to know the true tensions of the region. The last houses at the city limits in these island-like places seemed to define the contours of a shoreline, and after that it all dropped off. Beyond, the landscape was like an ocean, with a simple and usually empty horizon, people living in flyspecks in radically different ways—always much poorer and often speaking a different language, or so it seemed to me, an outsider both in the clutter of the urban island and in the empty green sea of the hinterland.

Greensboro, only thirty miles south of Tuscaloosa, lies under the horizon in that green sea, a small, pretty, somewhat collapsed town, much of its elegance strangled by poverty. Up the road from Greensboro, around Moundville, lies the farmland and still-substandard houses where James Agee and Walker Evans spent the summer of 1936 collecting material. Originally this work was planned as a *Fortune* magazine profile of three poor white families of tenant farmers. The twenty-thousand-word story was long, convoluted, and depressing; the photographs were melancholy; it was all too truthful to be publishable in a money magazine; and so the whole business was rejected. But Agee was from Tennessee. He knew the South and, passionate about his subject, expanded the text over several years and made it a substantial and somewhat experimental book. Published under the title *Let Us Now Praise Famous Men* in 1941, it sold a mere six hundred copies. Its commercial failure contributed to Agee's heavy drinking and early death at the age of forty-five.

The book had been inspired, and eventually overshadowed, by *You Have Seen Their Faces* (1937), a shorter and more straightforward book with a text by Erskine Caldwell and photographs by Margaret Bourke-White. But that book, once a seminal text of American radicals because of its portrait of Southern poverty, had long been out of print. Odd things happen in publishing. Twenty years after *Let Us Now Praise Famous Men* first appeared, it was republished, and in the early, more socially conscious 1960s it found many more readers and admirers, who understood its innovations. It was valued for its density, obliqueness, and poetic descriptions—whole chapters on old clothes, for example; pages of leaky roofs; lofty renderings of the textures of planks and shingles, of patches and slop buckets.

As a college student, I had a copy, and it pained me to think that I had such difficulty reading it. I could manage to get through it only by reading it aloud to myself, like a dim person struggling with literacy. I found the narration overwrought and self-consciously lyrical and wanted it (this was 1963, year of Southern strife) to tell me more about racial conflict. The photographs were tortured and memorable, classic images of poverty, but the text had too much Agee in it and not enough strife. The author in the foreground: that was a plus in the assertive sixties. Blacks were all but invisible in the text, and hardly mentioned. The manuscript of Agee's rejected piece was such a concentrated account of rural poverty that it is easy to see why it was turned down as a magazine article.

Cherokee City, in the book, is Tuscaloosa, and Centerboro is Greensboro, thirty miles south, the subject of some of Evans's photographs and where I was eventually headed. Agee's book had led me here to the middle of Alabama.

Agee and Evans had spent their time in Hale County and Greene County, in the Black Belt. Cotton country.

"Black for the fertile soil, black for the people," Cynthia Burton had told me. "The greater the number of farms, the more slaves that were needed—that's the reason for the high proportion of blacks in the area that starts south of Tuscaloosa and extends across the state."

The past wasn't dead, nor past. She herself was black, and was explaining the demographic of the Black Belt today by referring to slavery, still a visitable memory because of the persistence of its effects.

"Ah Mo Buy Me Some Popcorn, Set Me Down, and Watch the Show"

Rolling south out of Tuscaloosa, past Moundville and Havana, I had the idea of seeing some people in Eutaw at short notice. I called ahead and said I would meet them at a certain time in the afternoon, an hour apart, and then I allowed myself to be bewitched by back roads with lovely names — Raspberry Road, Finches Ferry Road — and a succession of small cemeteries, vegetable patches, and empty sunlit fields bordering on the Black Warrior River, named for the paramount chief Tuscaloosa.

And the town of Eutaw was beautiful too, a tiny place on a close grid of streets with a modest town hall and county courthouse. The town was named for the Battle of Eutaw Springs in South Carolina, commanded by General Nathanael Greene, whose name had been given to this county, Greene County. Eutaw's old street-front shops were quiet or abandoned, and hardly any pedestrians cast shadows on this hot afternoon except a few shoppers heading for the Piggly Wiggly grocery store. I drove in circles, sizing the place up, thinking how the sunshine made the mostly deserted town seem more melancholy.

I stopped at the town hall. Cynthia Burton had urged me to see the mayor, whose name was Raymond Steele. He was Eutaw's first black mayor, elected in 2000. He had served three terms and had been hoping for a fourth.

"But I lost the last election," Mayor Steele told me. He wore a baseball cap and a windbreaker. "I'm out of here in a few weeks, after twelve years. No matter. I have a good dry-cleaning business. Mr. Paul, I was in the military for twenty years. I was in the first Gulf War, in battle. Seen me some things. I have me a Bronze Star."

He suggested we drive around. He would show me the town and the plans he'd had for a new airport, for a playground, for a new sports field. No one had paid any mind to his plans. Twelve years as mayor: the voters felt he'd overstayed his welcome.

"This town of Eutaw is in the Black Belt. Black soil, black people — eighty percent black. Rich soil, more enslaved people as a result. My opponent was black, from the city council. But look what I've done. Enlarged that park. They never had no park. Put up lights on the baseball field. Got the housing going in 2007 and 2008. The first new houses since 1974. Low income, rent to own."

We drove up and down the side streets of Eutaw.

"Rosie Carpenter Haven — thirty-three new houses," Mayor Steele said. "Carver Circle — thirty houses."

The houses were well built and nicely kept, with small front lawns, brighter than the town itself.

"Business is not too good," he said. "We got the box factory, RockTenn boxes. We got the roofing company. We got catfish, SouthFresh catfish. You got catfish all over Greene County."

"But I heard catfish is going down."

"Going way down," Mayor Steele said. "Ain't no doubt about it. We losing citizens every day. It's now nine thousand, down from twel' thousand. That was part of my problem in the election. Our population has been regressing. But there were other problems."

"Such as?"

"Such as the election was dirty." He said his opponent had put up signs saying MAYOR STEELE HAS CASHED IN, and the S was a dollar sign. "Like I'd done something crooked. Which I hadn't, course."

"Now you can run your dry-cleaning business and let someone else try to solve Eutaw's problems."

"Exactly right. Ah mo buy me some popcorn, set me down, and watch the show."

"White Privilege"

I had one more visit to make in Eutaw. After a spell with Mayor Steele, who was instantly warm and forthcoming, I had the feeling that I was in for another friendly welcome. I was wrong. But that mistake, like many mistakes I made in the South, proved to be illuminating.

When I knocked on the door of the small office that fronted the sidewalk, and entered, I sensed an isolating darkness fall over me. It was an intimation that I was about to step into a hole or perhaps already stepped in one.

Two young women sat at desks, staring at computers in an alarmed way that suggested they were too terrified to look up. I said hello and, untypically—this was tiny, amiable, highly recommended Eutaw—there was no response.

"Who are you?"

I heard the demand before I saw the speaker, who was an older woman scowling under a mass of wild corkscrew curls, fierce-faced, wearing glasses that distorted her eyes. Her posture was that of someone repelling a threat, and her tone a bit too shrill, and her whole presence electrified and menacing.

I said my name, mentioned that I had made an appointment, emphasized that I was grateful that she was seeing me at short notice—and glancing around, I saw a man who could only have been the husband who had been described to me, seated silently at a desk in the corner.

"You're late," the woman said. "Why are you late?"

I began to extol the back roads, the groves of trees, the golden fields, the cotton bursting open, but I did not get far in this appreciation.

"You could have called," she said sharply, a note of menace in her voice.

"I did—to make an appointment."

"You didn't call to say you'd be late."

"I'm fifteen minutes late," I said, half laughing at the absurdity of this, appealing to the room—the women at the computers, the man in the back. (Was he at work, or was he cowering?)

I was standing in the center of the room, the fierce woman in front of me, now howling at me, berating me in a way that I could not remember ever enduring before—perhaps in the fourth grade, at the Washington School, by Miss Cook, for whispering while she was reciting the Twenty-third Psalm ("Yea, though I walk through the valley of the shadow of death ..."). In this office in Eutaw, in midafternoon, I was receiving a scorching denunciation, and I was so surprised I compounded my error by continuing to smile.

"You think I'm just going to sit here and wait for you to show up whenever you want to?" she said, and she made her mouth square so that I could see all her teeth.

My lateness did not seem serious enough for an apology, nor so serious that it merited this incessant bollocking from the woman standing before me.

So I said, "I'll leave then. Never mind."

She didn't want this. She wanted to continue. Scolders never want you to go away.

"I call that 'white privilege,'" she said, her voice remaining shrill, and now her screech and her wild corkscrew curls gave her a gorgon-like aspect.

I took out my small notebook from my shirt pocket and clicked my pen. "White privilege," I said, writing slowly. "Hmm."

"I'm sensitive to white privilege. Do you know what I mean by that?"

"Please tell me," I said, my pen poised.

"By that I mean you arrived late and were in a position to notify me ahead of time. But chose not to, because you assumed I'd be available"—I started to protest but she talked over me—"as I'm black."

She was not black at all. She could have been biracial, she could have been Sicilian, she could have been—and probably was—part Cherokee or Choctaw. "I'm black" seemed half protest, half boast.

"Who are you, anyway?"

I repeated my unusual name, and spelled it.

"'Paul Theroux' means nothing to me. I don't know who you are. I've never heard of you."

"That's why I'm here, to introduce myself," I said, suppressing another smile at her outbursts, which seemed as much for my benefit as for the benefit of the terrified typists and the man at the desk, who I now decided was cowering. I could see his apprehension: he held a big apple in his hand, the way a psychic holds a crystal ball. He merely studied it, scrying hard, seeming to discern an ominous visual, making no attempt to eat it.

"Paul Theroux!" The woman said in a fearsome way, making my name a poisonous substance. "You could be a member of the Ku Klux Klan. How do I know you're not?"

Affecting horror and disgust, she succeeded only in appearing truculent and unhappy.

"You could read one of my books, any of them," I said, "and I think you'd discover pretty quick that I am not a member of the Klan."

"I'm busy!" she said. "I have to stand vigil. I have to be watchful. My freedom as an individual is not guaranteed."

"Yes, it is, by the Constitution."

"That's just a document."

"It's legislation," I said. "And by the way, as I said, I'm a writer. Do you mind if I write down what you're saying?"

"Go ahead." Her tone was do-your-damnedest, yet she had an air of helpless melancholy that furious people often have. "The Constitution is just a piece of paper. Where's the protection here? We have to provide proof of identification everywhere we go. My daughter showed a policeman her ID driver's license. The man said, 'How do I know that's who you are?'"

"I'm noting that," I said, writing in my notebook, flipping pages, because she was talking fast.

"All these papers, all these questions, all this bureaucracy—to keep us down." She shook her finger in my face. "That's why we're still poor!"

"And that is why you're still poor," I said, in an echoing and intoning way, still writing, and when I finished I clapped my notebook shut.

"White entitlement, that's all we get. Now what do you want?"

I took a step back and said, "I think you've told me everything I need to know."

The man with the apple rose from his desk and crept nearer.

"This is my husband," the woman said.

The man winced but said nothing. He then performed an extraordinary act—to my mind at least. Facing me, he raised his apple and chawnked a big bite of it and chewed, with bits of apple flesh and juice gleaming on his mouth. This obvious eating—the chewing noise, the tooth-grinding, the pulpy noise, and his audible gulps and swallows—seemed more hostile by far than my being howled at by the woman, his wife. I could not remember anyone ever eating like that in my presence, defiantly masticating with such noise, with such spittle-flecked lips.

Both seemed a bit deflated when I said I'd be going, but before I left I drew their attention to what had just happened.

"I suppose this is a cultural difference," I said. "In the North it's considered bad manners to berate someone, especially a harmless stranger, in front of a roomful of people." I nodded to the terrified secretaries. "And it's really an insult to eat in front of a visitor without offering some."

"I wrote a book once," the woman said, but in a milder way, trying to get my attention, but by then I was half out the door and still shaking my head. She was well-off, well dressed, well educated, a businessperson and an organizer. She seemed to be doing very nicely. "That's why we're still poor" did not apply to her, though it could have been true of those cringing secretaries. But I couldn't condemn her. I suppose she was giving me a taste of the bumps and slights she'd received in her life.

We talked for a while, but to no purpose. The woman was offended. What I took to be the easygoing mood of the South had deluded me. It had never occurred to me that I would be perceived as entitled to be late because I happened to be white. But I also had the sense that she wanted to wipe that smile off my intruding face, seeing me as a throwback to the 1960s, a period that for her persisted in all its injustice to the present.

"She's paranoid — she hates white people," someone who knew her well told me later. "She always wants an argument. But I don't gee and haw with her."

Anyway, it was a good lesson to me, that for some, old wounds were unhealed. And she was a good example of the warping influences of the South.

Mary Hodge: The Burning

Some wounds were not old.

In Greensboro I met Mary Hodge, who showed me around — the library, the town hall, the churches. Mary was a beaming woman in late middle age, well dressed in a reddish suit and white blouse, proud of her daughter's recent law degree, eager for me to understand Greensboro, but the mention of the Klan cast a shadow over our talk, as she shook her head slowly.

"They're not gone," she said in a near-whisper. "Our church was burned by the Ku Klux Klan in 1996. The police first called it an accidental fire, but we knew it was arson. And the thing is, it was meant for Mrs. Singleton's church, not ours, Rising Star Baptist. Mrs. Singleton's is William Chapel, and it's a place that influential people visit all the time. And some people don't like that, a church that gets visited by influential people. No they don't."

"Wasn't the fire investigated afterward?" I asked.

"The police said it was electrical wiring, but surely it wasn't. The fire came at two o'clock in the morning. No one was there. How could it be electrical? It came out later that the Klan were involved, but that they hired other people to do it. One of the drivers taking out the fish truck saw them getting away."

"That's terrible — it must have been so demoralizing," I said. The act seemed so fiendish only platitudes came to mind.

"Not at all," Mary Hodge said, and smiled. "Volunteers came from all over to help us rebuild the church — from town, from the state, from the North. They stayed at my house for a long time. They did a great job. They were good people. I still hear from them."

I asked whether anyone had been arrested for starting the fire.

"The police never got to the true bottom of it all," Mary said. "My husband was a deacon at the church. He said it was no accident."

And it was, she said, the ninth Alabama church that year that had been either burned or vandalized. "There's this sense out there that [church burnings are] something that happened a long time ago, something that occurred during the battles of the civil-rights era and even earlier," activist Tim McCarthy said in *Harvard Magazine* in 2008. "It hasn't stopped. There are, on average, several dozen church-burnings per year." A church burning tore the heart out of a community, because a church was traditionally a meeting place, a source of joy and welfare, of social events and counseling, of hope. A burned-out church was an act of violence that a Northerner could scarcely comprehend, though many organizations in the North came to the aid of such wounded congregations.

Gathering Pecans

Passing some tall trees bordering a meadow, Mary Hodge and I saw a woman slumped in the grass under those trees. She appeared to be in distress, so I pulled off the road and called out to her.

She was seated on the ground but canted forward, and now I saw that she was slowly clawing at the grass, her legs flung out like someone re-enacting a Southern version of Andrew Wyeth's *Christina's World*, down to the large and seemingly unattainable house in the distance. Her straw hat was askew. She looked helpless, aimlessly combing the grass with her fingers. An elderly white woman seated awkwardly in a big field was not a common sight in Greensboro.

"I hope she's all right," Mary said.

"Hi there!" the old woman said, and we began to talk. She was Doris Torbert, gathering pecans that had fallen onto the grass, using both hands, bumping along on her bottom, and now I saw the bucket she was filling.

"I've been here all morning," she said. "We planted these trees about forty years ago. I got no one to help me, but I don't need help. I'm doing this for fun. And I can sell them at the market for seventy-five cents a pound."

"They have these pecan pickers," Mary suggested, and made a gesture with her hand, as though working an implement.

"I don't have any use for them. Fred at the hardware store has one. He declares that it picks them up fast, but I had two of them and I didn't like them. I'd rather pick them up this way with my hands. Anyway, those metal pickers cost forty dollars."

She went on scrabbling and grubbing, now and then flinging up one hand to adjust her sun hat.

"Crack some and eat them. You'll see they're real tasty. These are lovely trees, pecans."

Mrs. Torbert was friendly — that was her huge house in the distance, a white building with a row of tall white columns supporting the spacious porch.

"It's a good piece of land," she said. "We have about a hundred acres." But land and prosperity had not kept her from hopping and crawling in the grass, gathering pecans.

Greensboro: Mayor Johnnie B. Washington

Behind his tidy desk, in his small windowless office, wearing a ball cap and a windbreaker — it seemed the uniform of the rural Southern mayor — and looking more like a baseball coach than a politician, sat Greensboro's first black mayor, Johnnie B. Washington, known to the town as "JB." He gestured for me to sit and asked me what I wanted to know.

I had heard a bit about him from local talk. He had become mayor in 2004, and served briefly, but after some turmoil — accusations of voter fraud and a closer examination of absentee ballots revealing forged signatures and dubious postmarks — he had ultimately been disqualified by the findings of a team of handwriting experts. Campaigning again in 2008, he won fairly. In his mid-seventies, he was tall, slender, with the Cherokee features of his grandfather and a way of turtle-bobbing his head at most of my questions, as if enjoying a mild joke. He had made his living as the owner of a successful Greensboro funeral parlor, Washington and Page Mortuary, at the edge of the woods northeast of town on Highway 25. Easygoing, but with a soft courtesy — his reassuring mortician's manner — he gave me some background on the town.

"This is the Black Belt. The city and Hale County are both sixty-eight percent black," he said. "The town is divided into three groups." He counted by flipping his long fingers. "Black Greensboro. White Greensboro. And white — old guard." He chuckled, folded his fingers, and went on. "The old guard wants a bed-and-breakfast town, and whenever I come up with something to raise us economically, like a shopping center or a Walmart or any big store, there's pushback. They won't have it."

"You think a Walmart is the answer?" I asked.

"They'd bring jobs," he said.

"There's got to be another solution," I said, because Walmart had destroyed, not helped, many small towns in the South. I'd seen, up in

Brent, an example of Walmart blight. In that town of four thousand in Bibb County, about thirty miles north of Greensboro, the huge hulking Walmart, which had wrecked most of the other local businesses, had closed and become a vast gray collapsing building in the empty, ghostly town. A mile away, a much bigger Walmart Supercenter had opened, sucking the rest of the life out of Brent, and in its ugliness looking like the source of a poisonous virus, which in a way it had been. Now, apart from the Soviet-looking Walmart, the only other employment in Brent was a state prison, the Bibb County Correctional Facility. It was one thing to believe that a Walmart might solve your problems, but it was a monster that crowded out all other enterprises. And sometimes the unthinkable happened: after the Walmart had destroyed a town's businesses, the Walmart itself closed, and the town was finished.

I suggested this to Mayor Washington. He turtle-nodded at my explanation.

"Course, there's still some agriculture here — cotton, soybeans. And you see the water tower?" Greensboro's water tower was lettered CATFISH CAPITAL OF ALABAMA. "But catfish is going down, because the Vietnamese are exporting fish to the US. We cain't compete. It's farm-raised catfish, and there's a processing plant here and at Heartland over on 69. Used to have chickens. Massengale's chicken-processing plant went down in the 1970s. The meatpacking plant, Golden-Rod Broilers, closed a few years ago. Couldn't compete with the big chicken people."

All this was bad news, I said.

"The city is polarized, though lots of the whites support me, but secretly — they don't want the others to know. We had black and white schools. The East Campus of Greensboro High was black, the West Campus was white. They combined the schools. This caused white flight, the white kids going to school in Moundville, which is more white."

"When was that?"

"Four or five years ago, when they integrated."

"Is your main problem the economy?" I asked.

"Our main problems?" Mayor Washington said with a kindly smile. "How much time do you have? A day or two, to listen? It's lack of revenue, it's resistance to change, it's so many things. But I tell you, this is a fine town."

It seemed a fine town to me. Even mummified and peeling, the houses were beautiful, many of them antebellum mansions, like most in the South, of huge and superfluous dimensions and frivolous amplitudes. The churches were numerous and ranged from the brick Episcopal church in the center of town to the modest but well-kept wood-plank chapels on the side streets. The quiet, old-fashioned Main Street still had a hardware store, a furniture shop, and some clothing stores, but many were empty, collapsing, in need of repair.

Well-Wishers

Some Greensboro shops were being fixed up, put back into business, by a nonprofit organization called the HERO Project, the acronym standing for Hale Empowerment and Revitalization Organization. Though hardly changed architecturally since Agee and Walker's visit in 1934, and beautiful in a solemn, skeletal way, Greensboro was struggling. Its lovely bones, its weird time-warp quality, attracted well-wishers and volunteers, community development people by the score (including Cynthia Burton's housing activists), the Auburn Rural Studio (low-cost housing), and Project Horseshoe Farm ("tutoring, mentoring, and enrichment programs"), with a clubhouse in a restored shop on Main Street. HERO was larger than any of the other groups, and it was harder to define because it was involved in so many areas of Greensboro life. But the aim of all these groups — their primary movers newcomers to Greensboro — was uplift.

"You need to talk to Pam Dorr," I was told by several people in Greensboro. "She runs HERO. Those people are making a huge difference here."

But Pam Dorr was away — no one knew where.

I wandered Main Street, where some of the old shops were being renovated, one a thrift shop, another a workshop making bicycles from locally harvested bamboo, and a third, equipped like a schoolroom, with twenty or more youngsters in it, and a few adults — some of the youngsters performing, perhaps a recitation, perhaps a play.

"What's happening in there?" I asked a worker at HERO, an earnest young woman who was entering the altered shop space for this late-after-noon class. Half the children were standing, some seemed to be reading aloud from printed sheets; the others were seated in chairs and on the floor. They were clearly engaged in some sort of lesson.

"Those are kids in the after-school program," the worker said. "Maybe not a good idea to interrupt. When are you coming back?"

It was always assumed that I was merely drifting, and I suppose in a sense I was, but not "merely."

"In a few months, I guess."

"Maybe you can see Pam then."

I smiled at the "maybe."

This premise—that I would come back eventually—was one I kept hearing. I took it to mean that the traveler in the South, no matter who, would never light for any length of time, but keep returning, tumbling from one place to another. It was a conflicted assumption, perhaps the product of the aggrieved Southern feeling that the South was a place apart, deemed unworthy, weakened, misrepresented, hard to explain, but proud. The South was not a conventional destination, not a place where an outsider would fit in or a traveler would linger. The South was static, but gave the appearance of flux, offering a set of occasions to satisfy the wanderer's curiosity, and though the traveler might circle back for a bit, it was unthinkable that anyone would put down roots. We'd never under-stand the complexity of it. We were, all of us, just passing through, peering through windows.

The Horseshoe Farm After-School Program Competition Chart

Peering through the window of the renovated shop front on Main Street, I noted the names on the board, listing the children in the program, and it seemed to me a chant.

DE KEVION	JADEN
KEYONNA	QUA-DARIUS
JAIMESA	ANTONETTA
KIMBERLY	COURTNEY
JAKIRA	JAMIKHAEL
RASLYN	DEMARKUS
DEMAIS	TYRESHA
TRINITY	CURTIS
LOGAN	JONATHAN
TRAYMON	DAJUAN
JOLANDRIA	DAVID
TASHANTI	DEVONTAE
TREVION	KEONTAE
DE TYRICK	NEKENDRICK
KESHAWN	ARIANNA
SKILAH	ALEXIA
KIAJIAN	URIYAH
RONELL	TIMIYAH
TITIANA	QUINTARIO
JADA	SELENA
SONIJA	JARMEL

Mumbling at the window the litany of names to myself, I was reminded of some lines of the schoolteacher narrator in Lawrence Durrell's *The Black Book*: "Dazzling, in the flash of this last moment's reason, I question myself eagerly. Is this amusia, aphasia, agraphia, alexia, aboulia? It is life."

"Our Own Matlock"

Another day, walking down Main Street in Greensboro with Mary Hodge, she saw a man crossing the street. She said, "Here comes our own Matlock."

A tousled-haired man with a folder of papers under his arm was headed to the Greensboro courthouse, a glorious building of the colonnaded sort I saw all over the South, often the only building in town with a claim to the majestic, yet — to set this majesty in context — nearly always representing a history of injustice.

The man paused to say hello. We chatted awhile.

"How's business?" I asked, and got an unexpectedly long answer.

"Business is fine," he said. "But I don't care about money. The only time I ever consider it is when I have a debt. I pay it and then I go on with my life. What do you do with money otherwise? Fella comes to me and says, 'Have I got a deal for you! You just put some money in and I'll do the rest, and I know it's going to turn out good. What do you say, counselor?'

"'You're not going to like what I'm fixin' to tell you,' I said to him. 'The only thing worse than losing that money would be winning the money and having a big payoff. What would I do with it? I'd just give it away.'

"He didn't like what I said. When my son died I had an insurance policy on his life. The insurance company gave me the money. Quite a lot of money. I didn't need it. I didn't want it. I gave it away. Hear? I gave it away."

With that, he crossed the lawn to the courthouse, clawing at his hair and seemingly deep in thought.

"It was sad," Mary said. "A boating accident."

Reverend Eugene Lyles, Barber

Around the corner from Main Street, tucked into a brick building he'd financed himself, was Gene's, the barbershop of Reverend Eugene Lyles. He was seventy-nine but looked much younger, and not just physically fit but scholarly too. He was seated at a small table peering at his Bible, opened to the Acts of the Apostles, while awaiting his next customer. In addition to his barbershop, Reverend Lyles had his own church, the Mars Hill Missionary Baptist Church, just south of town. Next door to the barbershop was Reverend Lyles's own soul food diner, nameless except for the simple sign DINER out front.

I asked him for a haircut. Marking the page in his Bible with a tattered ribbon and shutting it, he went to the shelf beneath the big mirror and plucked his comb and scissors out of a jar of disinfectant. I climbed into one of the two barber chairs and he tied a bib around my neck.

In answer to my obvious first question, he said, "When I was a boy I bought me a pair of clippers. I cut my brother's hair. Well, I got ten boy siblings and three girl siblings — fourteen of us. One mother. I kept cutting hair. I started this business sixty years ago, cutting hair all that time. And I got the restaurant, and I got my church. Yes, I am busy."

"Tell me a little about Greensboro," I said.

He sighed, then took a deep breath before he spoke. "There are good people in Greensboro," he said. "But the white core is rooted in the status quo. And they have a way of indoctrinating their children and grand-children and great-grandchildren. You've heard the words 'separate but equal'? That means separate, not equal."

"But that changed, didn't it?"

"The school is separate yet," he said, snipping away at my hair. "When it was integrated the whites started a private school, Southern Academy. There's somewhere above a hundred there, all white." He laughed, put comb and scissors down, and spun his glasses off to polish them with a tissue. "History is alive and well here."

He sat in the other chair and said, "Very little work here requires marketable skills. There's no more sharecroppers. The military is a way out — lots of boys here join the army."

"Anyone in your family join the army?"

"Brother Benny," he said. "I have three other brothers who integrated the white school. This was in the late 1970s. There were no other black students. The law was on their side — no one else was on their side — but the law was distant. They were Amos, Daniel, and Frank, the first guys — and it was very hard. They had fistfights. The white kids would git 'em. Throw bricks at 'em. Call 'em names. My brothers wouldn't stand for it. They would respond."

Reverend Lyles sighed and got out of his chair and began to sweep the cuttings of hair on the floor at my feet, still talking.

"There was little fear in those days and no one helped them. Not the police. Not the teachers. The teachers were on the side of the enforcers."

"Was it like that for you?"

"I was older. I went to segregated schools. I grew up in the countryside, outside Greensboro, ten miles out, Cedarville. Very few whites lived in the area. I didn't know any whites. Whites say, 'All blacks look alike.' I thought all whites looked alike. I didn't know any whites until the sixties, when I was in my thirties."

I told him that there were many Northerners, even today, who had no black friends and who did not know any blacks. He said that was news to him, and returned in his talk to his childhood.

"Most of the land in Cedarville was owned by blacks," he said, saying that he was speaking of the 1930s and '40s. "There was a man, Tommy Ruffin, he owned ten thousand acres. He farmed, he had hands, just like white folks did, growing cotton and corn."

"Was your father one of those field hands?"

"My father was a World War One vet," Reverend Lyles said, speaking slowly in his methodical way. "It happened like this. He ran away from here in 1916—he was about twenty. He went to Virginia. He enlisted there in 1917. After the war, he worked in a coal mine in West Virginia. He came back and married in 1930, but kept working in the mine, going back and forth. He gave us money. I always had money in my pockets.

"Finally he migrated into Hale County for good. He bought some land. He was advised by a white man named Paul Cameron not to sell any of that land to a white person. Sell to blacks, he said, because that's the only way a black man can get a foothold in a rural area."

Now that the floor was swept and the comb and scissors put away, he approached me and turned the barber chair so that I faced the mirror. "How's that?"

We went next door to the diner. I ordered baked chicken, collard greens, and rice and gravy. Reverend Lyles had the same. His younger brother Benny joined us.

"Lord," Reverend Lyles began, his hands clasped, his eyes shut, beginning grace in an imploring voice. I reflected on his dignity, the nobility of his life, the integrity of his experience.

After lunch, he said, "Come back soon. We be waiting for you. I got some stories you won't believe."

The Klan in Philadelphia

I drifted west through the Black Belt via Demopolis, Alabama, and Meridian, Mississippi, past Collinsville, where I bought a drink at the Piggly Wiggly, noted Chunky Duffee Road and the crossroads at tidy Tucker, and drove toward Philadelphia, a place that had been on my mind for years.

In June 1964, near this small farming town, three civil rights workers were murdered by a lynch mob of the local Klan. The portion of Highway 19 that I would travel on was named the Chaney, Goodman, and Schwerner Memorial Highway, for those activists who'd been killed during the Freedom Summer—a season of voter registration and protest, of running battles and bloodshed. I had missed that tragic time. I drove on this highway almost fifty years later in a spirit of catching up on unfinished business, with a suggestion of atonement, because in that summer I had been so far away, in Nyasaland, preparing to celebrate the independence of Malawi.

Philadelphia had earned another, later footnote in political history. In August 1980, presidential candidate Ronald Reagan flew there to give the first speech of his campaign, at Philadelphia's Neshoba County Fair. It seems a wildly out-of-the-way place to kick off a presidential campaign: a small Mississippi town with one distinction in the history books, the site of a triple murder provoked by white supremacists.

But that was precisely why Reagan was there. He knew what he was doing, making a calculated, ingratiating speech to a large crowd at a county fair, and to white Southern voters in general, reminding them where he stood on the issue of civil rights. He stood squarely with the good old boys and the Klansmen.

He began by mildly mocking his opponent, Jimmy Carter, then he talked about the economy, and then he got to the point. He said, "I believe in states' rights, and I believe in people doing as much as they can for themselves at the community level and at the private level."

He then rubbished the role of the federal government in enacting laws that affected citizens at the state level. Speaking in a town that was the headquarters of the Mississippi Ku Klux Klan, he was saying: I'm on your side. Race was a factor in the 1980 election, which Reagan won.

Reagan was "tapping out the code," as the *New York Times* columnist Bob Herbert wrote many years later. Herbert added a detailed list of Reagan's opposition to civil rights measures while he was president: "He was opposed to the landmark Civil Rights Act of 1964, which was the same year that Goodman, Schwerner, and Chaney were slaughtered. As president, he actually tried to weaken the Voting Rights Act of 1965. He opposed a national holiday for the Rev. Dr. Martin Luther King Jr. He tried to get rid of the federal ban on tax exemptions for private schools that practiced racial discrimination. And in 1988, he vetoed a bill to expand the reach of federal civil rights legislation."

Philadelphia, like many towns in Mississippi, had an old, decaying town center of dusty streets and defunct and picturesque stores, surrounded on a bypass road by a scattering of shopping malls, fast food outlets, the usual Walmart, pawnshops, and gun retailers. It was the county seat, altogether a rather bleak place, much bleaker and nakeder in the glare of noon. On the sunny day that I spent walking its streets I was reminded that Philadelphia is still the headquarters of the Mississippi Klan. I easily found the headquarters and the free leaflets.

"The Original Knights of America, Knights of the Ku Klux Klan is a political activist organization," one of the leaflets explained. "We follow in the footsteps of our ancestors who were involved in the political process. It's a Klansman's responsibility to register to vote, campaign, and vote for conservative pro white candidates who will put America first and defend our nation's borders." On another page: "We the Ku Klux Klan have been fighting for the White Christian Race for over 150 years. We are the longest lasting and most respected White Civil Rights organization on Earth. We are no compromise and that's why we continue to be a feared organization."

"Feared" was indisputable, "most respected" was questionable, but it was obvious the KKK was a defiant group and, judging from the heavy inventory in the gun stores in Philadelphia, well armed. I was not there to reform anyone but only to listen.

"The Ku Klux Klan is . . . more than the embodiment of a tradition," Frank Tannenbaum wrote in an early and subtle analysis of the South's hidden impulses, *Darker Phases of the South* (1924). Tannenbaum was an Austrian-born criminologist, sociologist, Columbia University professor, and political radical who, as a soldier in the US Army stationed in the South, looked closely at the Klan. "[The Klan] expresses a deep-rooted social habit—a habit of ready violence in defense of a threatened social status." He explained the appeal, the grip, the danger of the Klan: "It seizes upon the monotony of a small town and gives it daily drama. It takes him who lived an uneventful life, one who is nobody in particular, and makes something of him. It gives him a purpose; makes him a soldier in a cause. The very existence of the Ku Klux Klan is proof of emotional infanthood. It would not be possible in a community where the people lived full, interesting, varied lives."

The Klan originated in the mid-nineteenth century, not with the poor whites but with the planter class, who used its terror to keep blacks working in the fields, to regulate labor, and to "perpetuate the South's repressive plantation system," in the view of the social historian Jonathan M. Wiener, in *Social Origins of the New South* (1978). But other historians have described how, after a period of relative inactivity, the Klan was revived at the end of World War One, growing rapidly after 1920, spreading north to Illinois and Iowa, because of the arrival there of new migrants, including Italians and Jews, whose religions the Klan abominated.

The Klan movement—its members convinced it was a stabilizing force—percolated through the classes of whites until it became a form of fantasy and "child's play" for the poorest whites, who had little else to animate them. Tannenbaum speaks about the double life of a Klansman, an ordinary drudge during the day and a crusader at night, in secret, with robes and hoods and a fiery cross and arcane rituals. "Then there is the opportunity to pry into other people's lives as a sacred duty."

On a maze of rivers and creeks in the wooded northern outskirts of Philadelphia, I found the Choctaw Native American reservation, marked by a large casino and two hotels. As the Pearl River Resort employed many from the tribe, I made a point of looking for some Choctaws to tell me about the land they had been allotted here, and how this gambling enterprise had improved it.

Without much prodding from me, one of the first men I spoke to mentioned, with a nervous laugh, how the nearby town of Philadelphia was "something else."

"Something else in a good sense?"

"Something else in a Klan sense," he said.

He was a solidly built Choctaw man of about thirty, with slicked-back dark hair and an olive complexion. He worked in middle management in one of the hotels. He happened to be in the lobby, and I asked him directions, and then he asked me where I was from. This led to the ambiguous remark about Philadelphia. Glancing around at the other people nearby, he walked me outside, still looking left and right but smiling the whole time. His smile never left his face, and it became brighter as he spoke, as though to fool anyone who saw him talking to me.

"There's plenty of them around here," he said with his mirthless grin. "I went to school with them. They come here all the time."

"So you know who they are."

"Everyone knows who they are," he said, and then fell silent. Three men in old clothes passed us, with the customary Southern greeting, pleasantries and nods.

"Them?" I asked.

"Could be," he said, and, still smiling, "It's not funny." He was very nervous now; he seemed giddy with apprehension. "Look, I can't talk anymore, but take my word for it."

Last Days on Gum Street

Larry Franey, a man of about sixty with a pearl-handled, nickel-plated .38 in a holster on his hip, was leaning against a porch post on Gum Street in Philadelphia, fretting. I walked by and said hello. We talked about guns for a while. Then he told me what he had on his mind.

"I reckon we're setting on Revelation—book of Revelation—with this election." The presidential election was two weeks away. "And the last election too. That something bad is coming. That God is behind Obama, that God put him in place to show the End is nigh. We are facing Tribulation. You cain't see it, but it's there—most of it out of sight, like a great trail of dominoes, and pretty soon they'll start to fall here and they'll keep dropping and we'll see where they are, afallin' from far off. We are facing the End, like it says in Revelation. Pacifically, the Mark of the Beast, the Scripture that says, 'There will be one world.' That's where it's all leading. China's gonna call in their debt, all the money we owe them, and then it will be over, sure enough. We'll be a Third World country, with China the only real country in the world, foretold in Revelation. We will be finished. It will be over."

"Is China mentioned in Revelation, Larry?"

Larry quoted: "'And they worshiped the dragon, for he had given his authority to the beast, and they worshiped the beast, saying, "Who is like the beast, and who can fight against it?"'"

"The dragon is China?"

"You said it." He rested his right hand on his pistol. "I know people who are stockpiling guns and food, gold and water, and all the necessaries. But it won't do them any good. We won't have a chance."

Bank Deserts

I stopped for the night at the Choctaw reservation's casino and resort, and the next day drove by way of Carthage to Jackson, in time for lunch with some housing development people.

In Jackson, a city of black paradoxes and white flight and stifling grandeur, with an unavoidable downtown ghetto and back streets of beautiful homes, the housing people encouraged me to look at the Delta, where they were hoping to help create some sort of financial stability.

"There are bank deserts in the Delta, and many other places," Bill Bynum, the CEO of the Hope Credit Union, told me. "Communities with no financial institutions. They closed, they went bankrupt, they moved. We buy some of them and help revitalize the community."

"Bank deserts" was an expression I had never heard before, not even in the wider world of acknowledged misery. In the small towns of Uganda and Kenya there was always a Barclays bank or a National and Grindlays. Some of the most unprepossessing towns in India had half a dozen banks or lending institutions. I had seen banks at the edge of Fijian cane fields and in the rural towns of Vietnam and the rice-growing hamlets of Thailand. The idea that there were communities in the United States where banks had departed and none now existed—in rural parts of Mississippi, Arkansas, and Louisiana—was news to me.

For eighteen years, the Hope Credit Union had been trying to improve the situation in which many people had no access to a financial institution. Its large budget was funded by a combination of private and government agencies. But this was working capital. They needed to double in size to be sustainable, and were now trying to raise twenty million dollars.

"Say they need a loan for a car, and can't get it," Bynum said. "If you don't have a car in these places—rural Arkansas or the Delta—you've got a problem. You can't move, you can't work, you stay poor. I tell you, some of the communities here are dying on the vine."

Mississippi was number one in the United States for people who had no bank account. Even where a bank existed, it was a forbidding thing.

"People—the poor," he said, "don't feel welcome in a bank. They're unused to entering a bank. They feel rejected and are very intimidated."

So what's the answer? I asked.

"We try to overcome that with the Hope Credit Union," he said. "In Utica a bank was going to close. It had twenty-three branches. We bought those bank branches and they became Hope Credit Unions. Our focus is business development in the Delta and first-time home buyers. We grant an average of about two hundred mortgages a year."

He added that thirty percent of the people who open an account have never had a bank account before.

"I took Assistant Treasury Secretary Cyrus Amir-Mokri down from Memphis," Bynum said. "We passed through Tunica, Mound Bayou, and Clarksdale, and ended up in Utica. Through the Delta. He just sat and looked sad. He said he could not believe such conditions existed in the United States."

Another of the men at the meeting then spoke up. "It's no good our telling you that thirty percent of the people in Utica live below the poverty line," he said. "You have to see for yourself."

Natchez Gun Show

I went by back roads, past pines, swamps, shacks, the small towns of Lorman and Fayette, a school flying a Confederate flag, and down one road on which for some miles there were large lettered signs with intimidating Bible quotations nailed to roadside trees: "Prepare to Meet Thy God — Amos 4:12" and "He who endures to the end shall be saved — Mark 13:13" and "REPENT"— Mark 6:12." Finally I arrived at the lovely town of Natchez.

Natchez is dramatically sited on the bluffs above the wide brown Mississippi, facing the cotton fields in flatter Louisiana and the transpontine town of Vidalia. It was my first glimpse of the river on this trip. Though the Mississippi is not the busy thoroughfare it once was, it is impossible for an American to see this great, muddy, slow-moving stream and not be moved, as an Indian is by the Ganges, a Chinese by the Yangtze, an Egyptian by the Nile, an African by the Zambezi, a New Guinean by the Sepik, a Brazilian by the Amazon, an English person by the Thames, a Quebecois by the St. Lawrence, or any citizen by a stream flowing past his feet. I mention these rivers because I've seen them myself, and written about them, but as an alien, a romantic voyeur. A river is history made visible, the lifeblood of a nation.

I feel a more profound connection to my own rivers, the Mystic River in Medford, flowing mystically into Boston Harbor and the sea, which filled my head with fantasies of travel and made me want to leave my hometown. The Mississippi meant everything to me, as a symbol, as a source of discovery and literary inspiration. It is the "strong brown god" of T. S. Eliot's poem "The Dry Salvages"; the "great river road" that enabled Lewis and Clark to travel to the Northwest; the military access route for Union soldiers to outflank the Confederates and lay siege to their towns; the river of Huck Finn, who's got to "light out for the Territory ahead of the rest"; a vision of liberation and the central artery of our country; and a symbol of self-belief, as Eliot, the poet from St. Louis, declared: "The river is within us."

The history of the river is like a metaphor for the South: the level is dropping, river traffic has slowed, riverside commerce has diminished, and the river towns and villages are struggling. The meretricious hotels and floating casinos represent the last gasp of commerce, gambling on riverboats that look unseaworthy and stay moored in the mud in Mississippi towns such as Natchez.

Natchez was once a French stronghold, Fort Rosalie, built with the forced labor of the Natchez Indians, whom the French had subdued in 1716. But when, thirteen years later, the Natchez regrouped, rose up again, and took control of the fort (and of course their own land), they were savaged so badly by the French and some loyal Choctaws that the Natchez as a people were exterminated. In the mid-1700s their name was given to the town. All that remained of the people was this word.*

A small, well-preserved city (because unlike defiant, besieged Vicksburg, Natchez surrendered to the Union Army and remained unburned); a city rich in history and river lore and architectural marvels—old ornate mansions, historic houses, churches, and quaint arcades; its downtown lined with restaurants; none of these metropolitan attributes held much interest for me. Here is a shrewd observation by Charles Shelton Aiken, writing about the Southern landscape and Faulkner: "One of the grandest creations of the New South was a mythical concept of an Old South." What people take to be an epoch was a matter of mere decades of pretension and an exercise in irrational nostalgia.

As in Charleston, South Carolina, the cultural event that got my attention was the Gun and Knife Expo I'd seen advertised the previous week, to be held at the Natchez Convention Center, in the middle of town. It was the main event in Natchez that weekend, and the arena was bigger than the one in Charleston. The same formalities at the entrance: eight dollars per adult, one dollar for children six to ten years of age, no loaded guns on the premises, but it was okay to carry them if they were secured with a plastic tie.

"Mississippi is the best state for gun laws," one man said to me soon after I entered. We were at the coffee and donut stall. "You can leave your house with a loaded gun. You can keep a loaded gun in your car in this state. Isn't that great?"

---

* It was one they never used to describe themselves. They called themselves Théocloel—the people of Thé, the name of their godlike original ancestor.

"Ever been to Arizona?" another man said. His beard and bib overalls were sprinkled with powdered sugar from the donut he held close to his face. "I was in a gun shop in Arizona. Man says, 'You interested in a gun?' There was a state trooper by the gun case. Trooper says, 'If you don't have a gun, I'll buy you one.' Ha!"

The Natchez show was almost identical to the one in Charleston and others I would see later in Southaven, in Laurel, in Jackson. At most of the shows I found the same people: the enormously fat man who sold ammo and sat among his crates and boxes; the handcrafted-knife man from Hot Coffee; the Taser stall; the Nazi memorabilia man, who was a New Zealander living in the middle of Mississippi; the old bearded man selling an assortment of his own leather holsters, who told me at one show that he always traveled with fifteen of his favorite guns ("This is my two-shot over-and-under, this is my Beretta nine millimeter") and at another show said, "That's my Judge. Forty-five caliber. That's for snakes—lots of cottonmouths in the country where we live."

Some men, too poor to hire a table, wandered the floor, conspicuously carrying a gun, looking like hunters, and in a way they were, hunting for a buyer, hoping to sell it.

"Can I have a look at that?"

"Sure thing. Aim it over there. Careful. It's single-action. Don't dry-fire it, hear."

One private seller had a thirty-year-old weapon, made of wood and stainless steel, a Sturm, Ruger .223-caliber Mini-14 assault rifle with a folding stock, the sort you see being carried by sharpshooters and conspirators in plots to overthrow wicked dictatorships.

"This is my baby," the man said, handing it to me. "I hate to sell it, but I have to. It's elegant, it's reliable, never jams. And it's pre-ban. They don't make them now. They'll never make them again."

"Seems very well made."

"She's a beauty. Not many of them around and none as nice. It's yours for twelve hundred cash. Private sale. Just take care of my baby."

I hefted the gun. It gleamed in my hands in an oddly sculptural way. I am not a gun nut, but as a Boy Scout, Troop 24 in Medford, Mass., I had a Mossburg .22, and though I have never killed an animal for sport, I have owned some sort of target-practice firearm ever since. This rifle tempted me to the point where I felt I should level with the seller.

"By the way, I'm from Massachusetts."

His face fell. He sighed, took the gun from me with meaty hands, and folded the stock flat, so that now it looked like a superior sort of pistol. "I wish you hadn't told me that."

"Oh, well."

"And how do I know you're not trying to set me up?"

"I'm not trying to set you up."

"You're not from around here."

"Right. I'm from up north. I'm just traveling—"

"The government's all over the place!" Now the man was talking to some bystanders who had watched me yanking the slider and cocking the rifle. "They're trying to shut us down!"

As I walked away, I heard him mutter, "God damn," not at me but at regulation generally—authority, the background checkers and inspectors and paper chewers, the government, Yankees.

That was when I began to understand the mood of the gun show. It was not about guns. Not about ammo, not about knives. It was not about shooting lead into perceived enemies. The mood was apparent in the way these men walked and spoke: they felt beleaguered, weakened, their backs to the wall. How old was this feeling? It was as old as the South, perhaps, for all they talked about was the Civil War, and they were oppressed by that and everything that had happened since, a persistent memory of defeat.

For the gun-show-goers the Civil War battles might have happened yesterday. Perhaps that's how it is with defeats, how they rankle, how the bitterness of humiliation never subsides. A person snubbed in childhood often carries the hurt through a whole life. The civil rights movement was another defeat for these Southerners who were so sensitized to intruders and gloaters and carpetbaggers, and even more so to outsiders who did not remember the humiliations of the Civil War. The passing of the plantation was another failure, as was the rise of opportunistic politicians, the outsourcing of local industries, the sinking of catfish farms, the plunge in manufacturing, and now this miserable economy in which there was so little work and so little spare money that people went to gun shows just to look and yearn for a decent weapon that they'd never be able to buy, an illusion of protection, a symbol of independence.

Over this history of failure was the scowling, punitive shadow of the federal government, hovering like a predator. "They're fixing to change this whole bidniss," as the man at the Charleston gun show had said—to take away the last vestige of Southern manhood. The general attitude wasn't one of defiance; what I sensed was the frustrated scowl and shallow breathing of people who felt lost and trifled with. The gun show was the one place where they could be themselves, like a clubhouse with strict admission and no windows. Yet the atmosphere was unmistakable: it was airless, self-conscious, rueful, watchful, and impoverished. Even putting on a brave face, the gun-show people radiated the feeling that throughout their history they had been beaten by outsiders and made to conform to laws that had no precedent and half the time caused more problems and required more laws—their world turned upside down.

The gun show wasn't about guns and gun totin'. It was about the self-esteem of men—white men mainly, the dominant ethnic group of the South, animated by a sense of grievance ("the heart of the Southern identity," according to one shrewd historian)—who felt defeated and still persecuted, conspired against by hostile outside forces, making a symbolic last stand.

Mrs. Robin Scott: "To Save My Children"

You hear talk of people fleeing the South, and some do. But I found many instances of the South as a refuge. I met a number of people who had fled the North for the South, for safety, for peace, for the old ways, returning to family, in retirement. A waiter taking a break outside a Mississippi restaurant said to me, "I'm from Detroit. My father got murdered there—he owned a little liquor store, the Pavilion. A man came to rob him. When my father gave him the money, the man shot him in the leg—femoral artery. He tried to drive himself to the hospital but he bled to death on the way. My mother had a breakdown because of it, so I took her here—she's got some kinfolk. It's better here, safer, happier, and my mother's improving day by day. I don't know if I'll ever go back north again."

I heard something similar at a laundromat in Natchez, doing my weekly wash. The efficient and friendly woman in charge changed some bills into quarters for the machines, sold me a cup of soap powder, and with a little encouragement told me her story.

Her name was Robin Scott, in her middle fifties, a brave woman with a powerful mothering instinct. She said, "I came here from Chicago to save my children from being killed by gangs. So many street gangs there—the Latin Kings, La Raza, Latin Eagles, the Popes, the Folk Nation, and more. At first where I lived was okay, the Garfield section. Then, around the late eighties, early nineties, the Four Corner gang and the BGs—Black Gangsters too—discovered crack cocaine and heroin. Using it, selling it, fighting about it. There was always shooting. I didn't want to stay there and bury my children.

"I said, Gotta get out of here. So I quit my job and rented a U-Haul and came down here where I had some family. I always had family in the South. Growing up in Chicago, we used to visit my family in North Carolina, a place in Halifax County near Rocky Mount."

I knew Rocky Mount from my recent drives, a pleasant place east of Raleigh, off I-95, where I sometimes stopped for a meal. It is also the birthplace of Thelonious Monk.

"I had good memories of Rocky Mount," Robin said. "It was country—so different from the Chicago streets. And my mother had a lot of family here in Natchez. So I knew the South was where I could save my kids. My first jobs here was all kinds. I worked at the casino dealing blackjack, but after a time I got rheumatoid arthritis. It's an autoimmune disease. It affected my hands, my joints, and my walking. It affected my marriage. My husband said, 'I don't want a cripple,' so he left me.

"Antibiotics are terrible for me, the way they affect me. I just can't get sick. I kept working, though, and I recovered from the rheumatoid arthritis, and I raised my kids. I got two girls, Melody and Courtney. Courtney's a bank manager. My boys are Anthony—the oldest, he's an electrician—and the twins, Robert and Joseph. They're twenty-one, at the University of Southern Mississippi. I'm proud of my kids. The twins used to talk to each other in their sleep!

"Natchez is a friendly place. I'm real glad I came. It wasn't easy. It's not easy now—the work situation is hard, but I manage. The man who owns this laundromat is a good man.

"I got so much family here. My grandmother was a Christmas—Mary Christmas. Her brother was Joseph. We called my grandmother Big Momma and my grandfather Big Daddy. I laughed when I saw that movie *Big Momma's House*.

"Mary Christmas was born on a plantation near Sibley. They were from families of sharecroppers. My grandfather was Jesse James Christmas. He passed, but when he was alive he used to get mail from a man in Vidalia across the river, by accident, also called Jesse James Christmas. So he'd save 'em up and then he'd go across the river to give the letters that were sent to him by mistake. That other Jesse James Christmas was a white man."

I mentioned Faulkner's *Light in August* and Joe Christmas, and how I'd always found the name faintly preposterous, heavy with symbolism. I told her the plot of the novel, and how the mysterious Joe Christmas, an orphan and bootlegger of black ancestry, passes for white.

In the novel, the foreman at the planing mill in Jefferson, speaking of the stranger, says, "His name is Christmas."

"His name is what?" one said.

"Christmas."

"Is he a foreigner?"

"Did you ever hear of a white man named Christmas?" the foreman said.

"I never heard of nobody a-tall named it," the other said.

And that was the first time Byron remembered that he had ever thought how a man's name, which is supposed to be just the sound for who he is, can be somehow an augur of what he will do, if other men can only read the meaning in time.

Before I could continue with the tale of Lena Grove and her child and the Christian theme, Robin broke in.

"Joe Christmas is my uncle," she said. "He's ninety-two. He lives in a care home in Natchez. It's a common name in these parts."

The Delta: The Round Table

In my ignorance, I had believed the Delta to be solely the low-lying estuary of the Mississippi River, round about and south of New Orleans, the river delta of the maps. But it isn't so simple. The Delta is the entire alluvial sprawl that stretches northward of that mud in Louisiana, the floodplain beyond Natchez, emphatically flat above Vicksburg, almost the whole of a bulge of western Mississippi, enclosed in the east by the Yazoo River, all the way to Memphis. It is a definite route, as well; it is Highway 61.

Continuing up that highway, past Fayette and Lorman again, I swung through Port Gibson, a town boasting that at least one road "looks much as it did in 1863," and some buildings too — General Grant spared it, saying the town was "too beautiful to burn." This was not the case with Vicksburg, just up the road, like Natchez a town on a bluff, but unlike Natchez it had been besieged, shelled constantly from Union barges on the river, in an assault that lasted forty days. And the siege ended in a significant defeat, a humiliating surrender.

The siege was still a memory. I joined eight strangers for lunch at the family-style Round Table at the Walnut Hills Restaurant in Vicksburg. Anyone at all could sit at the Round Table, among strangers or friends, and eat together. This bungalow on a side street had been recommended for its home cooking. Introducing myself, I said where I'd come from.

"Set yourself down," one man said.

But an older woman muttered in a resentful way, "You know what you did to us?"

The memory had become a taunt. The others at the table, all of them local, and most of them strangers to each other, though chatting amiably, went silent, waiting for my reply. They knew she was referring to the long siege of Vicksburg by the Union Army in 1864.

By then I'd toured the town of Vicksburg, with its lovely antebellum houses and landmarks of the war; the battlefield took up most of the town, and I heard about the suffering. "This whole city is a grave," Natasha Trethewey writes in her poem "Pilgrimage," about a visit to the place. So I didn't take the woman's accusation lightly. I said, as though to a cranky child, "I personally did not do anything to you. The South seceded. The North responded. All's well that ends well."

"You starved us," the woman said. "You made us eat rats."

This sort of response — sometimes heartfelt, sometimes a bitter joke, sometimes spoken with defiant nostalgia — is so commonly uttered in the South, always by whites, to a Northern visitor, that I learned not to say, "That was a hundred and fifty years ago," but instead listened with sympathy, because conquered people feel helpless, and the proof of this is the monotony of their complaint. Their nagging on this point, ancient to me but fresh as today in their minds, gives the North — of which I was the embodiment that morning — a fiendish magnitude.

So I commiserated, and asked some other questions. For example (I suggested), if the South had won the war, what would the national boundary of the Confederacy look like, and where would it end? How would we trade? Would the South have endured and still be backward-looking, with slaves and an aristocracy and a standing gray-uniformed army? How would that army have responded to international events, like the Spanish-American War and the Great War? And, assuming Hawaii had become a Union territory, how would the Confederate South have reacted to the bombing of Pearl Harbor?

Yet logic seldom overcomes the feelings of profound loss, or sentiment, or wounded pride. Much of the South still hurts because a great part of the South is still poor; and the air of defeat that I sensed keenly at gun shows was like a reminder of the Civil War — the losses, the deaths, the gratuitous burnings, the surrender. The sense, too, or the delusion, that a golden age had ended with the war — of ease, of mansions, of slavery — when what had happened was that the vigor of the South had been exhausted in its failed bid to be separate, turning it upside down and impoverishing it, making it a bitter place of tombstones and memorials and ruins.

"The South was created by the need to protect a peculiar institution from threats originating outside the region," the Southern historian Sheldon Hackney writes in his essay "Southern Violence" (1969). Consequently, "the Southern identity has been linked from the first to a siege mentality." Being Southern, he says, "involves a feeling of persecution at times, and a sense of being a passive, insignificant object of alien or external forces." Among these forces he lists abolitionists, the Union Army, carpetbaggers, Wall Street, civil rights agitators, the federal government, feminism, socialism, trade unionism, Darwinism, communism, atheism, daylight saving time, "and other by-products of modernity." And writers like me, nature's own subversives.

I often reflected that in the heart of Thomaston, Maine, under the tall maples and broad oaks, a Civil War soldier stands brooding on a granite block, and under him on the plinth, the inscription, *To the Memory of Soldiers and Sailors 1861–1865,* and *One Country — One Flag.* The 20th Maine Regiment, under the command of Colonel Joshua Chamberlain, in a heroic and decisive downhill bayonet charge against thousands of Confederates in the Battle of Little Round Top, helped turned the tide at Gettysburg. There are more than 150 such Civil War memorials in Maine towns, and a similar number in Massachusetts.

Virtually every community of any size in New England has a war memorial. One of the oldest, erected in 1866, is the stark obelisk that stands on the green in Centerville, on Cape Cod, the four sides of the base listing the names of dead soldiers — this tiny seaside fishing village, just a few hundred souls then, lost thirty-one men in the Civil War. My town of Sandwich on the Cape, with a population of 4,500 in 1861, sent 240 of its young men to that war. Fifty-four of them were killed and many wounded. One of the Sandwich veterans was a black man, Joseph Wilson, a freed slave, who fought with the 54th Massachusetts Regiment (the first to have black soldiers) at the siege of Vicksburg, and found his way back to Cape Cod after the war, to tell the tale.

But there is hardly a person today in Thomaston, Centerville, Sandwich, or elsewhere in New England who will mention that war, or even draw a visitor's attention to the melancholy memorials on the village greens.

After the woman had vented her feelings, I said something of this, and quoted the Chinese sage Lieh Tzu: "The reputation of a general is made on the corpses of ten thousand men."

When a Mexican in Charles Portis's novel *Gringos* complains that the Yanquis took half his country in 1848, the narrator, Jimmy Burns, says, "They took all of mine in 1865. We can't keep moping over it."

A younger woman said, "I was up north once. They talk a lot about the Revolutionary War up there. We never mention it here."

"War is hell," I said, and became acutely aware of the general I was quoting. I was glad when the conversation turned to food, and antiques, and the weather.

We all ate together. That was a tradition of the Walnut Hills Round Table. There was room for a dozen people around the big table. Anyone could sit down, and the food was served buffet style on a lazy Susan: bowls of fried chicken, bowls of stew and potatoes, rice and gravy, platters of fried fish, bowls of beans and collard greens. The turntable meant that a degree of consideration had to be observed toward your fellow diners. And as I had learned in my travels elsewhere, eating together is an occasion that humans have made into a peacemaking ritual; sharing food is sharing friendship, and so the talk of war subsided, and we spoke of the news of the day.

Unemployment was a topic. "Jobs are scarce," someone said.

One of the diners was a man whose business had been selling farm machinery. He was retired now. He said, "Mechanization has taken away all the jobs. I sold cotton pickers. The early ones only picked one row at a time, but even so, they did the work of forty men. These days they can do six rows, your spindle picker. Some can do twelve rows. How can any field hand compete with that?"

"And tell them what they cost," his wife said.

"Half a million dollars, some of 'em. Some a lot more."

"That's why no one's working here."

The woman who had said "You made us eat rats" asked me if I'd traveled outside the United States. I said yes, and I recognized this question as a cue for me to respond by returning it, asking about her European travels, because a person — and especially a traveler — asks a question in order to give information and state an opinion. "Ever been to Bhutan?" means "I have been to Bhutan and I would enjoy telling you about my trip for the next hour or so."

"I've been over there," the woman said. "Paris. London."

"What was it like?" one of the younger women inquired with enthusiasm.

"Hated it. It was nothing." The woman made a face. "America's lots better."

Delta Autumn

When I told a shopkeeper in Vicksburg that I was headed up Highway 61, he said to me, "Make sure you got a full belly and a full tank of gas. Don't stop on any account," which made me smile, because it was the sort of thing I'd heard all the time on the back roads of East and Central Africa: Keep on going, it's dangerous to stop, there's some hungry people on that road, they want what you have, and if you hit someone they'll snatch you and make life hell for you. But in this case it was the Blues Highway, the great river road.

"Soon now they would enter the Delta," runs the first line of Faulkner's story "Delta Autumn," from *Go Down, Moses.* It continues, "The last hill, at the foot of which the rich unbroken alluvial flatness began as the sea began at the base of its cliffs." This story, set in 1940, is a memory of deer hunting, an account of the passing of generations, of present events and past history—the reality of the war in Europe, mentions of Hitler and the intrusions of modernity, neon signs, big cotton gins, locomotives, "countless shining this-year's automobiles," the erosion and disappearance of the wilderness, the shrinking of hunting land, mentions of "Negroes" who worked the land. Near the remote hunting camp, the old Delta remains as deep woods and "the tall tremendous soaring of oak and gum and ash and hickory which had run to no axe save the hunter's."

Along with the philosophical musing about hunting by the patriarch Ike McCaslin, who is pessimistic about the future, there is an impasse at the center of the tale regarding race, a love story. This is the alliance between one of the hunters, Carothers ("Roth"), and a nameless light-skinned black woman, who is the mother of his child. She lives near the camp and shows up with their child, intending to see him. But he has risen early to hunt—to hide, it seems—and has guiltily left some money with Ike for him to hand over to her. As in much of Faulkner there is a great deal of genealogy and mingled blood behind this meeting, but in essence it represents the two branches of the McCaslin family, white and black, converging in the story.

Ike gives the woman the money and tells her to marry "a man in your own race." Justifiably indignant, because he has not considered the possibility that Roth and she were in love, she delivers the best line in the story. "Old man," she says, "have you lived so long and forgotten so much that you don't remember anything you ever knew about love?"

As she is taken away—to Leland, to board the train north to a new life—Ike regrets the change in the Delta, the destruction of the wilderness: "deswamped and denuded and derivered in two generations so that white men can own plantations." And in the present decline of the Delta he sees a much worse future: bankruptcy, miscegenation, people living "like animals."

Fiction often highlights a landscape and suggests a future, but fiction can be misleading. A good reason to travel is to put fiction in context. For Ike, the Delta was being destroyed by big money, intermarriage, and intensive farming—in a word, by Yankee culture, something Faulkner seems to have detested. The deforestation that Ike laments was occurring in the period when Faulkner wrote the story, and the tree cutting continued, the cotton fields sprawling farther to the margins of the swamps and backwaters, much as the landscape looks today. Ike (seeming to speak for Faulkner) predicts a conflict of races, ambitions, and commercial interests. What happened was simpler and more devastating: mechanization put field workers off the land and left them unemployed.

"When I was a boy, in the later 1940s and 1950s, we used to get up before dawn," a man named Will Thompson told me later, in Georgia. "This was in Jackson. A big truck picked us up and drove us in the darkness to the Delta, and we worked all day. I was just a kid, so young I couldn't pick any cotton at first. I was the water boy, going up and down the rows with a bucket and a dipper. After dark we were driven back to Jackson."

After high school, Will joined the army and served in Vietnam.

"One of my buddies was killed, and I was sent back to Mississippi to escort the body. This was 1968, that terrible year. We drove through those cotton fields from Memphis. It all came back. Soon as I got to Jackson I said to myself, 'I'm never going to accept being a second-class citizen ever again.'"

Many blacks in the Delta said the same thing; it was something Faulkner—and Ike McCaslin—had not foreseen: desertion.

In this Delta autumn of my trip, the countryside was beautiful — bottomland sloping toward the river looking moist and fertile, groves of oaks and gum trees and cypresses (Cypress Street was the old name of this southern stretch of Highway 61) — and I could sense the river beyond the trees from the clouds of insects over the nearer bayous and swampier distances and the quality of light, which was milkier and bluer, filtered through the stands of hardwoods and willows.

A little more than sixty years after the events of that short story, the landscape was hardly changed: no traffic, and only old or ruined houses. It was like driving into the past. The road flattened, straightened as I entered Sharkey County, cotton country, and the town of Cary, which had a ginnery and under five hundred people. Egremont, down the road, had far fewer. As I'd seen elsewhere, in South Carolina and Alabama, the cotton fields were an immense and linty whiteness of twiggy bushes, and no field hands, no pickers, no workers in sight. Flecks and scraps of cotton, blown from the fields, had snagged on boughs by the roadside, giving the impression of an immense untidiness, as if part of a bale load had blown from a passing rag truck.

Now and then I saw one of those gigantic cotton-picking machines the retired dealer in Vicksburg had described that cost half a million dollars. They were high-shouldered, they bulked over the throne-like cab, and they had a wide, gap-toothed lower jaw that entered six rows and stripped them.

No houses, and then bunches of them, and when I saw the beat-up house trailers, the shotgun shacks, the old rusted buses converted to habitations, I realized that this was the poorest part of the United States I had seen in my life, poorer than Allendale in South Carolina, poorer than the poorest village in Alabama, the meanest houses, as the Citizen rants in *Ulysses*, "mudcabins and shielings by the roadside."

The mobile homes, seeming decayed and abandoned, were clustered together in improvised settlements under the trees. These were not communities. They were encampments outside towns and at the edges of cotton fields, and there was no evidence that they had utilities. They mimicked the pattern of Gypsy camps in Britain: the huddles of house trailers, the heaps of garbage and litter, the clotheslines of drooping laundry, the idle ragged children, and in a weird, heartbreaking touch — because it was only October — a Christmas wreath with a red ribbon hung on the door of one shack, for color.

Don't stop, the man had said, but I stopped down the road at the town of Rolling Fork.

The large, stately, old stone Sharkey County Courthouse fronted the boarded-up shops, empty streets, and vandalized signs. But there was a Sunflower Food Store on one side of town and Sam Sing & Co, a Chinese grocery, on the other.

Walking around the town I met Leroy, a clerk at Sam Sing's, having a cigarette break. He told me what many others said, that the bluesman Muddy Waters had been born, as McKinley Morganfield, in Rolling Fork. Muddy had claimed this himself, but it was unconfirmed — he might have been born in an adjacent county, and he grew up in a shotgun shack on Stovall Plantation in Clarksdale, farther up the Delta. But Rolling Fork had so little to boast about, you have to give them the benefit of the doubt on the Muddy question.

"These shops used to be all of them real busy," Leroy said, "and now look at them — gone. But we farming still, cotton, soybeans, and corn."

Seeing Leroy talking to me, a woman approached. She was Ann Culpeper, formerly a guidance counselor at Rolling Fork Elementary School. She knew Leroy from the school.

"They integrated the high school in 1994," Leroy said, answering one of my questions.

"Must have been earlier than that," Ann said.

An old woman walking by asked, "What is it you want to know?" When Leroy told her, she said, "They don't know anything. Rolling Fork High School was white. When they integrated it, and blacks went there, a private school was started for whites."

Both of the women were white. Leroy was black. They argued among themselves about dates, and couldn't agree; recent history was a blur. It was perhaps an effect of the stagnation. There were so few events in this dying town that there was nothing to remember, nothing to associate with a particular year. They were in agreement on one issue: there was no work, no money, seemingly no future here.

Anguilla, about five miles up the highway, was desolate, a scattering of mobile homes at the edge of the road and bordering the plowed fields—decayed, rusted boxes, lying higgledy-piggledy with an air of disorder and desperation, like a refugee camp, which it was, in a way.

Worse yet, more wretched and bereft, was Arcola, a mile off the highway, a ghost town, every shop and some houses boarded up on the main street (and this main street was the former, curving Highway 61, not the straight road of today). I could read the faded names on the signboards of these doomed businesses—Four-Way Grocery and Club Tropicana and Roger's—everything shut except the Arcola post office.

The old backbreaking jobs were gone, and the newer businesses were failing—catfish farming, furniture making, and the Schwinn bicycle plant twenty miles away in Greenville that closed in 1991, with 250 workers laid off. There were also serious layoffs at the Viking Range plant in Greenwood.

Rotting, picturesquely hopeless, forgotten, these towns, all of them with a creek or a stream running through them, were backwaters, both literally and figuratively. They could have been any small, bereft agricultural town in the Third World where mechanization had taken hold, where tractors and picking machines had overtaken handpicking on the plantations. In these places people were struggling and making do, clinging to their routines, where life was precarious and everything—houses, shops, clotheslines, children's toys—looked improvised.

There was no wealth here, or if there was, it was hidden. The profits of the cotton crops did not appear to enrich anyone in the Delta. Probably someone in Jackson or Memphis lived well on this harvest.

I thought of Almeida Garrett, the mid-nineteenth-century Portuguese traveler and philosopher. An inspiration to me, Garrett had taken a trip in his own country, chronicled in *Travels in My Homeland* (*Viagens na Minha Terra*), and seeing the poverty, he had formulated a question: "I ask the political economists and the moralists if they have ever calculated the number of individuals who must be condemned to misery, overwork, demoralization, degradation, rank ignorance, overwhelming misfortune and utter penury in order to produce one rich man."

"Things Are Worse Than They Look"

"What you see in the Delta isn't how things are," a woman officer at a bank in Greenville told me.

"But they don't look good," I said.

"Things are worse than they look," she said.

She'd been raised in Hollandale, one of the bleaker towns on Highway 61 south of Greenville. She shrugged and asked me what I wanted to know. Her colleague Sue Evans, who was sixty or so, sat with her but said little, merely nodded in acknowledgment. We sat in their office on an upper floor of the bank, on a back street of Greenville on a dark afternoon, under a sky thick with bulgy drooping clouds. Scattered droplets of cold rain marked the broken sidewalks and potholed street. I had thought of the Delta, for all its misery, as at least a sunny place, but this was chilly, even wintry, though it was only October. For me the weather, the atmosphere, was something new, something unexpected and oppressive, and thus remarkable.

"Things are worse than they look" was one of the more shocking statements I heard in the Mississippi Delta, because as in Allendale, South Carolina, and the hamlets on the back roads of Alabama, this part of the Delta seemed to be imploding. The Bible is often the happy hunting ground of disturbed minds, but it was easy (as I kept finding among the biblically inclined in the South) to be drawn to the book of Revelation, with its signs and portents, and discern that instead of the parted clouds of salvation and the blare of trumpets, we were living in the sulfurous fumes of the Last Days.

"Housing is the biggest challenge," the bank officer said, "but we're in a Catch-22 — too big to be small, too small to be big. By that I mean, we're rural but we don't qualify for rural funding because the population is over twenty-five thousand."

"Funding from whom?"

"Federal funding," she said. "And there's the mind-set. It's challenging. It's short-term thinking, a misplaced value system."

I said, "Are you talking about the people living in poverty?"

"Yes, some of those people. For example, you see nice vehicles in front of really run-down houses. You see people at Walmart and in the nail shops getting their nails done."

"Is that unusual?"

"They're on government assistance," she said, and shook her head. Sue Evans murmured her agreement. "I'm not saying they shouldn't look nice, but it's instant gratification instead of sacrifice."

"What do you think they should do?"

"Tell you what I did," she said. "Because my value system is different. I grew up in a poverty-stricken town"—and having passed through the town the day before, I knew it was not an exaggeration: Hollandale looked as if the plague had struck it. "My parents had fourteen children, and at any given time there were never less than ten people in the house, plus my parents. One bathroom. This was interesting—we were never on any kind of government assistance, the reason being that my father worked. His job was at Nicholson Files. And he fished and hunted and gardened. His vegetables were really good. He shot deer, rabbits, squirrels. My mother fried the squirrels or made squirrel stew." She laughed and said, "I never ate that game. I ate chicken."

"I've had squirrel," Sue Evans said, her first contribution to the discussion.

"What happened to Nicholson Files?" It was a company that made metal files and quality tools, a well-respected brand among builders.

"Closed. Went to Mexico," the bank officer said. This was a reply I often heard when I asked about manufacturing in the Delta. "I could see there wasn't much for me here. I joined the Marines. I did three-and-three—three active, three reserve. I was based in Oceanside, California, and I can tell you that apart from salvation it was the best decision I've made in my life. The service provided me with a totally different perspective. It helped me to see things differently."

"I've heard that," I said. "The military as a way out and a way up."

"Made all the difference to me. Up to then, all I knew was the Delta. I went to Hollandale School, a typical public school in the Delta. It was integrated in, I think, 1969. The white school was on the other side of town, but it—miraculously, ha!—burned down just after that. Of course, they burned it so that they wouldn't have to deal with us. No one will be convinced otherwise. After it burned, Deer Creek Academy started in Arcola—a white school, still there, still white, or at least ninety-nine percent. There were some whites at my school, two or three. Though the ratio of blacks to whites in the Delta is sixty-forty, we still have an imbalance in Greenville. O'Bannon Elementary and High School is black. Riverside High School in Avon is mostly white. Those dynamics hurt us as a community."

"But Greenville is a big town." I'd been surprised at the extent of it, the sprawl, the downtown, the neighborhoods of good, even grand, houses. And a new bridge had been built — one yet to be named — across the Mississippi, just west of the city.

"This is a declining town. River traffic is way down. We've lost population, from about fifty thousand to less than forty thousand. This was a thriving place. We had so much manufacturing — trailers for big-rig trucks, Fruit of the Loom men's underwear, Schwinn bikes, Axminster carpets. They're all gone to Mexico, South America, China. There was an air force base here. It closed."

"What businesses are still here?" I asked.

"Catfish, but that's not as big as it was. We've got rice — Uncle Ben's, that's big. We've got a company making ceiling tiles, and Leading Edge — they put the paint on jet planes. But there's not enough jobs. Unemployment is huge, more than sixteen percent, twice the national average."

"People I've talked to say that better housing helps."

"It's fine to have a home, but if you don't have the subsidies to go with the home, you're just treading water. But that's how a lot of people live."

"Do you fix up houses?"

"Very few homes get rehabbed. Most are in such bad shape it's cheaper to tear them down than fix them. A lot are abandoned. There's more and more vacant lots."

"If Greenville happened to be a city in a Third World country, there would probably be lots of aid money pouring in."

"This was a federal Empowerment Zone — ten years, ten million dollars pumped into the economy."

"Ten million isn't much compared to the hundreds of millions I've seen in US aid to Africa," I said. "A small single country like Tanzania or Ghana might get seven hundred million. For schools or clinics."

"That's news to us," she said, and Sue Evans looked equally surprised. "We do what we can. Things have been improving slowly. There's Greenville Education Center. They have both day and night classes for people to study."

Later, I checked the curriculum of Mississippi Delta Community College, which was part of this program, and found that they offered courses in bricklaying and tilesetting, automotive mechanics, commercial truck driving, heavy equipment operation, electronics, machine tool expertise, welding, heating and air-conditioning, office systems, and much else. But there are few jobs.

"People get educated and they leave," she said. "There's a high rotation in doctors and teachers. We've got to come together. It doesn't matter how. Some healing has to take place."

Given the seriousness of the situation, and the blight that was general over the Delta, I wondered aloud why she persevered.

"Me? I was meant to be here," she said.

All this time, Sue Evans had sat in silence. But when I changed the subject, talked about the musical history of Greenville, the blues, the clubs that had been numerous up and down the Delta, Sue became animated. The subject of music was dear to her heart, she said.

"My mother had a jazz club in Leland," Sue said. I had passed through Leland, another farming town on Highway 61, known for its blues history. "She was a great gal, my mother — Ruby — everyone knew her."

There were still some clubs, she said. There was a blues museum. People came from all over the world to visit these places associated with the blues, and to see the birthplaces and the reference points — the farms, the creeks, the railways, the cotton fields.

"I heard that in Indianola there's a B. B. King museum," I said.

This produced a profound silence. The two women exchanged a glance but said nothing. It was the sort of silence provoked by an unwelcome allusion, or sheer confusion, as though I had lapsed into an unfamiliar language.

"He was born there, I understand," I said, flailing a bit, and wondering whether I had overstayed my visit.

Sue Evans had a mute and somewhat stubborn gaze fixed away from mine, while her colleague, smiling faintly, then spoke.

"Berclair," she said. "But he was raised in Kilmichael. Other side of Greenwood."

It seemed very precise and obscure information. I couldn't think of anything more to say, and it was apparent that this topic had produced an atmosphere in the room, a vibration that was unreadable, and that made me feel like a clumsy alien.

"Shall we tell him?"

"I don't know," Sue said.

"You tell him."

"Go ahead," Sue said.

This exchange, a sort of banter, had the effect of lifting the mood, diffusing the vibe.

"Sue was married to him."

"Married to B. B. King?"

Sue said, "Yes, I was. I was Sue Hall then. His second and last wife. It was a while back."

Sue was white and looked like a school librarian; her colleague was black and still had the forceful manner of a master sergeant in the Marines, which she had been. But now that the subject had been raised, both women were smiling.

"One night my mother booked him," Sue said. "He kind of looked at me. I was just a kid. I had an idea of what he was thinking, but my mother wouldn't stand any nonsense or fooling around. He played at the club a lot—a great musician. He waited until I turned eighteen—he waited because he didn't want to deal with my mother. He was afraid of her."

She laughed at the memory of it. I said, "This would have been when?"

"Long ago," Sue said. "We were married for ten years."

"Did you call him BB?"

"His proper name is Riley. I called him B."

I was writing down "Riley."

"Which was confusing," Sue was saying. "Because Ray Charles's wife was named Beatrice. We called her B too. We often got mixed up with the two B's."

"You traveled with him?" I asked.

"All the time. B loved to travel. He loved to play—he could play all night. He loved the audiences, the people, he lived to talk. But I got so tired. He'd say, 'You don't like to hear me,' but it wasn't that. I just hated staying up all hours. I'd be in the hotel room, waiting for him."

"Are you still in touch?"

"We talk all the time. He calls. We talk. He still tours — imagine. Last I talked to him, he said he had some dates in New York and New Jersey. He loves the life. He's still going strong."

And for that fifteen or twenty minutes there was no blight on the Delta. It was a cheery reminiscence of her decade with B. B. King, the man who'd brought glory to the Delta and proved that it was possible and could happen again.

"Jesus Is Lord — We Buy and Sell Guns"

My season of driving was ending. I continued up the Delta, then went east and crossed into Alabama. It was like traveling in the hinterland of a foreign country, the same solitude, the same poverty, the same birdsong, with unexpectedness and discoveries, as on the Alabama shop I passed with a yellow sign, enormous black letters, JESUS IS LORD — WE BUY AND SELL GUNS, which had become one of the mingled themes of my journey. Inarticulate in explanation but eloquent in its actions, the South never ceased to advertise its obsessions on big billboards. I had come to depend on its visibility.

After most trips you say, This is enough, I'll go home and write about it. This trip was done but the journey wasn't over, and my discoveries gave me an appetite for more. I had found that America had a peasant class, as hard-up and ignored and hopeless as any I had seen in the world. I thought of all the people I'd met — Reverend Virgin Johnson in Sycamore, Wilbur Cave in desperate Allendale, Cynthia Burton in Tuscaloosa, Mayor Washington and Reverend Lyles in Greensboro, the people in the Delta, Mother Scott, the former Mrs. B. B. King, and more. And all the folks who'd invited me back. The autumn landscapes were already turning cold and fading to gray. What would all this be like in the winter, and what would those folks be doing? My home was at one end of the road, my subject at the other end. Loving the long empty stretches, in the grip of white line fever, the satori of the open road, I drove home making plans to return soon.

INTERLUDE

The Taboo Word

At home the word I'd heard spoken by various people, and sung with joyful menace, was echoing in my head. It is perhaps the most explosive word in American English, which is noted for the vividness and originality of its robust vocabulary. Other racial or ethnic slurs do not come close to having its damning quality, its strength of insult, or its hint of infernality. Obscene words and vulgar references that were forbidden for their shock value when I was much younger are spoken these days on television shows for all the children to hear. But this racial epithet is in a category of its own, and as a writer who spends his days engrossed (as I am now) in contemplating the meaning, the effect, the sound, and the arrangement of English words in order to convey an experience, I can perhaps be forgiven for being fascinated that a word — a mere two syllables in this case — possesses such overwhelming power to enrage.

The handful of whites I met in the South who used this word in my presence did so in two different, almost opposing, moods, muttered it casually or enunciated it defiantly. And it was spoken by black and white alike — another paradox, it was used more frequently by blacks in my hearing, and with heartiness and zest and sometimes almost tunefully. It is impossible to say the word without showing your teeth.

It occurs in other languages, among them German, where the word is *Neger*. It was used by Nazi propagandists to induce fear or loathing (jazz was *Negermusik*), and in his speeches Reich Minister of Propaganda Joseph Goebbels raised the specter of a defeated Germany being overrun by *betrunken Neger* ("drunken niggers"). Germans have come to see *Neger* as an objectionable word (often replaced by *Farbige,* colored, or *Schwarze,* black), which is why *Negerkuss* ("nigger kiss"), the chocolate-covered marshmallow treat beloved by German children, was not long ago renamed *Schokokuss* ("chocolate kiss"). The French word *nègre* is not so insulting but has belittling implications — for example, *nègre* is also slang for ghostwriter. Defying the formality of the Belgian king Baudouin and other luminaries, in the celebration of the Congo's independence in 1960 in Leopoldville, Patrice Lumumba, the newly elected prime minister, angrily used the word, saying, "We have known sarcasm and insult, endured blows morning, noon and night, because we were 'niggers' [*nègres*]. Who will forget that a Black was addressed in the familiar *tu*, not as a friend, but because the polite *vous* was reserved for Whites only."

But none of these examples is as offensive as the English word. In America the word has the deepest roots, as the notable curse word of slavery — slavery, the South's enduring curse, which the use of this word seemingly perpetuates by calling it to mind and summoning up the image of a captive and despised individual. In his *Autobiography*, recalling his early days (the 1840s) in Hannibal, Missouri, Mark Twain writes, "The 'nigger trader' was loathed by everybody. He was regarded as a sort of human devil who bought and conveyed poor helpless creatures to hell — for to our whites and blacks alike the Southern plantation was simply hell."

Growing up in the North, I never heard the word in my house, though in the Boston streets at that time (late 1940s and 1950s) "nigger heaven" was the colloquial name for the top tier of any theater or sports arena; a cigarette might be "nigger-lipped" ("I hated it when a buddy took a greedy, wet puff, 'nigger-lipping' a butt before he passed it on to me," the black writer John Edgar Wideman wrote in a 1985 *New York Times* essay about growing up in Pittsburgh); "Eenie meenie miney moe" ended with "catch a nigger by the toe." In the corner shop that sold penny candy, the small black nuggets of licorice in a big jar were formally called "nigger babies" ("And five cents' worth of nigger babies, please"). These misguided uses of the word were common in a society that prided itself on racial fairness and where blacks and whites attended school together; using the word in the presence of a black person would have been regarded as gratuitously insulting.

My parents abhorred the word, even these conventional uses of it. They viewed it correctly as racist, betraying the bigotry and ignorance of anyone who spoke it. I can't think of another word in English that has such singular force: to speak it is to breathe fire. The word itself is historically a degrading synonym for "slave," and implies an inferior, even subhuman, being. In Faulkner's *Absolom, Absolom!* Rosa Coldfield (speaking to Quentin round about 1909) appears to set out the South's traditional categories when she rails, "What creature in the South since 1861, man woman nigger or mule . . ."

Uttering the word in some quarters is like an act of violence, causing ructions, riots, court cases, shame, disgrace, and summary dismissals. Though it has Latinate roots (from *niger*, black) and seems to be a coarse and mumbled variation of "Negro," even words that sound the same, such as "niggardly" (of Scandinavian origin, meaning stingy or parsimonious) and "niggard" (a stingy person), the verb "niggle" (to trifle with), and "snigger," a form of "snicker," have been execrated for their phonetic similarity and have gotten people who used them into trouble. None of these are cognates, they bear no relation to it, yet they seem like dark whispers of the explosive word, and people avoid them as they avoid using the word "crapulous," believing it to imply defecation rather than drunkenness.

This suggests paranoia, which is understandable. Yet it is just a word, and it is part of the South's subtext — there is hardly a work of Southern fiction, from *Huckleberry Finn* to the present, that doesn't use it somehow. "When John Rolfe recorded in his journal the first shipment of Africans to Virginia in 1619, he listed them as 'negars,'" Randall Kennedy states in his exhaustive and judicious examination of the word, *Nigger: The Strange Career of a Troublesome Word* (2002). The Oxford English Dictionary cites its first use in print as 1786, by Robert Burns, in his poem "The Ordination," characteristically dense with dialect, in these lines:

> *Come, let a proper text be read,*
> *An' touch it aff wi' vigour,*
> *How graceless Ham leugh at his dad,*
> *Which made Canaan a nigger . . .*

Coleridge also used the word (1849), speculating on the race of Shakespeare's Othello, and so did H. Rider Haggard (1889) in an aside about Allan Quatermain's wife. The Victorians understood the word was insulting. The explorer Richard Burton, known for his African exploits as "the White Nigger," seldom used the word but employed a variant, "niggerling," to denote a black child, in both his book on Brazil and his account of the Cameroon mountains. A significant distinction that Thomas Carlyle made in 1849, when he wrote his bigoted essay about the West Indian plantation economies and the inferiority of blacks, was that he titled it "Occasional Discourse on the Nigger Question," rebutted by John Stuart Mill in a wiser and more temperate essay, "The Negro Question."

In Britain the word, until about the 1960s, was an agreed-upon color. "They dropped an amused eye on the pale butter-colored waves in the white lambs' fleeces, the nigger-brown waves in the black lambs' fleeces," Rebecca West writes in her classic travel book *Black Lamb and Grey Falcon* (1941), making a casual observation in the course of her tour of Dalmatia. Black or brown dogs and cats were given the word as a name by many English owners, until its use made them self-conscious. "Nigger" was the name of the black cat on Captain Scott's Antarctic expedition. The mascot of the Royal Air Force's 617 ("Dam Buster") Squadron during World War Two was a black dog named Nigger, much loved and adoringly depicted in campaign photographs; though for a film recounting the heroic exploits of that squadron, the dog was renamed Digger.

Faulkner's writing, which is a fictional history of Southern life from the years of the dispossessed Chickasaws in the early nineteenth century until roughly the 1940s, bristles with it. In his most earnestly praised work we come across expressions such as "wild niggers," "monkey nigger," or, for a household slave, "monkey dressed nigger."

"All the niggers make fun of me because of the way she treats me," says redneck Lov Bensey, whose twelve-year-old wife, Pearl, refuses to sleep with him in Erskine Caldwell's *Tobacco Road*. Uttered through literature, the word has a wicked history, but the word persists.

Here is an apparent and bewildering paradox. Though it is construed in some circumstances as hate speech, actionable as a racial slur, and whites have been disgraced for using it, the word is blared constantly in popular music, especially in the lyrics of rap and hip-hop. In many songs it is the most often repeated word, usually in its more colloquial form, "nigga." Now and then a black commentator asserts that the words "nigger" and "nigga" are distinct lexical items, the former offensive, the latter acceptable; but of course the latter is a phonetic version of the former.

After the celebrated 2013 trial in Florida in which George Zimmerman was acquitted of killing the black teen Trayvon Martin, a prosecution witness, one Rachel Jeantel, explained the word in an interview on

CNN. Jeantel said, "People say it's a racist word. They change it around." For emphasis, she spelled it: "N-i-g-g-a. That means a male, any kind of male, even Chinese. A man. But nigger"— stressing of the second syllable as *gerrh*—"that's a racist word."

On the evidence of the songs, it sometimes implies a word of endearment among blacks, a way of saying "friend," or someone more intimate than a friend, a bosom buddy. The songs to this effect have similar titles: Lil Wayne's "My Nigga," Killa Kyleon's "My Nigga," Trae's "Still My Nigga," and many others, including the lyrics to the songs of Timothy Thedford (Jay Electronica), one of whose lines is "Kill a nigga, rob a nigga, take a nigga." Shawn Carter, who calls himself Jay-Z, a friend and donor to the campaigns of Barack Obama, a frequent guest at the White House, and an honored invitee at two presidential inaugurations, has an estimated worth of half a billion dollars, much of it earned from songs such as "Nigga What, Nigga Who," "Nigga Please," "Niggas in Paris," "Ain't No Nigga," and "Jigga That Nigga."

Pressed by Oprah Winfrey in a televised interview in 2011 on why he used the word so frequently, Carter/Jay-Z said, "By using the word so much we took the power out of it," and, unapologetic, he went on to explain that the word was used affectionately.

Still, in this twenty-minute segment neither he nor Oprah spoke the word. Oprah frowned and sourly referred to it as "the N-word." Carter called it "this word." At the close of the interview Oprah twinkled and said, "We'll have to agree to disagree," as Carter shrugged, muttering, "It's a generational thing." It is doubtful that Oprah would have smiled and been so cheerfully accommodating had she interviewed a similarly intransigent white person on that same subject.

In his book on the word, Randall Kennedy, who is black, quotes Oliver Wendell Holmes Jr. on a subtle distinction in words generally, how "'a word is not a crystal, transparent and unchanged' but is instead 'the skin of a living thought [that] may vary greatly in color and content, according to the circumstances and time in which it is used.'" Kennedy speaks of how the word was used in his household in North Carolina, and how "I learned at an early age that it could be said in many ways, put to many uses, and mean many things. Big Mama [his mother] peppered her speech with references to 'niggers,' by which she meant discreditable Negroes, a group that, in her view, constituted a large section of the African American population. If Big Mama saw blacks misbehaving, she would often roll her eyes, purse her lips, and then declare in a mournful tone, 'Nigguhs!' According to Big Mama, 'niggers can't get along, even in church' and 'are always late, even to their own funerals.' She swore that she would never allow a 'nigger doctor' to care for her and repeatedly warned that 'if you see a bunch of niggers coming, turn around and go the other way.'"

In his fair-minded and I think overlooked examination, Kennedy concludes that such uses of the word by Big Mama and others are examples of a black person internalizing black prejudice. Perhaps so, but there are notable contradictions. The confounding issue of the oddity, and license, of blacks using the word is summed up in an essay by two academics, on a scholarly website, the African American Registry, which is devoted to black issues:

> When used by Blacks, nigger refers to, among other things, all Blacks ("A nigger can't even get a break."); Black men ("Sisters want niggers to work all day long."); Blacks who behave in a stereotypical, and sometimes legendary, manner ("He's a lazy, good-for-nothing nigger."); things ("This piece-of-shit car is such a nigger."); enemies ("I'm sick and tired of those niggers bothering me!"); and friends ("Me and my niggers are tight."). This final habit, as a kind word, is particularly challenging. "Zup Niggah" has become an almost universal greeting among young urban Blacks. When asked, Blacks who use nigger or its variants argue that it has to be understood in its situation; repeated use of the word by Blacks will make it less offensive. It's not really the same word because Whites are saying nigger (and niggers) but Blacks are saying niggah (and niggaz). Also it is just a word and Blacks should not be prisoners of the past or the ugly words that originated in the past.*

I sometimes felt that hearing my Yankee accent, a Southerner, especially in a rural area, and nearly always uneducated and poor, said the

---

* "Nigger (the Word), a Brief History" by Phil Middleton and David Pilgrim, www .aaregistry.org/historic_events/view/nigger-word-brief-history, 2001.

word as a hostile taunt to challenge my sensibilities, to get a rise out of me. But the black rappers who spoke it, far from "taking the power out the word" or making it "less offensive," seem also to be testing it, uttering it as a dare, defying any white person to repeat it, and risk the penalty of saying it. Round about the time I was traveling, a celebrity chef from Georgia, the TV personality and restaurant owner Paula Deen, admitted in an obscure court deposition that she had sometimes used the word in the past ("but it's been a very long time"). When her admission became public, thunder crashed around her head: her TV show was canceled, she was abandoned by her sponsors, and though she wept in atonement in TV interviews, her reputation was seriously damaged, if not destroyed.

She was white and she was wealthy. But for many blacks, especially poor ones — poor in everything except their traditions — it is as though the word has value to them, because it has an unambiguous power to provoke. Certain words can have class associations; some people can be said to own their language. There is an upper-class manner of speaking in England, both in accent and in peculiar words and turns of speech. "We had a simply ripping time on our hols, masses of sunshine and bags of fun, and the chinky-chonks were just marvelous" is not the way a working-class English person would describe a vacation in Hong Kong.

In Tonga, you know from the way a person speaks whether he is a royal, a noble, or a commoner, and it is forbidden for a commoner to speak using words of a higher rank of person. Until about fifty years ago the emperor of Japan spoke in courtly language that was reserved to him; no one else was allowed to speak in this manner. And there is, around the world, the private language of the underclass that identifies the speaker and is exclusive to that group: Cockney, street slang, and thieves' argot, and verbal formulas that are distinct to secret societies, to baffle and vex and exclude outsiders. During the Harlem Renaissance in the 1920s, the writers Zora Neale Hurston, Wallace Thurman, and Langston Hughes, well-respected black literati, called themselves "the Niggerati."

Hughes's "Christ in Alabama," controversial, and powerful in its simplicity, is a poem he wrote in reaction to the nine black teenagers, falsely accused of rape, who became known as the Scottsboro Boys. First published in 1931, Hughes later reprinted it with slight changes, insisting on the word. The poem begins:

Christ is a nigger
Beaten and black
Oh, bare your back!

By implication, by insisting on the word in songs, irrespective of how it is spelled (because it is pronounced the same), and in their private lives, blacks are implying ownership, claiming it as a cultural artifact belonging to them alone. And rappers have created an outlaw priesthood of black exclusivity based on this word, while seeking white approval and white audiences for their music. But there is not a white person in America who could quote the words of these lingo-laden songs in public without risking his job or his reputation, or conceivably being accused of race baiting.

So what do we have here? We have not simply a word of abuse but a complex example of a taboo word. Taboo is the appropriate way of describing the word's aura, because the precise Polynesian motive for creating a taboo, such as the Hawaiian sanction, before *kapu* was outlawed, forbidding a commoner (*maka‘ainana*) from walking in the shadow of a noble (*ali‘i*), was to maintain power. Some shadows were sacred and had to be respected, others were not.

The subtitle of Jabari Asim's *The N Word* (2007) — *Who Can Say It, Who Shouldn't, and Why* — is a succinct definition of a taboo word and its paradoxical nature, and in the book, Asim — writer, scholar, and editor — is exhaustive in explaining the uses of the word in relation to the black experience in America from the early seventeenth century to the present. Like Randall Kennedy, Asim is African American. In spite of his provocative subtitle, though, Asim ends up conceding that the word is poisonous, demeaning, divisive, and unspeakable; nor does he deal with it as a taboo. Randall Kennedy comes down in favor of neutralizing the word by using it in specific ways, and he is against the elimination of the word by the outraged people he calls the "eradicationists," who would rewrite *Huckleberry Finn* and many other books.

As a white man I hear the word differently, as a strange ritualized artifact that has become a taboo. Declaring the word taboo is one of the ways — one of the very few ways — a black person can control a white, penalizing him for using a word that he, a black, in a subtler declaration, is licensed to speak freely. In this context, the use of the word by a white belittles (if not degrades) a black person by reclaiming the word, violating the taboo, infuriating and taking power from the black. As a taboo, it is not a forbidden word to all but only to some, as in the Polynesian instances where the sanction applies to commoners but not to nobles. Taboos are created by those who want power, in this case blacks, who can use it freely while punishing whites for violating the taboo. If the word were simply a racial slur, it would be forbidden to everyone who spoke it. As rap music shows, it is often used joyously.

Because of this social complexity the word has more power now than it has ever had. And as historically — etymologically — a white word, it is fair to ask whether in the distant past, in slave times, and during the civil rights era of the mid-twentieth century this word was used by blacks in common speech. Harriet Beecher Stowe thought so. The word appears on most of the pages of *Uncle Tom's Cabin,* spoken by slaves and slave owners alike. Here is part of a conversation between Eva, the slaveholder's daughter, and Topsy, the slave girl.

> "But, Topsy, if you'd only try to be good, you might —"
>
> "Couldn't never be nothin' but a nigger, if I was ever so good," said Topsy. "If I could be skinned, and come white, I'd try then."
>
> "But people can love you, if you are black, Topsy. Miss Ophelia would love you, if you were good."
>
> Topsy gave the short, blunt laugh that was her common mode of expressing incredulity.
>
> "Don't you think so?" said Eva.
>
> "No; she can't bar me, 'cause I'm a nigger! — she'd 's soon have a toad touch her! There can't nobody love niggers, and niggers can't do nothin'! I don't care," said Topsy, beginning to whistle.

We can doubt whether Harriet Beecher Stowe (a Northerner, who prior to writing her novel had no firsthand experience of plantation life) was accurately transcribing black speech. But Mark Twain's black characters often use the word, and so do Margaret Mitchell's. Of the hundreds of instances of the word in *Gone with the Wind,* none occurred in the movie adaptation, where the word "darky" predominated.

"My grandmother, born in the 1880s, was a small farmer, and she used the word 'darky' or 'darkies' all the time," a middle-aged white man was to tell me in rural Hale County, Alabama. "When I was growing up, most other whites around here said 'Nigra,' but without any sort of malice."

The word frequently appears in the work of black writers, notably Zora Neale Hurston, her novel *Mules and Men* being a vivid example. Hurston's best-known novel, *Jonah's Gourd Vine* (1934), was originally titled *Big Nigger.**

Upper-class blacks, "when angry with their children . . . accused them of talking or acting like 'common alley-niggers'" is one of the observations in *Deep South* (1941), a lengthy "social anthropological study of caste and class" in 1940s Natchez — called Old Town in the book. The fieldwork was carried out by two black and two white Harvard researchers, who lived for two years in the town, "with the same perspective and minimum bias which their fellow anthropologists have used . . . [among] the natives of New Guinea, the Indians of the Amazon, or the aborigines of Australia."

"We ought to give invitation dances and keep those common nigguhs out of here," one well-to-do black adolescent is quoted as saying; and another, "Those nigguhs don't know how to act or talk at a decent dance."

Among the oral histories recounted in *Plain Folk in the New South, 1880–1915*, by I. A. Newby (1989), is the memory of an old black field hand who recounted how some black children used to chant:

> *I had a little dog*
> *His name was Dash.*
> *I'd rather be a nigger*
> *Than po'h white trash.*

---

* *Nigger Heaven* by Carl Van Vechten, a close friend of Hurston's, appeared in 1926. Conrad's *The Nigger of the "Narcissus"* was retitled *The Children of the Sea* when it was first published in the United States in 1897, and in 2009 an edition was published under the title *The N-Word of the Narcissus*. The title of Ronald Firbank's *Prancing Nigger* was suggested by Van Vechten, who felt Firbank's title, *Sorrow in Sunlight,* was unlikely to attract notice — these days the novella is usually folded into other works under the title *Valmouth* or *Five Novels*. *Ten Little Niggers* (1939), by Agatha Christie became *And Then There Were None*. The comedian and activist Dick Gregory titled his 1964 autobiography *Nigger!*

I'd rather be a nigger
an' plow ol' Beck,
Dan a white hill-billy
Wid a long red neck.

In rap music, which is saturated with the word, Northern rappers accuse Southern rappers of being imitative, deriving their imagery from Northern songs that are now passé. The Southern rapper Percy Robert Miller, who calls himself Master P (and has an estimated net worth of $350 million, most of it earned from his music), has replied to this criticism by rapping that "New York niggas" called "southern rappers lame" while "jacking our slang."

I'd heard a snatch of a song by Marcus Delorean Roberts (who raps under the name DeLorean) at the gas station in Gadsden, Alabama, where I met Wendell Turley. His song "Southern Niggas" is, so he says, an assertion of black pride. Brad Terrence Jordan, a Texan who calls himself Scarface, describes himself as "the realest nigga to ever do southern rap." His hugely successful songs include "Bitch Nigga," "Funky L'il Nigga," and "Snitch Nigga." Another Southern rapper, J. Nics ("Polar Bear Mack") has defended his fellow rappers by naming one of his mix tapes SNAS, an acronym (described by a music blogger as "addressing the perception that rappers from below the Mason-Dixon line lack the lyrical depth of their Northern counterparts") meaning "Southern Niggas Ain't Slow."

In the profitable business of rap music, the word itself seems to have a high dollar value. A black farmer in Arkansas, speaking of the use of the word in rap and hip-hop music, told me disgustedly, "That word is all about money." Dr. Dre's 2001 hip-hop "gangsta rap" CD *The Chronic* (featuring such tracks as "Bitch Niggaz" and "Some LA Niggaz") has sold more than eight million copies. Dre himself (his birth name is Andre Romelle Young) has, at the age of forty-nine, become the first rap billionaire.

Money has raised the status of the rappers, not only in their communities but in the Ivy League. While I was traveling in the South, Harvard University established the Nasir Jones Hiphop Fellowship at its prestigious W.E.B. Du Bois Institute. The university's website explains the archive's mission: "to facilitate and encourage the pursuit of knowledge, art, culture and responsible leadership through Hiphop."

Nasir Jones's rapper name is Nas. Here are some examples of Nas's lyrics, by which a Harvard student might pursue knowledge, art, culture, and responsible leadership. In "Last Real Nigga Alive," he advises, "There's more shit than wanting to be this King of New York shit." And in "The Message," one of the messages is "You freak niggas played out, get fucked and ate out." He praises the high life in "Patience-Sabali," praises owning many acres, so that he can get a front-row seat and "watch niggas play the game like the Lakers." This view is modified in "Ether," where he disparages riches, because "y'all niggas deal with emotions like bitches."

So rapper Nasir Jones is a pillar of the Harvard community, his made-up name and his vulgar lyrics enshrined as part of the Crimson culture, his association with the university promoted with pride. He is rich, and he can rap, and is possessed of a fleeting fame in Harvard Yard. Not bad for someone from the projects in Brooklyn who dropped out of school in the eighth grade.

When the elevation of Nas to the Ivy League occurred, newspapers and critics of rap saw it as an ill omen. I am inclined to a different view. The fact that Harvard has endowed a hip-hop chair and has made rap and hip-hop scholarly subjects seems to me to signal a decline, if not a termination. Whenever an art form — music, book, drama, song — is dragged into the seminar rooms, it is finished as a force. Nothing is more deadly than the anatomizing of scholarship, since the study of art, any art — even the obscene, semiliterate yawp and grunt of rap — drains the life from it.

Still, even if it is on the wane, such music, such sentiments, such language — deconstructed, embraced, even celebrated by Harvard professors pretending that their slumming is scholarship — is the soundtrack of much of present-day black America, and it is loud in the black areas of the Deep South. But I winced whenever I heard it played, whenever I heard that word.

PART TWO

Winter: "Ones Born Today Don't Know How It Was"

Listen, stranger; this was myself: this was I.

— scratched on glass by Cecilia Farmer, in Faulkner's
Requiem for a Nun

Ten Degrees of Frost

Beyond the icicles hanging against my Cape Cod window like a row of overgrown crystal carrots, January snow lay thick on the ground—crusty, pitted, and hardened, some of it like the bubbly honeycomb of air-dried sea foam in the tide wrack down at the beach, the sort of snow that stays so long you get used to the intrusion of that world of uninvited white, a hooded subverted landscape, sparkling in the low flame of a sallow sunrise on a winter morning. And half the window itself was whitened and etched with frost.

The knifing wind had whittled the snow into beautiful contours like sculptural drapes, scooped it into folds, clumped it against the house, and wrapped it in scarves and shawls at the lumpy bases of tree trunks. My long driveway was white as well, but granular, with dark imprints, a parallel pair of wheel tracks, pebbles of gravel glazed in ice. The morning was clear and cloudless but cold, ten degrees of frost, a mute visible crackle in the air, like neurons sparking in ice chips, the winter silence broken only by the rasp and clatter of crows, beating the bumps and bandages of snow from the branches with their wings, startled by the crunch of my footfalls in the snow crust and the *ker-thunk* of my door slam.

Perhaps I am overdoing this. What was lovely to observe and describe was even lovelier to leave, which is perhaps why I was hyperventilating in a wordy way by seeing it as a winter wonderland, a cliché I was trying to avoid. It was an effect of my condition: I was in a mood of farewell. The relief of departure often brings on dishonest praise and grateful exaggeration ("Thanks! I had an outstanding time! Sorry I have to go . . ."). I was freezing and sick of it all. "Hooded"? "Subverted"? "Whittled"? "Sculptural"? Never mind. I was dying to get out of this cold and onto the road.

I set off briskly in sunshine, heading south, and by the time I got to the far end of Connecticut a storm front of solid cloud with a leading edge as blunt and splintery as an old desk drawer slid overhead and shut out the light, giving the sky the illusion of a falling tabletop, with an approaching wall of wicked plaster in the distance. The New Jersey sky sank to the level of my car roof and snow began to fall, light small tumbling flakes, whirled across the road by traffic. At intervals, cars tricked into collisions lay like smashed toys in the breakdown lane. In the evening darkness in Delaware snow poured in fat pellets past roadside lamps. The Beltway was sleety, slick and black, and drifts of snow were heaped all over northern Virginia.

After almost six hundred miles of snowfall I stopped for the night at a motel north of Richmond, and the next morning I continued into sunlight, happy again in the warm, winter-brown South.

This time I knew where I was going.

Lumberton

Caked with streaky layers of salt that frost and road slush had dried and turned into rime, my whitened car had a conspicuous, weather-struck, out-of-state look in the harsh impartial sunlight of North Carolina. And so I swung into Lumberton to clean the thing.

As I approached the wide-open entrance of a car wash and its dripping sprinklers, an old man in a military cap sidled over to me and waved me to a stop. He removed the cigarette from his mouth with a tweezing pair of stained fingers and stooped and leaned at me.

"Don't use this facility," he said.

"Is it closed?"

"No, sir. She's open," he said. He puffed on the cigarette, then snatched it down again.

"You work here?"

"No, sir, but I'm telling you, this facility is no good." He smoked awhile. "Use the one down the road. Just reverse and head on over there. You'll see it when you get close." He puffed again, then pinched the cigarette out of his mouth and said, "I know I don't talk good. I'm doing the best as I can, but I didn't have a real good education, on account of I'm a Lumbee. You know what a Lumbee is?"

And with that, I abandoned the idea of getting my car washed there. I parked and spent the next hour or so having a cup of coffee with this man, Robert Locklear, from Lumberton. He was thin, sallow, ill-looking—his slack chain-smoker's face lined like a biscuit—and he leaned on a cane to walk. His jacket was too heavy for this mild sunny day, suggesting that his circulation was poor. As soon as we found a bench to sit on with our coffee he became silent, as though embarrassed and exposed. But I was saddened by his yellow, beaky, tragic face.

I remarked on his patrol cap, which was lettered *Combat Veteran— Proud to Serve.*

"I was in Vietnam in '68, '69, the real hot years, in Pleiku, in the Central Highlands, right near Cambodia and Laos. We could walk right into those places, we were so near. And sometimes we did, and had some bad times. But I made it through.

"Come back here and it was the same as always. Lumberton was mainly segregated, not only white and black but Lumbee too. Most Locklears are Lumbees—anyone sees my name, they know who I am and where I come from.

"So, education. It was a problem for me. I couldn't go to a white school and they wouldn't let me into a black school. 'Cause I'm a Lumbee. The Lumbees had to be educated at the church. All the Lumbees got churches, and all the churches had a school inside, but it wasn't much. Look at me. I got nothing. I was fit for the army but nothing else. Coulda got killed in Vietnam. And what for?

"The segregation now is as worse as it was way back, and it was bad then. The Ku Klux Klan came over from Alabama and Mississippi in 1958 and burned some crosses in Robeson County here—they was as mean to the Lumbees as they was to the niggers, meaner when they come here. But that day we run out the Klan, and they were busted and as good as nekkid."

The Klan incident he referred to, I found, was the so-called Battle of Hayes Pond, in which a Klan Grand Dragon named James "Catfish" Cole led a group of Klansmen in a rally and cross burning in Maxton, twenty-odd miles from Lumberton, in the year that Locklear had mentioned. Small in number, they were overwhelmed and some injured by a larger group of armed and indignant Lumbees, who shot at them and harried them and beat them into the muddy thickets in the swamps at nearby Hayes and Maxton Pond. In the Lumbees' long history of defeats, this confrontation of the Klan was an event still celebrated every year by the Lumbee people, who are recognized as Native American by the federal government but denied any financial benefits, in part because their descent and ancestry is still a matter of dispute.

"I couldn't go anywhere, growing up, because of segregation—and look at me, I'm not black. I'm Lumbee," Robert Locklear said. "But Martin Luther King is a hero to me, and James Brown too. They hated the Lumbees, the people here. Still do. My cousin married a blond-haired, blue-eyed woman, and she come down here and thought she was going to be fine. Well, if you're a doctor or a lawyer maybe you're fine, but she takes out a credit card at Walmart, and they see her name is Locklear, and they treat her real bad 'cause they think she's a Lumbee. After a bit, she's so miserable here she went away."

Robert Locklear stamped out the cigarette he'd been smoking and removed his *Proud to Serve* cap. He inverted it and showed it to me, his thumb on the label inside.

"Look at this," he said. "Feel it. I was a weaver by trade, made cloth right here. But they closed the mills and sent the jobs overseas. So there's nothing here anymore. Now check out this label—see? 'Made in Vietnam.' And look what the hat says, 'Combat Veteran,' and that there is my vet facility."

The address indicated the name and address of a Disabled American Veterans office and clinic in Lumberton.

"I go there for counseling. I have bad nights. I get bad dreams about 'Nam and about the Klan and what-all. The US government give me that cap 'cause I'm a vet, *and the cap is made in 'Nam!*"

I sat with him on the bench and tried to offer some consolation. But I was merely a stranger passing through, writing down what he told me. He was silent for a while, then seemed to remember a question I'd asked a moment before.

"I don't know what's going to happen. One's as bad as the other. I almost died in Vietnam and now I have nothing, and I'm wearing this hat, made there—and people hereabouts still hate the Lumbees. Write this down. *Nothing's changed.*" He snatched my wrist and stared at me, wetting his lips. "I get *nightmeers.*"

Back Roads

From Lumberton, where at last I drenched my car and restored its color, I headed by side roads for South Carolina and the old familiar abandoned Route 301, the Doomsday road, where the burned-out motels and deserted Art Deco gas stations and scorched shells of restaurants lay by the roadside. But even in its desolation the road suggested a powerful sense of place, and also the best billboards, one enormous siding lettered: "So they said, 'Believe in the Lord Jesus Christ, and you will be saved, you and your household.'— Acts 16:31."

A man in Santee said, "It never snows here."

His wife said, "We got a little ten years ago."

Sunny, warm, pleasant, spring-like in January, on the back roads of the Lowcountry. But my pleasure was tempered by the shacks and the rusted trailers surrounded by plastic children's toys and old bikes and the absence of any industry. The poor in the rural South cast aside and existing like residue.

Sunday Morning in Sycamore

Drifting down the Confederate Highway from Orangeburg and Bamberg for a second visit to Reverend Johnson's Revelation Ministries, I came upon Sycamore, near Allendale. The church service didn't start until eleven, so I had time to kill. Some men were having their Sunday-morning coffee in Hardee's on Railroad Avenue. This being Sunday, the two other diners were closed.

"Set yourself down," one of the men said, and so I joined them, ten men at the tables. They were most of them older men, roughly dressed;

the only young one among them, a man of thirty or so named Barrett, wearing a dark suit, said he had to go. He was taking his mother to church.

The others were Sam, Freddy, Harold, Mose, Buddy, Clarence, Rewall, Charlie, and lastly Henry, who urged me to call him Sonny. They were all local men, they said, and had worked in the various factories in and around Allendale, before they closed.

"I was born right here in 1946," said Sonny Bryant, "but I spent most of my working life in other places — mainly Atlanta, then up in DC. I came back just a few years ago. I'm living outside Ulmer now with my grandparents. They're not the Bryant side, they're Jenkins — my grandfather Henry, my grandmother Sular Jenkins. Sular, it's an African name.

"We all grew up picking cotton. When I was six, I was picking with my whole family — my grandmother was amazing. She was always picking way ahead of us. By the time I was ten and up, I was picking pretty much five hundred pounds a day, at around fifty cents a pound. That particular cotton was owned by Mr. Kirkland and Mr. Bess."

Memories of picking cotton: everywhere I was to travel in the Deep South I heard these stories from older people — chopping cotton and picking cotton, of the long days in the fields before the onset of mechanical pickers, dragging a nine-foot pick sack and filling it. And everyone had memories of the amount picked. The 500 pounds that Sonny claimed was an impossible amount. In the 1930s James Agee estimated that the average for an adult male was about 250 pounds a day, and for a grown woman, between 150 and 200 pounds. Most of the people I met mentioned these amounts as their day's harvest.

But Sonny insisted that he picked a quarter ton of cotton a day. He also said — after mentioning the importance of Allendale in the past, its prosperity before I-95 cast its shadow, its fine restaurants and its nightlife, and his success at school ("It was black schools then, all the way up to high school. Segregation was hard. I seen some things") — that he had fled Allendale for Atlanta, where he had painted Martin Luther King's house.

"I met Martin in Atlanta. He talked to me the way I'm talking to you now. He hired me to paint his house. I learned painting from my grandfather Bryant, who was a painter here. He also played guitar. He taught me to play blues."

"So you were a painter who played the blues?" I asked.

"No, sir. I was a boiler technician for the municipal government in DC. I was away from here for forty years. And I done a lot of other things."

This seemed a cue for me to encourage him, so I did.

"Cocaine, for one," Sonny said. "I not only used it, I sold it, I cooked it, I cut it with baking powder, and I seen some strange things. But I'm here to tell you I made it through. Crack cocaine, I smoked it for years — years! I enjoyed every minute of it."

"Tell me why."

"Tell you wah. You think you got wangs. You think you can flah!"

"Crack cocaine. Good stuff, eh?"

"But it's poison, like a lot of great things you can do. I gave it up fourteen years ago and never took it again. I been with people who've been using it, but I just watched — I didn't take any myself. I just stopped. And I came down here, back home. I should never have left."

All the men had listened to Sonny's story, and when he was done, one of them, Sam, said, "Maybe you met Martin in Atlanta. But you never did pick no five hundred pounds of cotton in one day."

"We Love You—Ain't Nothing You Can Do About It!"

The back roads were empty on this Sunday morning, empty and beautiful, along the margins of more twiggy cotton fields, many of them puddled and muddy, the ripe tufts — the linty so-called locks — in open sodden bolls and the bushes beaten down by yesterday's rain. The wet earth steamed in the morning sunlight, tall trees lined the edges of fields, and cows grazed. Small wooden shacks of sunburned cedar, with splintery porches and roofs of curling shingles, crouched and bent over amid groves of enormous beech trees.

I passed through Ulmer and found the church, eager to listen to Reverend Virgin Johnson, who in our previous conversation had been a fund of wisdom and hope and humor. Just down the road, diagonally across from the black church, was the meetinghouse of the Sons of Confederate

Veterans at Barker's Mill. A detailed sign in front memorialized the local militia who skirmished, on February 2, 1865, with the troops of General Francis Preston Blair Jr., whose soldiers were a flank of General William Tecumseh Sherman's March to the Sea. The Union Army shouldered its way through this farmland, looting and burning houses and firing back at snipers. The fight at Barker's Mill had not accomplished anything except checking for one day the progress of the victorious army in its crossing of Jackson Branch, a narrow stream that flowed southeasterly. The sign indicated the skirmish, a delay, a defeat, another humiliation, actually; but the meetinghouse was still active, flying the Confederate flag.

"In the South there's a church on every corner," Reverend Johnson had said to me when I'd met him in Orangeburg and he'd invited me to his church service. Today, sixty cars or more were parked in the muddy field in front, and in the foyer I was greeted with a hug and asked to sign the visitors' book. A group of older men, formally dressed in neatly pressed suits and sober ties, welcomed me and introduced themselves as deacons and ushers. One usher escorted me into the church, where a woman in a frilly dress and a big white hat was seated at an organ, repeatedly planting her splayed-out fingers on the keys, playing urgent music as an emphatic background to the earnest preaching of a woman in a purple gown. The church hall was full, about three hundred people, the majority of them women and children.

Over the stage, a scroll-shaped sign in gold: REVELATION MINISTRIES —"REVEALING GOD'S WORD TO THE WORLD — WE LOVE YOU — AIN'T NOTHING YOU CAN DO ABOUT IT!"

This reminded me of the sign that had thrilled Henry Miller on his *Air-Conditioned Nightmare* trip through the USA in 1940: GOOD NEWS! GOD IS LOVE! I had been in a handful of Southern homes, poor ones mostly. I had been in busy pawnshops and rowdy bars. They had been revelatory. And the gun shows had left a powerful impression of a prevailing mood of bitter defeat. These experiences helped reveal to me the texture of the South. But I did not come to a full understanding of the sense of community in the rural South until I entered a church. A church was more than a church; it was the beating heart — the vitality, the hope — of a Southern community.

And knowing that, I had some sense of what a devastating event it was when a church was blown up, as happened often in Southern history, and significantly almost fifty years before, on September 15, 1963, in Birmingham, Alabama, at the Sixteenth Street Baptist Church, when sticks of dynamite planted by Klansmen killed four small girls and wounded twenty-two others. That Baptist church was not merely a place of worship, a gathering place for friends, it was a meetinghouse for civil rights leaders and voter registration activists, and it was a resource for welfare and guidance. The dynamite in that church, a landmark event in the civil rights movement, had created martyrs and heroes, and hastened civil rights legislation.

A church burning or bombing might devastate a congregation, but it was a desperate act. The church was always rebuilt and was stronger afterward, as a necessity, because people attended church to find hope, dignity, love, consolation, fellowship, and advice. The church was central to life here in a way I had never seen elsewhere in the United States — certainly not where I was born. A church in the South resembled the life around a mosque or a temple in India or Africa.

Shortly after the service began, my name was announced ("Mr. Paul, visiting from Boston") — they'd gotten it from the visitors' book — and the service was suspended for me to be greeted by almost every person in the church in turn, man and woman, young and old, with a hug or a handshake. They were beautifully dressed, women in satin, many wearing hats and gloves, most holding Bibles, and men in well-cut suits, and even the children squirming on seats or chasing each other in the aisles were formally attired. They lifted their arms and smiled, approaching me, crushing me in an embrace.

"Welcome, brother."

A man read announcements about activities for the coming weeks, spiritual, social, gustatory: welfare projects, church outings, get-togethers, visits to neighboring churches. Then the rousing music played again, and for the next hour or so a chorus of women in silken dresses sang and preached, and one of them — singing a blues song — riffed on her life, which had been one of tribulation and spiritual renewal, and she punctuated her mellifluous narration with asides of "Thank you, Lord!"

This was all prologue, an opening act that settled the crowd, theme music to the filing in of stragglers and latecomers. When the church was full, the familiar dark-suited figure of Attorney Virgin Johnson Jr. rose from his high-backed, throne-like chair, and in his Sunday role as Reverend Johnson he began to preach, a well-thumbed Bible in his right hand, his left hand raised in admonition. He was only partly the man I'd met on the street in Orangeburg—the lawyer helping a stranger. Today he was a preacher, with a commanding voice that occasionally was liltingly persuasive, with Deep Southern tones.

"Hear me today, brothers and sisters," he began, and lifted his Bible to read from it. "Luke one, thirty-seven. 'For nothing will be impossible for God.' Now look at Mark nine, twenty-three. 'Everything is possible for him who believes.'"

They were simple, lucid texts that gave hope, offered reassurance, spread some balm in an uncertain world. He repeated them and let his words sink in.

"And consider Jeremiah twenty, nine–eleven." Reverend Johnson's voice was reasonable and encouraging. "'I know the plan is a plan for yo' welfare—not disaster.'" I could not tell whether he was quoting or paraphrasing Jeremiah—it didn't matter anyway. I looked up the verse in the Bible at my pew and found he was paraphrasing: "But the Lord is with me as a mighty terrible one: therefore my persecutors shall stumble and they shall not prevail: they shall be greatly ashamed," etc. He had taken charge of the congregation, as the authority figure, the explainer, the exhorter.

"Tell yo' neighbor: God has a plan for you!"

The woman in front of me, the man beside me, even the video camera operator who was ten feet away, took turns to say to me in a grand gulping tone of delivering good news, "God has a plan for you!"

"The children of Israel had been taken into captivity in Babylon," Reverend Johnson went on, his voice rising. "The prophet Jeremiah sent a letter to them. It said"—and now he was leaning toward us and enunciating carefully—"it said, 'Even though it look like stuff mess up in yo' life, it gon' be all right after a while! Stop distressing, stop worrying. Even though yo' circumstances don't look prosperous, you gon' be all right!'

"That's Jeremiah. And I'm here to tell you it's gon' be all right." Gesticulating, his tissuey Bible pages fluttering, he said, "It's irrelevant what's gon' on. If you connected to God, it's gon' be all right. My life is not dependent on whether the president is right or wrong. Because why? Because Ah mo put my trust in Jesus. God will not fail you! In the midst of slavery and oppression — the children of Israel in Babylon — Jeremiah said — what did he say? He said: 'It gon' be all right! God gonna make a way out! God gon' work it out. All signs are positive!'"

Now some women in the congregation were calling out "Yes!" and "Thank you, Jesus!" Other men and women rose to their feet to clap and sing.

"Some of us are enslaved in our mind — in our lives and in our addictions. Nemmine! God says, 'Ahm gon' give you a future and a hope. My future is gon' to be better than my today.' Because you can only see today. But God can see the future!"

"Tell it! Tell it!"

"Get ready, because you gon' to know tomorrow. God says, 'Hold on till you get there!'"

"Yes, Lord! Hold on!"

"There's three parts of this, three parts of 'God has a plan for your life.' Num' one. God's plan may not be your plan. Submit and obey God's plan."

"Oh, yeah! Praise Him!"

"Num' two. Yo' may not understand God's plan. But accept what He tells you. You may think" — and Reverend Johnson paused to mask his face with a scowl of befuddlement — "Why this happenin' to me?" He smiled and propped himself on the lectern and said, "Listen, be patient. Stop hurryin' to mess up! Think real hard!

"Think of the eagle and the buzzard in famine times. The eagle says, 'I'm not used to waitin'.' But what does the buzzard say? He say, 'I'm used to waitin'!' Jes' wait! Because num' three is this: God has his own time! Your time and His time may be different."

"Praise His name!"

Now many people were standing and swaying and crying out, and the woman in the big white hat playing keyboards was leaning forward and slapping at the keys and squeezing out blurting chords. A drummer had joined her and was rattling his sticks on the cymbals, and a man playing the electric guitar was canted back, worrying the strings on his instrument with his clawing fingers.

Reverend Johnson, continuing to preach, reminded me of Reverend Shegog at the end of the Dilsey section ("I seed de first and de last") of *The*

Sound and the Fury, preaching on Easter Sunday ("I got de ricklickshun and de blood of de Lamb"), and in preaching — gaining in inspiration and becoming more colloquial as he spoke — Reverend Johnson turned into a prophet, conveying the voice of God, and God's message of hope and love, as Bishop Palmer had done in Tuscaloosa, sounding just as certain as the prophets he was quoting, Jeremiah and Isaiah.

And when Reverend Johnson said, "Thus sayeth the Lord," it made sense, because he was a resonant and oracular and vatic presence, all confident encouragement now, in his Deep South accent, "po' boy" as he described it to me, the message of "Don't hurry" and "God has a plan" and "Don't give up."

"What did Jeremiah say to the children of Israel? 'You gon' be all right!'"

Then the music began in earnest and the whole church was rocked in song. Envelopes were passed out; we folded money into them; men wearing white gloves carried chunky baskets up and down the aisles and collected the envelopes. Still there was singing, and in the singing I picked up a Bible and looked for a passage in Proverbs I remembered from long ago: "These six things doth the Lord hate: yea, seven are an abomination unto him: A proud look, a lying tongue, and hands that shed innocent blood. A heart that deviseth wicked imaginations, feet that be swift in running to mischief. A false witness that speaketh lies, and he that soweth discord among brethren."

Words to live by.

Then we all hugged again and filed out into the sunlight, rejoicing. The small children twisted and slipped past our legs, running ahead of us like scalded rats.

Lucky

The next day, somewhere on the back roads, I glided through a junction and missed the turn to Orangeburg. When I pulled over to reverse direction, I saw a freestanding store, a shed really, set back under a spreading tree of bare boughs, with a hand-lettered signboard, LUCKY'S GUN

REPAIR, a woolly sleeve of smoke twisting out a rusty chimney pipe and flattening in the chilly breeze.

People who dealt with guns were generally talkers, I'd learned. Usually they had a gripe with the government and strong views on neighbors or crime, and felt put-upon and slighted. A man with a weapon was a man with something on his mind.

So I parked and went in.

A man in a black cowboy hat, a greasy shirt, and a thick vest sat behind a workbench, metal pieces spread out, pistol parts, but no whole gun visible anywhere. His hands were as dirty as the greasy parts, and he was holding a pistol's trigger assembly.

"Help you?"

"I'm looking for the road to Allendale."

"That way." He gestured with the trigger assembly. "Down about six miles. Left at the gas station. Keep going."

"Thanks. Are you Lucky?"

"Uh-huh. I'm Lucky."

"You sell guns?"

"Fix 'em. I don't have the capital to keep any inventory."

"So you don't have a gun?"

He smiled. "I got plenty of guns. Over in the house."

"Thinking of selling any of them?"

He pondered a moment, more than a moment, perhaps mentally ranging over his gun collection.

"Got me a nice forty-five I've been fixing to sell."

"That's a big gun."

"Big and useful." He shoved his chair back. "I'll fetch it."

I said, "I'm not sure."

"Have a look. No obligation."

He walked across a weedy field to a large decaying house, overhung by tall trees, while I sat in the shed among disassembled pistols, a catalog, a calendar, jam jars filled with rusted screws, a tin tray of small oily tools, the woodstove clucking and crackling.

A few minutes later he stepped through the door and passed me the gun. It was heavy in my hand, a deadly heaviness, a thick handle. It was scratched and bumped and looked unloved.

I said, "Thanks. It's too big for me."

"Won't know that until you shoot it," he said.

"Where would I do that?"

"Over there," he said, and pushed the door open and walked past a torn-open sofa and a tipped-over barrel of punctured oil cans. I followed. He was wearing battered cowboy boots and high-stepping through the trash.

"How much for the gun?"

"Three hundred. But you want to shoot it first." As he spoke, he took a bullet the size of a peanut, or so it seemed to me, out of his shirt pocket. "Aim over there."

He indicated a six-foot-high pile of old truck tires. We were no more than fifty feet from the main road, cars going past, the occasional truck, a school bus, a motorcycle with high handlebars, the rider sitting with his feet straight out as though in a barber's chair. I sensed derangement in the neighborhood of poor houses. But here I was with Lucky, who was friendly and holding a serious gun.

Instead of filling the magazine, he slipped the bullet into the chamber and handed the gun to me. "Aim at the middle of the pile, the fat part."

I did so, gripping the pistol with both hands and holding it so the kick-back of the recoiling slide wouldn't take my thumb off. And then *bam,* and as my head rang, the pistol became weightless and lifted in one bounce.

"What do you think?"

"Nice. But I don't need a gun this big."

"Everyone needs a gun this big, or bigger." He fed another bullet into the chamber. "Blow some more lead, buddy."

I shot again, and again. Then he took two shots, nailing a Coke can that had been tossed in the tire pile. I remarked that the gun did not move in his hand when he fired. He showed me a trigger squeeze that was almost imperceptible and kept the pistol motionless.

"How'd you get the name Lucky?"

"Not from my daddy. From other people." He looked rueful. "You don't give yourself names like Lucky."

"Nice name."

"Effen it was true." He laughed. He hefted the gun in his hand, holding it like a dangerous toy, which it was. "Make me an offer."

Instead of making one, I changed the subject. I asked him about Allendale. He said, "It's tough down there," and then with a smile, "Tough everywhere. I got no money, never had no money, I worked my whole damn life. But no one got any money—no one I know. No sense complaining. But if you buy that gun I'd have me three hundred dollars."

I left without the gun. I felt that I had wasted his time, and I said so. But I had just dropped in, which was permissible in the South. It was strange to be firing this big weapon so near the road, into a stack of old tires, cars going past. He had not given it a thought: walk a few steps and *bam bam bam*. He let me pay for the ammo and said, "Come back, you hear? We'll shoot some more lead." He said he owned plenty of guns; I had expected a gun nut with a grievance, but, hard-up like everyone else, Lucky seemed to be a reasonably happy man.

"The Future Is a Faded Song"

I had last seen Allendale in sunshine, people in the streets greeting each other, children playing. It had looked like the end of the world, but there it was, animated by conspicuous citizens. On a winter morning, a sky threatening rain, no one strolling or even sitting under trees, the town looked utterly desolate. Yet studying its ruination I saw it was the same, really: three months had wrought no alteration. It was then I realized that part of the appeal of my traveling in the South was that I could return and pick up where I left off, because in the rural parts where I had chosen to look, nothing changed. If anything, much of it was sliding slowly backward, the past persisting, and "the future is a faded song."

Because of this shrinkage, the slipping into greater poverty, people—many of the ones I spoke to—had a clear memory of the past, of how things had been long ago, and what their hopes had been.

Wilbur Cave was waiting for me. I had called ahead and suggested we meet for lunch at the soul food diner O Taste and See.

"How's things?" I asked, over baked chicken and beans and cornbread, after he finished saying grace.

"We're still at it," he said. "Trying to make a difference."

"If possible, I'd like to meet some families — people you've rehoused or helped. Or people behind the eight ball."

"I'll make some calls. Can't do much unless I get their permission," he said.

Saying so, he made a note on a memo pad. I thought of all the people I'd buttonholed in my traveling life, the doors I'd knocked on, the confrontations, my history of intrusions. And how, here in my own country, where I spoke the language and posed no threat, where I presumed to be one of them, I needed an intermediary, and more than that, needed to make an appointment. But of course I was not one of them, and I was a stranger.

"What've you been doing?" Wilbur asked.

I told him I'd recently attended Reverend Johnson's church service, and from that casual piece of information flowed the familiar topics: religion, music, race, guns, unemployment, poverty, the past.

"I'm older than Reverend Johnson," he said — he was sixty-two — "so in 1966 I was in the ninth grade in Barnwell High School, living up the road in Kline. You could call it an integrated school — what Reverend Johnson would call 'voluntary integration.' It was known as 'freedom of choice.' Pretty big high school, and there were five of us, African American, but I was the only one in college prep."

"If all the other students were white, you must have felt — how?"

"Isolated," he said. "But it wasn't too bad. You talk to older people and you'll hear they had a harder time. I was on the track team, ran the hundred, the two-twenty, the four-forty. I held the school record in the two-twenty, but it's been broken by now."

"Isn't sports one way of distinguishing yourself, getting respect?"

"Track's funny," he said. "It isn't like basketball or football. People don't pay much mind to it. You don't get famous for running fast."

"Anyway, you were headed for college, so you had to study, I guess. Were the teachers helpful?"

"Some were real helpful," he said. "My English teacher Miss Masuski was encouraging. She asked us to choose a novel, then read it and select a passage from it that meant something to us personally. On the day, we got up in front of the class and explained the passage. I can't remember the novel, but I recall being in front of all those people and saying, 'So here's what it means. It's just this. We know more than we think we know.'"

"That's good. Did they like it?"

"Miss Masuski clapped her hands and shouted, 'That's my favorite!' I felt great. It meant a lot to me." He ate some more, reflecting on this, then said, "There were other times, different times. A football game, would have been around 1967, a home game. We were playing Branchville High — it's the other side of Bamberg. They had one African American on their team, a running back. He was their star player."

"You wanted to see how he'd play?"

"Dying to see him," Wilbur said. "My parents dropped us off. We watched the game, but instead of staying until the end and getting a ride home, we left early. We were walking down the road when some white guys in a car saw us and chased us. We ran!"

"You were fast, though."

"My running ability helped," he said. "We ducked into a field and ended up laying for a long time on the field of soybeans."

"Who were the guys?"

"I'm sure I knew who they were. I hate to think what they would have done if they'd caught us."

"A beating?"

"Oh, sure — or worse. But you know, just a few wanted to cause problems. The majority were okay. In the early 1970s at the University of South Carolina there were twenty thousand white students and only a few hundred African Americans."

"How did that make you feel?"

"You know you're in an environment where you're not wanted," he said. He finished his meal and nodded gravely. "I'll go to my grave remembering it."

On our way back to his office, in a cubicle in the mobile unit that was parked near the Allendale courthouse, Wilbur talked about how he had come back to Kline and run for the South Carolina legislature and won, and after a political career he'd become involved in nonprofit community development, the small-scale but effective Allendale County Alive.

"Housing is what we do, one person at a time." Around 150 houses had been fixed up or rebuilt in and around Allendale and Fairfax. But there were other needs. In cold weather like this, people asked for space heaters; they also asked for food, shelter, clothing, loans to prevent foreclosures — other agencies in Allendale helped with these things, if the people qualified by having an income that was eighty percent below the median income of the county.

"Many?"

"More than we can handle."

Talking about hunger and the homeless, of people living in poverty, many with no water or electricity, a vast number without jobs, I was put in mind of what I had seen in Africa and Asia — the talk of funding and the hopes of development, that mood of remoteness and neglect when the world seems distant. Yet this was the real world, a town in crisis on a road that was easily reachable from my home at the other end of it.

"Like I said, I'd like to see some people you're helping."

Wilbur picked up the phone and asked his assistant to request permission for me to see some families who'd been helped, and others seeking housing.

"Do people let you do all the work," I asked, "or do they participate?"

"We have a new initiative," he said. "In order to get help — as part of getting rehab assistance — people will be required to volunteer in community service."

"I like that."

"We'll make a list of things they can do. Clean up trash. Read to a child. Work at a homeless shelter. Or they might have a skill. If so, share it. We want to make it a requirement: Hey, you're getting something, so give something back."

The phone rang. Wilbur picked it up and listened for a moment.

"The people you asked to see, they're having a hard time. They're not ready now. Maybe when you come back?"

If this had been Zimbabwe, which it much resembled, I might have said: This is urgent. I don't know when I can come back. Isn't there anything you can do?

But I said, "Okay. I'll come back some other time."

The Inevitable Mr. Patel

All the convenience stores, the three gas stations, and the one motel in small, unpromising Allendale were each owned by Indians from India, each Indian rejoicing in the same name, the inevitable Mr. Patel, as I had learned on my first visit.

One of the gas stations, decrepit but busy, was also a convenience store full of hand-scrawled signs, a rack of violent black-themed DVDs, cheap T-shirts, gum, candy, and beer. Since beer was sold by the single container, the place was also a hangout for men boozing out of cans or bottles wrapped in brown bags. I had stopped to buy gas. When I went inside to pay for it I got a whiff of the East — incense like scorched sugar and a thick cloud of curry-scented air, which you could break down into fragrant eye-watering aromas, cardamom and turmeric and fenugreek. Mr. and Mrs. Patel.

"I came here two years ago from Broach," Mr. Suresh Patel told me from behind the counter of his cluttered shop.

Broach is an industrial river city of half a million in the state of Gujarat. Many Indian shopkeepers — *dukawallahs* I knew in East and Central Africa — claimed Broach as their ancestral home, where the Patel surname identifies them as members of a Gujarati Hindu subcaste. And Mr. Patel's convenience store in Allendale was identical to the *dukas* in East Africa, the shelves of food and beer and cheap clothes and candy and household goods, the stern hand-lettered sign NO CREDIT, the same air of frugality with a whiff of incense and curry.

Mr. Suresh Patel could barely speak English, or perhaps his mumbling was caused by the lump of *pan* he was chewing, the betel leaf and betel nut bundle that is the postprandial digestive favored by Hindus and masticated in a cud-like lump, like a chaw that turns the teeth crimson and produces the gouts and squirts of russet spittle you see staining the multitudinous Indian sidewalks incarnadine, painting the plaster red.

He'd been a chemist in India. "My cousin call me. He say, 'Come. Good business.'"

Mr. Patel hopped on a plane with his wife and son, and took over the management of a shop and gas station, one of the three shops and gas stations in Allendale now owned by Patels. In the roughly 150-year history of the town, which was the county seat, none of these businesses had ever been owned by an African American.

A week before, on my way down Five Chop Road, near Orangeburg, at another gas station, a man named Evers had said to me, "The whites sold these stores and the gas stations and the motels to the Indians." He happened to be eating. He swallowed and finished his thought: "Who are taking over."

Now I understood them a little better, having done some homework. The journalist and scholar Tunku Varadarajan had written a piece in 1999 on this subject for the *New York Times Magazine*. He had reported the fact that more than fifty percent of all motels in the United States were owned by people of Indian origin, a statistic supplied to him by the Asian American Hotel Owners Association. Yet the Indians who owned and operated these motels were most of them first-timers, many of whom had been either shopkeepers in East Africa or farmers in India, or as I had seen in Virginia, immigrant Indian medical doctors who had managed to secure a visa waiver, arriving as physicians, then gravitating to or moonlighting in motel ownership.

An immigrant Italian running a pizzeria, or a Japanese owning a sushi bar, or a Turk opening a kebab stall was a logical linear transition, but an Indian operating a motel was anomalous. American-style motels are so rare as to be almost unknown in India, and so, Varadarajan wrote, "America's motels constitute what could be called a nonlinear ethnic niche." He explained this rarefied sociological term: "A certain ethnic group becomes entrenched in a clearly identifiable economic sector, working at jobs for which it has no evident cultural, geographical or even racial affinity." It's also known as "occupational clustering," like the Korean-owned deli in New York or, in the England that I knew, the Greek-owned fish-and-chips shop.

It seems that Indian immigrants turned to the business because the demands of running a non-chain motel (or a mom-and-pop convenience store) did not include a mastery of English or having to answer to an American boss, only the need to work long hours. Running a restaurant was a problem, as another Patel told me later in my trip, because the owner would have to taste the food, and that was out of the question because it might be beef, an abomination to the vegetarian Hindu, who regarded the cow as sacred.

The Hindu kinship system was an advantage. Other Patels, the extended family, might help when a trusted partner or a loan of advance money for a down payment on the business was needed. Investigating the phenomenon more thoroughly, Varadarajan discovered that "70 percent of all Indian motel owners – or a third of all motel owners in America – are called Patel." That was in 1999. The figure is much higher now.

The domination of one sort of business by one recently arrived ethnic group, unused to such work, seems improbable. Trying to imagine a comparison, I thought of the *paanwala*, the betel leaf seller, a traditional feature of every city and town in India, and I conceived a situation in which eighty percent of the *paanwala* shops in India began to be operated by immigrant American Baptists named Smith.

The cash flow was a distinct incentive, but one of the greatest benefits was that a motel included living quarters for the owner. The convenience stores did too (behind the beaded curtains), just as the shop (the *duka* in the bush) did in Africa. Living on the premises also meant there was no downtime, no commute, and rarely did I see any of these places employing non-Indians, except as menials, clerks, or sweepers in Housekeeping. The typical Patel-owned non-chain motel was usually a modest structure, and many were grubby and inexpensive enough to fit the owlish observation of Charles Portis, in "Motel Life, Lower Reaches": "There should have been a pair of signs out front, flashing back and forth: NOT QUITE A DUMP — AT DUMP PRICES."

Indians – in particular the Patels of Gujarat – constitute one of the South's subcultures, and the deeper I went into the South, the more of them I met, like Suresh Patel in Allendale, nearly always running convenience stores and gas stations and motels. Mention them to some people and they reply, "Like *Mississippi Masala*" – a movie made in 1991. But the reality was not like that movie at all, which is about a passionate love affair between the daughter of an Indian motel owner and Denzel Washington. The Indian family had been thrown out of Uganda by the dictator Idi Amin, and because of this the father applies his anti-African prejudice to Southern blacks.

The flaw in the film is the assumption that Ugandan Indians are anti-African or anti-black. But I lived among them for six years and got to know them, and they spoke of their pride in having been part of Uganda's independence struggle. (The same was true for the Indians in colonial Kenya, who helped to bring about Uhuru with money and legal assistance and their own anticolonial press.) They knew Amin to be an aberration. Over several generations, Ugandan-born Indians learned how to adapt, which is why they became so successful in Britain. They were not fazed by being aliens; they had lost so many of their Indian prejudices that they chose to go to Britain rather than to India, a country unknown to most of them. Some have returned to Uganda and their businesses, and have flourished.

Most of the Indians I was to meet in the South had, like Suresh Patel in Allendale, like Hardeep Patel whom I'd met in Virginia, like most of the Patels and Desais I met on my trip, arrived straight from India, were fearful of the new country, and were comforted by their ancient pieties. Virtually all the Patels I met were caste-conscious, mutually supportive, ardently superstitious, highly sensitized to ethnic differences, ignorant of local history, jittery in the presence of blacks, and suspicious of anything or anyone who might represent a threat to their religion or their notions of racial purity. They too might have objected to their daughter's marrying Denzel.

Some of these nonlinear ethnic niches, in the form of back-roads motels, were clean and well run, but many were dire to the point of disgusting. One of these motels, where I spent a night on Highway 68, near Collinsville, Alabama, was among the filthiest places I have stayed in a life of resorting, out of desperation, to flophouses. Masses of dime-sized brown beetles on the walls of my Travelers Inn room were creeping to the ceiling, where they clustered and dropped in gobs, pinkle-pankling onto my face, disgusting sheets stiff with dirt and stains of unknown origin, the mattress all hogged down and wallered out in the middle (as they said in these parts), a bathroom that had the features and the reek of a vomitorium, an entire floor of dust bunnies—the room was filthier by far than almost any I've found in Africa or China, or for that matter India. The desk clerk, Mr. Patel, smiled at my complaints ("I woke up itching") and boasted that every (filthy) room was occupied.

He had also been a student. More than any other immigrant group I'd ever encountered, Indians had a keen instinct for queue-jumping on the fast track. The complete story of the Indians of the South has not been written; it is secret and subtle, just whispers, emerging now and then when a politically ambitious Indian American becomes a public figure, like Piyush ("Bobby") Jindal, the governor of Louisiana, or Nimrata Randhawa (Nikki Haley), the governor of South Carolina, both children of Punjabi immigrants, both converts to Christianity, both right-wing Republicans, supporters of the death penalty, and dismissive of welfare programs. And both have distanced themselves from their parents, who are tradition-minded and perhaps a bit too exotic to appeal to Southern voters, even though Sikhs, and many Punjabis, consider themselves Indo-Aryan people.

The Indian shopkeepers and motel owners, many of them now American citizens, were unquestionably hardworking, but many preserved the Hindu caste rules, including the highly developed abhorrence of racial taint. As I had noticed on my first visit, there was something weirdly colonial about the presence of Indians in the rural South, which reminded me of Africa: the Indian shop in the dusty upcountry town, the overpriced and grubby merchandise, the locals squatting under the trees, giving parts of the South an even more dramatic, sleepier, unfixable Third World appearance.

Off the Grid

On my way back to Alabama, I crossed Georgia on the country roads, beginning with the evacuation route out of Allendale and the radioactive road past the Savannah River Site. Emerging from the Talladega National Forest south of Pell City, I took a blissful all-day meandering ride on the back roads, Route 231 to 25, through Childersburg, Wilsonville, and Columbiana, moody in the winter mist under a gray sky.

I stopped at a pawnshop in Calera, a crossroads, and inquired about the guns they stocked.

"We got plenty, but I cain't sell you one because you from out of state."

"So what'll I do?" I said, just to provoke him.

And it worked so well I was sorry for my insincerity, because the man looked pained on my behalf. "I know. You off the grid. You really need one in these parts. Me, I wouldn't drive around here without one."

"But it all looks beautiful to me."

"They's some strange places here. God, I only wish I could help."

He did not mean the narrow rolling road through the wooded backland, where the offices of timber companies squatted amid piles of logs and acres of orange sawdust, nor the cattle farms, nor Shelby Springs and its green ponds, nor the cotton fields. He must have meant the sudden settlements, the pockets of dereliction, the house trailers and motor homes that looked like old oversized cigarette cartons, the decaying houses and some outright shacks — the obvious hunger and poverty in the beautiful pinewoods. *Seems a land out of time,* I had written at a chicken restaurant I'd found at a crossroads, where I fell into conversation with a man on his way to Montevallo. He was a former marine, just retired, wishing to join the Montevallo Police Department. He chose Montevallo because he had children: the high school was small and friendly, and the town quieter than Hoover, where his girlfriend lived.

After the tall, slender, starved-looking pines in the Talladega Forest, and the shacks and poor houses outside Greensboro, traveling down Main Street was like a homecoming to me.

The Rosenwald Gift

At the edge of County Road 16, ten miles south of Greensboro, a white wooden building stood back from the road but commanded attention. It had recently been prettified and restored and was used as a community center. When I inquired, I was told it had started life as a two-room schoolhouse, built for black children in about 1917 — and what caught my attention was that all those years ago it had been built at the instigation of a Chicago philanthropist who had somehow seen a need for such a school in distant and deeply segregated Greensboro, rich in cotton but reluctant to teach blacks to read or give them a vote.

"That's the Rosenwald school. We called it the Emory School," Reverend Lyles told me when I stopped by his barbershop in Greensboro to ask about it. "I was enrolled in that school in 1940. Half the money came from Sears, Roebuck. Folks here put up the difference. My mother also went to a Rosenwald school, the same as me. The students were black, the teachers were black. If you go down Highway 69, down to the Gallion area, there is another Rosenwald school, name of Oak Grove."

Julius Rosenwald, the son of German-Jewish immigrants, made a success of his clothing business by selling to Sears, Roebuck, and in 1909 became the CEO of Sears. In later life his wish was to make a difference with his money, and he hatched a plan to give his wealth to charitable causes, but on a condition that has become common today: his contribution had to be met by an equal amount from another party — the matching grant. Convinced that Booker T. Washington's notion to create rural schools was a way forward, Rosenwald met the great educator, and thus began the Rosenwald Fund to build schools in the backlands of the South, many of them in Hale County.

"The school population of Hale County is five black to one white," James Agee wrote in 1937 in an essay that was rejected by *Fortune* magazine, his employer at the time, and published only recently in book form under the title *Cotton Tenants: Three Families*. He continued: "And since not a cent has gone into Negro schools, such neat buildings as this [in Moundville] are possible: for white children. Negroes still sardine themselves, 100 and 120 strong, into stoveheated oneroom shacks which would reasonably house a fifth of them if the walls, roof, and windows were tight. But then as one landlord said and as many more would agree: 'I don't object to nigrah education, not up through foath or fift grade maybe, but not furdern dat.'"

Five thousand schools were built in fifteen states beginning in 1917, and they continued to be built into the 1930s. Rosenwald died in 1932, around the time the last schools were built, but before the money he had put aside ran out, in 1948, a plan had been adopted through which money was given to black scholars and writers of exceptional promise. One of the young writers, Ralph Ellison, from Oklahoma, was granted a Rosenwald Fellowship, and this gave him the time and incentive to complete his novel *Invisible Man* (1952), one of the defining dramas of racial violence and despair in America. Rosenwald Fellowships also went to the photographer Gordon Parks, the sculptor Elizabeth Catlett (who later created Ellison's memorial in New York City), W.E.B. Du Bois, Langston Hughes, and many other African-American artists and thinkers.

The schools built with Rosenwald money (and local effort) were modest structures in the beginning, two-room schools like the one in Greensboro, with two or at most three teachers. They were commonly known as Rosenwald schools, though Rosenwald discouraged naming any of them after himself. As the school-building project developed into the 1920s the schools became more ambitious, brick-built, with more rooms. The simple style that identified them — because they looked alike — was the result of detailed plans from a Tuskegee University study by two architecture professors, Robert R. Taylor and W. A. Hazel, who had published their ideas in a 1915 pamphlet, "The Negro Rural School and Its Relation to the Community."

One of the characteristics of the schools was an emphasis on natural light through the use of large windows. The assumption was that the rural areas where they'd be built would probably not have electricity. Paint colors, placement of blackboards and desks, and the southerly orientation of the school to maximize the light were specified in blueprints that had been fastidiously elaborated by Rosenwald's chief administrator, Samuel Leonard Smith, who was both an architect and an educator.

Though Booker T. Washington had died in 1915, before Rosenwald began building, his ideas were incorporated — a key one was that a school in such a remote area would be more useful if it could also function as a meeting hall, a community center, a gathering place, or an auditorium. To this end, some of the schools were fitted with movable inner walls that could be folded back to create larger rooms as needed.

The simple white building outside Greensboro was a relic from an earlier time, and had Reverend Lyles not explained its history and his personal connection, I would have had no idea that almost a hundred years ago a philanthropic-minded stranger from Chicago — white, Jewish, humble, craving anonymity — had tried to make a difference here. And by the way, through his fellowships he had helped enrich American literature with classic accounts of the black experience.

"The financing was partly the responsibility of the parents," Reverend Lyles told me. "They had to give certain stipends. Wasn't always money.

You've heard of people giving the doctors chickens for their payment? That's the truth—that happened in America. Some was given corn, peanuts, and other stuff, instead of cash money. They didn't have money back in that day. When folks started getting paid in money, that was in the middle or late 1940s."

Tuition was paid in kind: Reverend Lyles, who came from a farming family, brought produce his father had grown, and chickens and eggs.

"Why was your school called the Emory School?" I asked.

"The school received its name from a gentleman name of Agnew," Reverend Lyles said in his precise way, speaking slowly, and I was again reminded that though he usually sat in one of his barber chairs when we talked, and we were next door to his soul food diner, Eugene Lyles was first and foremost a preacher. "The man Agnew was in cahoots with a man name of Tommy Ruffin. He owned land in that area. And Agnew gave the land for the school on the grounds that they would name the school for his son. His son was named Emory—he had passed away."

"Did you know that man Emory?"

"My father did. My father and the others who were born around his time, they helped put up that school building. And just recently Pam Dorr and the HERO people made a plan to fix the school up."

I asked him whether he'd been involved in the renovation.

"Not the renovations as such," he said. "But it made me proud that I was able to speak when it was reopened as a community center. My father would have been proud too. My father and Mr. Agnew's son was contemporaries, around the same age. Old folks then—my grandfather was born in 1850."

I thought I had misheard. Surely this was impossible. I queried the date.

"Correct—1850." So Booker T. Washington (1856–1915) was younger than Reverend Lyles's grandfather. "My grandfather wasn't born here, but he came here. He remembered slavery. He told us all about it. I was thirteen years old when he passed. I was born in 1934. He would have been in his nineties. Work it out—he was ten years old in 1860. Education wasn't for blacks then. He lived slavery. Therefore his name was that of his owner, Lyles, and he was Andrew Lyles. Later on, he heard stories about the Civil War, and he told them to me."

Miss Cotton Blossom

Blue Shadows Bed and Breakfast became my home for a while in Greensboro. Apart from the semiderelict Inn Motel on the other side of town (Mr. Patel, prop.), which never had cars in its parking lot or any guests that I saw, there was no other place to stay. An older bed and breakfast, Muckle House on Main Street, had closed. The nearest roach-free motels were twenty miles south, on the bypass road outside Demopolis.

Blue Shadows was a large, squarish house of obvious pretension, set in a grove of trees just beyond Hale County Jail, on the farming outskirts of Greensboro. My room was an addition atop the garage, which suited me for its being separate from the house next door and its constantly playing theme music, the owner's favorites, show tunes mostly.

The owner and occupier, who lived on her own, was an elderly widow and former beauty queen, Mrs. Janet May. In writing this (elderly woman, once glamorous, loner, innkeeper, big old house), I am aware that I am treading on the slippery ground of the Southern grotesque, as if describing someone out of Carson McCullers, the aged coquette in *The Ballad of the Sad Café* springing to mind, in which Miss Amelia Evans, living alone in her small Southern town, welcomes into her house an enigmatic hunchback, Cousin Lymon, who becomes a prisoner of her love until, in a dark frenzy, he robs her and breaks her heart. But Janet May was kindly and generous, eager to please, and without an ounce of rancor, a pillar of the Methodist church and a capable cook.

"Former beauty queen" was not her boast but my discovery: on a high shelf in a closet in my room where I was snooping, I found a trophy inscribed with Janet's maiden name and her achievement, *Miss Cotton Blossom* — 1949. I worked out from hints dropped and events mentioned that Mrs. May was now eighty-seven years old, and her achievement was that she ran this bed and breakfast competently, without much fuss, though her manner was drawlingly effusive.

She had known a few years of glamour as a Powers model in New York City. "A junior model," she explained. "Because I wasn't tall enough." Originally from Chattanooga, she'd settled here in Greensboro, her late husband's home, and they'd raised five children in this house — Blue Shadows had been in the May family for several generations. John May had had a career as an airline pilot. He had died some years ago. Janet employed a housekeeper, Elmira, who had worked for John May's family for many years. Janet loved Elmira and was grateful for her help, especially in the solitary days of her widowhood.

A wonderful Southern touch was related to Elmira. One morning, years back, Janet said, gushing and grateful, "Elmira, why are you so good to me?"

The elderly black woman paused in her sweeping and said, "Mr. May and me was kinfolks."

I heard that not from Janet but from someone in town who swore it was true. And I realize as I write it that that, too, sounds like dialogue from a piece of Southern fiction.

Janet casually mentioned to me that one of her sons spent part of every year in Africa as a volunteer in some sort of community development. "Helping people."

"Where in Africa?"

"Zambia," she said.

Suppressing a mocking laugh, I remarked to her that parts of Greensboro—the decaying houses, the areas of shacks, the dirt roads, the boarded-up shops, the Indian-owned gas station and the moth-eaten Inn Motel, the many idle youths, the odors of woodsmoke from burning blue gums and the pong of freshly plowed land, the red roads, the lumber mill—so much here bore a distinct resemblance to places in Zambia I had seen. And this being the case, why wasn't her son provoked to do anything in Greensboro?

"Now that's a good question," she said. "I wish you'd talk to him. I often think that myself, I sure do. I have no idea why he insists on going to Africa."

I suggested that for her son's next birthday she give him a copy of *Dark Star Safari: Overland from Cairo to Cape Town*.

The motives of Janet's son were undoubtedly idealistic. Many Southerners went to Africa to proselytize: the hinterland of Malawi and Uganda, I'd seen in the 1960s, had been thick with them, usually a preacher and his wife, and sometimes a small family, living next to their small bush church that had been built with donations from home.

"Even though white Protestant missionaries were being sent to Africa to save the souls of heathen black natives," Erskine Caldwell wrote in *Deep South: Memory and Observation,* his 1966 book-length essay on Southern churches—his own father was an itinerant preacher—"at home it was feared that Southern Negroes might rebel against staying in their assigned place if they became imbued with too much of the spirit of Christian brotherhood and would presume to be privileged to fraternize socially and politically as well as religiously."

One day Janet said that the next evening there would be a potluck supper at her church, First United Methodist, in town—and really I ought to go, because the food would be delicious and I would be welcome. As it happened, I was busy that evening—I had planned to see Reverend Lyles. And that appointment inspired a question.

"Will there be any black people at the potluck?"

"Oh, no—no blacks ever come," she said. "Blacks and whites don't socialize here."

"Not even at church?"

"Paul," she said in a reprimanding tone, as though to a simpleton, and in a Southern accent a reprimand sounds especially belittling. "They have their own church."

"So no mixed gatherings?"

Janet shook her head. "My neighbors over yonder are teachers in a black school, but I know for a fact that though they sure enough teach them, they don't socialize with them at all. Blacks have never been in their house. I expect you're wondering why. But that's how things are."

She was slow-talking and long-winded and dithery. Yet I grew to like her and found her amazing—at her age to be running this place, shopping, solving the many problems of scheduling and cooking, and apart from a little mopping and dusting by Elmira, doing it alone.

Dusting such a place was not simple. The house was sensationally cluttered, crammed with knickknacks: plaster pigs, dancing frogs, Betty Boop dolls, golfing trophies, cute signs and plaques (*Shalom, Y'all* was a stairwell greeting), tassels, Christmas wreaths, souvenirs from all over—New Orleans, Nashville, Disney World—movie posters, a mounted deer head, doilies, throw rugs, coasters, stenciled mugs, and a really toxic smell, the mingled aromas of mildewed carpet and air freshener.

Yet I admired Janet for her humor, her fortitude, her grace, and her independence. She was a very old woman doing a much younger woman's work. It would have been so easy to poke fun at her, or mock her for "They have their own church," or for her elaborate makeup, the rouged cheeks, the sooty mascara, the hot-pink lipstick. But she was from another age, even the way she stood, canted slightly backward in her haughty Powers-model posture, legs together, one hand upright, a finger on her cheek, looking slightly drunk as coquettes often do: Miss Cotton Blossom.

At times I felt trapped, but I had the privacy I wanted. I needed solitude to transcribe my notes and conversations into description and dialogue. I did not use a tape recorder. Early one morning there was a storm. It came with strong winds and heavy rain, all of it unimpeded, blowing and soaking this flat farmland, great sweeping curtains of rain borne out of Mississippi, drowning the yard of Blue Shadows, beating down the big white bushes of mock orange and rose of Sharon, the wind snatching and twisting the bare tree limbs, all this with thunder and lightning. A great overwhelming storm of water and wind clapped over us, altogether different from any storm I'd experienced in the North, more like a monsoon downpour in India, its suddenness, its drenching way of paralyzing everything. The loudness of the rain smacking the muddy yard was Asiatic. All I could do was wait, sit it out, watch it slapping at the Blue Shadows shingle sign and making it swing back and forth so hard I thought it would be torn from its hinges. I was reminded in that storm that I needed this house as a refuge.

"Ones Born Today Don't Know How It Was"

On the evening of the Methodist potluck I was at Gene's barbershop, talking to Reverend Lyles about the various church events in Greensboro — and I had in mind Janet May's invitation. He held up his hand to prevent me from wasting my breath.

"I know very few white people here," he said, without bitterness, simply stating the fact to let me know that he was in no position to judge what was happening on the other side of the racial divide, though he had lived in Greensboro for the entirety of his seventy-nine years.

As for entering a white church, he shook his head.

"We're not welcome," he said. "I know from experience. It was a funeral — I went because my friend wanted to go, and I was there to help him out. When we walked in, everyone turned their head. I thought, Oh, my. I said to my friend, 'I don't want to create any scenery.' So I left. Forty years ago they'd fight you if you tried to go in. Less than forty years ago a man took a swing at my friend."

"In a church?"

"Just outside the door." He pondered this. "Everyone who lived through it remembers. Trouble came to Greensboro, the protests in '59 and '60, somewhere like that. And Dr. King came to Greensboro three times in '62 and '63, and spoke at St. Matthew's African Methodist Episcopal, and St. Luke's."

"Was it secret?"

"Oh yeah, oh yeah. And there's the Safe House in the depot area, where he hid from the Klan in '68."

The Safe House, one of the landmarks in the civil rights struggle, was now Greensboro's Safe House Black History Museum. This shotgun house memorialized the efforts of the many nameless unsung foot soldiers in the movement, and the overlooked sites, such as this small wood-frame house, and the timely rescue by passionate locals who had saved Martin Luther King from a murderous mob on the night of March 21, 1968, in a corner of Greensboro.

"The days he came we knew he was coming," Reverend Lyles said. "We had connections. And when he spoke it was standing room only."

"What did he say?"

"His message was nonviolence," Reverend Lyles said. "Voter registration. Don't fight back with guns and weapons. That's history. But look all these years later, Hale County is still on the edge. For various, certain people there's still distrust between the races. We just elected an African-American probate judge, and the mayor is the second African American who served in the seat. That's JB — Johnnie Washington — he's a contemporary of mine."

"I met him last time I was here," I said. "We talked. He mentioned the problems."

"There's a lot of division," Reverend Lyles said. "But one of the things that you have to take under consideration is that change just don't happen overnight—and it mostly change through generations. School integration made big changes. When kids go to school together they see life different from the ones that was separated."

I mentioned that people here greeted each other, unlike in the North, where strangers avoided eye contact and hellos.

"You would have to live here to understand it. People are sometimes distant, but they come together with that greeting, that hello. You and I are talking, but that is different from the past, when the two races didn't speak in particular. Remember my brother Benny?"

"Yes, he'd been in the army." I had met him in the soul food diner, we'd eaten together, and he'd told me about his visits to the North.

"Back aways, my brother—you wouldn't have spoken to him particular like you did, I mean a white person. You'd never say a word. That changed when blacks began to get into public office and began to mingle with other people and realize that you and I might have similar views."

"So things are changing?"

"Some. I've seen some changes made tremendously. But if there's going to be real change, you have to find the people to make that change with. And so therefore someone goin' to have to reach out. We can't just sit back and hope there's a change. Number one is finding the resources to make a change. If you don't find the resources, you have to find an individual with the kind of commodity that it takes. Also, if he has the resources, then he has to seek my labor."

"It seems to me that you spent your life being self-sufficient, doing your own thing."

"I'm the builder of this building—brick building, well made. It took me months and months. I went to the mayor to get a permit. Wasn't easy. And once I obtained a permit, then I had to go through all kinds of struggles and straining."

"How did you borrow money?"

"Wasn't easy at all. I went to bank after bank after bank. Finally a banker told me, he said, 'I'll look into it.' It was 1962. I was in my twenties. The man who loaned me the money, his statement to me was 'Those people would rather see anything happen than for you to be economically supportive in Greensboro.' He was an older man. White. He said, 'They would rather see you fail.'"

"But you succeeded."

"I was a barber. I wanted a barbershop of my own. I bought all new chairs. I wanted what I'd seen in other cities. I said to myself, 'I'd like to see this in Greensboro.'"

"Do you have any other white customers?" I asked, because the previous day I'd stopped in as Reverend Lyles was shaving an older white man. This was a sight, because the man was not white but pink, and plump, seventy or more, seemingly one of the Greensboro old guard, and he lay slightly supine in the chair as Reverend Lyles, his fingers poised on a cutthroat razor, scraped his neck slowly with the glittering blade, with the concentration of the mutineer Babo shaving the captive Benito Cereno on the deck of the *San Dominick,* witnessed by Captain Delano in the Melville tale. But this was pure fantasy on my part.

"That man you saw yester morning—might be his fifth time. But he's lived here his whole life. The change comes with time. Since the last two-three years, some whites come here. Time makes the difference. Used to be a barbershop on Main Street that was white. No mo'."

"Did you ever go there?"

This made Reverend Lyles laugh hard and shake his head. "Man, I couldn't even stand in front of that barbershop. They didn't allow it, no standing on that sidewalk, no talking, nothing—wouldn't allow it when I was young. That's the change that I lived."

"How did you feel?"

"It made me angry." He frowned, remembering. "So when the time came for voter registration, we was on the front lines. But if you don't have blacks and whites now talking together, and with a vision, it's going to be no business and stores closed and no work. We have blacks on the city council, the county commission. Our congressman is black—Terri Sewell."

Terrycina Sewell, representing Alabama's 7th District—much of it in the Black Belt—was a highly educated woman of fifty, born in Huntsville and raised in Selma, where her parents were closely involved in the civil rights movement. A graduate of Princeton, with postgraduate degrees from Harvard Law School and Oxford University, Sewell had worked for ten years at a Wall Street law firm before returning to Alabama as a partner in a firm in Birmingham specializing in public finance. She became Alabama's first black congresswoman in 2012 after winning a landslide election.

"That was the objective of the civil rights movement, to have equal representation in government," I said. "It's been achieved. And now there's more financial hardship than ever. So what next?"

"These people have to sit down and start brainstorming what is the most feasible thing they can do economically to make a change," he said. "But many people oppose business in Greensboro today. Old families have the status quo mentality — quite a few of those old families are in the white race. The mind-set that they have is that if business comes to Hale County that offers a fair price for labor, it forces them to offer more for their labor. Also, this is a farm area, and they would like to keep it that way. Cattle, soybeans, catfish."

CATFISH CAPITAL OF ALABAMA was painted in tall letters on Greensboro's water tower. Catfish was regarded by some as an economic engine, but for others it was the plantation all over again, as an Alabama journalist, Patricia Dedrick, observed in 2002 in the *Birmingham News*: "At Southern Pride [Catfish Company, in Greensboro], unskilled men, single mothers and inmates from the state prison ranch in Faunsdale make up the bulk of the work force. The company also buses in Hispanics from Tuscaloosa and beyond, deducting the cost of transportation from their pay." The pay was poor, and the whole business, especially that detail of convict labor, smacked of the outlawed nineteenth-century practice known as peonage, an abuse widely found in the South.

"Still got some catfish," Reverend Lyles said. "But you have a plant here already close less than a month ago. It's a high-risk business, though. When Mercedes came to Tuscaloosa, it was a shot in the arm for Hale County. We need something closer to town."

I was about to leave when I saw that he had a book on his reading table, where he usually studied his Bible. He showed it to me: *Carry It On: The War on Poverty and the Civil Rights Movement in Alabama, 1964–1972* by Susan Youngblood Ashmore, an American history professor at Emory University. He had met the author on her visits to Greensboro and shared his civil rights–era experiences, which had been nightmarish.

Looking through the book, I came upon the description of an incident in Greensboro in July 1965 when a Ku Klux Klan demonstration against a peaceful protest march erupted on Main Street. Local white men banded together with robed Klansmen carrying signs: *Fight Communism, Fight Race Mixing, Protect the American Way.* These men had attacked the marchers with sticks, rubber hoses, and hammers. Seventeen people were taken to the hospital, all black. Two black churches were burned. By the end of July, 435 black protesters had been jailed on a number of charges relating to illegal assembly and breaches of the peace.

"We were afraid to come out at night," Reverend Lyles said. "And much later the whites were worried too. Even today they're worried yet, thinking, The blacks you beat back then might recognize you. So that keeps people apart, that fear." He shook his head. "Ones born today don't know how it was."

"Our Randall Curb"

One morning at my Blue Shadows breakfast, rolling her eyes and with a surrendering sigh at my many questions, Janet May said, "Do you know our Randall Curb?" Her tone indicated that since I was a writer I must know this man, who was also a writer. I said I hadn't heard of him.

Then I smiled. "But maybe he's heard of me."

She screamed, "Paul, you are a stitch!"

She began to think hard. She had a habit when ruminating of clapping her hands to each side of her done-up and wound-around hair, like a Sikh straightening his turban, and she did that now for a few moments, then said, "He's a historian. He can answer all your questions."

I said fine. She got him on the phone and handed the phone to me. We talked a little bit and, in the Southern way, Randall Curb said I was welcome to drop in anytime. He gave me his address.

"How about later this morning?"

"Perfect. I'll be looking out for you."

Just before I left Blue Shadows, Janet hummed to get my attention and said, "Randall's pretty much blind, and it slows him down, but it doesn't stop him none."

The white house with the shutters at the corner of First and Main, near the center of town, with the screened-in porch, as he described it, was easy to find. I parked on his lawn, at his suggestion, and he came to the door the moment I knocked. Randall Curb was a big, pale, slightly breathless man, about sixty, with a full face, boyish in its openness, with blue widened eyes and the eager, slightly off-center gaze of someone near-sighted. He searched for me with his outstretched arms and found my hand, and, shaking it warmly, tugged on it.

"You're Paul," he said. "Now, you come on in."

I was at once among many books, and smiling, recognizing the names of writers and titles I loved on the packed shelves. And we were just passing through the foyer; there were more bookshelves beyond. This was unusual. I had not so far met any readers on my trip; none of the houses I'd been in had books on view, though many had had bookcases. The shelves usually held mementos and souvenirs, like Janet May's dancing frogs and plaster pigs and painted saucers.

This was why, whenever I mentioned I was a writer, most people smiled in what I took to be pity, as though I had just disclosed a personal failing, but a lovable, forgivable fault. Because to nonreaders a book is a riddle and a challenge; and not knowing what to say next, and baffled, they mildly blame me for putting them on the spot, the way a dinner guest among carnivores takes a seat at the table and says, "By the way, I'm a vegan."

Another feature of meeting Randall was that, in what became a year and a half of my traveling in the South, and hundreds of encounters, he was the only person I met who knew my name or had read any of my books. This was an advantage: anonymity is freedom.

In my traveling life, it had never been a hardship for me as a writer to live among illiterates. For most of the years I spent in Africa, I lived contentedly with people for whom books were little more than unfathomable but potent fetishes. The unlettered person has other refined skills and is often more watchful, shrewd, and freer in discussion than the literate person with a limited experience of literature, who believes that all the answers to life's questions can be found in the pages of the Bible, say, or the Koran. And then there are the laziest and most presumptuous of people, those who can read but who don't bother, who live in the smuggest ignorance and seem to me dangerous.

A reader meeting another reader is an encounter of kindred spirits. The pleasure of such a joyous event is impossible to describe to a non-reader, and why would I bother? But you, with this book in your hand, are familiar with the phenomenon, and so it is not necessary. I have written about this elsewhere, of my chance meeting with the great scholar Leon Edel on a beach in Hawaii. Leon had written one of my favorite books, his five-volume biography of Henry James. I had resigned myself to the insularity and philistinism of Hawaii: there was so much else to enjoy on the islands, the delicious food, the beautiful weather, the marine sunlight, the mounting surf, the emblematic rainbows.

So I was content in Hawaii, satisfied with sunshine and my own work. But when I met Leon Edel, who, like me, was married to a local woman, I realized that there was a part of my brain, an area of my experience, a way of expressing myself, an entire possible conversation, the language of books, that I was again able to use. It was as if (I wrote later) I were meeting a fellow alien from my home planet: we were two people who looked like everyone else, yet we were from the great race of readers, and spoke the same language. I met Leon often after that, for lunch, over drinks, and when he died, I grieved for him and for myself, isolated again under the sunny skies of Oahu, chatting in Pidgin, or basic English, in rubious generalities about nothing much.

It was a satisfaction to me that on one shelf of Randall Curb's library there rested the five thick volumes of Leon Edel's *Henry James*. And seeing them gave me an opportunity to tell him my Leon Edel story and to say what a pleasure it was to meet another reader.

"I reviewed your *Mosquito Coast*, way back when it came out, for the paper in Birmingham," he said. "I could actually read then."

We were now seated on a sofa in his parlor, among more books, and paintings — nineteenth-century landscapes — and decorative glassware and cushions. Classical music was playing, the first classical music I heard in any home in the South. And sunshine filtered through lace curtains struck the ruby vase on a polished mahogany table and gave it life in the form of crimson pulsing in its depths and catching on its gilded lip.

"I was born legally blind, with optic atrophy," Randall said. "I can't read anymore, but I still buy books. I like to hold them, I like to feel them." He was holding one now, a life of George Orwell. He'd listened to an audio version of the book and talked a little about it. Then he asked me what I was doing in Greensboro.

"A little like Orwell," I said. "Think of *The Road to Wigan Pier,* or *Down and Out in Paris and London.* I'm visiting the South, driving around, sticking to rural areas."

"I've never been able to drive, though I love to travel. I'm so envious of your driving around."

"You were born here?"

"Yes, I was. In a doctor's clinic on Main Street, and never left, though I spend long periods of time in England every summer—London, Oxford, all over."

"How do you manage to travel with limited vision?"

"I get some help. But the wonderful public transport system in London makes it real easy. The summers here are unbearably hot. London is freedom to me. You're a traveler, so you know that."

"Janet May describes you as a historian."

"That's Janet hyperbole. Isn't she sweet? Greensboro's full of characters like her," he said. "One dear old lady from a distinguished family on the other side of town was afflicted with a severe case of coprolalia, swearing every time she opened her mouth. She published a book of poems—very good ones," he said. "I've written some things about the town. I edited a book, *Historic Hale County.* It was published locally about twenty years ago."

"It was *Let Us Now Praise Famous Men* that gave me the idea of looking at the South and visiting Greensboro."

"Oh, yes, other people say that. They come here and they're disappointed that they don't find sharecroppers."

"I'm not disappointed. This is my second trip. I aim to keep coming back."

"Lots of people pass through Greensboro and like it so much they buy a house," Randall said. "In some cases, they stay. In others, the charm wears off. They sell, they lose money on the mansion they fixed up, and they move away."

"Some of the houses are really grand, though a little faded," I said. "They must have been beautiful in Agee's time, but he leaves them out of his book."

"He concentrated on the sharecroppers, the poor whites. But this was a very wealthy area before the Civil War. It was the center of the cotton industry. These big houses were the town houses of the cotton barons. They also had big houses on the plantations. Early on, the plantations were right here, next to the town."

We talked about James Agee. Randall was steeped in the lore of *Let Us Now Praise Famous Men*, and I was thinking, as he talked, how you meet such men as Randall in Chekhov's stories. Indeed, you meet a great number of Southerners who seem Chekhovian—not only the provincial and isolated intellectuals who gather for tea, but the common ruck of poor country folk, as near to peasants as anyone in the United States: struggling smallholders, people living in shacks, with the folk memory of Southern slavery, like the folk memory of Russian serfdom. (The dates of the emancipations are close—Lincoln's of the slaves in 1863, Tsar Alexander II's of the serfs in 1861—and both are linked to wars, the Civil War and the Crimean War.)

Randall was like a scion of a former landlord, Reverend Lyles the descendant of slaves—both intensely evocative of the complex past. Reverend Lyles was passionate, wronged, godly, forgiving, and still hopeful; Randall was kindly, generous, even sweet, eager to share his knowledge of Greensboro, of which he was the unofficial historian. Both men grateful for a visitor.

I tried to explain to Randall my feelings about *Let Us Now Praise Famous Men*, how, because it is so self-conscious, digressive, and determined to be innovative, it remains a literary artifact rather than a reliable document of the condition of sharecroppers. In what seems sheer perversity, Agee ignored the existence of blacks, who were being lynched in Hale County when he visited. And blacks would have been in the majority then.

What I admired about the book, I said, was the way it incorporated the vignettes of concentrated close-ups: the descriptions of people's clothes, the floorboards of the shacks, the frugal meals, the feral children with tangled hair and in rags. Walker Evans captured these in his images too. In parts it was an inspired book; as a whole it seemed off-kilter, mannered, and highly wrought. No surprise that it sold poorly, but fared better when it was reissued twenty years later, which was when, as a college student, I first read it and was struck by—in a William Blake phrase—its "articulation of minute particulars."

My criticizing its prose style provoked Randall to say, "I find it incantatory. I read it aloud and it makes more sense."

"Incantatory" seemed just right, the repetitive prose like the words of an ancient chant, and as Agee was as much a poet as a prose writer, this remark would have pleased him. Agee was a brilliant man but a fitful writer, deeply conflicted, self-destructive, alcoholic, abusive to his three wives. Because he was born in Knoxville, Tennessee, his writing a book about this corner of the South meant everything to him, though it was out of print, as was everything he'd written, by the time he died, of a heart attack at the age of forty-five, believing he was a failure. The notion of the book began as a magazine article, but the long piece he wrote for *Fortune*, where he was a staff writer, was turned down by the editor. That piece, published as the short book *Cotton Tenants* in 2013, is a model of clarity and quite unlike the larger book that grew out of it.

Some of the descendants of those white sharecropping families, which Agee had named Ricketts, Woods, and Gudger (whose real names were Tingle, Fields, and Burroughs), still lived a bit north of Greensboro, near Akron. From time to time (notably in an atoning *Fortune* piece by David Whitford in 2005), reporters have returned to the area to discover that the families are angry because of what they considered the stigma of Agee's characterization—his making them famous—feeling that they'd been misrepresented in their poverty and violated in their trust of the two strangers in whom they'd confided. It was "a tribal shame," Whitford wrote, "still keenly felt, both by the families Agee wrote about and Evans photographed, now spread several generations wide, and by those of another class who knew the families, and considered them white trash, beneath contempt."

"They were the worst possible representatives of the South in people's minds," Randall Curb had told Whitford. "Of course that's the big irony, because that's what Agee was trying to tell people they were not."

The most detailed return visit to the *Let Us Now Praise* families was re-counted in *And Their Children After Them* (1989), written by Dale Maha-ridge and photographed by Michael Williamson. Its title, like Agee's, was also derived from Ecclesiasticus 44. It had been respectfully reviewed and awarded a Pulitzer Prize, and though I had merely glanced at it, Randall had read it thoroughly.

"It's venomous, it's unwieldy, and a lot of it is biased," Randall said. "They talked to white people, and the slant was how racist they are. I'm not denying that racism and bigotry are rampant, and that a large per-centage of white children grow up not knowing black children, but they missed so much, especially that things really are so much better now than what they were here. Look what we lived through."

Hearing this, I recalled Reverend Lyles speaking of how a stroll on the sidewalk of Main Street was forbidden to him.

"And now all the public schools are fully integrated," Randall was saying.

"But there's still resistance," I said. "For example, the all-white private academy here."

"Like all similar places in the South," Randall said with a fatalistic shrug. "That's a fact of life."

"What about the churches? Eugene Lyles — Reverend Lyles in town — told me that he would never dare set foot in a white church for fear of be-ing thrown out."

"No one would be turned away, black or white," Randall said. "Twice a year in Greensboro, at Thanksgiving and Easter, there's an ecumenical service, community-wide, all the races together at the service."

He went on to say that the whole social fabric of the community was found in the church and that the church was so much a part of the black identity that no black person had a desire to leave the protection of his or her own church. "Protection" seemed a shrewd word for church member-ship.

"Most people attend the church they grow up in," he said. "When new people come to town, the churches vie to bring them in. I sometimes won-der how any new people manage without going through a church."

"That's a useful tip I learned in the South," I said. "Go to church and you meet people. Gun shows too. Barbershops, football games."

"And books. Southern fiction," Randall said, speaking of how to get acquainted with the South. He gave talks — on Agee, on Faulkner, on the English writers he loved, on historical figures such as Ben Franklin. He knew the writers well.

I agreed with him that Faulkner wrote the definitive fictional history of the South, but said that I found some of it unreadable. I unburdened myself with my exasperation with the man, who was even more maddening because he was brilliant, along with being uneven and at times opaque in an Agee-like way. I liked his humor; I hated his mannered obliquity. In Randall's book-lined parlor, we railed at the Southern gothics for their freak show of horror costumes and macabre cobwebs, and agreed that Truman Capote was overrated and William Styron underrated and Charles Portis entirely neglected. These men were considered dated, faded, old hat, and all passé.

"Not many people write about the new problems," Randall said. "The new tensions are more delicate than the old tensions. The old tension was complete incomprehension. The new tension is 'How do we do it?'"

"Who writes on that theme?"

"Do you know Mary Ward Brown's writing?"

I said I had not come across it.

"You should meet Mary T," he said to me, his way of referring to her. She lived in Perry County, east of Hale, in the town of Marion. "She writes short stories, very good ones."

Randall told me a little about her. She had married into a farming family and still lived alone in the old family house in a remote area.

"She's ninety-five," Randall said. "Ninety-six in a few months."

"Perhaps you could introduce me," I said as I left him.

Some days passed. I read some of Brown's short stories in *Tongues of Flame* and was impressed by the truth of their description, by the unaffected prose; many stories were episodes of social awkwardness in small towns, of misunderstanding — some of it racial — and hard feeling. And they possessed a simplicity of line, as in the opening to "The Fruit of the Season": "The Deep South is at its best in early May, when the last cold spell is over and the heat has not yet arrived. Leaves and grass are still the tender green of Easter. Wild flowers liven the countryside and, above all, the magnolia starts to bloom. Days grow long and fireflies light up the slow-falling darkness. In early May of 1959, dewberries were ripe in Alabama."

It was a story about three black children, their berry picking, and a small crisis that arises when they offer them to the white woman who owns the berry patch.

I called Randall and said, "I'd like to see her soon."

"Maybe when you come back again," he said.

I heard that a lot. Normally on a journey I might insist on a meeting, but this was not a normal journey, not a traverse of China or a tour of Africa in search of a book; this was something else, a road trip, a coming-and-going, a way of life, a series of seasonal returns, and now it was winter.

"Maybe in the spring," he suggested.

"She'll be ninety-six years old then."

It seemed presumptuous to delay a meeting with someone who was so old, but Randall said that she was in good health and was looking forward to meeting me in a few months.

Hero of Greensboro

A corner shop on Main Street was now a café, called the Pie Lab, well known locally for its variety of homemade fruit pies and its salads and sandwiches. It had been a project of HERO, the Hale Empowerment and Revitalization Organization, which I'd heard about on my first visit.

"The idea was that people would drop in at the Pie Lab and get to know someone new," Randall Curb had said. "A good concept, but it hasn't worked out—at least I don't think so."

Shaking his head, he had somewhat disparaged it as "a liberal drawing card."

Yet the next day, quite by chance, having lunch at the Pie Lab, I met the founder and organizer of HERO, Pam Dorr, whom I had wished to meet in the fall and had not gotten around to calling. And here we were, drinking coffee and eating quiche Lorraine, known to some folks in Greensboro as "quickee Lorraine."

The more attractive of the skeletal, fading towns in the South attracted outsiders, in the way Third World countries attracted idealistic volunteers, and for many of the same reasons. With a look of innocence and promise, the places were poor, pretty, and in need of revival. They posed the possibility of rescue, an irresistible challenge to a young college graduate or someone who wanted to take a semester off to perform community service in another world. These were also pleasant places to live — or at least seemed so.

The desperate housing situation in Greensboro, and Hale County generally, had inspired student architects of the Auburn Rural Studio (an undergraduate program of the School of Architecture, Planning, and Landscape Architecture at Auburn University) to create attractive low-cost housing for needy people. The Auburn houses are small but simple, and some of them brilliantly innovative and attractive, looking folded out and logical, like oversized elaborations of origami in tin and plywood. Because affordability was a primary objective, the price of a newly built Auburn house in Greensboro — the "20K House" — would be no more than $20,000, the highest mortgage amount a person on Social Security can afford.

Hearing about the Auburn Rural Studio, Pam Dorr had traveled from San Francisco to Greensboro ten years before to become an Auburn "outreach fellow." It was a break from her successful career as a designer for various clothing companies, including Esprit and Gap and, more recently, Victoria's Secret ("I made cozy pajamas"). She had come to Greensboro in a spirit of volunteerism, but when her fellowship ended, she was reluctant to leave the lovely but struggling town.

"I realized there was so much more I could do," she told me at the Pie Lab, which had been one of her entrepreneurial ideas. She had many ideas. She had created her San Francisco apartment out of "free and found materials" — she showed me pictures of her colorful rooms, the tables and chairs she'd gotten at dumps and yard sales, and refinished. Repairing, reusing, and rehabbing were her passions; Greensboro was badly in need of improvement, and it had the raw materials — beat-up houses and shops to make habitable, a dying downtown that was still revivable, and plenty of wild invasive bamboo growing in canebrakes in the pinewoods that could be put to good use. Pam's idea to make bicycle frames out of bamboo resulted in Hero Bikes, one of the businesses Pam had overseen since starting HERO in 2004.

"We build houses, we educate people on home ownership, and working with nontraditional bankers, we help people establish credit."

The local banks had a history of lending mainly to whites. Blacks could get loans but only at extortionate rates — twenty-seven percent interest was not uncommon.

"It seemed to me a prime opportunity to start a community again." Pam said. "We have thirty-three people on the payroll and lots of volunteers. HERO is in the pie business, the pecan business — we sell locally grown pecans to retail stores. We have a day-care center and after-school program. A construction business, a thrift store. The bike business."

Some of these businesses were now housed on Main Street in what had been the hardware store, the insurance agency, the opera house. HERO had redeveloped or improved eleven of the defunct stores on Main Street, buying them when the owners were desperate to sell ("when the roof falls down or the ceiling caves in").

At Hero Bikes I fell into conversation with the bike builder and manager, Patrick Kelly. He was an example of my notion that the outsiders who worked to improve Greensboro were the sort one might find working in Third World countries.

"I wanted to go to Nigeria, to work in development," he said. "But the project wasn't approved. So I went to Korea for five years, to teach. And I also learned bike building there. Then I came to Greensboro."

Pam Dorr was also like the most inspired and energetic Peace Corps volunteer imaginable. Smiling, upbeat, full of recipes, solutions, and ideas for repurposing, still young — hardly fifty — she had wide experience and a California smile and an informal manner.

"I worked free for two years," Pam said. "We got a HUD grant, we got some other help, and now, because of the various businesses, we're self-sustaining."

Being from California set her apart. The way she dressed, in a purple fleece and green clogs, made her conspicuous. Her determination to effect change made her suspect. Outsiders in the South are often objects of suspicion. What do they want? Why are they here? What is the point of their trying to change things? Such people are regarded as agitators, even if all they are trying to do is build inexpensive houses, or harvest bamboo, or keep the children of working mothers busy after school: De Kevion, Keyonna, Jaimesa, Kimberly, Jakira, Raslyn, Demais, Trinity, and the rest.

"You find out a lot living here," she told me. "Drugs are a problem. Drive along a side road at night and you'll see white girls prostituting themselves to get money to support their habit. Mothers pimping out their children to men. Thirteen-year-olds getting pregnant—I know two personally, but there are plenty of others. It's not a black thing. White girls at Christian schools who get pregnant wrap their stomachs tight with belts to abort the child, because there's nowhere for white pregnant teen-agers in Alabama to go. They'll be kicked out of school if they're found to be pregnant."

"What does the town think of your work?" I asked.

"A lot of people are on our side," she said. "But they know that change has to come from within."

"Reverend Lyles told me you had something to do with fixing up the Rosenwald school here."

"The Emory School, yeah," she said. "But we had help from the University of Alabama and volunteers from AmeriCorps—lots of people contributed. Reverend Lyles was one of our speakers at the reopening dedication ceremony. That was a great day." She took a deep, calming breath. "But not everyone is on our side."

"Really?"

This surprised me, because what she had described, the renovation of an old schoolhouse in a hard-up rural area, was like a small-scale development project in a Third World country. I had witnessed such efforts many times: the energizing of a sleepy community, the fundraising, the soliciting of well-wishers and sponsors, engaging volunteers, asking for donations of building material, applying for grants and permits, fighting inertia and the naysayers' laughter, making a plan, getting the word out, supervising the business, paying the skilled workers, bringing meals to the volunteers, and seeing the project through to completion. Years of effort, years of budgeting. At last, the dedication, everyone turned out in clean clothes for a change, the cookies, the lemonade, the grateful speeches, the hugs. That was another side to the South, people seeing it as a development opportunity, and in "workshops" talking about "challenges" and "potential."

"So who's against you?" I asked.

"Plenty of people seem to dislike what we're doing," Pam said. She rocked in her clogs and zipped her fleece against the chilly air. "Lots of opposition. Lots of abuse. They call me names." She laughed, saying this. "Now and then someone walks past and spits on me."

"Reason for Visit"

I remembered the visitors' book from my previous visit to the office of the Community Service Programs of West Alabama, in a low building at the edge of Tuscaloosa, behind an old high school. I had driven there from Greensboro one morning. This time, as before, I studied the column titled *Reason for Visit* and noted the scrawls next to the names: "Food," "Clothes," "Water," "Light bill," and more: "Utilities," "Assistance." "Food" was the reason most frequently cited, and the others listed almost as often. That was just today's tally, and it was not yet eleven o'clock in the morning.

I had come again to see Cynthia Burton, to get an update on the housing situation and to make appointments.

Cynthia was as welcoming as ever, but did not look well. She admitted she'd been ill, and so instead of asking her whether she had been in touch with anyone I might see, I inquired about her health.

"High blood pressure," she said, "and I have a blood clot. I need surgery on my knee, but the problem is that for that procedure I have to take medication. The medication might make me bleed. It's a question of stabilizing my condition."

In spite of her ailments she worked long hours every day in this small spare building, and she seemed to me to be as hard-pressed as the people she was attempting to help. While the desperate people wrote "Food" and "Clothes" and "Water" in the visitors' book, the things they needed, Cynthia would have written "Time" or "Health," perhaps.

Having just come from Greensboro, I mentioned the HERO projects:

the renovations, the shops, the bike building, the pecan harvesting, the after-school program, the Pie Lab.

Cynthia listened with a lopsided smile of such obvious incredulity, I asked her why.

"They have caused divisions," she said. "And they could have avoided that."

"Pam Dorr seems to me a motivator."

Cynthia shook her head and laughed softly. "Pam Dorr is from California, and she thinks she knows better. She believes she can walk right in and have the answers to everything she sees—the California way. But, Paul, this is Alabama. This is not California."

"Still, she gets grants for her projects."

"Some money from HUD. But she's lost a few grants."

"Isn't HERO fixing up houses and building some too?"

"Not like us," and by "us" she meant the house building and renovation work of the Community Service Programs of West Alabama.

I now understood that in the scramble for grants, for recognition, for Housing and Urban Development funds, there was spirited competition among the nonprofits. Though both women had been frank with me, I did not know enough to take sides. They were both strong women, and I was grateful for their straightforward opinions. Neither of them dodged my questions, and they gave me more information than I'd asked for. Pam Dorr was an outsider, though, and as I kept hearing, an alien new to the South and determined to make changes was often characterized as an agitator—seen as a competitor by the local nonprofits, dismissed as a meddler by the old guard.

So I changed the subject and said, "What else is new?"

"Tell you what," she said, "we got a newly elected probate judge, Arthur Crawford. How he won is historical. He was prevented from being on the ballot, disqualified because of some technicalities. So he started a campaign for write-in votes. He went all over, he told people how important it was to vote. All they had to do was write in his name as a candidate and spell it right. The incumbent, Leland Avery, was a three-termer, but Crawford beat him with the write-in votes." Cynthia gasped a little in her excitement, then said, "Isn't that something?"

The write-in vote that had turned the tide was unprecedented in

Alabama. That Arthur Crawford Jr. was black and Leland Avery was white—and now Avery was facing serious ethics violations—led us to discuss the issues of voting that were at the heart of the 1960s protest marches.

"As you well know, this is the fiftieth anniversary of the civil rights movement," Cynthia said. "I think about how far we've come. I want to talk about how people have benefited. I want to celebrate the families that didn't get notoriety. So many people contributed to that struggle—it was a war, they were soldiers in that war. No one knows their names. They were ordinary people, taking big risks."

I mentioned the 1965 confrontation provoked by the Klan and the "Fight Race Mixing" whites in Greensboro that Reverend Lyles had described, elaborated in the book he'd shown me, Susan Ashmore's *Carry It On*: the street fights, the many injuries, the arrests of the black protesters, the connivance of the police, the indifference or hostility of the white politicians.

"It surely was a war," Cynthia said. She sighed and reflected for a moment. "I try to imagine the pain of Beulah Mae Donald when she saw her son hanging from a tree." Saying so, Cynthia became tearful. "That poor woman."

The death of Michael Donald had been recent in Alabama terms, and was an outrage, the last recorded lynching in the state. A local horror that had not resonated much beyond the state line, it had happened in Mobile in 1981. It had begun with a murder trial and a hung jury and the consequent acquittal of a black man accused of murdering a white policeman. Infuriated by this turn of events, the Exalted Cyclops (presiding officer) of the local Klavern, Bennie Jack Hays, summoned a meeting of his Klansmen and demanded a revenge killing. His son Henry and James Knowles, two young Klansmen—the youngsters known as Ghouls or Knights—obeyed him. They drove through the back streets of the city looking for a black man, any black man, to punish as an example.

Late on the night of March 21, 1981, Michael Donald, nineteen years old, was walking alone, on his way to buy cigarettes at a convenience store. Slowing down near him, the two Klansmen called him over to their car, claimed they were lost, and asked him for directions. When Donald obliged, answering them, they seized him, dragged him into the back seat, and drove to the next county where they clubbed him to death. For good measure, they slit his throat. They then brought Donald's corpse back to Mobile, tied a rope around his neck, and hanged him conspicuously from a tree on a city street.

"I can hardly imagine the sorrow of a mother," Cynthia Burton said, "and what this poor woman went through."

What she went through was the horror of seeing her son lynched, and then falsely accused by the police of being a drug dealer (this being the supposed pretext for his murder), and enduring two and a half years of justice denied, of agony and appeals and interventions (by, among others, Jesse Jackson), before the FBI became involved and the murderers were at last caught, sent to trial, and found guilty. When the younger of the two defendants, James Knowles, from his place in the dock after his conviction, in June 1983, told Beulah Mae Donald that he was sorry, he asked for her forgiveness.

"I do forgive you," the bereaved Mrs. Donald said. "From the day I found out who you all was, I asked God to take care of y'all, and He has."

Because Knowles had agreed to a plea deal and testified against his accomplice, he got life in prison. Henry Hays was sentenced to death. He spent fourteen years on death row in Holman Prison (called "the Slaughterhouse" by prisoners), about fifty miles northeast of Mobile. He was executed in June 1997, in Holman, in the electric chair, painted yellow and known to Alabamians as "Yellow Mama."

Cynthia and I talked about this tragedy and its implications. She said, "Nothing like that happens now. But people don't have an appreciation of the sacrifices that have been made. And we have a distance to go."

After a while I said, "About those appointments."

"Oh, yes, there's some people I want you to meet when you come back here and I'm feeling better."

"Black Day"

Instead of making another roundabout tour via Philadelphia and Choctaw, I drove south and west out of Alabama, through Mississippi, on the back roads of beat-up bungalows and small, white-painted wood-frame churches. I had crossed from Lincoln County to Jefferson County. Jefferson had the distinction of being home to the most obese Americans, and paradoxically it was also one of the poorest counties in the nation. I headed to Fayette, Jefferson's county seat, and went from there to Union Church, a small town of 830 people (and five good-sized churches), where I planned to turn north into the Delta and return to Highway 61. Eventually I got to the lovely town of Vicksburg.

In Vicksburg again, I returned to the Round Table at the Walnut Hills Restaurant, because eating with the eight white people had been such an unexpected immersion ("You made us eat rats") on my previous trip. This time three women, just finishing their meal, welcomed me; the two questioners — mother and daughter — were having dessert, and a more exotic woman, their friend, was sipping coffee.

"We like the Round Table," the mother said in a good-humored way, pressing her fork tines slantwise into a wedge of pie. "We like to eat, as you can see."

They were, each of them, heavy and pale, resembling one another in their bulk and their friendliness, but chewing hard, a bit breathless in their eating.

"I'm part Cherokee," the exotic woman said. She was dusky, her black hair in a long braid. "I do some writing too. Poetry mainly."

They asked me, off the bat, whether I was married, and where was my wife, and what did I do for a living. These were the sort of questions I was used to when traveling in Africa or India or on a Pacific island, a concern for family, the fascination and distrust of someone traveling alone.

"Mama, look at the time."

"Oh, golly, we gotta run," the mother said. "We from across the river, north of Tallulah, near Lake Providence, Louisiana." She added with a slight boastfulness, "That there's the poorest town in the whole United States."

It was not true, but it was close: fifty percent of Lake Providence's population lived below the poverty line.

With that, they upped and left, and wished me safe travels. I sat and ate alone for a while, spinning the lazy Susan, and then three more women entered the room and took their places at the table. They were Deborah

McDonald and Carmen Brooks, two black middle-aged women, both of them attorneys in Natchez, and Carmen's aunt Lola. They'd come up to Vicksburg for the day, for the pleasant drive, to look around, to shop. It was a Saturday, a free day for them, and they were fond of the freedom of the Round Table, choosing dishes at will.

"I went to Alcorn," Deborah said, "and then law school at Ole Miss. John Grisham was one of my classmates."

Alcorn State University, near Lorman, which I'd passed through, was a traditionally black institution, founded in 1871, as its brochure explained, "to educate the descendants of formerly enslaved Africans." There were now two other campuses, but the enrollment was still predominantly black.

At the University of Mississippi, Deborah was one of thirteen black students in the law school class (1979–1982) of three hundred. When she laughed at the memory of her years there, I suspected her laughter to be pure exasperation, so I asked for details.

"It was always very hostile, which is really strange, because James Meredith had been there years before," she said. "For example, the other students would hide books from us. We'd have required reading and the books would be nowhere in sight — not on the shelves. That's just mean. And the teachers would ignore us. But they'd call on us now and then, and some days they'd call on three black students. We'd laugh about that. We'd call that Black Day."

Randall Curb, a reasonable man, had said to me, "The tables are turned. In a lot of places in the South, the whites are out of power. The blacks have taken their place. There are hard feelings on both sides."

I mentioned that to Carmen.

"That's true," she said. "But the whites want to come back — and they might. They field their own candidates, like Jonathan Lee in Jackson, a right-wing black candidate — that's their man. Jackson is now seventy-five percent black."

But in the event, Lee lost in the Democratic primary to an activist attorney, Chokwe Lumumba, a sixty-five-year-old civil rights lawyer who had gained fame in a 1993 successful defense of the rapper Tupac Shakur, who'd been charged with assault. Born in Detroit and educated in Michigan, Edwin Taliaferro had renounced what he called his "slave name" and renamed himself Chokwe Lumumba. It seemed to me an eccentric choice: the Chokwe — properly, Lunda Chokwe — are an Angolan tribe (and it is not a first name among those people, though Edwin is), and Lumumba was the martyred patriot of the Congo. Chokwe Lumumba became Jackson's mayor in July 2013, promising renewal and fairness, and at his inauguration he gave a black power salute and shouted, "Free the land!" A local paper described his program as an "all new, progressive Black agenda committed to self-determination, self-governance, self-economic development." If whites had felt somewhat distant before, Mayor Lumumba had arrived to offer them no encouragement, and to tell them that their place was at the back of the line. (Mayor Lumumba died suddenly, six months into his term, on February 25, 2014.)

"I live in Fayette," Deborah said. "Charles Evers was the mayor of Fayette way back, from 1969 to '74. He was a great friend of Robert Kennedy."

They asked what I'd seen so far in the South. I mentioned that I had been unprepared for the sight of such extensive poverty, of the sort I'd seen in Third World countries.

"What we got now are the working poor, just keeping their heads above water," Carmen said. And then she said something I thought of often afterward: "One medical problem can propel you down."

She talked about Natchez, how the south of the city was mainly white and had its own school; north Natchez was black, its high school ninety percent black. Natchez's recent history had been turbulent. The Klan had a large membership (six thousand Klansmen in this part of Mississippi, in fifty-two Klaverns) and had been active in and around Natchez into the late 1960s, in a particularly violent incarnation, as an offshoot called the White Knights of the Ku Klux Klan. For many, including the aunt, Lola, this was a recent memory.

Recalling this, Deborah became emphatic, like the lawyer she was, delivering a closing argument, a summation at the end of an important trial, enunciating each word.

"We have been living, black and white, *forever,*" she said. "No point saying we're strangers! We have been friends. We have been neighbors — intermarrying, living together, talking all the time. We know each other better than we know anyone else."

"So what needs to happen?" I asked.

"People have to change in their hearts," she said, then dropped her voice. "It's hard."

Delta Winter

The cold mist and the gray sky seemed to flatten the Delta and made the road bleaker, the muddy fields beside the long straight road, raised like a levee, the chilly wind from the river that tore leaves from the trees. In its nakedness the Delta had a stark beauty and simplicity, the stripped trees, some of the dark fields evenly combed of their stubble by a harrow for planting—cotton, I guessed; the sprawl of it had not been obvious to me on my previous trip. Denuded in winter, the land had a desolate grandeur. But those were the fields and the woods and the sloping swamps of the bottomlands and the sodden grass, the bayous and the backwaters.

The human communities were another story, and a sad one. The decaying house trailers sat in clusters outside the decaying towns, all of them more shocking for being so visible. And because of the cold day, few people were outdoors, a Doomsday vision, a road through a depopulated landscape. No wonder the notion of Last Days was something I met often in the South, the famine, tribulation, and false prophets mentioned in the book of Revelation. Going up Highway 61 you could be persuaded (if your church helped you along by drumming the passages into your fearful mind) that you were seeing the dire disclosures of the Seven Seals—deception, devastation, hunger, civil unrest, persecution, tribulation, and—the Seventh Seal—the revealed mysteries.

Arcola was a cluster of poor houses and shacks and shuttered shops on a grid of streets. One house had six gravestones in the front yard. A small school, a police station, the post office—but no one outside. Dee Jones, whom I had met in Greenville on my last trip, had a sister here, Ruby Johnson, and Dee had suggested I look her up if I wanted to know a bit more of Arcola. Ruby was Arcola's postmaster.

"Miss Johnson's away this week," the woman at the counter told me.

This was Vivien Weston, who was filling in for her. "You come back and you'll find her."

"How's things here?" I asked.

"It's nice and quiet around here," Miss Weston said. "I like it."

That was a characteristic of the Delta: no matter how down-at-the-heels a place looked, the local people talked it up and found something to praise.

I bought some stamps.

"Course, when the fish farm closed in Hollandale," Miss Weston said, handing me my change, "that was real hard."

"What happened?"

"They was no more work," she said, and in her Delta way gave the word a lilt and made it into *woik*.

At the Leland crossroads, I called to make an appointment to see Sue Evans again, to catch up, and perhaps to learn a bit more of B. B. King. But she was busy.

"Next time you come 'round this way, please stop by."

The Ghostliest Structure in the South

So, instead of turning left at Leland, I went right, drove another forty miles or so to Greenwood, and up Money Road to the place called Money.

Hardly a town or a village, Money (pop. 94) was no more than a road junction near the banks of the Tallahatchie River. There, without any trouble, I found what I was looking for, a one-hundred-year-old grocery store, the roof caved in, the brick walls broken, the façade boarded up, the wooden porch roughly patched, and the whole wreck of it overgrown with dying plants and tangled vines. For its haunted appearance and its bloody history it was the ghostliest structure I was to see in the whole of my travels in the South. This ruin, formerly Bryant's Grocery and Meat Market, is at the top of the list of the Mississippi Heritage Trust's "Ten Most Endangered Historic Places," though many people would like to tear it down as an abomination.

What happened there in the store and, subsequently, in that tiny com-

Country road in the Ozarks, near Lamar, Arkansas

Reverend Virgin Johnson of Revelation Ministries Church. "God sends us a storm. I need this storm. What would I do without my storm? It makes me turn to the Lord. And so I say, 'Thank you, storm!'" Sycamore, South Carolina.

Photographs © Steve McCurry

Ruby Johnson, postmaster, folding the flag at the end of the day, Arcola, Mississippi

Janet May, the proprietor of Blue Shadows Bed and Breakfast, on her lawn, Greensboro, Alabama

Andre Peer, a farmer, explaining the frustrations of farming, after supervising the loading of his soybean crop onto a river barge, Helena, Arkansas

Melvin Johnson on the porch of his family's nineteenth-century house, which he's lived in for more than fifty years without plumbing or electricity, Razor Road, Allendale, South Carolina

Shuquita Drakes with her month-old child, D'Vohta Knight, at the Sam Chatmon Blues Festival, Hollandale, Mississippi

Jessica Badger in a bedroom of her mother's house, indicating the leaky roof, Allendale, South Carolina

Delores Walker Robinson on her farm near Palestine, Arkansas. "I'm looking ten years down the road. I want to build up the herd and do this full time."

Mary Ward Brown, writer, in the home her father built, two months before she died, at ninety-five, in Hamburg, near Marion, Alabama

Abandoned shop by the railroad tracks in Demopolis, Alabama

Paul Theroux outside the ruin of Bryant's Grocery Store, Money, Mississippi

Ernest Cox, Delta farmer, in the early evening after a long day at harvest time, near Marvel, Alabama

Late afternoon in Natchez, Mississippi

A decorated window of an old house in Greenville, Mississippi

Former sharecropper's shack near the Little Tallahatchie River, Money, Mississippi

"Most of this community is lower class. All poverty level." Chester Skaggs in the bedroom of his newly renovated house, Holman Community, Ozarks, Arkansas.

Abandoned motel, Route 301, Sylvania, Georgia

Bridal dress shop in the center of Philadelphia, Mississippi

Massoud Besharat at one of his granite quarries, Elberton, Georgia

Prison laborers, convicted of misdemeanors, sweeping the streets under a guard's supervision, Marianna, Arkansas

Abandoned gas station, Route 301, Allendale, South Carolina

Lester Carter in front of his shack on a winter afternoon, Cotton Plant, Arkansas. Penniless, unemployed, and hungry: "I got nothing to eat but some rice."

Reverend Eugene Lyles in his Greensboro, Alabama, barbershop. "Ones born today don't know how it was."

Reverend Lyles's annotated Bible, on the desk in his barbershop

Abandoned garden, Elberton, Georgia

Paul Theroux and Steve McCurry, Allendale, South Carolina

munity of Money was one of the most powerful stories I'd heard as a youth, and it was unforgettable, which was why I was there today. As was so often the case, driving up a country road in the South was driving into the shadowy past. A "Mississippi Freedom Trail" sign in front of the store gave the details of its place in history. It was part of my history too.

I had just turned fourteen, in May 1955, when the murder of the boy occurred. He was exactly my age. But I have no memory of any news report in a Boston newspaper at the time of the outrage. Our daily paper was the *Boston Globe,* but we were subscribers to and diligent readers of family magazines: *Life* for its photographs, *Collier's* and the *Saturday Evening Post* for profiles and short stories, *Look* for its racier features, the *Reader's Digest* for its roundups from other magazines. This Victorian habit of magazines as family entertainment and enlightenment persisted until television overwhelmed it in the late 1960s.

In January 1956, our copy of *Look* carried a story by William Bradford Huie, "The Shocking Story of Approved Killing in Mississippi," and it appeared in a shorter form in the *Reader's Digest* that spring. I remember this distinctly, because my two older brothers had read the story first, and I was much influenced by their tastes and enthusiasms. After hearing them excitedly talking about the story, I read it and was appalled and fascinated.

Emmett Till, a black boy, visiting his great-uncle in Mississippi, stopped at a grocery store to buy some candy. He apparently whistled at the white woman behind the counter. A few nights later he was abducted, tortured, killed, and thrown into a river. Two men were caught and tried for the crime. They were acquitted, and afterward gloated, telling Huie that they had indeed committed the crime, and they brazenly volunteered the gory particulars of the killing. They had gotten away with murder.

"Let's write them a letter," my brother Alexander said, and did so. His letter was two lines of threat: *We're coming to get you. You'll be sorry.* And signed it *The Gang from Boston.* We mailed it to the named killers, in care of their post office in Money, Mississippi.

No one was ever convicted of the murder, though the killers and accomplices were known. But as the commemorative sign in front of Bryant's store said, ". . . Till's death received international attention and is widely credited with sparking the American Civil Rights Movement."

The depositions in the case and the transcripts of the 1955 trial of the accused were believed to have been lost. But in 2004 the FBI found water-damaged copies and transcribed them, releasing them in 2005, fifty years after the events, with a 110-page "FBI Summary Prosecutive Report of the Investigation of the Murder of Emmett Till."*

The FBI investigation reported that Emmett Till, fourteen years old, and at 150 pounds big for his age, arrived in Money from Chicago, in August 1955, to visit his great-uncle, Mose Wright. Before he left home, his mother, Mamie Bradley, gave him his late father's silver ring. The ring was inscribed "Mar. 25, 1943" and "LT," for Louis Till.

Louis Till had a strange and violent history. To avoid being imprisoned on a charge of assaulting his wife, Till enlisted in the US Army in 1943 and served in the Italian campaign. While in Italy he was convicted of the murder of an Italian woman, and the rape of two others, by a military court. He was jailed in Pisa (the poet Ezra Pound was detained in the same military prison, on a charge of treason) and hanged there in 1945. None of this was known to Till's ex-wife and young son, who believed he had died in combat. The ring was to prove significant in identifying Emmett Till, the only unviolated item on the naked mangled body.

Emmett had lived for a week with Mose Wright in Wright's small house in East Money, three miles from the crossroads. Wright was known locally as Preacher Wright (he was a part-time pastor at a small church nearby). Emmett had last visited there when he was nine. Known as Bobo or Bo, he had a slight speech impediment, a stammer, but was known for his practical jokes, his teasing, and his ability to amuse his friends. Popular with the other children, he had Chicago confidence in this rural and backward part of the Deep South.

Late one afternoon, after a day of picking cotton, Emmett and eight other youngsters, including a girl, went to Bryant's Grocery for soft drinks and candy. The store was owned by Roy and Carolyn Bryant. Roy had been a paratrooper in the 82nd Airborne Division from 1950 to 1953 and was a big man, six feet, 190 pounds. He was then twenty-four years old.

---

* This "Prosecutive Report" is a summary of the FBI's 8,000-page report of its investigation of the murder, dated February 9, 2006, filed at the Jackson, Mississippi, office. The report also includes the 354-page transcript of the 1955 murder trial of J. W. Milam and Roy Bryant. See www.emmetttillmurder.com.

Carolyn was two years younger and clerked at the store when Roy was away, as he was on the fateful afternoon.

Emmett went into the store and asked for some bubble gum and paid for it.

"Till exited the store, and shortly thereafter Carolyn Bryant, the store owner's wife, exited as well," the FBI report reads. "Upon Carolyn Bryant's exit, Till whistled. The relatives accompanying him knew his whistle would cause trouble, and they left in haste, taking Till with them."

That was the version of the bystanders watching from outside the store, and there was a suggestion that perhaps it was to impress his friends with his big-city bravado that he whistled at Carolyn Bryant.

Carolyn Bryant's version was different. She claimed that when Emmett paid for the bubble gum, he grabbed her hand and said, "How about a date, baby?" and then, when she pulled away, he followed her and used "one unprintable word." Frightened, she hurried to her car to get her pistol from under the front seat, and as she did so, Emmett Till, who was lingering by the front porch, whistled at her and then got into a car and was driven away. The sun had set, and by then Money was in darkness.

Carolyn Bryant's story was disputed by one of Till's friends, who had gone into the store shortly after Till entered, and was with him when he paid for the gum. According to the friend, Till had not said the words attributed to him. But the wolf whistle was not in dispute. One of the friends said, "Everyone knew Till's whistling was trouble."

For a few days nothing happened. Then, four days after the event, on August 28, Roy Bryant and J. W. Milam, his thirty-six-year-old half-brother, met and conferred. Milam was a veteran of World War Two, having served in the 2nd Armored Division in Europe from 1941 to 1946. They decided to look for the boy Carolyn Bryant had described, and drove the roads near Money, where they found a black boy walking alone. They captured him and showed him to Carolyn, but she said he was not the one from the store.

The Southern white woman was central to the drama. Long before this incident, Frank Tannenbaum wrote, in *Darker Phases of the South* (1924), "The simple truth of the matter seems to be that the tremendous protection which the South throws about the white women is the compensation for the lack of protection which the colored women have to endure." His prescient observation continues by conjuring up the images of Roy Bryant and J. W. Milam: "The idealization of the white women in the South is thus partly the unconscious self-protection on the part of the white men from their own bad habits, notions, beliefs, attitudes, and practices."

Suspecting that the children who'd come to the store were associated with Mose Wright, Bryant and Milam went to his house in East Money that night and made demands and threats. Milam had a pistol in one hand and a flashlight in the other. He said, "I want the boy who done the talking down at Money."

Emmett was roused from his bed at the back of the house. As Emmett was putting his clothes on, Mose's wife, Elizabeth, begged the men to leave Emmett alone, and said she'd pay them anything they asked if they would not take him away. How much money did they want?

They did not reply to that. Milam said, "We're just going to take him up the road and just whip him."

They dragged Emmett to their car. A woman's voice said, "That's the one."

("The amount of whipping usually depended on 'the humor of the madam' rather than the behavior of the slave," Louis Hughes wrote in *Thirty Years a Slave* in 1897.)

Later that night, Bryant, Milam, and some others (possibly including Otha "Oso" Johnson and Levi "Too Tight" Collins, two black farm hands) drove Emmett in the back of a pickup truck to a barn in Glendora, where they brutally beat him, whipping him and smashing his skull. Milam described the beating to a friend, who later reported Milam saying, "During the beating Till was never respectful to the men and did not say 'Yes, sir' or 'No, sir.' Things got out of hand and Till stated something to the effect of 'he was as good as they are.'"

"The Negro, when addressing a white person, is expected to use a title such as 'Sah,' 'Mistah,' 'Boss,'" observed the field researchers in the Harvard study *Deep South* (the 1941 sociological account of Natchez in the late 1930s), adding, "while the white must never use such titles of respect to the Negro but should address him by his first name or as 'Boy.'"

Emmett Till broke all the rules. He defied his abductors, and even while being whipped he was not deferential or humble; he didn't know his place; he was uppity. If he'd been good, he would have accepted and expressed his inferior social position. As the *Deep South* scholars described a white man's account of a beating in Natchez, "They were bad niggers and were getting biggity."

What happened to Emmett Till, brutal though it was, had happened many times before. In his confidence in the store, and his defiance afterward, he had broken "the strongest taboo of the system." A white planter, quoted in *Deep South,* explained the penalty clearly: "We often have to whip one of them around here who gets too uppity or insolent or does something. We don't run them off, because it usually does more good to let them come back to work, so the other niggers will know about it . . . We took [one man] out and whipped him and told him to be back at work the next day. Ever since then, whenever he sees me, he tips his hat and has been a good nigger ever since."

AT LAST, AFTER beating Emmett Till until his skull was broken and his face smashed, the men shot him in the head and loaded his bleeding corpse into the pickup truck. ("It's a deer," Too Tight Collins explained to a man who pointed out the blood running from the truck bed to the ground at a stop the next day.) They drove to the Tallahatchie River and, using barbed wire as an attachment, weighted his body with a seventy-five-pound fan from a ginnery, then dropped the corpse into the water.

Within a day Bryant and Milam were arrested on suspicion — people had talked — and a few days later Emmett's body, "hung up on a snag," was sighted by a fisherman and dragged from the river at a place called Pecan Point, above Philipp, about ten miles north of Money. The decomposed corpse, the face crushed ("extensive trauma to the head"), was unrecognizable, but the ring with the initials "LT" on a bloated finger proved it was Emmett. A week later in Chicago, Emmett's brutalized body was put on view. Thousands of people, over four days, filed past to see Emmett's remains in (as his mother insisted) an open casket.

A month after the murder, Bryant and Milam went to trial at the Tallahatchie courthouse in Sumner. The evidence against them was irrefutable. Incriminating witnesses were called. Mose Wright testified and famously rose from the witness chair and pointed to the men, identifying them as Emmett's abductors. A guilty verdict seemed certain. But after a brief deliberation by the white jury, Bryant and Milam were found not guilty of murder and were later cleared of kidnapping. They were photographed smoking cigars, hugging their wives, openly gloating outside the court-house.

And, for a fee, the men cooperated with William Bradford Huie in his *Look* article, published four months after the trial. Huie paid the men $1,500 each for the interview, and their lawyer got $1,000. Milam, the most talkative, was unrepentant in describing how he'd kidnapped Emmett Till with Bryant's help, how they pistol-whipped him in a shed behind his home in Glendora, then shot him and disposed of his body.

Though many of Milam's details of the killing were inconsistent with the evidence, and the time line was skewed, everything he said was incriminating. There was a general outcry in the North, and my brothers and I talked of little else for months. Yet there was no response from the authorities. The reaction by Southern blacks was momentous, and unusual because it was nonviolent. On December 1 of that same year of the Till trial, 1955, in Montgomery, Alabama, Rosa Parks refused to surrender her seat to a white passenger on a city bus. She was arrested for her act of disobedience, and she became a symbol of defiance. Her stubbornness and sense of justice made her a rallying point and an exemplar.

What was the reaction to the Emmett Till murder in the nation's capital? Mississippi senator John C. Stennis released to the press the details of Louis Till's court-martial and his hanging in Italy for rape and murder. This was intended to taint the case and sway public opinion against Emmett. Immediately after the trial, Mamie Bradley sent a telegram to President Eisenhower, begging for justice: "I the mother of Emmett Louis still am pleading that you personally see that justice is meted out to all persons involved in the beastly lynching of my son in Money Miss. Awaiting a direct reply from you."

She got no reply, but her telegram eventually generated an interoffice memo. Among the many documents in the Till file is that White House memo, dated October 23, 1956, from Max Rabb, Eisenhower's secretary of the cabinet and his adviser on minorities, to James C. Hagerty, the White House press secretary. Mamie Bradley was a tool of the Communists, the memo began; the woman was "a 'phoney'." Rabb went on, "Any recognition of her would have been used to further Communist causes in this country . . . Mrs. Bradley was discredited for using her son's death as a means of making a living."

"Practically all the evidence against the defendants was circumstantial evidence" was the opinion in an editorial in the *Jackson Daily News* on September 25, 1955. "It is best for all concerned that the Bryant-Milam case be forgotten as quickly as possible."

But the Jackson paper published a more robust piece by William Faulkner. The crime itself was like a dark Faulkner story, with all the Southern small-town elements, even the cast: the young white shopkeeping wife, the boastful peckerwood murderers, the panicky black children, the intimidated black preacher. It was one of the most damning and gloomiest accusations Faulkner ever wrote — and he normally resisted the simplifications of newspaper essays. His anguish shows in the scathing broadside, written hurriedly in Rome while he was on a State Department speaking junket. The piece was released through the United States Information Service and published in the *Jackson Daily News* when the two men were acquitted of Till's murder.

Faulkner first spoke about the bombing of Pearl Harbor and the hypocrisy of boasting of our values to our enemies "after we have taught them (as we are now doing) that when we talk of freedom and liberty, we not only mean neither, we don't even mean security and justice and even not the preservation of life for people whose pigmentation is not the same as ours." He went on to say that if Americans are to survive, we will have to show the world that we are not racists, "to present to the world one homogeneous and unbroken front." Yet this might be a test we will fail: "Perhaps we will find out now whether we are to survive or not. Perhaps the purpose of this sorry and tragic error committed in my native Mississippi by two white adults on an afflicted Negro child is to prove to us whether or not we deserve to survive." And his damning conclusion: "Because if we in America have reached that point in our desperate culture when we must murder children, no matter for what reason or what color, we don't deserve to survive, and probably won't."

Nowhere in the piece did Faulkner use Emmett Till's name, yet anyone who read it knew whom he was speaking about.

"Don't Be Fourteen (in Mississippi)," a poem by the Mississippi writer

Jerry W. Ward Jr., was a direct response to the killing, and a powerful one. Ward, who is black, was close to Emmett Till's age when the murder occurred and, as a teacher, is still resident in the state. "Racism is a permanent feature of life in Mississippi," he said, "and that produces its own set of headaches."

Forget Emmett Till, the Jackson paper had said in its editorial, but the case was not forgotten. On the contrary, it became a remembered infamy and a celebrated injustice, and Emmett Till was eulogized as a hero and a martyr. Suppression of the truth is not merely futile but almost a guarantee of something wonderful and revelatory emerging from it, creating an opposing and more powerful and ultimately overwhelming force, sunlight breaking in, as the Till case proved.

I never forgot it. And that was why, late that afternoon in Money, Mississippi, I parked near the ghostly ruin of Bryant's store and noted the sentiments on the sign in front. I walked around in the chill air — no one outside on this winter day. Just walls, and not strong ones; it was hard to imagine how the building was still standing. Enclosed in a tangle of vines and the roots of parasitic trees, like a cracked structure of rusticated stone in Angkor Wat, the store was perhaps held together for the same reason, by the clinging claws of roots and vignettes.

Not a soul stirred at this crossroads, no one near the bleak cotton sheds of corrugated tin, an ancient cotton gin behind it, a faded sign, MONEY, coated in red dust above a loading dock. No one on the road or near the tracks of the north-south railway line that passed the level crossing by the front of Bryant's store, where I stood in the failing light.

A whistle sounded, the two-note moan of an oncoming train, *whoo-eee*, a lonely cry, especially so in this haunted place, a crossroads in the dark plowed land in the flat heart of Mississippi. Banging on the rails, the train went past, the anvil-clang echo vibrating on the skeletal walls of Bryant's store and the tin of the cotton sheds and the gin. It was a wonder to me that in the fifty-nine years since the crime, the indifferent thunder of this passing train had not shaken down the walls of this old store.

I drove east down Whaley Road, past Money Bayou and some narrow ponds, hoping to find Dark Ferry Road and the farm of Grover C. Washington, where Mose Wright's little house had stood, where he'd worked as a sharecropper. My map didn't help, and there was no one to ask, and some parts of the past had been erased, but negligible parts. It was dusk when I drove back to Money, the same sort of darkness into which Emmett Till had been dragged.

Traveling up the empty road out of Money (renamed the Emmett Till Memorial Highway in 2005), I passed a sign, GLENDORA. I turned off and even in the failing light saw that Glendora, unlike Money, was an actual town with a main street, or it had been before the decay had set in. Near these mean huts and trailers and bankrupt shops, Emmett Till had been beaten to death, in J. W. Milam's barn, and where Milam had lived, a free man, until he died in 1980.

On a later sunny day I returned to Glendora. Sunshine can be cruel; pitiless light can turn a sad place into something awful. Glendora was worse than a ruin. It was shocking, a hideous street of shacks and hovels, a poor grocery store, the porch of a bar where men in rags, with glazed dog-like eyes, sipped from bottles and cans. The squalor of Glendora made it seem a living museum of Southern poverty — drunks, stumblers in broken shoes, some of them supine and snoring in the grass, idle men in the middle of the sunny day, near the plot of land and the house the murderer J. W. Milam had once owned — the house torn down, a sign indicating where it had stood. These black Glendora men and dazed defiant boys were the inheritors.

In more than a year of travel in the Deep South, I never felt menaced or sensed that I was in the presence of danger from anyone. I did not feel endangered here, but the vibration of hostility on this potholed road of Glendora was something that made me feel like an intruder and caused me to be watchful. Perhaps it was something simple, the shame of poor people, suddenly self-conscious in the presence of a stranger, drunks feeling conspicuous in their jostling among someone sober, the poor rooted in their decrepitude, hating to be observed, resenting me for having arrived, resenting me for so easily being able to depart.

Down this Glendora lane I saw a former cotton gin, a plain, two-story, looming structure of corrugated metal sections — tin walls, tin roof — with the additional horror of having no windows. This obsolete building, on its own in the middle of fields at the edge of Glendora, housed the Emmett

Till Historic Intrepid Center (ETHIC) and the museum associated with his name.

Outside the building, a woman walking to her car smiled at me. I said hello, and then, to engage her, "What did you think of the museum?"

"You have to see it," she said. She was dressed formally, as though for church or a social, in a red dress, wearing a white hat, and carrying a substantial handbag. "This is a very important place. Everyone should see it."

Her name, she said, was Cherraye Oats. She was probably in her late forties, and in her dignified clothes looked unlike any other person I'd seen in Glendora.

I said, "I remember when it happened."

"I'm too young for that," she said. "But it deeply affected my aunt"—and she paused, then added—"who was Fannie Lou Hamer."

Fannie Lou Hamer, one of the bravest and most outspoken of the activists in voter registration in the Freedom Summer of 1963, founded the Mississippi Freedom Democratic Party the following year as a response (which proved contentious) to the all-white state delegation to the Democratic National Convention in Atlantic City, New Jersey. Severely beaten, imprisoned, and fired from her job for her views, Fannie Lou Hamer became one of the memorable voices of the civil rights movement and was politically and socially active until her death, at the age of sixty, in 1977. Her gravestone is inscribed with one of her remarks about segregation: "I am sick and tired of being sick and tired."

Cherraye Oats and her daughter Courtney were organizers at the Fannie Lou Hamer Center for Change in Eupora. Cherraye had been raised in Ruleville and now lived in Eupora, small towns not far from Glendora. The daughter of a sharecropper named Townsend, one of twenty children, Fannie Lou must have had many nieces and nephews, but in her passion and presence Cherraye was in the Hamer mold. We talked awhile—she asked how I happened to be there and where I was headed.

"I'm glad you're here," she said. "But I'll tell you, very little has changed."

This cotton gin building had provided the seventy-five-pound fan that had been wired to Emmett Till's corpse to sink it in the river. A similar gin fan was on view, along with farm paraphernalia—just old tools, but they looked sinister and brutal in the context of the murder: barbed wire, hammers and pitchforks, axes and sickles. One display was an old Ford pickup truck like the one the abductors had used. Another was of Emmett's bed and bedroom, and one a mock-up of Bryant's storefront. In a macabre tableau, a life-sized replica of Emmett Till lay in his coffin, his smashed and mutilated face modeled in plastic. Much of this was appropriately gory, but the details of the crime and its chronology were also set out: it was a worthy memorial and an essential footnote to history.

"It was a terrible thing," said Benjamin Saulsberry, the curator of the museum. Saulsberry was just twenty-nine, but knowledgeable about the crime, and about the area. He directed me to a part of the museum that was devoted to the life and career of the bluesman Sonny Boy Williamson, who'd been born on a plantation near Glendora a hundred years ago.

"Do you get many visitors?" I asked.

"Ten or twelve people a week."

Fewer than two a day, another melancholy number. Cherraye Oats had driven away, the dust from her car had settled, and apart from Benjamin and me, there was no one else in the building. This look of abandonment lent an added ghoulishness to the exhibits. A stack of leaflets offered fifteen-dollar day tours to places associated with the Till murder, the store, the house site, the courthouse, the river — places I'd already seen. There were no takers this morning, and the only signs of life were a short walk away, near the shops at Glendora: the derelicts and drunks and, at the edge of this poor village, their flyblown and malodorous shacks.

"People Are Buying Guns That Never Wanted No Guns"

In the early darkness of the Mississippi winter, the towns north of Glendora, Batesville and Southaven, were a blaze of lights, rising from the roadside as sudden and sprawling communities, bursting with life — or seemed so. In the South such places might look like important metropolises, but that was misleading; in reality they were no more than overbright blights of fast food joints, discount outlets and malls, and enormous parking lots, glittering in the darkness, yet empty.

Southaven, one of these dazzling mirages, is so far north in Mississippi it is like a suburb of Memphis. I easily found a motel there. I was wearing a US Army camouflage patrol cap as I idled by the front door, wondering where to eat.

"Whereabouts you hunting at?" a man asked me, approaching from the parking lot. He had a similar cap.

I said I wasn't hunting. But he was — duck hunting. He had just arrived from Tennessee with three small boys and a rifle in a carrying case. He named the lake where he'd be tomorrow.

"I'm here for the gun show," I said.

"That's real popular," he said. And he said I was smart to go, because ammo was in short supply, but they might have some at the show.

Another gun show for me, and for a better reason than just gawking, though gawking was my usual pastime. Gun laws were in the news, because six weeks before, on December 14, 2012, at Sandy Hook Elementary School in Newtown, Connecticut, a heavily armed twenty-year-old named Adam Lanza had murdered twenty children and six teachers with an assault rifle before shooting himself in the head. When the mayhem ended, it was discovered that he'd killed his mother that same morning before leaving home. He had used his mother's guns, and it was she who had taught him to shoot — an odd choice of skill for a mother to impart to a child who was troubled, solitary, withdrawn, hated to be touched, perhaps delusional, subject to explosive fits of temper, and housebound. Knowing that her son was borderline insane, she gave him a gun.

One of the deadliest episodes by a solitary shooter in US history, the Sandy Hook school killings had reopened the gun debate in Congress and caused a rash of assault rifle purchases. The news was that, far from discouraging the buying of guns and ammo, the condemnation of weapons had created a panic among gun owners and potential buyers. So many guns and so much ammo were bought in the aftermath that the rumor had gone around (as the hunter at the motel had told me) that there was a national shortage, especially of Bushmaster assault rifles, like Adam Lanza's, and supplies of the .223-caliber ammo that went with them.

The Tri-Lake Gun and Knife Show, the weekend event at the South-aven Arena, was the boast of the town. It was similar to the other gun shows I'd seen, and the arena also resembled many of the larger churches I'd passed on Sundays in the South, the same three or four acres of parked cars, the same industrial, church-like building resembling a warehouse topped with a steeple, a thousand unwavering believers inside, and a friendly buzz of welcome.

The Southaven crowd was orderly, pacing among the hundreds of tables that were stacked with rifles, handguns, and knives. Other tables stocked miscellaneous items: Tasers, leather goods, and signs such as *Because of the Cost of Ammo There Will Be No Warning Shot — No Trespassing*.

Almost the first voice I heard was that of a man, bouncing with anger beside his table, ranting about the school shooting.

He was saying, "If someone had had a weapon, they could have stopped him! Teachers should have been armed."

Because I had seen that gun shows were attended by well-armed, well-behaved people, any show of excitement drew a crowd, and this man had attracted listeners and a chorus of murmurers.

One man: "Schools should have marshals as a regular thing."

Another man: "Bet your life."

A third: "They weren't prepared."

Most of the men were wearing a sidearm, but conforming to gun show regulations, they were empty of any magazine and the firing mechanism was secured with a plastic zip tie.

This was my third gun show, and I now realized that in spite of the improvisational, flea-market appearance, there was a pattern that repeated in each show: the tables of rare and elegant guns — engraved shotguns, fowling pieces, dueling pistols; the back tables piled with old handguns; the array of assault rifles; the sign sellers, knife sellers, and Nazi memorabilia sellers; the purveyors of army surplus — old canteens, belts, mess kits, gas masks, trenching tools; the specialists in ammo clips, many of them the thick, curving, high-capacity thirty-shot magazines that were illegal in most states. And there were the automatics, the simplest and meanest of which was the AK-47, essentially a machine gun, something you might need if you were waging war or taking out a detachment of Taliban fighters.

But the AKs I'd seen three months before for $1,500 cost almost $2,000 here — the same gun. I remarked on this to the dealer.

"It's because of Obama," he said. "See this baby?" He lifted a plastic assault rifle and handed it to me. "This used to be two hundred bucks. After the ban it went up to five hundred. All this talk about the school shooting, it's fixing to go higher. It'll be a thousand 'fore you know it."

The interest was intense, gun-show-goers shuffling from table to table, remarking on the qualities of the weapons: "That's the limited edition," "That thing's air-cooled," "Look at the engraving on that little beauty," "That's the broomhandle Luger — sweet." They clearly loved looking at the guns on view, but not many people were buying. The parking lot of the Southaven Arena would have given the reason for slow sales. It was filled with old pickup trucks, muddy cars, and dented SUVs, and the shuffling people — men mostly — were poorly dressed country people, garage mechanics with black-rimmed fingernails, farmers in bib overalls and feed store caps or in hunter's camouflage. There was a smattering of well-turned-out men, more eager buyers than the others, perhaps looking to pick up the newest Sig Sauer 9-millimeter beavertail, which was also in Adam Lanza's — or his mother's — arsenal of weapons.

A man standing behind his stall of Civil War percussion pistols was talking loudly into his cell phone as he surveyed the crowd: "Jes' walkin' around, lots of people, no spending."

I walked from table to table, reminded again of the extreme courtesy and politeness that prevailed at gun shows. A zapping noise from an adjacent table got my attention. Two black men — the only black men in the huge hall of perhaps a thousand people — were demonstrating Tasers and stun guns, one of them holding a Taser in each hand and squeezing off a cluster of bright blue electric shocks between them.

I talked with them for a while. Business was poor, they said, but it would pick up later.

"Those are illegal in Massachusetts," I said.

"But you're not in Massachusetts now," one of the men said, working a Taser, shooting sparks. "So maybe time to pick up a few. Give some to your friends." *Zap, zap.* "Check out that voltage. That would knock down a big dude."

"My name's Paul," I said.

"Matisse," the man said, and before I could comment, he added, "Yes, like the painter."

These Tasers and stun guns were made in China, they said, which was why they were so cheap. And unlike the gun sellers, most of whom were local, these men, from Jackson, Mississippi, went from gun show to gun show, peddling what they called "products for personal protection."

"There's a show every week or so."

I said, "Excuse me, but I don't see any other black people here."

"Black people don't sell their guns," Matisse said, laughing softly.

"'Deed they don't," the other man added.

The tables at the back were stacked with old weapons and manned by eager-to-bargain young men, but in the center of the hall and up front were the larger concessions of bona fide dealers, supervising the filling-out of paperwork for registering their guns.

I tried to purchase a gun from one of these dealers and my request was politely declined: "If you're from out of state, I can't sell you a handgun."

But at the back tables the young men hung on. "This Glock is in good shape. I've fired it myself. Three hundred and it's yours. Okay, two seventy-five, and I'll throw in an extra mag and a box of shells."

"I'm from out of state," I said, to let him down gently.

"Private sale. This is for personal protection. Make me an offer."

I went to one of the many tables stacked with ammo, surrounded by a dozen men, and got into line.

"I hear there's a shortage," I said to the man in front of me wearing a camo jacket.

"Hell, I got enough ammo to last me until the next Civil War," he said.

I said to the dealer, "I'm interested in hearing about the ammo that's scarce."

He didn't hesitate. "No twenty-two long rifle. No two-two-three. I'm low on nine-millimeter. People probably hoarding. But I got everything else. What do you want?"

"I'm just asking."

"If you're not buying, do me a favor and step aside, sir."

In the prevailing politeness and good humor of a gun show, his stern tone was like naked aggression.

"The Democrats are scared," one stallholder was saying a few tables over, standing in front of his array of handguns. "They'll back down or else there won't be a Democrat in the whole of Washington. They blame the guns!"

"It sure ain't the guns," another man said.

"A guy on parole gets a gun and kills someone," this dealer said, "and they blame the gun dealers! Why not look at the whole foolish parole system? They're penalizing the wrong people. The mental health lobby is even worse—they blame the gun people too! They're scaring Americans and putting the prices up."

"People are buying guns that never wanted no guns!" the other man said. "They're buying guns because they think it'll be impossible in the future to own a firearm, and now it's all panic buying. Where will it end?"

It was a bazaar, and like any bazaar it was also a social occasion, with men swapping stories over paper plates heaped with cheese fries. Some stalls sold T-shirts, others raffle tickets, and one was operated by gun rights advocates, soliciting signatures and offering to explain the fine print in state gun laws.

The tribal air of like-mindedness, which was also an air of grievance, was something I'd seen at other gun shows: the defiance of people who care less about shooting guns than owning them, and indignant that their rights are being threatened—more change in a region that hates change, and among people who have had to accept changes, and now the federal government coming after them again.

Yet I loved being at the gun show for what it said of the South. I was a stranger here, I didn't know a soul, and so it was a relief to step inside this building and be welcomed among so many people. I could have struck up a conversation with any of them, because it was assumed we were all in agreement on guns, and therefore in agreement on everything else—politics, war, religion, hunting, child rearing, food choices, TV shows. In that way it resembled a large, hospitable church. For a traveler, this meant a great deal. I was not there to challenge them in their beliefs but only to watch and listen.

At the Southaven gun show I saw how white Southerners needed to gather, to remind themselves who they were and what they stood for, how in the tribalism and monotony of their beliefs and the convulsions of their history they felt compelled to affirm that they were not like other Americans. They were more social than people I grew up with in the North, and families — fractured as they were — mattered more than the community. The whites felt like a despised minority — different, defeated, misunderstood, meddled with, pushed around, cheated. Blood mattered, so did history and old grievances and perceived injustices — all the themes of Faulkner, who grew up near here, in Oxford, Lafayette County.

I decided to drive there.

Rowan Oak

Oxford, where Faulkner had lived and died, was the university town of Ole Miss, just an hour's ride from Southaven, twenty-five miles east of Interstate 55. Off well-traveled Route 278, the town vibrated with the rush of distant traffic. There is hardly a corner of this otherwise pleasant place where the whine of cars is absent, and it is a low hum at Rowan Oak, the house of William Faulkner, which lies at the periphery of the campus and its vividly pompous splendors.

The road noise struck an odd and intrusive note because, though Oxford is "Jefferson" in Faulkner's work, the town and its surroundings are in all respects as remote from Faulkner's folksy, bosky, strife-ridden, plot-saturated, and fictional Yoknapatawpha County as it is possible to be. Oxford is unexpectedly mild and lovely, and though everything standing near this busy highway tingles in the continual hum of passing road traffic, the university is classically beautiful in the Greek Revival Southern style, of columns and bricks and domes, evoking a mood both genteel and scholarly, and backward-looking.

And for a century this esteemed place of learning clung to the old ways, segregation and bigotry among them, overwhelming any liberal tendencies. So here is an irony, one of the many in the Faulkner biography, odder than this self-described farmer's living on a side street in a fraternity-mad, football-crazed college town.

Faulkner, one of our greatest writers and subtlest thinkers — a shy man but a bold, opinionated literary genius with an encyclopedic grasp of Southern history, impossible to ignore for anyone traveling the South — lived his whole life at the center of this racially divided community without once suggesting aloud, in his wise voice, in a town he was proud to call his own, that a black student had an immediate right to study at the university. All in good time was his view. The Nobel Prize winner stood by as blacks were shooed off the campus, admitted as menials only through the back door and, when their work was done, told to go away. Faulkner died in July 1962. Two months later, after a protracted legal fuss (and deadly riots afterward), and no thanks to Faulkner, James Meredith, from the small central Mississippi town of Kosciusko, was admitted as the University of Mississippi's first black student.*

Half a dozen years before the James Meredith showdown, Faulkner had written in *Harper's Magazine,* "To live anywhere in the world today and be against equality because of race or color is like living in Alaska and being against snow." The racism he saw over the admission of Autherine Lucy to the University of Alabama he regarded as "a sad commentary on human nature." Yet he asked for a gradual approach to integration, and as he wrote in *Life* magazine, he was against militant integrationists or the interference of the federal government — "forces outside the South that would use legal or police compulsion to eradicate that evil overnight." We'll do it ourselves, when we want to, was his approach, but nothing happened until the federal government — the South's historical villain — intervened and Meredith was escorted onto the campus by US marshals.

Faulkner's 1844 house is a little older than the famed Lyceum, the university's oldest building. The beauty of the campus, the harmony of its architecture, was a surprise to me. And its newness too: it's a mid-nineteenth-century university that did not have a large student body, or many buildings, until the turn of the twentieth century, about the time the Faulkner family moved there in 1902 from New Albany, Mississippi, when little Billy was turning five.

---

* And a life-sized bronze statue of James Meredith was erected on campus, depicting him striding forward. On February 16, 2014, a few months after I visited Ole Miss, three white students vandalized the statue, hanging a noose around the neck of the figure and draping it in an old Confederate battle flag from Georgia. Meredith made a characteristically temperate comment about the incident, but in an interview with the *New York Times* he spoke disapprovingly of the very existence of the statue: "It's a false idol, and it's an insult not only to God, it's an insult to me."

Restless when he was not writing, always in need of money, Faulkner traveled throughout his life. But Oxford remained his home, and Rowan Oak his house, even when (it seems) a neighborhood grew up around the big, ill-proportioned farmhouse ("the Bailey Place"). He renamed it Rowan Oak for the powers of the wood of the rowan tree, as the docents at the house helpfully explained to me. The first owner and builder of the house was Robert Shegogg — the odd name, slightly altered, recurs in *The Sound and the Fury,* where Reverend Shegog is a black preacher from St. Louis, whose robust sermon makes Dilsey cry.

The house lies at the end of a suburban street, and this street — orderly, bourgeois, well tended, tidy, conventional — is everything Faulkner's fiction is not, and is at odds with Faulkner's posturing as a country squire. On this road of smug homes Rowan Oak rises lopsidedly, like a relic if not a white elephant, with porches and white columns, windows framed by dark shutters, and stands of old, lovely juniper trees. The remnants of a formal garden are visible under the trees at the front — but just the symmetrical brickwork of flower-bed borders and walkways showing on the surface of the ground, like the remains of a neglected Neolithic site.

Faulkner was anchored by Oxford but lived a chaotic life; the surprising thing to me is that from this messy, lurching existence, which combined the asceticism of concentrated writing with the distractions of binge drinking and passionate infidelities, he produced an enormous body of work, a number of literary masterpieces, some near-misses, and a great deal of garble. He was no scholar, he was self-made, and — Mark Twain aside — no Southern writer of his stature preceded him.

The rooms at Rowan Oak were austerely furnished, with a number of ordinary paintings and simple knickknacks, a dusty piano, the typewriter, and the weird novelty of notes, puzzling out the plot of *A Fable,* written by him on the wall of an upstairs room. Notes to clarify the multilayered if not muddled plot for Faulkner was a good idea, and would serve a reader too. Nothing to me would be more useful than handwriting on a wall, explaining the plot, as a fixture for readers of Faulkner's novels. Baffled by seven pages of meandering prose, you glance at the wall and see: "Charles is the son of Eulalia Bon and Thomas Sutpen, born in the West Indies, but Sutpen hadn't realized Eulalia was of mixed race, until too late . . ."

"We'll be closing soon," the docent warned me.

I went outside, looked at the brick outbuildings, sheds, and the stable, and lingered in the plainness of the yard among the long shadows of the junipers in the slant of the winter sun and the remnants of the formal garden. From where I stood the house was obscured by the trees at the front, yet it had the look of a mausoleum, marked — you might say — by the myriad coruscations of immolation and abnegation and time, or simply peeling and weather-beaten. I was moved to think of Faulkner in those rooms, exhausting himself with work, poisoning himself with drink, driven mad in the contradictions of the South, obstinate in his refusal to simplify or romanticize its history, resolute in mirroring its complexity with such depth and so many human faces — all this before his early death, at the age of sixty-four.

Tupelo Blues

A penetrating melancholy possessed me in the gathering Mississippi darkness. Writers often exaggerate the difficulties of their lives, but Faulkner didn't complain, and in his work he aimed higher than anyone I had ever read. And I had felt, in his house and in his town of Oxford, that there was something fatally stubborn in the man.

It was an hour to Tupelo, and all the way there the words to "Tupelo Blues" were playing in my head — "A dark cloud rolled, way back in Tupelo" — the soft lament of John Lee Hooker (who was born elsewhere in Mississippi), singing of the Tupelo flood. The name of the town comes from the tupelo tree, a black gum tree, known in the North as a pepperidge — a tall, noble one stood at the end of my Cape Cod road, its horizontal branches flung wide apart. My sadness was also the effect of the look of Tupelo at twilight, a large, still-working town surrounded by fast food joints, with the aura of Elvis hanging over it: his two-room house — an improved shack, really — built by his father; the church where he sang gospel.

The mood of the South is powerful and the weight of its history is palpable in people's faces, their postures, their clothes, the houses and shacks, the look of abandonment. You wonder, after all that has gone before, what's going to happen next. Impossible to travel through the South and not ask: Who will inherit this land and its conflicts?

I chose a small motel at random after dark, intending to look at the town more leisurely in the morning, Elvis's Tupelo — the house just outside of town. No sooner had I stepped inside the motel lobby than I recognized the aromas of the New South, that whiff of Hindustan, the eye-tickle and nose-buzz of smoking joss sticks, a reek of burnt sugar and scorched onions, the tang of bubbling curry, odors undreamed-of by Faulkner or Elvis.

The manager appeared and squinted as if to underline the thought: I am inevitable. Whom else were you expecting?

"Single room, one night, nonsmoking," I said.

He licked his thumb and pushed pages with it. "I will see what I have available."

"Thank you, Mr. Patel."

He smiled. "How you are knowing my name?"

Bluegrass

That there were no direct roads from Tupelo across the state line to Huntsville, and only a zigzag route on narrow roads after that, was a blessing. All that slow country way I listened to bluegrass on the radio, *Front Porch Fellowship* in Mississippi, then "bluegrass gospel." Under January skies clotted with clouds, down the empty road, the easy talk and spirited music of East Tennessee radio, "Clinch River Breakdown," the bluegrass specials, the Hill Benders, fiddles and banjos, "neighbors," "salvation," and the repeated assurance "You gonna be all right."

Over to Chattanooga, up to Knoxville, and past Bristol, the way I'd come on my first trip. It was chilly in East Tennessee. Light snow began to fall, and after that, fat icicles and frozen drip hung or bulged from the roadside cliffs, flurries farther on, deep snow in Virginia, and all along the Appalachians cold and snowy hills, sleet blowing on the road, poor visibility, into the blur of winter again, northward.

INTERLUDE

❧

The Paradoxes of Faulkner

The memory of my visit to Rowan Oak stayed with me, and in the time I spent preparing for my next drive to the Deep South, I reread Faulkner. I contemplated his life, which was one of paradoxes, a certain amount of posturing, and many secrets. He was undoubtedly a writer of genius; he was also a writer of flapdoodle and a successful Hollywood screenwriter. His education was sketchy, yet he was immensely learned in the oblique and selective way of someone self-taught. He seemed to come from nowhere, but he put his Nowhere on the map. That's what I mean by his paradoxes.

"Once you have counted James Branch Cabell," H. L. Mencken wrote in 1917 in "The Sahara of the Bozart," a broad mocking piece about the philistinism of the South, "you will not find a single Southern prose writer who can actually write." Mencken regarded the South as the bunghole of America, a cesspool of Baptists, a miasma of Methodism, snake charmers, real estate operators, and syphilitic evangelists. And an artless place, to boot. "Georgia is at once the home of the cotton-mill sweater, of the Methodist parson turned Savonarola and of the lynching bee," he writes with contempt. And again, "The most booming sort of piety, in the South, is not incompatible with the theory that lynching is a benign institution. Two generations ago it was not incompatible with an ardent belief in slavery."

Perhaps provoked by this spleen, thirteen years after Mencken's essay appeared, Faulkner sent Mencken himself a short story, which (heavily edited by Mencken) appeared in his magazine, the *American Mercury,* as "That Evening Sun," in 1931. In the meantime, Faulkner had published his first novel, *Sartoris,* and he kept writing until he died, defying Mencken by turning Southern literature into a peculiar art form, and hallowing through fiction the particularities of Southern life. He is the writer all aspiring American writers are encouraged to read, yet with his complex and speechifying prose he is the worst possible model for a young writer. He is someone you have to learn how to read, not someone anyone should dare imitate, though unfortunately many do.

My introduction to Faulkner — the book most students read first — was *The Sound and the Fury*. Confused by its multiple narrators, one a thirty-three-year-old idiot struggling to make noises, and by the tangled Compson family history, I became lost in it but discovered much to love. I was still young enough to see its excesses and flourishes as triumphs rather than faults. I would come to a sentence such as this, of Dilsey weeping at Reverend Shegog's church service: "Two tears slid down her fallen cheeks, in and out of the myriad coruscations of immolation and abnegation and time," and I did not dare to say this was ridiculous and purple.

Faulkner taught himself how to write and wished to be distinguished by his excesses and his obscurities. It's clear from his prose and the structure of his narratives that his literary inspiration came less from books than from the talkers he'd known in his early life — his writing often has the endless ear-bending yak-yak of monologues over cracker barrels, or that preacher's thump of damnation from the pulpit. In Wyndham Lewis's crisp denunciation, Faulkner was "the moralist with a corn cob." You might agree when Faulkner delivers such judgments as, "People need trouble — a little frustration to sharpen the spirit on, toughen it. Artists do; I don't mean you need to live in a rat hole or gutter, but you have to learn fortitude, endurance. Only vegetables are happy."

Often, amid the cadenzas and the phantasmagoria that he makes of the South, there is a passage of pure brilliance, such as this: "the first seconds of fall always seem like soar: a weightless deliberation preliminary to a rush not downward but upward, the falling body reversed during that second by transubstantiation into the upward rush of earth." The trouble is that these lovely lines are buried in one rolling six-thousand-word sentence in the "Jail" section of *Requiem for a Nun* that continues breathlessly for almost forty pages. It's "like farting 'Annie Laurie' through a keyhole," as Gulley Jimson remarks in *The Horse's Mouth*. "It may be clever but is it worth the trouble?"

FAULKNER KNEW FIRSTHAND how the marvelous self-deceiving paradox of falling seemed like flight. Still in his teens, he signed on as a pilot in the Royal Air Force, intending to fly in the First World War, though he was disappointed that he didn't see any action. Later on, in 1933, when he had the money, he bought his own airplane, a Waco-210 monoplane, quite a boast for anyone in Mississippi, or elsewhere for that matter.

He was full of surprises, living overlapping lives that were various and contradictory: dependable highly paid screenwriter, innovative poorly paid fiction writer, supporter of a large extended family, part-time fox hunter, occasional binge drinker, fantasist and sometimes fop (hunting pinks, top hat, white gloves, shiny boots). It is part of his legend that he failed as a student at Ole Miss, failed as a postal clerk, and worked briefly and unwillingly at the Ole Miss power plant. But all that time he was writing, first poetry, then *As I Lay Dying,* among the boilers of the power plant.

It is a measure of how well Faulkner knew the mind of rural Southerners that people who have never read him are able to paraphrase his sentiments. They may not have known his stories, but many people I met were living his narratives and could easily have fitted themselves into his fictions. Reverend Lyles had the dignity and defiance of Lucas Beauchamp; Robin Scott, the valiant mother I met in Natchez, was the granddaughter of another Joe Christmas; the Snopeses are still scheming everywhere in the rural Deep South.

Though it's hard to find many people outside a university English department who read him for pleasure, some of Faulkner's South still exists, not on the land but as a racial memory. Early in his writing life he set himself a mammoth task: to create the fictional world of an archetypical Mississippi county where everything happened; to explain to Southerners who they were and where they'd come from. Where they were going didn't matter much to Faulkner. Go slowly, urged Faulkner, always the gradualist.

He gave Southerners heroes and villains and good ole boys; he added names and histories to Southern stereotypes: the Major, the Colonel, the Lawyer, the Landowner, the Preacher, the Runaway, the Alien, the Jailbird, the Criminal, the Meddler, the Interloper. And he differentiated among the Indians and the categories of blacks, all sorts — the mixed-race characters in *Absolom, Absolom!* and *Light in August,* upright and falsely accused black Lucas Beauchamp in *Intruder in the Dust,* the enduring housekeeper Dilsey ("I seed the first en de last"), the field hands, and the ambiguous accomplices: Levi "Too Tight" Collins, the black laborer who helped dispose of Emmett Till's corpse, is Faulknerian right down to his name. Faulkner's most memorable characters are his villains, Popeye in *Sanctuary*, the Tall Convict in "The Old Man," and all the Snopeses, especially the wicked and wily Flem Snopes, who succeeds as the ideal of a Snopes, set forth (in *The Mansion*) in the words of his cousin Montgomery Ward Snopes: "All right ... every Snopes will make it his private and personal aim to have the whole world recognize him as THE son of a bitch's son of a bitch."

Faulkner's lurid narratives ("A Rose for Emily," *Sanctuary*) were his most commercially successful. My favorites remain *Light in August, As I Lay Dying*, the stories in *Go Down, Moses* (especially "The Bear"), *The Wild Palms, Sanctuary*, and the Snopes trilogy: *The Hamlet, The Town, The Mansion*. I reread them for this Southern trip, and still admire them, and though they still seem like textbooks from my college dorm room, they have lasting value.

Ralph Ellison, the author of *Invisible Man*, once said, "If you want to know something about the dynamics of the South, of interpersonal relationships in the South from, roughly, 1874 until today, you don't go to historians; not even to Negro historians. You go to William Faulkner and Robert Penn Warren."

But Warren, like Ellison and many Southern writers (Mark Twain, Thomas Wolfe, William Styron, Willie Morris, Truman Capote, Tennessee Williams, Carson McCullers, Richard Wright, and others), fled the South for the glory and the hospitality and praise and full employment in the North: Warren in New Haven, Ellison in New York. In *North Toward Home*, Willie Morris writes, artlessly but to the point, "Why was it, in moments just before I leave the South, did I always feel some easing of a great burden? It was as if someone had taken some terrible weight off my shoulders, or as if some old grievance had suddenly fallen away."

"You go north. You became expatriated, exiled," says a character in Styron's *Lie Down in Darkness*, "yearning to repudiate the wrong you've grown up with."

A *Paris Review* interviewer asked Barry Hannah, writer of wild stories and inspired novels, why so many Southern writers "have felt this need to leave." Hannah replied, "They have indeed, and they write their best Southern fiction when they're in Vermont."

Hannah eventually came to rest in Mississippi, where he was born. He ended up in Oxford, like Faulkner, who stayed put in the town where he'd grown up, obsessed with remaining a provincial. His characters are of the same mind—determined to remain in the South, not inward-looking but backward-looking and embattled, resigned to their fate. In their stubborn provinciality (and you could say the same about Faulkner) they cannot imagine a life elsewhere.

Something about his isolation and inwardness must have contributed to Faulkner's prose style; perhaps a twitch of his compulsiveness as a binge drinker is indicated, too, in his garrulous and tipsy and tumbling narration. But if at first glance he seems slapdash, even careless, piling on the effects, on reflection you may conclude that he wrote this way because at bottom he knew he had a scheme he wished to disguise. Self-conscious about formality, he hung his verbosity on a superstructure that was rigid and socially sound, on families and people whose background he knew intimately, determined to write a novel without a center, a text that radiated outward. He was old-fashioned in the way he lived, but as a writer he was a modernist. As for his "eye-blinding, mind-stunning" modernism, which took the form of incantations, the English critic V. S. Pritchett once wrote, "Faulkner clutches at every sight and suggestion with the avidity of suspicion and even mania, and all manias create monotony."

Faulkner insisted on how different Southerners are from the rest of Americans; it is a belief that many Southerners cling to, and it explains Faulkner's appeal. His fiction is an elaboration of this difference, which is also insisted upon by Flannery O'Connor in her forceful but self-serving essay "The Regional Writer." Southern identity is not a matter of local color, quaintness, biscuits, white columns, dusty roads, and so forth. "It lies very deep. In its entirety, it is known only to God, but of those who look for it, none gets so close as the artist." This is a spirited explanation for the peculiar detail of Faulkner's fiction, and her own.

But what of the eye-blinding mannerisms? "The artist, journalist, or historian who ponders the South for a living," the distinguished Southern journalist Edwin Yoder writes in his foreword to John Shelton Reed's *The Enduring South*, "must at times be haunted, as I am, by the fear that the regional 'differences' he traffics in are essentially obscurantist when you get down to it: elegantly so, it may be, but obscurantist all the same."

This deflecting, shrouding manner is often employed when a writer (Joyce in *Ulysses* is a good example) suspects that his work suffers from an excess of design; the oratory and hyperbole and special effects are ways of distracting from the big plan. But Faulkner was a genuine homegrown experimenter in language and narrative form. It must have taken courage to write like this in the narrow and disapproving world of literary Mississippi, and it also explains why all his books were out of print when Malcolm Cowley discovered the figure in the carpet, and guided readers back to the man's grand design with his *Portable Faulkner* (1946). That anthology showed that all along Faulkner knew what he was doing, and he went so far as to provide Cowley with a detailed map of his imaginary Yoknapatawpha County, its landmarks and its citizens.

SO MUCH FOR the contradictions in his fiction. Another paradox looms. It is Faulkner the Hollywood screenwriter, the go-to scenarist for the director Howard Hawks. As a fiction writer, Faulkner was uncompromising—look at the tangled prose on any of his pages and you have to conclude it was printed as it was typed out on the manual typewriter on view at Rowan Oak. His manuscripts would have been a copy editor's nightmare had his publisher not sent a memo saying that not a word, punctuation mark, or lengthy italicized passage was to be changed. A six-thousand-word sentence? Leave it as is was Faulkner's wish. Keep the semicolons and the neologisms, make it more opaque, bury the message, cloud it with hyperbole, obscure the speaker, force the reader to solve the puzzle.

That sort of obliquity, beloved of English departments, is unacceptable in Hollywood, where the rewrite is constant, collaboration is the rule for writers, tradition is the method, whoring is the necessity, and easy money is the objective. Not a natural fit for the likes of Faulkner, and yet—medicating himself with booze—he thrived there, was well paid, and was much in demand. Many brilliant writers in the thirties, forties, and fifties found work in Hollywood—Aldous Huxley, James Agee, John Steinbeck, John Collier, F. Scott Fitzgerald, Lillian Hellman, Dorothy Parker, Nathanael West—yet even the most earnest moviegoer would find it hard to name a film written by any of those writers. But Faulkner was serious and successful, and his scripts—for *The Big Sleep, To Have and Have Not, Land of the Pharaohs,* and *The Left Hand of God*—are well known. His commitment to the work is clear when you discover that he wrote the last two movies in that list after he won the 1949 Nobel Prize in literature.

Scriptwriting is drudgery, a massive insult to the brain of a person who cares about the nuances of language; it is no more literary than elaborating a recipe for clam chowder. I have written nine screenplays (God forgive me these chronicles of wasted time), and anyone who has written one knows the tedium of such a task, the inexact science of the script, the approximation of description and Byzantine camera angles, the baroque technicalities of shooting, the frustration of dealing with a team of bullying know-it-alls and domineering money men and often the trickiest actors in the bleak land of the Philistines.

And that is not the worst of the awful craft, which is the epitome of the rejection business. The hack aspect of it is that it is a long experience of compromise, the antithesis of great (and especially Faulknerian) fiction writing. It is a study in strict time limits and the attention span of the dimmest moviegoer, negotiation, teamwork, script conferences, let's-try-it-another-way, multiple versions, rewrites, second-guessing, and deliberate vulgarity, all in the aid of pleasing the moviegoing public and of getting bums on seats. Never again for me. How did Faulkner stand it?

Faulkner and his many biographers claimed that he wrote scripts to make money, but can he have been so hard-up? His Nobel Prize was $30,000, a large sum at the time, yet he continued to write scripts after he was flush with that windfall. As his fiction demonstrates, he was adept at writing dialogue, so that part of his Hollywood experience would have been easy money. But Faulkner is on the record as saying that he did not enjoy going to movies, especially his own.

There is a further and more devastating awfulness. As all scriptwriters know, many scripts are exercises in pure futility. The first draft is written, a rewrite is ordered, other writers are summoned to doctor the thing, script conferences are called for, and after all this work, time, compromise, argument, and editing, the project is put in turnaround, or shelved, or killed outright. An utter waste of time and brain power.

Faulkner must have known a good deal of this humiliation. And that is perhaps why, though we have *The Last Tycoon*, *The Day of the Locust*, and other vivid novels of Hollywood, Faulkner — who worked as a screenwriter for more than twenty years, who knew directors intimately and many actors (Bogart and Bacall, for example) — never wrote a word of fiction about the place and never mentioned it except in grumpy letters. And he worked longer in Hollywood and knew it better than his screenwriting contemporaries Scott Fitzgerald and Nathanael West, who wrote those novels.

Given the stark difference between the order, blandness, and strict chronology of a movie script, and the apparent disorder, florid description, and disjunction in time of Faulkner's books, it is worth considering that his experimental fiction was a reaction to the discipline of his scriptwriting — that it was an acting out of an impulse of "manic defense."

This combative-sounding psychological term, coined by Freud's pupil Melanie Klein, elaborates on Freudian theory to explain a form of evasion. "By adopting a triumphantly scornful attitude toward psychic reality, the patient uses this kind of defense to avoid the depression associated with the conviction of having destroyed an internal object." A scriptwriter, subjected to all sorts of idiot opinions, brusque readings, and demands for rewrites, might, in private time, on a personal project, write a sixty-page sentence with arbitrary punctuation as a form of assertion — or so it seemed to me, on the basis of my course in Psychology 101. "Manic defenses are typified by three feelings, namely control, triumph, contempt."

Hollywood for Faulkner was also an escape from the tension in Rowan Oak, his fractious marriage, and the provincialism in Mississippi, and it gave him opportunities — as it has so many others — to indulge his libido. Faulkner may have been reserved in public, but he was privately passionate. Of the howlers associated with the authorized, two-volume, 2,100-page biography by Joseph Blotner, one is the omission of Faulkner's extramarital love affairs (several of them crucial to his literary work), and another is the circumspect treatment of his adulteries. Yet that biography is fastidious in the inclusion of such irrelevant details as dinner menus and the names of Little League baseball players Faulkner had casually met.

His paradoxes aside, Faulkner remains original and indispensable. No other region in America had a writer who was blessed with such a vision. Sinclair Lewis defined the upper Midwest and showed us who we were in *Main Street* and *Elmer Gantry,* but he moved on to other places and other subjects. Faulkner stayed put, he achieved greatness, but as a writer, as a man, as a husband, as a delineator of the South's arcane formalities and its lawlessness, his was a life of suffering.

"To understand the world, you must first understand a place like Mississippi," he said. And one of his wisest characters, Ike McCaslin (in "The Bear" in *Go Down, Moses*), seems to speak for him when he cries out to the black stranger, "Don't you see? This whole land, the whole South, is cursed, and all of us who derive from it, whom it ever suckled, white and black both, lie under the curse? Granted that my people brought the curse onto the land: maybe for that reason their descendants alone can — not resist it, not combat it — maybe just endure and outlast it until the curse is lifted."

PART THREE

Spring: Redbud in Bloom

Tiny things take on significance when I'm
away from home. I'm on the alert for omens.
Odd things happen when you get out of town.

—CHARLES PORTIS, *The Dog of the South*

Mud Season

In the misleading twinkle of early spring, an afterglow of sun-struck afternoon drizzle ("I shine in tears like the sun in April"), the mud around my house was just another illusion of the season, a sodden surface of squashy soil and puddled lawn; and in the woods, with its tweedy gradations of brown and the same tweedy itch, the only hints of green were the bristling elbows of cedar boughs and the wicked needles of pitch pines; and on the woodland floor, a clutter of rain-blackened leaves. Beneath it all, and a few inches under the slab of blobbed and gummy mud, was a substratum of frost left over from winter.

This leakproof layer of ice kept the water – the new melt, the recent showers – from draining away. It was the month of dirty hands and spattered pant cuffs and wet shoes, of deep footprints in the dark green grass that brimmed with muddy water, of that teasing sparkle on some days and raw wind on cold ones, with mornings of heavy dew, sometimes a stammer of warmth and the slow drip that suggested a faint pulse, the swelling of life and the setting in of the annual thaw.

Mud season. The world was softened by the dribble of dampness, the soaked granite boulders of the garden wall shining, the lawn like a hog wallow, and troughs of wheel tracks along the unpaved driveway. Walking across the bare ground was like tramping through a shelf of chocolate cake, sinking into the fudge and gunk thickened by standing water. Some of the trunks of doomed saplings were whitish and peeled, some teeth marks visible, the edible bark having been gnawed by hungry voles, starved in the winter snow. Tiny, almost imperceptible buds had begun to sharpen on twiggy branch ends.

Spring was also a prism of damp smells radiating in a rainbow of aromas, and there was hope in those exhalations of spring – a change from the unreality of odorless, nose-pinching winter cold. Rising from the mud was the tobacco blast of old leaf mulch, the sour honk of saturated earth, the prickle of evergreens, the sweet breath of damp grass, and in places wisps of dusty vapor rising from wrinkled seams in the warmed dirt. The tang of these sensations directed my attention downward to the nub of sprouting bulbs, smooth and hopeful, some tulips like inch-high knuckles, the bird beaks of crocuses, the fiddleheads of ferns, the thin green slips of irises, others with sharpened tips, onion domes of new lilies putting out tapers, all of it climbing from the slick and crumbly mud.

Leaving footprints in the soggy lawn, I tramped to my car, slung my gear in the back, and drove 580 miles to Fredericksburg, Virginia. There I slept soundly. I woke and drove 450 miles more, where I left the superslab of the interstate. I rode slowly down a side road through the sunshine and the dogwoods and azaleas, and the redbud just starting to bloom, to the town of Aiken, South Carolina.

Steeplechase in Aiken

"Here for the steeplechase, sir?" the woman at the Hotel Aiken asked me at the front desk. Her name was Amanda. The hotel was old-fashioned and roomy, unfussy and comfortable, with the smug solid ordinariness of an English coaching inn, on the main street, which itself resembled a high road in an English market town, shop fronts squared against the wide sidewalks, and the whole tidy community in great shape — thriving, or so it seemed.

"Oh, right, the steeplechase," I said, a beat too late, because that was not the whole truth.

I was in Aiken for its contradictions. Many towns in the Deep South are full of oddities and ironies, but Aiken had more than most, and there was another merit to the town: it was not seedy, it was bursting with life, a very pretty and spirited place, and especially welcoming on this festive weekend.

"I have a single room for you," Amanda said, her finger on a page of her reservations book. She gave me a frank stare, a faint smile floating at her lips. "But I have to warn you that you won't get any sleep. We have two bars and a live band, and it's going to be real noisy. Everyone's going to be partying, and most of them will be drunk, and we won't close up until about two a.m. Unless you're a drinker too."

"I'm not much of a drinker." And I thought: God, I hate the word "partying."

"This here's the biggest weekend of the year, people coming from miles around for the steeplechase. The horse people, the race people, the rich people, the college kids – oh, yeah, the gamblers, the hat people. And they all like a real good time."

"The 'hat people'?"

"There's a kind of informal competition. 'Best hat.'" She was nodding with certainty and slipped into a heavy drawl, with the self-conscious jocularity Southerners sometimes use with outsiders in an effort to be persuasive. "Ah mo tell you somethin'. It gon' to be real loud here, so if y'all want a good night's sleep, y'all go somewhere else."

I thanked her, left the Hotel Aiken, drove to the edge of town to the Days Inn. There I was checked in by the owner, who said there was a complimentary breakfast (I knew in advance it would be Froot Loops in a Styrofoam bowl) and introduced himself as Mike.

"Mike?" I said in a querying, clarifying tone.

"Mike Patel."

Solicitous, deferential, helpful, anxious to please, in a ball cap and a bum-freezer, the inevitable Mr. Patel.

Aiken was the complete Southern town, and though it was of modest size, it was in character larger than life and had a number of claims on my attention. Its outskirts were radioactive, as I had discovered on my last ride down Atomic Road, which passes a few miles southwest of it, on the river. Aiken's big houses – some of them manor houses – were lovely and well maintained, and the main part of the town was laid out on symmetrical broad boulevards. Aiken was Southern in its disparities: mansions on the boulevards here at the center, shacks on the notorious streets at the periphery, and racetracks, polo fields, the occasional gun show at the fairgrounds, and this week the Imperial Cup Steeplechase.

On my autumn trip I'd seen that Aiken was the nearest town to the nuclear plant, the Savannah River Site, and to the deceptively rustic, radiation-soaked banks of that river. (You need lots of water if you're splitting atoms, and there are often messy spills.) Many of the scientists, technicians, and support staff lived in Aiken. I went there out of sheer curiosity, and it couldn't have been a better decision.

This well-proportioned and prosperous-looking town was a horsy place with a history as a winter colony for wealthy visitors from the North, including John ("Jack") Astor IV and his nineteen-year-old wife, Madeleine Force Astor (Jack died on the *Titanic*, Madeleine survived), New Yorkers Charles and Hope Iselin, and later Fred Astaire, who was as keen on breeding racehorses as he was on tap-dancing, and some of whose wife's family lived in Aiken. Many others had left their mark, prettifying the small town with their wealth.

One of the earliest railways in America ran from Aiken to Charleston in 1833, built for hauling cotton bales from the huge plantation near Aiken that was owned by Captain William White Williams. Like many another Southern town, Aiken (the name came later) was a cotton plantation that became a community, a marvelous early example of American urban design. Around 1835, a master plan had been imposed on it, drawn up by a Harvard-trained surveyor, Alfred Dexter, who had fallen in love with a local beauty, Captain Williams's daughter Sara. At his father-in-law's suggestion, Dexter planned a town with streets wide enough to allow cotton wagons to make U-turns easily. As an orderly town with a good climate, Aiken attracted wealthy Northerners, some of them interested in "equestrian living" (as the town advertises its culture today) — horse breeders, riders, polo players, fox hunters.

The "Blessing of the Hounds" took place every Thanksgiving weekend, with solemnity and drinking; the equestrian calendar of Aiken was dense with fox hunts, the winter sport. Some were live hunts, chasing foxes, but most were "drag hunts," the scent of a fox laid with a trailing rag through Hitchcock Woods and nearby fields. The drag-hound pack and mounted hunters chased the foxy odor over obstacles as a test of horsemanship.

The snowbirds and the horse people and the cotton barons had built grand houses, planted gardens, formed clubs, and set out golf courses. This social infrastructure would have been unsupportable without cheap labor in the form of domestic staff, servants, gardeners, field hands, cooks, nannies, and sweepers, the workforce of the underclass that traditionally propped up and helped create the economy and society of the South.

And so Aiken also had—and still has—a substantial black community, a third of the population, at the bottom of the heap in income. In stark contrast to the conspicuous magnificence of Aiken proper, its orderly tree-lined thoroughfares, its substantial houses set in well-tended gardens of trumpet vines and irises and honeysuckle and the local yucca called Spanish bayonet, are the simple, run-down, slab-sided houses of the blacks, enslaved at one time, then segregated, and now simply poor. They endure, living humbly as Aiken's peasantry on potholed roads at the periphery of the town and farther afield in the seedier corners of Aiken County. But everywhere, rich and poor, redbud was in bloom, a froth of purply pink flowers on bare branches.

"I'm going to wear a big old hat I made myself," a young waitress, Rachel, told me that night at a restaurant. "I've been working on it for ages. It's all decorated with ribbons. And a real pretty and colorful dress."

"I got me my new corduroys, I got my beads—these here are from Kenya," Gregory Jefferson told me in the Polo Bar of the Hotel Aiken, where I was loitering. He was stylishly dressed—a dark vest, a flowered shirt, strings of beads around his neck. He laughed when I asked him whether he would have been welcome in this bar when he was younger. "No, man, this was a Jim Crow town," he said. "But it's okay now. You can go anywhere."

He was celebrating at the hotel but was not sure whether he'd be at the steeplechase. He didn't pay much mind to horses, he said.

"You're going to see some amazing clothes tomorrow—yellow pants, green hats, pink shirts," a frat boy named Lyle, wearing a Lambda Chi pin on his blazer, promised me.

This was at the racecourse at sundown, the evening before the steeplechase. Lyle was there with his frat brothers Chance and Brian. The University of South Carolina at Aiken was not far away, and gave the town added prestige, as well as a casual labor force. In the gathering darkness these students were parking attendants at the annual dinner, a formal affair in a big tent near the steeplechase's grandstand.

"Everybody's going to be drunk," Chance said. "When I say everybody, I mean every damn person you see tomorrow is going to be falling down."

"What about the race?" I asked. "The Imperial Cup."

Brian said, "Hey, I was so shitfaced last year I didn't even see a horse."

We stood in the thick, dew-drenched grass, watching the diners getting out of their luxury cars, the men in tuxedos, the women in ball gowns, wearing high heels, tittupping across the turf of the racecourse to the lighted tent.

"Who are these people?" I asked.

They were the most obviously wealthy and best-dressed people I had seen in all my travels in the South, and I had never seen so formal an event on so large a scale in such a provincial place. Perhaps the very provinciality of the remote place was an incentive for these partygoers to assert themselves as socialites. Where do you find elaborate dinners, stiff-collared men, and bejeweled women? Often you find them in the boondocks, where in their finery they are making a statement, the assertion that they are not hicks.

"These are the horse people, the polo people, the real well-to-do people," Lyle said.

"The white people," I said.

"I guess."

Greeting one another, calling out, shaking hands, exchanging kisses, the elite of Aiken and the nearby horse farms filed into the enormous tent, where there was color and light, food and wine and gaiety. This was the annual dinner party for the Imperial Cup Steeplechase, "Blossoms and Bow Ties—a Garden Party Gala." At $120 per person the event drew a select crowd, and because it was a self-conscious reenactment of an earlier time of social exclusion—an extension of the plutocratic culture of the Aiken winter colony—it could be easily satirized as squires and stuffed shirts on parade. Yet it was far too good-humored an occasion to be mocked; it was a feast, a reward, a celebration. And as the Aiken Steeplechase Association advertised, some of the revenue was used for charity, helping hard-up people and neglected animals in and around Aiken.

It was a cold night. The frat boys had wandered away. I stood in the clammy darkness, peering at the many hundreds of elegantly dressed people in the warm bright tent, laughing among the ice sculptures and flower arrangements, eating and drinking.

"There is always a certain element of insolence in being well-fed, as in every aspect of power," Anton Chekhov wrote to a friend in 1892 while living in Melikhovo, a provincial town smaller than Aiken but with a distinct

resemblance: farms, horses, landlords, classy people, overworked peasants. "And that element expresses itself chiefly in the well-fed preaching
to the hungry."

At dawn on the day of the steeplechase, cold rain fell on Aiken. "It
should clear by noon," I heard someone say as I walked along the boulevard of Richland Avenue, which was the town's main street. When I got to
the racecourse there was no letup, and toward noon the rain came harder,
thrashing the oaks at the perimeter of the racecourse, gusts of wind driving against the tents and shelters of people who lined the enclosure adjacent to it. I was reminded of how bad weather in the South seemed worse,
more punishing, than in most other places I knew, more dramatic, because it came and went quickly.

The rain did not faze the racecourse people. They were there to drink,
to grill hamburgers, to have a good time, and were undeterred by the driving rain and cold wind. They stood in wet feet, in extravagant and brightly
colored clothes — striped blazers and straw hats for the men, flamboyant
wide-brimmed hats and gauzy dresses for the women. They drank with
the determination of sailors weathering a gale and shouted into the wind.

Though it somewhat resembled a tailgate party, to simplify the occasion with that name was to do it an injustice. It was an enormous, well-
organized picnic set out like a camp meeting, a thousand people roistering
in the rain, pouring drinks from coolers stacked in the back of their SUVs
or pickup trucks, huddled in tents or around gas grills and barbecues.

This peripheral event was a celebration of horsemanship, friends and
family, and money. It would be a brave outsider who dared to join this
group unbidden, but when I told a man I was a stranger, he said — and
it was the second time in the South someone said this to me — "Ain't no
strangers here," and he insisted I have a drink with him.

I remarked that in spite of all the drunkenness — not yet noon and people were staggering and falling in the mud — it was fairly orderly.

"These here are designated spots," he said. "Very hard to get one. They
keep them in the family and get handed down."

The race was not the point; gathering was the point, and dressing up
and being happy. The party was the pride of the town, and as everyone
said, it was greatly anticipated. Some people showed me their albums with
pictures of last year's steeplechase — sunny and hot, people sprawled in the

grass. Months of planning had gone into this, and as for the bad weather, it was something to laugh about, and toast, and use as a way of joking with me.

The race was still a few hours away, but for them the race was just another aspect of the binge. It was steeplechase day—not old or even continuous in Aiken: the Steeplechase Association had started in 1930, foundered for twenty-five years, then restarted in 1967. Now it was enshrined as a tradition, in a town—you could say a region—that needed rituals that could be passed down to a new generation, especially rituals that were local, demonstrated community pride, and had the flavor of exclusivity.

Here is what struck me. The wealthy people at the pre-steeplechase party were predictably classy, perhaps snobbish, and easy targets. But the steeplechase had a wider reach than that. Almost the whole town had turned up. I had not expected so many people, from all parts of the town, the locals, the tradesmen, the real estate brokers, the shop girls and store clerks, the college students, the high school kids, the women and girls in homemade hats and summer dresses, the boys and men in blazers and silly hats. They were having a good time, even the ones who were wandering among the tents and stalls in groups, watching the games, being happy in the rain.

And you could be heartened by such a display of enthusiasm and hospitality and good will. All you had to do was pretend that blacks did not exist in Aiken.

The Secret Life of a Segregationist

A few months before I arrived in town, a woman from Aiken died, and her death revived an old story. Her name was Essie Mae Washington-Williams. Her obituary appeared in the *Aiken Standard* on February 5, 2013: "Biracial Daughter of Strom Thurmond Dies at 87."

Strom Thurmond, the ardent segregationist, was born in 1902, about twenty miles up the road from Aiken, past the peach orchards, in the small town of Edgefield. But his preferred place of worship, the First Baptist Church, was in Aiken—an imposing steepled structure of red brick and white columns. He had owned various homes in Aiken, and his second wife, Nancy, had been born in the town. Aiken had a right to claim him. He lived for a hundred years, and he embodied in his century all the contradictions of the South—like the Aiken steeplechase, a joyous and heartening celebration until you realized that it was by tradition a purely white event, the very sort of occasion that Strom Thurmond advocated for much of his life, as a believer in racial separation.

A Clemson University graduate, a decorated soldier in World War Two (in combat in the Normandy invasion), later a lawyer and attorney general and one-term governor and (in 1948) presidential candidate, Thurmond was elected to the United States Senate in 1954 and remained there until his death in 2003. He was one of the longest-serving senators in American history, forty-eight years of ranting and filibustering on behalf of the South's antiquated racial policies, and against civil rights legislation, with an especial vehemence for the Civil Rights Act of 1957.

He was also, from his earliest years, an advocate of states' rights and later an initiator of the "Southern Manifesto," a document of rage and racial exclusion, which was written in defiance of the 1954 Supreme Court school desegregation ruling. "Without regard to the consent of the governed, outside mediators are threatening immediate and revolutionary changes in our public school systems," the document proclaimed. "If done, this is certain to destroy the system of public education in some of the States." In another part, it spoke "with the gravest concern for the explosive and dangerous condition created by this decision and inflamed by outside meddlers."

Now here is the oddity, and a revelation of the secrecy of the man, and a clue to the inner life of the South. And, you might say, a reason for an outsider in these parts to take nothing for granted, or at face value.

At Thurmond's home in Edgefield, one of the black housemaids was sixteen-year-old Carrie Butler, known affectionately (and obscurely) as "Tunch." In this household of segregationists, Strom Thurmond took her as his lover, and afterward, in 1925, their daughter, Essie Mae, was born in Aiken—Thurmond's first child, and Carrie's too. He was twenty-two at the time, an undergraduate at whites-only Clemson, studying horticulture, preparing for the farming career he hoped to have: a vision of cotton fields, an Aiken boy's dream.*

Thurmond, of all people, would have been keenly aware that in 1925 miscegenation was a crime throughout the South, punishable by one to five years in prison in most of its states. Anti-miscegenation laws were enforced, more or less, though in 1932 South Carolina reduced miscegenation from a felony to a misdemeanor. To keep the birth a secret, and to resolve what was obviously an awkward as well as unlawful situation, Carrie Butler arranged for her aunt Essie Washington (after whom her daughter was named) and Essie's husband, John, to adopt Essie Mae when she was six months old. They took her to live with them in Coatesville, Pennsylvania. There Essie Mae remained, raised by the Washingtons (and Aunt Essie's sister Mary), whose surname she took as her own, not knowing who her real father was.

Abandoning the idea of being a farmer, Thurmond went on to earn a law degree and set himself up in an office in Edgefield. He was an unmarried local boy, but with helpful political connections; he was appointed county attorney, then circuit judge, and the war in Europe got him thinking of joining the army. He had no idea what had happened to Carrie or the small girl whose name he did not know, but was soon to learn.

Sometime in 1941, Carrie Butler, who had since moved to Chester, Pennsylvania, to be near her daughter, visited Essie Mae at the Washingtons' in Coatesville. Carrie said, "I'm going to take you to introduce you to your father."

Essie Mae was then sixteen, the same age Carrie had been when she'd been seduced by the son of her white employer. Love was not a factor in the situation, Essie later said; nothing like Thomas Jefferson and his black slave Sally Hemings, whose romance had resulted in six biracial children, four of whom survived—a love story that unfolded over many years and two continents, from Monticello to Paris and back.

Essie Mae had no idea who her father was or even that he was white. Her mother had not spoken about his race, Essie Mae recalled later (to Dan Rather on *60 Minutes,* in a 2003 interview from which many of these

---

* Clemson's first black student, Harvey Gantt, was admitted in 1963.

quotations are taken). "And when I met him, I was surprised, because she'd never mentioned that he was white."

Thurmond said, "That's a beautiful daughter you have."

Carrie said, "She's your daughter too."

"And he was glad to meet me," Essie Mae said, "because of course, he had never seen me. And it was a very nice meeting. And we talked about various things such as what I planned to do in life."

Peering at the teenager, Thurmond remarked, "Well, you look like one of my sisters. You've got those cheekbones like our family."

This seemed a tacit admission of Essie Mae's being his daughter. In her autobiography, *Dear Senator: A Memoir by the Daughter of Strom Thurmond* (2005), she was clear-sighted about the mood of the meeting. "He didn't ask when I was leaving and didn't invite me to come back. It was like an audience with an important man, a job interview, but not a reunion with a father."

But she did see Thurmond again. And as well as giving advice, he gave her money, at first hundred-dollar bills stuffed in envelopes, which Essie Mae picked up at his Senate office — a day's travel back and forth from Pennsylvania — and then, to save her time, he put personal checks in the mail. Keen for her to get an education, he urged her to study at South Carolina State University in Orangeburg. She did so, and from time to time he visited her, not disclosing the relationship to anyone but continuing his financial support.

"Well, whenever I was in need, he would help me out financially," Essie Mae said. After the early death, at forty-five, of her husband, she was in need again, and Thurmond sent money to help the thirty-nine-year-old widow in raising her four children. This arrangement continued until her children were grown.

Inevitably, there was talk, but it was local gossip. In Edgefield and Aiken, "among the black people it was common knowledge." Yet here is another paradox of the hugger-mugger business. Because blacks and whites were kept so separate, little information was passed from one community to the other. "[Blacks] didn't do too much talking to other people."

Nor did Essie Mae speak about it. "It wasn't to my advantage to talk about anything that he had done," she said. "And he, of course, didn't want it to be known." Thurmond had not forbidden her from saying any-thing—there was no "agreement," as she put it. There was simply no point in talking. And she was well aware that Thurmond's political position would have been at risk had the secret been revealed. Essie Mae said, "I didn't want to do anything to harm his career."

Even so, after Thurmond became governor, he visited Essie Mae at her college in Orangeburg, and she paid him visits at the governor's mansion in Columbia. They would sit in his office, and he would talk, and Essie Mae would listen. Thurmond revealed himself as something of a health nut and life coach. "His talks were always on health, exercise, nutrition, and what I was going to do."

While still in college, and visiting Thurmond, Essie Mae asked him directly about his racial politics. "Why was he a racist, a segregationist, at that time?" she wondered. "And he said, 'Well, that's the way things have always been.'"

He had not originated the concept of segregation or Jim Crow laws, he said. All that was a cultural legacy. He was merely upholding them as traditional legislation. "You know, that's the way it was in the South," Essie Mae said afterward. She felt that he was not at heart a racist. "I think he did what he did to promote his career."

Bill Clinton said something similar at the funeral of Robert Byrd: the implied dictum of Southern politics, that ethical beliefs and strong moral positions are for suckers and losers—you have to compromise, fiddle, and be a hypocrite to hold office in Dixie. Byrd was another long-serving Southern senator—and he had held high office as Exalted Cyclops of his local branch of the Ku Klux Klan in the 1940s. "He was a country boy from the hills and hollows of West Virginia," Clinton said in his mellifluous eulogy in Charleston in 2010. "He was trying to get elected."

In other words, like most politicians, animated by pretension. But after Byrd was elected his views did not change much, nor did Thurmond's, until long after the tide turned and overwhelmed them, and both men turned and went with the flow. Like Thurmond, Byrd was opposed to moves toward integration, and he remained an obstacle to civil rights legislation, a filibusterer against the Civil Rights Act of 1964, and a de-nouncer of so-called race mixing.

"No decent and self-respecting Negro would ask for a law to force people to accept him where he is not wanted," Thurmond said in a speech in Jackson, Mississippi, in May 1948, where he was firing the opening volleys in a run for president. "They themselves do not want social intermingling." Fielding Wright, the Mississippi governor, was present at the gathering. The day before, he had advised blacks who asked for equal opportunity to "make your home in some state other than Mississippi."

A few weeks later, tipped to be a presidential candidate on the States' Rights Democratic Party ticket, Thurmond screamed at a crowd in Birmingham, Alabama (a Movietone News film was made of this speech): "But I want to tell you, ladies and gentlemen, that there's not enough troops in the Army to force the Southern people to break down segregation and admit the nigger race into our theaters, into our swimming pools, into our homes and into our churches."

That was the year Carrie Butler, the black mother of his child, died at the age of thirty-nine, when Essie Mae was a student in Orangeburg.

For a while the financial arrangement between Essie Mae and Thurmond continued. Essie Mae married, became Mrs. Washington-Williams, and bore four children (Wanda, Monica, Ronald, and Julius), and still father and daughter kept in touch now and then. Essie Mae aged gracefully; Thurmond got a hair transplant and dyed his plugs reddish brown. In the 1960s, *Ebony* magazine attempted to do a story on the rumored relationship, but Essie Mae demurred, saying she had nothing to reveal, and wouldn't cooperate. She sent the reporters away. She kept silent for sixty years, and worked as a respected schoolteacher in Los Angeles.

Then, in 2003, Strom Thurmond died. And reflecting on her own age, nearly eighty, and her children, and the fact that Thurmond could not be hurt by anything she said, she came forward five months after his death, in December of that year. Standing before reporters in South Carolina, she told her story, saying, "I am Essie Mae Washington-Williams, and at last I am completely free."

Her health was poor, her children were grown — it was they who had persuaded her that her story needed to be told. She said she felt she owed it to history to declare who she was. She wasn't looking for money. "I am not suing his estate. I just want to tell the truth."

"My children deserve the right to know from whom, where and what they have come," Ms. Washington-Williams said at the press conference. "I am committed in teaching them and helping them to learn about their past. It is their right to know and understand the rich history of their ancestry, black and white."

It was a relief, she said afterward. "I would say 50 or 60 years now this thing has been following me. So the fact that I am coming up now to talk about it is like a burden lifted. Because I had this secret. And even though many people did know about it, I hadn't gotten it off my shoulders." It was, she said, "a legacy."

She had by then moved back to South Carolina from Los Angeles. She died in Columbia, not far from Aiken, where she was born, just a few months before I was rambling around Aiken and Edgefield, and pondering the paradoxes of the South.

The Bomb Factory: Mutant Spiders

"Aiken is a real cute place," one of its proud residents said to me in a coffee shop. It was true — so tidy and bright. And just down Atomic Road was the Bomb Factory. Everyone in Aiken talked about it, and I had passed it the last time I'd been this way, driving from Allendale. Its existence was no secret, but there were rumors of chattering Geiger counters and dangerous spills and radioactive soil and failed attempts at cleanups. I had been turned away at the main gate of the nuclear facility in the winter, so I thought, since I was in town, I'd gather anecdotal evidence.

Gregory Jefferson, whom I had met a few days before at the hotel on the eve of the steeplechase, had mentioned it. I had kept his cell phone number. I called him and met him for a drink.

"Atomic Road," I said after a while. "That's an amazing name."

"Amazing place down there. It's because of the bomb plant, what folks call the Savannah River Site. It's from the 1950s, I guess. Happen this way. Government bought the town of Dunbarton, so they could build it there. They moved all the people, thousands of them, to Ellenton, and built New Ellenton."

"So there was a town where there's now a nuclear facility?"

"Not much of a town, though, way back," he said. "Top-level people from the Bomb Factory, white folk, they live in Aiken, with the horse people. It's all secret, they won't let you near it, though the road goes right along it, and along the Savannah River."

"Makes sense. Nuclear reactors need water for cooling," I said.

"Folks say there's spills, maybe spills in the river. Maybe you heard about the accident at Graniteville. Chlorine gas pollution. And there's the other thing. You got a nuclear facility and what happens? You're in trouble. Folks used to say that when the Russians send a bomb over here, the first place they'll hit is us. We're a target."

"The Russians were planning to bomb Aiken?"

"We was in the crosshairs, sure," he said, seeming to derive a measure of community pride by being a target of the Soviet Union. "Never mind, Aiken is a premier place to live."

We were joined by his friend Willie, who said, "And there's the other stuff, spent fuel rods and nuclear waste. That stuff is still lying around."

"You're sure of that?"

"We know it. We got high cancer rates, birth defects, lots of secrets."

You could say: This is all anecdotal. You meet a couple of local guys and listen to their stories that sound like hearsay, and in your casual way (the credulous mood of a traveler) you draw dire conclusions. But Gregory and Willie were not wrong. The truth was much more alarming than anything they told me. I had asked a simple question about Atomic Road, because the road was so fragrant with pine needles, the river so placid, the air so fresh. Aiken itself was a pretty place, with its orderly town center, its golf club, and its racecourses, and the flat green meadows and stately homes and the paddocks and friendly board fences of horse country. Real cute, as the lady said.

But after Gregory's chatty account of the history of the nuclear site, I talked to other people, just chatting.

"They make atom bombs there . . ."

"Lots of employment . . ."

"Very secret . . ."

"Sir, you be real careful . . ."

And a young military man named Kevin, on leave at his home in Augusta but running an errand in Aiken, said, "They's some strange things happening there."

"Strange in what way?"

"Full-on security, for one thing. You will never get inside that place. And strange regarding the animals."

"Which animals?"

"Ones in the woods. Ones in the river." He smiled, but it was a grim smile. "They got different colors. Not the colors you used to. Alligators in the river."

"There are alligators in the Savannah River?"

"But not green ones. They yellow. They pink. Some of them white. They real different. From the radioactivity."

Pink alligators? From radioactive and heavy-metal contamination? Records show that some *Alligator mississippiensis* have become unusually large. It has been argued that these giants (up to a record thirteen feet long) achieved their size not because of genetic mutation caused by radioactivity but for the opposite reason, because their habitat has been undisturbed. Yet in February 2012, strange webs of "string-like material" were found in a nuclear waste dump at the Savannah River Site, and it was theorized that they came from mutant spiders.

The site outside Aiken had been chosen by the Atomic Energy Commission in 1950, with the intention to build a plant to produce fuel for thermonuclear weapons. When the plant was finished it had five production reactors, fuel fabrication facilities, a research laboratory, heavy-water production facilities, two fuel reprocessing facilities and tritium recovery facilities.

Later, I found authoritative reports claiming the place — road, river, air — was blighted with "significant site contamination" and radioactive "ground water migration" throughout the 310-square-mile site. One EPA report cited that "multiple buildings and facilities at SRS have been contaminated with radioactive contaminants of concern, including cadmium, cesium, cobalt, plutonium, tritium and uranium."

The site had been largely decommissioned, and as a Superfund cleanup site it had become a billion-dollar headache. And here was the EPA's promise: "All inactive waste sites [at the Savannah River Site] posing an unacceptable risk to human health, ecological receptors, surface water or ground water will be cleaned up, and any contaminated ground water will be cleaned up or undergoing cleanup, by 2031."

Gregory, Willie, and others had spoken of the Savannah River Site being a target of the Russians. More recently, Joseph Trento, a security analyst, investigative reporter, and president of the award-winning Public Education Center, wrote an alarming report on the site. He described it as being a prime target of Al Qaeda or any homegrown terrorist wishing to make a point by starting a plutonium fire, a dire consequence: "A nuclear accident has a beginning but no end." This nuclear facility, hidden by the dense pinewoods on the banks of the Savannah River, contained "one of the greatest concentrations in the world of radioactive material . . . enough weapons grade plutonium to destroy the world multiple times. Here plutonium in its purest form can be found by the ton."*

That the site was large and vulnerable ("a geographic nightmare") was bad enough. Much worse was the fact that it was not guarded by the US military. This was something Trento described in detail. A private security firm, Wackenhut, was responsible for protecting "massive amounts of high-level nuclear waste, huge amounts of bomb-grade plutonium." Wackenhut, renamed G4S Secure Solutions, was a Danish-British firm "with a long record of botched security operations from Afghanistan to London to Oak Ridge, Tennessee."

The Oak Ridge breach was still in the news. Three antinuclear activists (a Vietnam vet, a house painter, and an eighty-two-year-old Catholic nun, Sister Megan Rice) managed (with bolt cutters and saws) to cut through the perimeter fence of the nuclear facility at Oak Ridge in July 2012. These three unlikely saboteurs, outwitting the guards, crept under cover of night to the Highly Enriched Uranium Materials Facility and left graffiti (verses from Proverbs, Isaiah, and the book of Habakkuk: "The fruit of justice is peace" and "Woe to the empire of blood," among others), hung symbolic yellow crime-scene tape, and splashed blood on the walls from a deceased activist, Tom Lewis, in his memory. They hammered at the guard towers,

* "The Bomb Plant: America's Three A.M. Nightmare," National Security News Service, November 2012.

breaking off bits of concrete, then stayed and waited to be discovered. They remained in the facility for two hours. Seeing a guard, they offered him food and began singing. He arrested them. (They were finally sentenced in a court in Knoxville in February 2014. Sister Megan was given three years, her two male accomplices five years each.)

Wackenhut/G4S has as many as eight hundred armed guards on duty at the Savannah River Site. Even so, in the view of experts the site is underguarded and has too many access points on its perimeter. A well-planned suicide bombing could be effective and catastrophic, because the plutonium stored there is volatile, and there is too great a concentration of weapons-grade material on the site. "If an explosion disturbs it, then we could face a massive fire with a plutonium flash and large scale exposure," one of Trento's informants said, later adding, "It looks very impressive at the front gate but around back, a chain link fence is really all that separates the American public from a zealot or lunatic with a cheap pair of bolt cutters trying to inflict as much harm on the nation as possible."

Just up the road from this nuclear-disaster-in-the-making is Augusta, Georgia, where you never hear the horror stories of nuclear contamination that will take seventeen more years to clean up, but only the whispered delights of playing golf.

"Even though signs said not to stop, not to get out of the car, there was not a single security patrol in sight during the entire trip," Trento wrote in his analysis, recounting his drive on the narrow state highway, Atomic Road. "Gates were left open on either side of the highway. It seemed like the entire Site was open to the public."

That was my experience too, as I drove out of Aiken and through the pretty pinewoods, not far from the nuclear waste dumps and the millions of gallons of high-level nuclear waste. I was heading southeast down Atomic Road, from happy, well-heeled Aiken toward poor, benighted Allendale County.

The Savannah River that slipped past the trees as I drove appears in *Tobacco Road* as an image of salvation, a refuge from sharecropping. "The best thing you can do, Jeeter," his neighbors tell him, "is to move your family up to Augusta or across the river to South Carolina."

A Glimpse of Wrens

Just across the Savannah River, which forms the state line, about thirty miles to the west of Atomic Road, is the small town of Wrens, Georgia. Wrens is the Cotton Belt town where Erskine Caldwell, son of a preacher, lived as an impressionable teenager. Much of his fiction is located near here, notably *Tobacco Road,* and many of his best short stories.

Caldwell was so hated by his fellow Georgians, who felt he'd made them a laughingstock, he left the South, lived in San Francisco and New York City, and for some years in a small town in Maine. He traveled in Europe and the Soviet Union, where he worked as a war correspondent, and was also regarded as a chronicler of peasant life in the United States. He wrote books about his trips, including several investigations of the Deep South. With his much younger fourth wife, he ended his days in Arizona, still writing, still prolific, but with a diminishing readership.

Though his literary star dimmed, Caldwell retained the distinction of having popularized the notion of Southerners as grotesques — toothless, incestuous, ignorant, coarse, and bigoted, quite a different cast of characters in *God's Little Acre* (1933) from those of his fellow Georgian and near-contemporary Margaret Mitchell, chronicler of life at Tara in *Gone with the Wind* (1936). Her nostalgic version of a stylish and sophisticated South, passionate, wealthy (ball gowns, balustrades, ormolu clocks), violated by war, and wrecked by Yankees, is the one that many white Southerners cling to.

Deep Trouble at the House of Love:
"Accused Means Guilty"

On a rainy night in Orangeburg — I had driven the country way, via the flyspecks of Blackville and Denmark — I was back at Ruby Tuesday, waiting in a back booth to meet Reverend Virgin Johnson. Because he did not in the least resemble anyone else at the restaurant, he created a vibe of murmurs when he arrived, and this susurration reached me on his approach. Reverend Johnson is a tall and athletic man with a preacher's mildness and a lawyer's confident bearing, and when he strode among the tables in his dark pinstripe suit and silk tie, people naturally looked up—white and black alike—compelled by his presence, his dignity, his bearing, a procession of one, bringing me a smile.

"Brother Paul," he said, giving me a hug, and then he ordered sweet tea and explained his choice: "It would just not look right if one of my congregation saw their preacher imbibing alcohol. Sweet tea is just fine for me."

"Speaking of which, how is your congregation?" I asked.

He smiled and nodded, but it was a complex smile with a world of worry behind it.

"That's a story," he said. "I'll tell you in a little while, but what I want to hear is, how you doing, man?"

"I've just come from Aiken," I said. And I began to recount a bit of the story of Essie Mae Washington-Williams, but no sooner had I said her name than he tapped the table and said, "Strom Thurmond." I went on, "Funny that a racist like Thurmond would have had an affair with his black servant."

"Maybe he wasn't much of a racist, ever think of that?" Reverend Johnson said slowly, steadying his straw with pinching fingers and sipping his tea. "You got to understand that in many cases these white Southern politicians weren't really deep-down racists." He smiled again. "In spite of what they said."

"But what they said lots of times was bigoted and inflammatory. How about that?"

Reverend Johnson laughed, as though at my innocence. "They had to toe the line! If they didn't, they wouldn't get anywhere."

"Where does their racial talk put you?"

"We know what they're thinking. We understand the double-talk. Strom Thurmond did a lot of good things for this state."

"He said a lot of dreadful things," I said, with—I realized—prissy Yankee sanctimony. "And what about his black child?"

"It's the Southern way," Reverend Johnson said, and then went back to sipping from his straw.

"And all that segregation talk." Out of delicacy, I avoided quoting Thurmond's speech about admitting "the nigger race" into schools and churches.

"It's the Southern way!" Reverend Johnson said.

"Doesn't it bother you?"

"We know what he's saying. We can translate it," he said. "Remember George Wallace? He ran for governor of Alabama, not a bad man, maybe even a moderate man in some ways. In the campaign he refused the support of the Ku Klux Klan — didn't have any time for them, he said." Reverend Johnson sipped more sweet tea. "That was his downfall. They would have helped him. The NAACP backed him. He was looking for the black vote. And he lost to the white man who took a hard line and had the Klan's endorsement. 'I was outniggered,' he said. 'I'll never be outniggered again.'"

Reverend Johnson was laughing as I asked, "It's the Southern way?"

"It's the Southern way."

Our meal was served. Reverend Johnson, over his lobster tail and steak, voluble and full of stories again, talked about growing up "po' black" and what it was like at school to sit at a table in the cafeteria and watch thirty white boys get up and leave. "But I stood my ground. Eventually I got respect. I earned it." And things had changed, he said. We talked about earning respect.

"I've got a fighting spirit," Reverend Johnson said. He thought a moment. "Well, that's what I was going to talk to you about. I got a little problem. I mean, there's a case coming up and it's vexing me."

"Serious case?"

"A bishop, with a church down in Allendale," he said, and paused — a preacher's pause, suspenseful and intended to seize my attention — "charged with child molestation."

This accusation sounded especially pernicious in his deliberate way of saying it, chewing each syllable: *chahl moh-les-ta-shun.*

"Did he do it?"

"No way. Lord no. I have known this man my whole life, and I have a feeling what happened — it is a gross misunderstanding." He sipped more tea. "And it is a tragedy."

"If he's not guilty, then he'll be cleared and he'll be fine."

"You don't understand," Reverend Johnson said. "He's been accused of child molestation. *Chahl moh-les-ta-shun.* He will never recover, even if he's cleared. He will be ruined. His name is tarred. Accused means guilty."

He gave me some general details. The man was Bishop Bobby Jones, fifty-four, a resident of Allendale. His church, the New Life House of Love, on Oswald Drive at the edge of town, was about the same size as Revelation Ministries, but it was connected to a bigger organization, the New Life Pentecostal Holiness churches. The New Life Pentecostal Holiness House of Love Church advertised its motto as "Pursue, Overtake, and Recover All!"

"Hard-line Pentecostal," Reverend Johnson said, clenching his fists and raising them to emphasize the sect's tenacity.

From an early age, Bobby Jones had clung to the faith. He started as a six-year-old choirboy in Allendale, singing in a church group called the All Star Angels. They became so popular they were invited to other churches. They renamed themselves the Pilgrimaires, for their evangelizing, and traveled the South, singing their faith, finding adherents.

"He received the Lord when he was nine, studied hard, and preached his first sermon when he was fourteen," Reverend Johnson said. "Dedicated his life to the people around here — people in Allendale, people in need. Thirty years he's been preaching and fellowshiping."

Pastor Bobby Jones was promoted to bishop. He was popular, known for his preaching as well as his singing. In accordance with local church protocol, his wife was referred to as "First Lady" Brenda Jones. He had six children and ten grandchildren. Altogether, as Reverend Johnson outlined it, an admirable man.

I said, "What about this child molestation charge?"

"Criminal sexual conduct with a fourteen-year-old," Reverend Johnson said, and *fo'teen* sounded especially young. The incident occurred sometime in January of this year, 2013, but he had recently been indicted, and was out on $50,000 bond.

"So what's the story?"

"Like I said, he's a hard-line Pentecostal, born again," Reverend Johnson said. "For them there are no exceptions. The letter of the law. No sex before marriage. The way I understand it, in a general speculative way, his daughter might have come to him saying she was feeling things — normal physical desires. The bishop listened. He is a patient and godly man."

"What was his advice?"

Reverend Johnson lifted his hands, curling his fingers, seeming to hold an object. He said, "I don't know. But say he went out and bought her a dildo."

In his pronunciation, *dee-aw-doh*, it sounded like a large and very technical device.

"Did he do that?"

"I don't know. I'm just theorizing," he said, with an attorney's surmise and circumspection. "And, let's say, when the child went to school she could have told a friend what her father had given her. And that friend could have told someone else. The teachers learned of it. And they went to the sheriff. And the sheriff brought in state law enforcement. And the news got out." Reverend Johnson gazed at me in a mournful way. "And Bishop Bobby Jones is in deep trouble, and so is the House of Love Church."

Under the strict terms of his bail, the bishop could not have contact with anyone under the age of eighteen, and that meant he had to steer clear of some of his children and all of his grandchildren. His name was smeared with the accusation.

"Lewdness with an underage person is a crime in this state," Reverend Johnson said. "Like I say, even if he's found not guilty, he will suffer. He deserves to have the best trial lawyer he can find."

"Might that be you, Reverend?"

"I'd do the best I can," he said. "But the problem is that some of my congregation don't see it my way. They have girl children and grandchildren. From what they hear, they see Bishop Bobby Jones as a guilty man who should be punished."

"What do you think?"

He smiled and nodded. "I see Bishop Bobby Jones as a man who should have his day in court."*

---

* As of this writing, the daughter had recanted, withdrawn her accusation, and refused to testify. No other witnesses had come forward, the case was still pending, and Bishop Bobby Jones remained out on bail.

"And not everyone agrees?"

"There's haters," Reverend Johnson said. "Oh, dear me. There's haters."

Sermon with a Subtext:
"What Would I Do Without My Storm?"

Revelation Ministries Church was, unusually, only half full on this Sunday morning, but as if to make up for it, the singing was more full-throated, and the Revelation combo was loud, playing their hearts out. The preliminary preaching, by a woman in a dress of watered silk who was gesturing with her Bible, seemed particularly intense, and when she called out "The Lord is here today!" she was answered with "Tell it, sister!"

All this time, Reverend Johnson had been sitting quietly in his throne-like chair, under the gold, scroll-shaped sign REVELATION MINISTRIES—"REVEALING GOD'S WORD TO THE WORLD—WE LOVE YOU—AIN'T NOTHING YOU CAN DO ABOUT IT!"

When he rose to preach, there was a hush as he lifted his battered Bible and spoke a chapter and verse from the Acts of the Apostles.

"After they had evangelized that town and made many disciples, they returned to Lystra, to Iconium, and to Antioch," he intoned, quoting, speaking quietly, "strengthening the hearts of the disciples by encouraging them to continue in the faith, and by telling them, 'It is necessary to pass through many troubles on our way into the kingdom of God.'"

He had struck the deliberate note at once, his theme being that there is no salvation without a severe test. Everyone knew he was alluding to Bishop Bobby Jones, accused of child molestation, but the man's name was never spoken. The sermon was entirely concerned with hard decisions, Saint Paul's, and Job's, and Christ's, and others'.

"What is popular is not always right," Reverend Johnson said. "What is right is not always popular. And so I gotta ask you, do you want to be unpopular with the Lord?" He mused awhile about bad weather — stormy weather was another theme of this sermon: "The rain comes and folks say, 'Oh, it's raining hard!' But there's something about the rain — a peacefulness and a calm. You can go into it and be with the Lord."

I had seen this congregation on its feet before, calling out, yelling their praise — "Tell it!" "Oh, yeah!" — echoing lines in the sermon. But now they stayed seated, listening with uncommon reserve, and Reverend Johnson seemed to be using his trial lawyer's rhetoric rather than his preacher's poise to persuade them, as though they were jurors. But then, both sounded similar in a church.

"When I came to you, brothers, announcing the testimony of God to you, I did not come with brilliance of speech or wisdom," he said, quoting Corinthians. "I was with you in weakness, in fear, and much trembling."

Being weak, enduring hardship, resolving conflict: it was all about Bishop Bobby Jones, except for the stating of his name, and it was clear that Reverend Johnson was trying to hold on to his congregation using his powers of persuasion.

"God sends us a storm," he thundered. "I need this storm. What would I do without my storm? It makes me turn to the Lord. And so I say, 'Thank you, storm!' Because it sends me to the Lord. I have to be willing to put it all on the line for the Lord — by faith and not by sight."

He moved from the podium, and as he did, as if his movement was a cue, the woman in the white hat and veil at the keyboards brought her fingers down on a loud chord that became a diminuendo before it trickled away, and the woman seated at the drum kit rattled her snare drum into a hush.

"The darkness of night," Reverend Johnson continued. "Nighttime does not have any limits. It can last a long period of time. It can test your faith. Job lost his possessions and lost his family. But he never left God. Hold on just a little while longer to see what the end gon' be. Never leave your relation with the Lord, though you be tested so bad you want to howl in misery!"

This mention of howl, the word "howl," made him howl, and the spirit moved him as he chanted and moaned and threw his head back, gargling. This was so effective, the congregation began to call out to him in tones of support and encouragement, as though shouting to a man struggling to come ashore. And all this while the Revelation combo kept playing, the woman at the keyboards planting her hands on the keys and producing thunder and lightning.

"Weeping may endure for a night, but joy cometh in the morning," he said at last in a tone of delivering good news, quoting Psalm 30, and repeating it.

And it worked: the faces of his congregation were happy, even beatific. The storm had passed; he was no longer chanting. He spoke now in the modulated and consoling voice of a friend. He began telling stories about his life.

He had first told me these stories over dinner months ago. Perhaps his flock had heard them before too, but if so, they did not let on. They sat seemingly fascinated by his tale of taking the first bus, the white bus; of being alone, tested by the white students, encouraged by the only blacks in the school, the janitors, who smiled at him as if to say, "Hold on, son. Hold on." The school stories, the stories about being alone, being the only black student among a hundred whites.

"I lost all my friends. I learned at an early age that you have to stand by yourself," he said. "What happens when you let other people make your decisions? You become incapable of making your own decisions."

At this the church went silent.

"I have a fighting spirit. I've been doing it since I was a child." And now I saw his link, his sympathy, with Bishop Bobby Jones, the child singer and precocious preacher, the man who had spent thirty years evangelizing. "It's destiny."

A chord rose from the keyboards, then a sizzle and smash from the snare drum and a crash and smash from the cymbals.

"I want you to know that I'm leaning," he said, and this was the nearest he came to declaring that his decision to defend Bishop Bobby Jones was coming. "And I want you to know that I love y'all. And if you talk to the haters, y'all tell them that I love them."

It was a powerful sermon. Yet not long after that, Reverend Virgin Johnson declared that he would not be representing Bishop Bobby Jones in the child molestation case. He told me that he had found him an excellent attorney from elsewhere in the county.

Cresent Motel

On a damp morning, the smell of the back streets of Allendale was the malodorous hum of poverty, and the neighborhood of poor houses was a littered encampment. I had come back via the familiar route on the four-lane obsolete highway, desolation road, past the rusted and faded signs of the defunct restaurants (LOBSTER) and the abandoned gas station plazas (INTERSTATE, ESSO) and the bleak broken motels (EXECUTIVE INN), all of it like a foray into Dystopia Dixie. More than that, like arriving at the end of the world.

And it was another return for me. A travel book is usually based on a journey on which the traveler confronts places for the first time, describes them vividly, then moves on and never goes back. This portrait of the place, the way it looked that hour, that day, or that week, in that weather, is the one that is clapped between covers for its peculiarity to be given permanent form. This generalizing—the snap judgment of the traveler—is the reason travel writing can seem so crisp, so insightful to the reader, and so maddening to the person who knows the place well, or who inhabits the area, who does not recognize his or her home from the brisk description of the wisecracking wayfarer.

The single visit ("Then we stopped for lunch in Chittagong") also accounts for the distortions and sour notes in travel narratives—not gratuitous or mean-spirited, but merely the blur of haste, the glance of someone passing through. The traveler's conceit is that one visit is plenty, that travel is not a study but a summing up, personal and partisan. I have lived much of my traveling life that way, well aware of the reductiveness and dissonance and smirking self-regard in the breezing through, conscious that my journeys were as much about my life as about the places I was experiencing. What seemed to work in Africa and India and China, however, was insufficient and misleading in the Deep South.

On my third visit to Allendale I saw things I had missed the first two times. Some of the town was improved, even in six months: the derelict movie theater was being renovated. Another soul food restaurant had opened, Carolina Diner, next to one of the three Patel-owned Stop-N-Go gas stations in town, this black-operated eatery on South Main Street. The

New Life House of Love Church on Oswald Drive looked moribund, its parking lot empty, its doors locked, while its bishop, now on bail, languished under a cloud, disgraced on a charge of lewdness with an underage person — that was a new development too.

The first time I'd seen the old sign CRESENT MOTEL, I laughed at the spelling and the rusted star above it, while fascinated by the look of abandonment of the mock–Art Deco brick building behind it, with its faded, numbered doors, the old-style, flat-roofed, one-story "motor lodge" from the 1950s. On a later visit to Allendale I walked around the premises, kicking doors open, stepping over broken glass, marveling at the big, derelict swimming pool, surrounded by a chain-link fence and secured by a locked gate, with a foot of green water at the bottom. These were my fall and winter visits.

This springtime a flicker of life was evident at the Cresent Motel, some rooms were occupied, a few people were going in and out of them, a woman with a baby, a man with a bag of groceries. A man in a folding beach chair outside one room was staring with suspicion at me. Two battered cars sat side by side in the parking lot that was otherwise empty but for a flock of dirty pigeons strutting clumsily past the puddles. At first I took the people to be squatters or campers: they were poorly dressed, they squinted hard at me, and though they said hello, they wouldn't answer any of my questions. The big man in the beach chair glowered at me and said softly but menacingly, "Git."

The door with the painted OFFICE sign on it was broken, and as it was ajar I could see the clutter of papers and plastic soda bottles on the floor, an oil can tipped over and leaking, a wing chair losing its stuffing and hanging sideways. All these interiors looked to me like crime scenes.

Then the wing chair swelled and came alive and spoke to me.

"Kin Ah," the man breathed, "he'p you?"

Jamming his cane into the cement floor, he clutched it and hoisted himself and rose to greet me. He wore a heavy coat and under it a wool sweater that was unraveling at the collar, a dark cap, and trousers baggy and torn at the knees. He moved slowly, emerging from the office, stabbing his cane into the cracked asphalt, then he saluted me.

"Are you the manager of the Cresent?"

"Me, I'm maintenance." He was still limping toward me, grunting from the effort.

"How are you doing?" I asked in a sympathetic tone, because he was clearly struggling.

"Knee surgery," he said. He was lopsided but still moving forward. "Hip surgery."

"Take your time."

"Had my knees done. Had my hips done. It's the arthuritis got me." His name was Leon Williams, he said; his job was to keep this place running. As it was visibly falling apart, and he was unwell, this was not an easy job. "It sure needs a new roof, needs new electric, needs a lot. Old plumbing fixtures, old everything."

Yet, amazingly, it was occupied — seven rooms, anyway — by single men, and some couples, and a small family, each paying eighty dollars a week for a room. I had seen motels just like this, ones built by optimistic Portuguese settlers in Mozambique, bullet-ridden and broken down, hollowed out by conflict, occupied by poor African families after the long civil war ended: the same sort of haggard women, scowling men, and bewildered children, standing in front of cracked walls and smashed windows by the seaside in Beira. It was Doomsday housing, desperate people scuttling and living rough in urban ruins.

Leon lived about twelve miles east, in Brunson. He drove down Railroad Avenue from there in his pickup truck most days to look after the Cresent, which was now more a refuge for the truly hopeless and homeless than a motel for the casual traveler. Leon, born and raised in Allendale, said he preferred Brunson, a tiny crossroads community with a population of about 500. It had once been locally celebrated for its old town hall, a wood-frame octagonal building purposely upraised on stilts, so that Brunson's citizens could sit under it, relaxing in its shade, and talk. The new town hall was a small brick structure that would never get in the news. Leon remembered the better days in Allendale — days when there had been employment in the town.

"My folks, mother and father, worked at the mill, and me too. They was good jobs."

"They milled lumber?"

"Two-bah-fo's. One-bah-fo's. Plahwood. Made telegram po's. Made everything."

Leon was sixty-six but, ailing, he looked much older in his limping discomfort. He had three children; they'd grown up here, but with nothing to do and no opportunities, they had fled to New York City.

"They come down here but they don't like it, 'cause it too slow," Leon said. "Me, I likes it slow."

"But Allendale must have been lively way back, when all the tourists stopped here at the motels and restaurants"—the fallen buildings that were bomb craters now.

"They was plenty of nightlife, specially on Flat Street. That was where they was hangouts."

Flat Street was tucked behind the main road, Railroad Avenue, and ran parallel to it, in its shadow, so to speak, and somewhat hidden. It was hard to imagine any sort of nightlife on that bleak street, but in that other age Allendale was a boomtown.

"The hangouts was lively but they was a problem—the drinkin' and the fightin'. They was women too. But they put a new police station down on Flat Street, and that eliminated the problem."

"Pretty quiet now."

"The interstate killed us."

Leon gave me his address in Brunson and invited me to stop by anytime. Then he returned to the Cresent Motel office to await a call for maintenance.

Allendale had a bright spot. A few miles south on Allendale's empty superhighway, I found Christiana Estates, a subdivision of pretty, well-kept houses on large lots, not visible from the main road and casually gated, proof that not all of Allendale was in a state of decay or incurably hard-up, as I had believed.

Saying Grace

After a solemn prayer of grace over chicken, rice, gravy, biscuits, and cabbage at the soul food diner O Taste and See, Wilbur Cave said "Amen" and began eating.

He'd suggested months before that I come back if I wanted to see more of his work in Allendale as an urban developer, and here I was. I wanted to visit some families that Allendale County Alive had helped, or ones that were looking for help.

"I put in a call," Wilbur said. "We need permission if we're going to visit. Some people don't want visits or drop-ins. They're sensitive about their position."

Ninety years ago, not far from here, the great muralist and painter Thomas Hart Benton encountered those same sensitivities. He mentions it in his chapter on the South in his memoir, *An Artist in America* (1937). He was sitting on a curb in eastern Georgia, making a drawing of a white-washed shack.

"Some colored folks sitting on the porch went inside when they caught sight of me," he writes. "Pretty soon a tall Negro with very much patched but clean overalls came out of the shack and walked over to me hesitantly. 'Howdy,' I said, seeing that he wanted to speak. 'Sir,' he said with perfect English, 'I beg your pardon, but my mother thinks you are making fun of her house and wants you to please go away.' I went."

A whole district in Allendale within easy walking distance of the main street was made up of inhabited shacks, which Wilbur Cave was attempting to improve with the limited resources of Allendale County Alive. He reminded me of his operating budget of $100,000, which was not much, but his organization was self-sustaining through the revenue from derelict houses they'd renovated and rented. His was a small operation but an efficient one, and it seemed to me that it was successful precisely because it was small; Wilbur could account for every dollar that flowed through his office, which was not the case when many millions were spent.

We talked over a lunch of chicken and rice about Allendale County, which was small and poor, and about the town, which was seventy-two percent black, the highest percentage in the state. When I mentioned Leon Williams, who with his parents had worked at the mill, Wilbur enumerated the businesses that had left the town — not only all the restaurants and garages and motels, and their support services in the heyday of Route 301, but Allendale's manufacturing.

"We made furniture here," he said. "We had textile factories, weaving cloth and carpets right into the 1980s."

"What happened to them?"

"Went to China. Went to India."

"A lot of jobs lost, I guess."

"All the jobs went. There is nothing here now," he said. "And we never had highly educated people. You don't need much of an education to work in service industries or a carpet factory or agriculture. And so all these people were left. They're struggling now. Those are the people we're trying to help."

"What would it take to transform this county?" I asked.

"I'll tell you. We have significant amounts of undeveloped land. Think of people who want to retire to a good climate or who want to migrate. We're near Columbia, Charleston, and Augusta, easy driving distance." Now he was sounding hopeful, gesturing to the surrounding countryside. "It's possible that we could grow that way. You could buy five acres and put a nice home on it. You might pay three thousand an acre, or even one thousand. Imagine, for a small amount of money you'd have a sizable piece of land in a pretty place."

He answered his ringing cell phone, spoke briefly, and ended the call.

"I can introduce you to some folks."

Razor Road

The abandoned houses on Razor Road gave it the look of having been in the path of a terrible storm, and blighted by it, leaving rat-haunted ruins. Razor Road — a menacing and memorable name — ran through the poorest district, from near the center of Allendale, where it began, to a perimeter of farmland at its eastern limit. The farmland stretched for miles, a margin of darkness at night.

Many of the houses had been reduced to rubble or were shacks. The oldest, strangest, most ramshackle one was a single-story house of age-blackened hand-hewn planks with a patched tin roof. This dwelling, primitive even when it had first been built, had existed in this place in the period General Sherman passed nearby, in February 1865, meeting two days of resistance at Broxton Bridge, his vindictive soldiers marching ever deeper into the state, burning farmsteads and barns. This house, a stark example of endurance, had lain far enough from the marauding army to have been spared.

It was an enormous antique, sensational in its decrepitude, with a cookhouse attached to the rear. But its dimensions looked original, and it could not have changed much since it had been put up; it had simply weathered the storms and gradually deteriorated. The roof was rusted, the porch sagged, the windows were broken and patched with cardboard; it had no evident indoor plumbing. A chimney rose from the middle of the roof peak, a feature of the oldest houses.

"Looks abandoned," I said.

"It was fully occupied until last year," Wilbur said. Then, hearing some-one kicking through the tall grass beside the house, he said, "And here is the owner. Hello, Melvin. I want you to meet Paul."

Melvin Johnson was an older man in blue bib overalls. I was surprised when he told me he was fifty-seven, because he looked much older—it seemed everyone below the poverty line aged prematurely here, as else-where. We shook hands and he smiled and said, "Want to have a look inside?"

"Melvin's been poorly," Wilbur said.

"I'm in recovery," Melvin said, "from colorectal cancer."

"How you doing?"

"Taking it slow," he said. "Wilbur helped me a lot."

"I got him into the housing program," Wilbur said. "But Melvin did all the work to get a new home. He enrolled in a class to learn about manag-ing money. He studied hard. He found finance. He got a mortgage."

"Got me a new house," Melvin said.

It was a small one, shotgun-sized but new, two streets away from Razor Road, and there he lived with his two sons.

To have moved a couple of streets away, from this wreck of a house to a modest new one, might seem a small achievement, but to me it was huge. I thought of the vast sums of money spent on projects, and the boasts, and how ultimately they made little difference. And I reflected on Wilbur and his attention to detail on a modest budget. Lines from William Blake's *Jerusalem* came to mind:

He who would do good to another must do it in Minute Particulars.
General Good is the plea of the scoundrel, hypocrite, and flatterer.

"Better than this one, that's for sure," Melvin said, pushing the old door open.

The smell of house rot, of damp rags and worm-eaten wood and dead mice and wet, half-dissolved newspapers, was overpowering. Melvin switched on a light—the only bulb in the room, dangling from a cord—and I saw, as though a glimpse of an earlier age of poverty and hardship, the clutter: the flattened cardboard boxes nailed to the wall to serve as insulation; the floor strewn with old shoes, torn pillows, twisted quilts, splintered chairs, piled boxes, ill-sorted papers, and rags; the accumulation of decades, like the desperate nest of a burrowing animal. Paper portraits of Jesus decorated one wall, and perhaps some of the newspapers had been tacked up because of their photographs or headlines, but they were yellowed beyond any legibility. A cracked mirror was the crowning touch, lending a hint of horror.

Melvin sat on a torn sofa and tossed a blanket aside, where it lay over a soot-blackened and scorched woodstove. The spring day was bright and warm, but no sunlight penetrated this chilly, stinking interior. Blankets were hung against the windows, the inner doors were shut, and it was not the clutter that disturbed me but the smell, which was the smell of death, and the notion that it was the sort of setting that I associated with the Cresent Motel, a crime scene; all it lacked was a corpse.

"I was born here," Melvin said. "I lived here, mainly with my grandmother."

"What did you do for water?"

"The well, yonder."

"What about the toilet?"

"Had us an outhouse 'round back. Still there."

"How long did you live here?"

"Fifty-six years," Melvin said. "Moved out last year, into the new place." He looked around the littered room and marveled. "Ain't this something? Six generations lived in this old house. My grandmother died in that room." He indicated a door, which was nailed shut, with a mass of clobber piled against it.

"Do you know much about your family history?" I asked.

He replied with an extraordinary statement, diving into the nineteenth century, saying eagerly, "Oh, yes, sir. It was Bruce Eady sold us into slavery."

Flowers Lane

On this sunny day, in the poorest part of the poorest town in South Carolina, I saw that Flowers Lane was not really a lane; it was about two acres of wasteland softened by the recent rain, with dirt tracks imprinted on it. And the houses scattered around this area of mud puddles and stony ground were not houses; they were hovels and decaying trailers, the sort I'd seen in the poorest towns of the Mississippi Delta. That was where Assistant Treasury Secretary Cyrus Amir-Mokri had passed through in 2011 and gazed on the ruination and the ragged people, remarking that he could not believe conditions like this existed in the United States. Perhaps that was less a comment on the United States and more a judgment on this privileged Iranian-born bureaucrat, who should have known about our "submerged twentieth." Flowers Lane was in South Carolina, but it could have been in the Delta, and—as I kept thinking—it could have been in Zimbabwe too.

"You know the people here?" I asked Wilbur.

"I know them some," he said. "This family asked for renovation. They're on our list. Maybe we can help. That's why I'm here—to do an assessment."

The low, flat-roofed rectangular house, mobile-home-sized, had been faced in white plastic, and at first glance it did not look half as bad as the rotting trailer across the field, or the shack messily bandaged in blue plastic next door. Looking closer, I could see that the white plastic was merely a cheap cosmetic covering splintered wood walls, that the window cracks were taped, that the porch was unstable. When I stepped on the porch planks—and on the floorboards inside the house—my feet sank as though I was walking on soft, wormy wood that was giving way.

An old woman met us at the door and seemed dismayed that there were two of us. She knew Wilbur, but who was I?

"I'm just looking," I said.

That seemed more dismaying to her — not that I blamed her. The front room was cluttered and obviously falling apart, and it was crowded: a tiny room with seven people, old and young, draped on chairs and sprawled on the floor. They were watching a soap opera, *The Young and the Restless*, on a television set that was flickering in the far corner.

What do people do when they have nothing to do? I had wondered this when I'd set off from home months before. The family in this poor house on Flowers Lane provided the hint of an answer. Such people try to keep warm. It was not the television show they were watching, or that some were lying on the floor, one boy under a low table, a small girl in an older girl's lap. It was the fact that they were huddled together in this ru-ined house, in this much-too-hot room. They stared at me and said hello when I did, and now I saw the assortment of ages, and that the only one of them in a proper chair was an old woman, with a steady gaze and a heavy shawl on her shoulders. There was a stump where her right foot should have been, and this amputation was the more emphatic for the red sock pulled tight on it. Her name was Janice Williams, and she might have been ninety, or older.

Her daughter, the one with the dismayed expression, who had let me in, was Sharlene Badger.

"This is Willie, and this is Roger," Sharlene said, indicating two older boys in their late teens or early twenties. They smirked at me in a taunting way. Then one of them stood up — they had been lying on the floor — and put his face against mine.

"You can call me Roger Rabbit," he said. "If y'all got any questions."

"No questions yet," I said.

I was slightly alarmed by Roger's wolfish alertness and his dirty clothes. He wore a torn T-shirt with the motif of dark gesturing hands, each with an upraised middle finger, and over it, *Fuck Y'all Records*, not a music label that I was familiar with.

"Get Jessica," Sharlene Badger said. "Jessica can answer your ques-tions."

"I think Wilbur's got the questions," I said.

The small room was very hot, and it stank of dirty cushions and human feet, and the heat made it all the smellier, as of roasted flatulence.
It was the smell of poverty, a stink that no one, not even someone in the
submerged twentieth, could get used to, and it was intensified by a hissing
gas fire attached to the wall, giving the alarming impression that the wall
itself was in flames.

From the moment I'd entered the room, I'd been aware of the hiss.
Outside, a spring day — of sunshine, with a light breeze — in the mid-seventies perhaps, shirtsleeve weather. Inside, the huddled family, with the
gas fire blowing heat into the room. These people were cold on a warm
day, indoors, with nothing to do except to keep warm.

Four generations of them: the old woman, the matriarch; Janice her
daughter; her grandsons Roger and Willie; an older girl, a granddaughter, who turned away when I asked her name; and the girl's daughter, age
six, who told me her name, Shaquavien Thompson, as her hair was being
braided.

"That's a hazard," Wilbur said of the gas fire mounted on the wall,
spewing flames. "That needs to be vented."

A painting of Jesus on black velvet had been hung on one wall, with
family photographs, and other pictures of Jesus, above a shelf of plastic
trophies, a snow globe, a model of the Eiffel Tower, a dirty baseball, a mass
of tangled beads, souvenir ashtrays, two propped-up postcards of New
York City, some thick gold tassels on a thick gold braid, and a dish of loose
buttons. The chairs were jammed together so tightly there was scarcely
room to walk, and I found myself sidling from the entrance to the back of
the room, trying to avoid the oddly leering face of Roger.

It was not poverty as an absence or an insufficiency of things, but poverty as a great unsorted accumulation of decaying and broken possessions, crowding the room the way the people did, like tide wrack heaped
on a beach, the sort of debris a storm had deposited. Doing a rapid calculation, I realized that in that hot tiny room, hiding on this afternoon
in spring on the dirt road that was Flowers Lane, in this four-generation
family, there was no sign of a breadwinner.

"Here she is, here's Sweetpea," Sharlene Badger said as a smiling girl
stepped into the room from the flash of sunlight outside, and greeted us.

This was Jessica. She was tall and wore a green sweater and black tights. Her hair was braided and colored with gold highlights, and had long, closely woven hair extensions. Her vitality was unmistakable—I could see why her mother had summoned her to speak for the family. She was worldly, she'd done a course in cosmetology, she said; she'd traveled a little bit. She wasn't fazed by Wilbur or me. She led us down a narrow passage, showing us the house, the stained ceiling tiles, the bedrooms that had no windows and seemed to be a mass of quilts and blankets and mattresses on the floor.

"We got leaks," Jessica said. "The rain comes through up there—see this puddle?"

But it wasn't a puddle, it was a soggy blanket, darkened by water, in the shadowy and airless room. Jessica lived there too. Altogether, she said, nine people inhabited the four-room house—three small bedrooms and this stifling front room. I could not imagine the disposition of bodies at bedtime.

"I'm thinking of relocating to Ohio," Jessica said.

"Show them the kitchen," Sharlene said over the hiss of the gas fire and the squawk of the soap opera.

"The kitchen real bad," Jessica said. "That ceiling falling down, the floor's gone too."

This was a tiny room tucked at the back, with a greasy, gummy stovetop, a chipped refrigerator, a sink stacked with dirty dishes, a counter full of torn-open cereal boxes. Outside, a patch of yard was scattered with Shaquavien's toys, some old car tires, and a broken swing set.

"If we knew you were coming, we would have cleaned the place up," Jessica said.

"That's okay," Wilbur said.

"Think you can do something?" she said.

"We can help. We can vent that stove and shore up the floor," he said. "Might be able to fix that ceiling." He was making notes as he talked. "Patch the roof."

As he spoke amid the squalor, I admired his calm and reassuring demeanor. I had no doubt that he would do as he promised, and make improvements.

The rest of the family kept watching the midafternoon soap opera—a romantic dispute onscreen, a quarreling young white couple—as Wilbur and I thanked them for allowing us to visit and went outside, where we stood in the mud of Flowers Lane and surveyed the damaged house.

"What do they live on?" I asked.

"That old woman you saw, she's the key. Probably gets Social Security. Other than that ...." His voice trailed off. He was thinking what I was thinking: food stamps, disability payments, unemployment insurance, government cheese, welfare, handouts.

It was just one poor house, one poor family—one of millions—but a vivid glimpse of poverty and hopelessness, of isolation and idleness.

Wilbur was still sizing up the house. He said, "You know, this is going to be a big job. It would be better to gut the whole place and build it all again. But we don't have the money."

Roger and Willie had followed us outside. They were sitting on old bicycles, smiling at us, rocking back and forth. They were too big for the bikes, and because of that they seemed playfully menacing, straddling the bikes, jerking them at us and laughing. Jessica had wandered out to the porch, holding the six-year-old Shaquavien by the hand. In the sunshine they all looked different, more exposed, sadder.

Walking away, Wilbur said to me, "We'll do something."

"Yes, living with them was frightful, but still they are human beings," the narrator says, speaking for Olga, at the end of Chekhov's story "Peasants." "They suffer and cry like human beings, and there is nothing in their lives for which justification could not be found ... And now she felt sorry for all these people, painfully sorry, and kept looking back at the huts as she walked."

The Fall

I drove from Allendale, back along Atomic Road to Aiken and Augusta, then across Georgia and into Alabama again, by way of Talladega and Childersburg to Greensboro, where I had an appointment that week. There I had an accident. Killing time at the edge of town, I walked to examine the run-down Inn Motel (Mr. Patel, prop.), near the junction of Route 69 and State Street. It was hideous and looked uninhabitable.

As I left the parking lot, I stepped off the sidewalk, fell forward, and kept falling. Anticipating a flash of catastrophe and pain, and in a moment of panic too quick for me to form words in my head, I saw images of myself: a broken arm, a smashed face, a cracked skull, a messy death.

I tumbled into a cement culvert and crumpled in shock. I lay like a badly plinked squirrel for a minute or two. Then, crawling upright, my right forearm bleeding and sore, both hands raw, I blessed my luck that I had not broken a bone. My head ached, and the dirt jammed into my bleeding hands worried me. I squatted in the dust for a while to compose myself, then went to the nearby drugstore and bought bandages and anti-septic. After that, I sat in my car and dressed my injuries.

My fall was shocking and annoying. I might have died, people say. But I was angry with myself for being inattentive, for assuming that the sidewalks of Greensboro were as symmetrical and safe as the sidewalks where I came from.

I gave myself a day off and drove to Demopolis, where I found a motel on the bypass road. In my room, aching badly, I fell into a deep sleep. I woke up twelve hours later, still hurting, still feeling lucky.

Vernell Micey

In Demopolis, which is an exhausted yet pretty town on the Tombigbee River, of sedate houses, several lovely mansions, and mostly empty shops, I met Vernell Micey and tried to understand what he was trying to tell me. Vernell had the strongest local accent that I had yet encountered in the South. He recommended a restaurant called the Red Barn, but he gave the name four jaw-twisting haws: *Rey-oh Bow-un.*

He was in his early twenties, a senior in college, studying accounting, a small, friendly, excitable fellow, scowling through large eyeglasses.

When I complimented him on the serenity of Demopolis, he became indignant.

"I want to leave this town," he said angrily. His snarl made it almost comic, yet with a hint of pathos. "I want to leave this state."

"Where would you go?"

"I'd like to go north, to New York City, or somewhere, anywhere. I want to get away from here. I want to get away from my family."

"Ever been up north?"

"I've never been out of Alabama," Vernell said. "That's why I want to go. I don't care what's it like. It's got to be better than this."

Demopolis was an island surrounded by open fields and groves of trees, areas of outstanding natural beauty. Here and there, at a shack or near a cluster of decaying trailers, a woman would be hanging washing on a line, or a man under a propped-up car hood, leaning over an engine block. For miles there was no sign of modernity; you could not tell what year it was; the decrepitude and the clutter and the simplicity of the settlements suggested an earlier time. The poorer places seemed to exist outside time. It was not strange that Vernell wanted to leave, but he seemed more urgent than others, even frantic.

Pawnshop

Like many similar towns in the South, Demopolis was known for its several antebellum mansions: Bluff Hall, an early-nineteenth-century cotton planter's home of majestic proportions, a Federal-style building that had been Grecianized in 1840; Gaineswood, a squat manor of white plaster built a decade later, more solid, more Greek, but sitting too close to the modern, red-brick Demopolis High School to possess much grandeur now; and Lyon Hall, with its porticoes, colonnades, hipped roofs, balconies, belvederes, and domes. As for the unwelcome fact that they were built by slaves, you could say the same about the pyramids, but the Egyptians had better excuses for using forced labor.

Such oversized houses, the McMansions of the slave states, were touted as sights for visitors, and some had been spruced up. But just as many or more had fallen into ruin, calling to mind the words of Rebecca West: "There is something especially terrifying about a house that is very big and very poor . . . a Blenheim of misery."

In any case, Demopolis was also a town of modest bungalows, dogtrot houses, shotgun shacks, an area of decaying huts, and the remnant of a downtown with a defunct movie theater and shops struggling to stay alive. The motels, eating places, strip malls, gas stations, and banks lined the bypass road, which was also the road into Mississippi.

The exception, the busiest store in Demopolis proper — and the exception in most Southern communities in this condition — was the pawnshop, Trade and Traffic, in the center of town on the corner of Washington and Walnut. The pawnshop was thriving, multiracial, full of life — people selling, people buying. The shelves and display cases were filled with pawned tools, household appliances, clothes, jewelry, coins, Civil War and World War Two items, bayonets, helmets, canteens, and the usual Nazi memorabilia. Against one wall were shelves of weapons, with a selection of rifles, pistols, and knives, an arsenal being examined by earnest browsers in slouch hats and blue jeans.

And like most of the other pawnshops I'd looked at in the South, the mood of the place was hospitable and helpful. A dozen people shuffled through the shop, picking through the merchandise, and one happy man was surrendering an old chainsaw for a sum of money.

A black man with a bristly beard and a hunter's cap sidled in past the stuffed deer head and the rusted harrow still with dirt in its blades, said hello to the browsers in his path, and made for the back of the shop, where a very fat man at the firearms section was leaning against a display case of revolvers. The man leaning was the clerk, and it was midmorning, and he was eating a takeout hamburger with such gusto he'd snagged the wrapper in his teeth and was chewing paper.

"What's going on, heavy man?"

"I ain't got no idea," said the man, chewing.

"Effen you don't, then no one do."

"Bleeding Like a Hog"

Down the country lanes, past catfish farms, cattle ranches, and open fields — a horse nudging a foal struggling on spindly legs — past hedges growing out of control, the white froth of cherry trees, and bouquets of peach blossoms, I drove to Greensboro again, where more redbuds were in bloom.

The spring day was hot, and Main Street was a glare of sunlight blazing against the metal sides and dazzling windows of parked cars. I sat down on a bench on the shady side of the street near the Pie Lab, because the man seated on the other side of the bench smiled at me. He was very old and had one arm, a stump articulated at the elbow.

A brown beaky cap was jammed slightly tilted on his head. The thick lenses of his eyeglasses suggested cataracts, and he wore a heavy wool coat in spite of the spring heat. His smile was welcoming, and he patted the bench with the only hand he had. I took him to be about eighty, and he had the vaguely Native American cast of features that some black people had in this part of the South. His name was Floyd Taylor.

"The gun was loaded," he said at last, after we'd passed the time of day and I'd asked the obvious question. "Because you never know what you're going to find, and we was hungry, and depended on squirrels and such to eat. I was watching for squirrels, the gun leaning against me. The hammer was on the outside—they don't make them like that no more. I had the safety switch off, and I picked it up by the barrel and trigger, and it come up and blow my arm off. I was bleeding like a hog for three quarters of a mile. But they fixed it and sewed it up and that's what I got left."

"Must have been a problem finding work, with only one good arm," I said.

"We was farmers," Floyd said. "It wun't much of a problem. I drove a truck on the farm for a while, and then I worked at a cee-ment place, making cee-ment. And then I worked on the roads, when they got busted. Drove a truck and sprinkled water on the roads, a water truck."

"With one arm?"

"Done it all with one hand," he said. "That was in Demopolis and Greensboro about thirty years ago, maybe forty or more, now I think about it."

"You grew up around here?"

"I'm from Greensboro, but the country outside." He canted his head back and smiled at the blue sky. "Life was pretty good here, but we never had no work. Even now we're trying to get some industry here. They had some things going, but they couldn't get labor cheap like before. They used to find it, the cheap labor, but they cain't no more."

"There's work in Tuscaloosa," I said.

"Nothin' here, though. If you cain't find work, you just stay at home. We didn't need much money."

I smiled at this, and remembered. *We weren't poor,* Thomas Hart Benton said of life as a struggling painter; *we just didn't have money.*

"When I was a boy my parents were farmers," Floyd went on. "We had corn, cotton, and outside of those fields we raised a few things to eat. We had watermelons, a big patch of watermelons. We never sold them. We just give 'em away. My pa didn't believe in selling. We raised sweet potatoes for ourselves. We made syrups and molasses."

"How do you make molasses?"

"Molasses we made out of cane and sorghum," he said. "Ribbon cane was top of the line. They had another one called POJ."

POJ, I found, was a variety of hybrid sugarcane developed in East Java, Indonesia, by the Dutch in the 1920s; the initials stood for Proefstation Oost Java. These imported rot-resistant hybrids saved the diseased cane fields of the South in the twenties and thirties.

"You take the cane and strip it. Then you take it to the syrup mill, where you had a thing like a crusher. You put the cane up there and hook your mule to it. And you had a pan, called a syrup pan, about four foot wide, and the syrup run into that pan, and up the front, that's where the heat stays. Like a skillet. You boils it and th'ows the top away with a ladle. That molasses was prime."

"It seems you could feed yourselves."

"We was poor, so we made our own food," he said. "Gutting and smoking hogs. Bleeding them, cutting them up, smoking them for about two-three days. We done everything ourselves."

"How much land did you have?"

"Forty or fifty acres, we rented it from a white man who had a lot of land. I have nothing bad to say about that white man. He had a tractor, though, and we had nothing but two mules."

"Mules instead of a tractor."

"Sure enough. Hook 'em up to the plow, but they only plowed one furrow at a time, not like a tractor that could do two or more."

We went on talking about the old-fashioned farm, cotton picking, foraging, hunting.

"My father went out hunting almost every day," Floyd said. "He shot rabbits and squirrels and deer, and we et 'em." He smiled, perhaps thinking of those meals. Then he said, "Not like today. People are hungry today but all they do is sit around."

Paralyzing Despair

"When you come back again," Randall Curb had said, in the no-hurry way of the South, assuming that nothing would change, because so little had changed. And he hadn't finished the sentence.

People often said "Come back," and consequently what I had thought of as a trip with a destination, like many I'd taken before to write about, became circular and seasonal, and I was not sure how it would end, or when.

The idea, which Randall eventually explained, was that he and I would drive over to Marion, the seat of Perry County, and see Mary Ward Brown, the short story writer, who in about a month would turn ninety-six. Randall was confident that when I came back, Mary T, as she was affectionately known to friends, would be eager to see me. More than that, she would still be alive, alert and talkative and healthy.

Randall had told me about Mary Ward Brown's work, and after I read three of her books — two collections of stories and her memoir — I was eager to meet her. Her writing was direct, unaffected, unsentimental, and powerful for its simplicity and for its revealing the inner life of rural Alabama, the day-to-day, the provincial manners and pretensions, the conflicts racial and economic. No gothic, no dwarfs, no twelve-year-old wives, no idiots, no picturesque monstrosities, nothing that could be described as phantasmagoric.

From her girlhood, Mary T had yearned to be a writer, and had begun some stories, but she had put her writing aside to raise her family. In her sixties she resumed writing; her stories were published by some New York magazines and university quarterlies; and she gained notoriety to the extent that she was invited on a tour in the 1980s to the Soviet Union. She was someone who spoke for the rural South. But until Randall mentioned her name, I had never heard of her. Her stories were a surprise and an enlightenment.

Randall was also a surprise. In his house full of books, he was welcoming—singular and solitary, with a sweetness in his nature; and as a local son he was well connected in town. He had lived through the town's segregation, had been an eyewitness to the civil rights battles on Main Street, and had chronicled much of this strife. He was not only the most widely read person I met in the South; he was one of the most widely read persons I'd met in my life. He'd been a teacher and a critic and a contributor to magazines and newspapers. He was modest about his writing, and as for his reading, he said that was how he spent his days, immersed in books.

He was blind now—a gradual blindness had descended as the years had passed, as the blind Argentine writer Jorge Luis Borges had described his similar progressive blindness. "Not that perfect blindness which people imagine," Borges said, because Borges had some ability to see, as Randall did. "In my case, that slow nightfall, that slow loss of sight, began when I began to see. It has continued since 1899 without dramatic moments, a slow nightfall that has lasted more than three quarters of a century . . . The pathetic moment came when I knew I had lost my sight, my reader's and writer's sight."

In "Blindness," the essay from which I am quoting, Borges writes, "Being blind has some advantages. I owe to the darkness some gifts," and he speaks of how he discovered other ways of perceiving that blindness has given him, and describes the many blind people (Homer, Milton, Joyce, and others) whose lives have been devoted to literature. Randall seemed to me one of those unusual and gifted people, a rare person living alone, among his many books, in a small town in rural Alabama that had become famous for its poverty and isolation.

I was happy to return. The first time I met him, Randall was recommended to me as the cheerful local historian. Like many private people who are devoted readers, he was happiest at home, and he rarely had a chance to speak to anyone about the books he was reading—or rather, these days, the audiobooks he listened to. I'd left him listening to *Time Regained,* the seventh and last volume of Proust's vast novel *In Search of Lost Time.* He was an enthusiastic reader of writers whom I admired, many of them uncelebrated today, such as Henry Green, Jean Stafford, Joyce Cary, and the other Elizabeth Taylor — the English short story writer. He had read all of Faulkner, all of Waugh, all of Henry James, all of Muriel Spark. In a world where books are decorative, or trophies, where books serve to furnish a room, Randall had read every book that rested on his shelves, and many more besides. He was brilliant and modest and solitary, and did not realize how unusual he was in this setting.

It was a relief to see him, to be able to talk about books, to hear his verdict on his completion of the Proust, to sound him out on my Faulkner confusions. As I'd felt before, when we first met, we had a common language and the common experience of books.

"Welcome, welcome," he said, pawing the air between us, to seize my hand and shake it. "Great to see you. Mary T's not expecting us until noon, so come on in and have a drink."

We sat among his bookshelves, the radio softly playing a Chopin nocturne, and talked about books, and the weather, and Greensboro. He spoke with enthusiasm, and yet between bursts of information, taking a breath, or listening, he seemed subdued, even sad, and lapsed into a silent pause.

"I haven't been well," he said after one of these pauses.

"You're better now, though?"

"A bit," he said, and became quiet again, blinking, as if sentences were running through his mind.

The room at once seemed to darken, and the books to cast shadows, as a silence descended — so odd, on this spring day, the sun so bright on his lawn, the cherry blossoms on the tree in his front yard. This difference reminded me of the poor shadowy room in the house on Flowers Lane, filled with the family goggling at the soap opera, the gas fire hissing up the wall, while outside the mud puddles sparkled in the sunshine and new leaves fluttered on the trees. Randall was still thinking.

"I suffer from clinical depression," Randall said at last. "I have had it my whole life."

"What form does it take?"

"It is a paralyzing despair," he said, but there was no self-pity in his voice, merely the stating of a condition, like naming a color.

"You've experienced it recently?"

"These past weeks, yes."

"'The black dog,' Churchill called it."

"All of that," Randall said with a wan smile.

"How do you deal with it?"

"I can't deal with it. There's nothing to do. I'm helpless."

"You can't function?"

"I can't think about functioning," he said. "I lie in bed. I can't get out of bed. I don't see the point of getting up."

"How long does it last?"

"Days pass. I have no willpower. I lie there and think to myself, Can I raise my arm? I consider this awhile, lying there. Then I think, Probably not."

He sat with his hands in his lap, saying that he was better now, but that at any time the melancholy might return and hold him in its paralyzing grip. I told him what William Styron had mentioned to me, of the physical effect of melancholy, the severe and monotonous pain, the brain ache, for which there was often no relief. Randall said that he had read Styron's *Darkness Visible*, and not only knew the lines from Milton, but felt that the words reflected his own melancholy.

> *No light; but rather darkness visible*
> *Served only to discover sights of woe,*
> *Regions of sorrow, doleful shades, where peace*
> *And rest can never dwell; hope never comes*
> *That comes to all; but torture without end . . .*

"What makes its slightly worse is that I have no one to look after me, only my mother, bless her," he said. "And she's eighty-five."

The fact that Randall was blind made his condition of melancholy more intense, more alienated and isolated, perhaps triggered it at times. But he wasn't looking for sympathy, he was explaining his fatigue.

"We're going to have a good time," he said, reviving a little, and smiled.

"Mary T is dying to meet you. I made a reservation at Lottie's in Marion — that's the best Southern cooking you're going to find around here. And look, it's a beautiful day."

"Limbic Resonance Is What You Need"

When I came to the town of Marion, I realized how moribund Greensboro was. The shops in Marion were still in business, and the town had a majestic courthouse, a large military institute, and Judson College, which Mary T (she insisted on the name, which was short for Mary Thomas) had attended. There were bookstores in Marion and the well-known soul food restaurant Lottie's. Martin Luther King's widow, Coretta Scott King, had been raised in Marion, and voting rights activist Jimmie Lee Jackson had been shot by an Alabama state trooper in the town in 1965, during a peaceful protest, a catalyzing event in the civil rights movement that provoked the confrontational and historic protest marches from Selma to Montgomery.

"Notice how it's desolate here," Randall said as we drove through the farmland outside of town. Though he was unable to see, he had a clear memory of the flat land, the fields of stubble, the wet clay roads, the thin patches of woods, the absence of any houses, now and then a crossroads. "You'll know it when you see it. It's the only house here."

That was true. After five miles of fields he said, "This must be Hamburg." Less than a minute later, a white bungalow appeared on the right-hand side of the road, and on the porch — we had called ahead — Mary T and a much younger woman in an apron.

"Is Ozella with her?" Randall said, twisting his head, trying to see. He explained that Ozella was the daughter of the previous housekeeper, Eula Mae Thomas. Ozella was standing next to Mary T, who was tiny, watchful, like a bird on a branch, and smiling in anticipation and fully alive. Very old and upright people have a dusty glow that makes them seem immortal.

"My father built this house in 1927," Mary T said after we were introduced, and I praised the house.

The modest two-story bungalow was squat and solid, fronted by the bulging porch, a dormer above it, so unlike the shotgun shacks and rectangular houses and pretentious mansions we'd passed at the edge of Marion. Inside, the walls were paneled in dark wood, a planked ceiling, an oak floor. Like Randall's house, it was filled with books, in bookcases that were fitted in all the inner rooms and upstairs. I paused in front of a painting of two women seated at a window.

"That's a Crawford Gillis."

She had three paintings by this artist, done in the 1980s. His was a new name to me. Born near Selma in 1914, Gillis had studied in New York and concentrated on depicting the rural poor, black and white, in a simple, powerful, rather slopy style, slightly distorted for effect, in the manner of Thomas Hart Benton but with gloomy colors. He was a regionalist, associated with the New South School (this pedantry I learned from a gallery blurb), who'd known success in the 1930s, but after the war had become a part-timer and an experimenter. Like Mary T, whose stories I had by now read with enormous pleasure, he was little known outside the South — apparently outside Alabama — yet a painter of considerable gifts, someone she had called a friend.

I told Mary T how pleased I was to meet her. As a short story writer she was the real thing, with a perceptive view of the South today. She wrote about the new tensions, her neighbors and her town, without affectation, in the clearest prose.

The very fact that there is such a person as a Southern writer (and not a Northern writer) seemed odd to me until I spent some time in the South. Southern fiction was an English department category, the most confining and dubious of pigeonholes, and in its stereotype it is filled with grotesque characters and prose so convoluted it was as though there was something the Southern writer found so painful or shameful he or she did not want to state it plainly. I was reminded of Conrad's Marlow saying (and it has a distinct Faulknerian echo), "It was the stillness of an implacable force brooding over an inscrutable intention" — waffling vaguely because Conrad does not want to write about cannibalism.

I had read Southern fiction all my adult life — not just Faulkner and the gothics but the lesser lights and the poets, the playwrights, the explainers, the apologists, the memoirists — yet for all the reading I had done, few of the books I'd read had prepared me for what I found in the South: the un-complaining underclass that amounted to a peasantry; the opportunistic newcomers, Northerners and foreigners, taking advantage of the South's accommodating culture; the powerful few, black and white, animated by their pretensions; the poverty, not the colorful kind of Catfish Row and Tobacco Road, but the grim and seemingly ineradicable hardship of Razor Road and the back lanes of the Delta. It was a region in which books — apart from the Bible — hardly mattered to most people, and why should they, when people spent their days struggling to get by? Freaks and goofballs were well documented in Southern fiction; the working poor not so much.

Mary T opened a bottle of blueberry wine from a winery in Harpersville, and though it was a warm noontime, a fly buzzing behind the hot white curtains in the small back dining room, we stood and clinked schooners of the wine and toasted our meeting, the ancient Mary T, the nearly blind Randall, and me, the disoriented traveler passing through. Something about the wood paneling, the quality of the curtains, the closeness of the room, the sense of being in the deep countryside holding a glass of wine on a hot day — all of it was like being in old Russia. I said so.

"That's why I love Chekhov," Mary T said. "He writes about places like this, people like the ones who live here, the same situations."

Chekhov's provincial towns, as one of his biographers, Ronald Hingley, has written, "are the scene of inspissated boredom which is only thrown into sharper relief by their inhabitants' pathetic attempts to diversify lives essentially dedicated to 'eating, drinking, and sleeping,' that common Chekhovian formula." Carson McCullers, who grew up in Georgia, has said that the paradoxes and grotesqueries of the South — they are the stuff of her fiction — resemble those in the fiction of peasant Russia, and she specifically mentions Chekhov, as well as Dostoyevsky, Tolstoy, and Gogol, in her 1941 essay "The Russian Realists and Southern Literature."

"The South and old Russia have much in common sociologically," McCullers writes. "The South has always been a section apart from the rest of the United States, having interests and a personality distinctly its own. Economically and in other ways it has been used as a colony to the rest of the nation. The poverty is unlike anything known in other parts of the country." She goes on to speak of the South's class system, the character traits, the peasant class, and much more as being like old Russia's—and she makes her point, which is almost like a boast, by Russifying these fields and farms.

"He loved the singularity in people, the individuality," Eudora Welty said of Chekhov in her *Paris Review* interview. "He took for granted the sense of family. He had the sense of fate overtaking a way of life, and his Russian humor seems to me kin to the humor of a Southerner. It's the kind that lies mostly in character. You know, in *Uncle Vanya* and *The Cherry Orchard,* how people are always gathered together and talking and talking, no one's really listening. Yet there's a great love and understanding that prevails through it, and a knowledge and acceptance of each other's idiosyncrasies, a tolerance of them, and also an acute enjoyment of the dramatic."

What is remarkable is that what she described almost seventy-five years ago is still pretty much the case today in the rural South—yet another reason why travel in these parts was such a melancholy pleasure.

The sunny day, the bleakness of the countryside, the old bungalow on the narrow road, no other house nearby, the smell of the muddy fields penetrating the room—and that other thing, a great and overwhelming sadness that I felt but couldn't fathom. Perhaps it was the effect of what Randall had told me, his devastating phrase "paralyzing despair."

"And Isaac Babel," Mary was saying. "'The Story of My Dovecote.'"

Babel, too, wrote of small towns, of back streets, of family life, especially in his autobiographical tales, and of Cossack settlements in other stories. Counterparts to the American South abounded in Russian fiction.

"Have a slice of pound cake," Randall said, opening the foil on a heavy yellow loaf. "My mother made it yesterday."

Mary T cut a crumbly slab and divided it among us, and I kept thinking: This could only be the South, but an enlightened and special niche of it, a house full of books, the dark paintings, the loudly ticking clock, the old furniture, the heavy oak table, something brooding and indestructible but looking a bit besieged. And that unusual, almost unnatural tidiness imposed by a housekeeper—pencils lined up, magazines and pamphlets in squared-up piles—Ozella's hand, obvious and unlikely, a servant's sense of order.

In *Fanning the Spark* (2009), a selective, impressionistic memoir, Mary T tells her story: her upbringing as a rural shopkeeper's daughter, her becoming a writer late in life—she was sixty-three when she published her first short story. It is a little history of surprises: surprise that she became a writer after so long, a period she called "the twenty-five-year silence"; surprise that her stories found favor; surprise that her stories won awards, the PEN/Hemingway, the PEN/Faulkner, and four others. Later, on the strength of a prize-winning story set in the rural South, "The Cure," and included in a Soviet-American anthology, *The Human Experience,* she was chosen to visit the Soviet Union in 1990 with a delegation that included other American writers, one of the highlights of her literary life.

She had been happily married, but it was brief; she was widowed in her forties. Her son, Kirtley, who had fought in Vietnam, had returned to Alabama and become a lawyer in Marion. He was now retired, but teaching at the military academy.

Setting her glass of wine down on the thick disc of coaster, she said, "I'm hungry for catfish"—the expression of appetite a delight to hear from someone ninety-five years old.

She put on a wide-brimmed black hat—the diameter, it seemed, of a bicycle wheel—and a red cape-like coat. Helping her down the stairs, I realized she was tiny and frail, but her mind was active, she spoke clearly, and her memory was good. Her bird claw of a hand was in my grip.

"That redbud is not doing so well. It needs some care," she said of a tree in the front yard. "We'll have to futtilize it."

All the way to Lottie's diner in Marion, on the country road, she talked about how she'd become a writer.

"It wasn't easy for me to write," she said. "I had a family to raise, and after my husband died it became even harder, because Kirtley was still young. I thought about writing, I read books, but I didn't write. My sister-in-law encouraged me. And I think I had an advantage. I could tell literature from junk. I knew what was good. I knew what I wanted to write. And when I came to it—I was over sixty—I rewrote hard. I tried to make it right."

I was driving out of what seemed the theoretical settlement of Hamburg—no other houses here—down the empty road that was as narrow as a track, enjoying her reflections, negotiating the occasional crossroads. At one of these crossroads, marked by small green signs, trying to read the name of her road, I asked her what it was.

"They renamed it," Randall said from the back seat before Mary T could speak. "It used to be Route 2. Now it's Dr. J. J. Howard Road."

"He was a quack," Mary T said.

We were now rolling down Marion's main street, Washington Street, past the military academy and the courthouse, past Green Street and beyond it Pickens, the site of Mack's Café — the places associated with the shooting of Jimmie Lee Jackson, now on the Black Heritage Trail. We passed churches with stout steeples and arched doorways, the stately white churches; the black churches were tumbledown and smaller, on the back streets. We came to Lottie's. I parked in front and eased Mary T out of the passenger seat and into the diner.

"I've been reading a book about interviews with people who are over a hundred years old," Mary T said, perhaps reminded of her frailty in her unsteady progress from the car to the door of the diner. "It was called something like *Lessons from the Centenarians*."

"What sort of lessons?"

"All sorts. But the lesson to me was, I don't think I want to live that long."

People seated at their meals looked up from their food as Mary T entered, and many of them recognized her and greeted her. While Mary T moved slowly along, lifting her hand to greet them, she talked about writing, saying, "Limbic resonance is what you need . . ."

This exalted expression in the humble diner was a bit startling and obscure. I wrote it down, and later found it was defined as "mood contagion," an instinctive understanding of others' emotions — in a word, empathy.

Meanwhile, Mary T and Randall had seated themselves and were ordering sweet tea. There followed that menu-perusing silence of hungry diners. Lottie's offered all sorts of chicken, fried and baked; fried catfish, grilled catfish, catfish fillets; mashed potatoes, mac and cheese, and three kinds of boiled greens. Everyone got a biscuit.

"See, the Yankee's having the grilled catfish," Randall said after we ordered. "We stick with the fried."

I asked Mary T about her childhood, living on the top floor of her father's general store, the Munden-Ward Store, in the small settlement of Hamburg. She was happy to reminisce, speaking slowly, and I wished I could have recorded it, because she spoke in the accents of a hundred years ago.

"My mother worked in the store. She was too busy to raise me," she said, pausing after each sentence, a bit breathless. "I was raised by our black housekeeper. She was also the cook. I called her Mammy. I know it's not good to call someone Mammy these days, but I meant it. She was like a mother to me. I leaned on her."

"If my mother ever sat and held me as a child I don't remember, but I do remember the solace of Mammy's lap," she had written in her memoir, *Fanning the Spark*. "Though she was small, light-skinned and far from the stereotype, her lap could spread and deepen to accommodate any wound. It smelled of gingham and a smoky cabin, and it rocked gently during tears. It didn't spill me out with token consolation but was there as long as it was needed. It was pure heartsease."

"And you know she may have saved my life," Mary T told me. "I had colitis. I was just a small child and I was starving, about to die. Mammy understood. She gave me a tablespoon of buttermilk every day, and then more. Little by little she increased it to half a cup, and then a cup. The black people were so poor they couldn't afford to go to the doctor. They had their own remedies. That was one of them. Buttermilk. It saved my life."

I mentioned another tradition I'd heard of, so-called potlikker. The broth from boiled greens, usually discarded, was drunk by the poor in the South and was so nutritious it helped keep them healthy, and especially prevented pellagra.

But Randall, his mind on Mammy, was talking about the changes in the South that he knew. That provoked Mary T to indignation.

"It's all different these days," Mary T said. "The black people here look at me with hatred. It's because of the difference. It's not because of something I did. It's a resentment. It makes them vote for Albert Turner." This was Albert Turner Jr., the Perry County commissioner, son of a civil rights leader and Selma marcher.

"What's his story?" I asked.

Mary said, "He tells people they're poor because of slavery and the white people who held them down. But is that so? Think of all the people on welfare. You find families where there's three generations on welfare, who've never had jobs, and with children too."

What will happen here? I wondered.

"Time will help," Mary T said. *Tahm will he'p.*

While she talked, people dropped by the table to say hello, in the courteous way that Mary T had mentioned as being a characteristic of Alabama. One woman gave me some pamphlets and mentioned Jimmie Lee Jackson; another introduced herself, saying "Hah, y'all," and reported on someone Mary T knew ("He's getting new knees"), and then, "Y'all take care." Mary nodded and smiled and, after she was out of earshot said, "She's the upper crust in Marion." But it was Mary whom they'd gone out of their way to pay court to—Mary the ancient inhabitant, Mary the writer, Mary the witness.

Randall had been frowning at "Time will help." He said, "I'm a bit hopeful. I mean, I saw the worst of the civil rights struggle—the fighting, the bombs, the demonstrations." He rested his fork against the feeble and spiny skeleton of a catfish on his plate. "I think about where we were, and it's seems there's been considerable progress."

"But the divisions will always be there—the racial divisions," Mary T said.

In one of her best stories, "Beyond New Forks," a white woman is driving her elderly black housekeeper home and is reminded how awkward subjects come up, contrasting their lots in life, black and white:

> And suddenly the whole Pandora's box of race, with all the unconscious, unintended, even unrecognized withholdings of respect, status, privilege, even rights we never thought about, much less understood at the time, embedded as they were in custom and usage, would open up to silence us completely.
>
> We never tried to examine or explain such things in words, as some claimed to do. We would simply look at each other hopelessly, after which one or the other would change the subject and start getting ready to go.

And I reminded myself that Mary T had been born in 1917. She had been in her twenties during the Depression. She was only six years younger than James Agee, so she had known the poverty and the share-croppers, the poor whites and the poor blacks, the lynchings of the 1930s in the Black Belt — a harrowing history. The somber Walker Evans photo-graphs of the storefronts and the streets and the white folks of Hale and Perry counties constituted an album of Mary T's early life.

"Let me tell you about the school," she said. "When I was growing up, the black people on the farms didn't go to school. Then, after some years, and they went to school, the schools were poor. They didn't have much of a start. They were so far behind. So when things changed, we all had to back up."

"Some people do take education seriously," Randall said in his earnest and generous way.

"I knew a woman," Mary T said. "She was a good woman. But the hus-band was sorry. She drove every day to Marengo Mills in Demopolis to work. Then she went to school and got her degree. She became a nurse. She worked, she studied, she made such an effort. Her husband did noth-ing at all."

I said, "That's the sort of situation you've written about in your short stories."

"Yes, I have."

"What does your family think of your writing?" I asked.

This question made her laugh so hard her laughter became a cough, and she covered her mouth with her bird-claw hand and became short-winded.

"As far as I know they don't read it!" she said at last. "No one ever men-tions it — that I write. I don't think they care!"

And she laughed again, not the bitter laugh that I expected, but genu-ine amusement, as though she was commenting on utter silliness, and of course she was. And I thought of the ingratitude and philistinism of a family that studiously ignored the genius and witness of this woman's work.

"I did my best," she said. "I told the truth."

"Amen," Randall said.

On the way back to Hamburg, she told me a story relating to a family estrangement. She told it well, each phase of it, at first without emotion, but then in a tremulous voice. It was so dramatic and complete in her telling that I urged her to write it. She said she had not written a story in years. I said that this one would be perfect. After I dropped her at her remote house, the sun lowering into the fields, she waved from the porch, Ozella beside her. I dropped Randall in Greensboro and hit the road again.

The following week, Mary T sent me an email, remarking on something I'd written, saying I was a real writer — praise from her was like a garland. "You can tell one in a sentence or two, can't you?" she wrote. "Thank you for the book. It was a privilege to have you in my house." In response, I mentioned the factual account of the family estrangement from her own experience that she had told me, and said I thought it would be a corker of a short story.

"I do too," she replied, "and it's roiling around in my subconscious but as fiction. I've always wanted to write a short-short story, and this could be it. In its uniqueness and coldness it seems to need isolation, like a photograph. Or so it seems at the moment."

I wrote again in the following days. I received a brief reply — "Not feeling well" — and then there was silence. Randall wrote to say that Mary T was ill and in the hospital. About a month after we met, she died. The cause was given as pancreatic cancer.

By then I was home, as though in another country, at the far end of the road that led to the South.

INTERLUDE

~

The Fantastications of
Southern Fiction

Reading made me a traveler; travel sent me back to books. When I got home, I immersed myself in Southern fiction. The Faulkner I had read in my last interlude, and the places I had seen in the spring, made me curious to know how the novels and short stories located in the Deep South might give me better access to the reflective interior of those states, so passive, so mute. Many Southern writers are defiant in their belief in a nebulous concept of regionalism — that they are expressing in their work the heart and soul of the South. Faulkner's conviction in this was so strong that his fiction seemed to define the South, its history and its people. Though the more I read him, the greater my realization that, for all his obsession with detail, he left unwritten, undefined, the simple fact that for his entire life he lived at the edge of a university campus that demeaned its black workers and excluded black students. Fascinated to the point of mania by the past, he seemed bored, annoyed, and uncomprehending of the enormous events of the present to which he'd been an eyewitness.

On my previous trip, on the banks of the Savannah River I had passed by Wrens, Georgia, childhood home of Erskine Caldwell, who, apparently inspired by the country folk he knew, wrote *Tobacco Road* (1932), one of his earliest and most successful novels. This is the saga of the sharecropper Jeeter Lester, his wife Ada, who has no teeth ("she dipped snuff since she was eight years old"), his son Dude, who marries a much older woman named Bessie (who has no nose), his daughter Ellie Mae (who is mute and has a harelip), and his daughter Pearl, whom he marries off to his friend Lov Bensey when she turns twelve. This twelve-year-old wife sleeps on the floor, refusing to share the marital bed with the much older Lov, who is aggrieved at his child wife's disgust. What the *hail* is going on here?

In his works of fiction, once immensely popular for the very coarseness for which they are belittled now — they sold in the tens of millions in the 1930s and '40s — Caldwell created a popular image of the South as a landscape peopled by grotesques. Most of his white characters seemed to come from Dogpatch, L'il Abner's hometown, which first appeared in the Al Capp comic strip in 1934. *Tobacco Road* and *God's Little Acre* (1933), just as outlandish in its cast, along with Faulkner's *Sanctuary* (1931), set the tone for the Southern novel of tenants and sharecroppers in which the freakish and the darkly comic predominated — bizarre characters, unspeakable crimes, unnatural acts, shocking sexual situations — almost as a form of literary indirection. Why does this seem like a trick? Because black life, the racial rejection, and the peasant misery only obliquely enter these narratives.

Though Caldwell's novel *Trouble in July* (1940) and his long story "Kneel to the Rising Sun" (1934) concern the lynching and harrying of innocent black men, and Faulkner's *Light in August* (1932) has a near-lynching that ends in the shooting and castration of Joe Christmas, these works are exceptional. Southern fiction and its grotesques, sometimes termed "Southern gothic," seldom touched upon (and seemed to accept) the day-to-day injustices of the 1920s and '30s. So we have a nightmarish literature of dwarfs, hunchbacks, albinos, night hags, and deviants (in *Sanctuary*, the impotent Popeye, who has "yellow clots for eyes," rapes Temple Drake with a corncob), but little mention of forced labor, racial violence, extreme segregation, and the lynching of blacks. You see this Witches' Sabbath of freaks throughout Flannery O'Conner and Carson McCullers and in the early Truman Capote.

"The Artificial Nigger," Flannery O'Connor's much-praised story in the collection *A Good Man Is Hard to Find* (1955), shows black life as a grotesque netherworld. In another tale in this collection, "Good Country People," a bogus Bible salesman runs off with the prosthetic leg of a woman he has failed to seduce. Good fun, you think, but O'Connor's intention is often spiritual redemption and high-mindedness, as in her brilliant short story "Revelation," from *Everything That Rises Must Converge* (1965), describing the enlightenment of Mrs. Ruby Turpin, which buds in a doctor's waiting room and blooms in a pigpen. The story is about class, race, and God's grace. Here, in a paragraph of Southern paranoia, Mrs. Turpin tortures herself with a farcical dilemma:

> Sometimes at night when she couldn't go to sleep, Mrs. Turpin
> would occupy herself with the question of who she would have cho-

sen to be if she couldn't have been herself. If Jesus had said to her before he made her "There's only two places available for you. You can either be a nigger or white trash," what would she have said? "Please, Jesus, please," she would have said, "just let me wait until there's another place available," and he would have said, "No, you have to go right now and I have only those two places so make up your mind." She would have wiggled and squirmed and begged and pleaded but it would have been no use and finally she would have said, "All right, make me a nigger then — but that don't mean a trashy one." And he would have made her a neat clean respectable Negro woman, herself but black.

Carson McCullers's novel *The Member of the Wedding* (1946) is the story of a twelve-year-old Southern girl, Frankie Addams, and her assorted friends and family. By chance, she meets a soldier on furlough, who persuades her to visit his hotel room, where he attempts to rape her. Her black cook, Berenice Sadie Brown, blind in one eye, wears a blue glass eye: "It stared out fixed and wild from her quiet colored face." A transvestite, Lily Mae Jenkins, puts in an appearance. An important experience for Frankie is her visit to the House of Freaks at the Chattahoochee Exposition, where she sees the Giant, the Midget, the Fat Lady, the Alligator Boy, and the Wild Nigger, though "some said he was not a genuine Wild Nigger, but a crazy colored man from Selma — he ate live rats." Later, Frankie wonders whether she will grow into a freak, and, she reflects, the near-rape by the soldier was "like a minute in the fair Crazy House."

Hardly fifty pages into Capote's debut novel, *Other Voices, Other Rooms* (1948), we have met a witch-like woman ("long ape-like arms . . . a wart on her chin . . . dirty-nailed fingers"), a black dwarf ("a little pygmy"), a one-hundred-year-old man named Jesus Fever, and a long-necked woman, a cook, who "was almost a freak, a human giraffe." Colorful, perhaps, but you have no notion that this narrative is taking place in a bleak segregated town; the horrors of the everyday are an accepted fact, not worth mentioning.

To Kill a Mockingbird (1960) seems on the surface to be a worthy evaluation of small-town Southern values, even if it is tediously plotty, overwritten, and predictable: the black laborer on trial for manhandling, throttling, and raping the white woman has a withered arm and could not possibly have done the deed, but he is found guilty and ends up shot to death. The critic Jeffrey Meyers has referred to the novel as "a sentimental, simple-minded rip-off of [Faulkner's] *Intruder in the Dust.*" And my brother Alexander has called attention to its "ecological fascism," asserting that while the novel insists "it is wrong for anyone to kill a mockingbird which so sweetly sings its heart out for us, it is nevertheless all right to shoot blue jays – this, when the headline theme of this so-called heartfelt, liberal novel unapologetically attacks the extremes of racism, bigotry, and ethnic selection." With a cast of stereotypes confirming every conventional prejudice against the Deep South, the book has sold in the millions.

Look closer and you see that *Mockingbird,* which most readers took to be a tale of the intolerant 1950s South, is set (decorous courtroom talk) "in this year of grace 1935," and it, too, has a lineup of freaks, including Misses Tutti and Frutti and the hideous racist Mrs. Dubose: "Her face was the color of a pillowcase, and the corners of her mouth glistened with wet, which inched like a glacier down the deep grooves enclosing her chin." Turns out Mrs. Dubose is a morphine addict. Boo Radley, taken to be a weirdo, turns out to be a hero. The news that Harper Lee was releasing another novel, *Go Set a Watchman,* written before *Mockingbird* and apparently rejected by her publisher, filled me with gloom.

The tall-tale tradition of Southern life as a malignancy – "gothic" is an elevating misnomer meant to ornament or dignify it – has persisted. The work of the late Barry Hannah, a Mississippian (born 1942), is an example. His fiction, too, has been described as "darkly comic" and "set in a phantasmagoric South." His stories, especially those in *Airships* (1978), have an unusual garrulity and undeniable power, a tipsy love of language, and broad humor; they are memorable for the utter absurdity of their situations. The same can be said for Charles Portis, whose name is solely attached to the comical Western *True Grit.* Portis was born and still lives in Arkansas, and his work is inspired by life in Arkansas even when the work is not set there. *The Dog of the South,* a brilliant road book – a manic drive from Little Rock to the Honduran jungle – is a good and hilarious example of this, and so is *Norwood,* which features an ex–circus midget,

Edward Ratner, "the world's smallest perfect fat man." Most of the gringos in *Gringos,* which is set in Mexico, are misfits and fantasists.

The best of these outlandish writers is Portis, because of the consistency of his humor, his fluency, his ear for the nuances and inflections of Southern speech, and his comic purity—his wish (nearly always achieved) to produce laughter. His characters, such as the con man Dr. Reo Symes, enlarge themselves with their talk, which is usually paranoia or bluff. "A lot of people leave Arkansas and most of them come back sooner or later" is one of the compact observations in *The Dog of the South.* "They can't quite achieve escape velocity."

Hannah and Portis broadened and deepened the same furrow that was plowed in the Southern soil by Caldwell and Faulkner, and the fantastications of their extravagant prose seem like a diversionary tactic. In the work of these writers, something odd and evasive is also taking place. It is as if an alternate reality, verging on a crude surrealism ("phantasmagoric"), in the form of mutilated and misshapen whites and freakish blacks, a sideshow of distraction, was invented to deflect from the bald facts of Southern life, the boredom and poverty and fatigue, the pedestrian cruelties and common abuses, the sorrows, the fatal misunderstandings.

This was why I felt so strongly about the writing of Mary Ward Brown, modest in scope but unsparing in its scrutiny. And the interconnected stories in Eudora Welty's *The Golden Apples* (1949) were a masterly evocation of a Delta town in Mississippi. I was not a fan of Harper Lee's solitary (and I think overpraised) book, preferring her fellow Alabamian William March (1893–1954), best known for his last novel, *The Bad Seed,* and the obscure author of earlier ones, *Come In at the Door,* and *The Looking-Glass,* and many great short stories, as well as a superb war novel with multiple narrators, *Company K.* His story "Runagate Niggers," in *Some Like Them Short* (1939), is an ironic account of racial injustice and debt slavery. His work is without fantastication and is to my taste; to the land and people it depicted, it is devastatingly truthful.

All of these writers are white Southerners. The South's black writers, by contrast, have no need to resort to fantastication: the truth behind their fiction is so bizarre that the grotesque comes firsthand, ready-made. From the South's earliest black novelist, William Wells Brown—who partly based his 1853 novel, *Clotel; or, The President's Daughter,* on Thomas Jefferson's relationship with Sally Hemings — through Zora Neale Hurston, Ralph Ellison, Richard Wright, and Ernest Gaines, Alice Walker, the works of black writers are more factual, contain more obvious self-portraiture, are often polemical in their sentimental rage, and are emphatically racial in their indignation. And with the exception of Gaines, none of these writers remained in the South. For example, Brown, an escaped slave, died in Boston in 1884.

PART FOUR

Summer: The Odor
of Sun-Heated Roads

Don't never drive a stranger from your door,

He may be your best friend, you don't know . . .

—SAM CHATMON, Delta bluesman,
"Make Me Down a Pallet on Your Floor"

Chasing Summer

Under the impartial dazzle of the sun, late-summer exhaustion on Cape Cod had begun to set in with a visible sigh, a last gasp of heat fading the shrubbery with a distinct desiccation, a general wrinkling and shrinkage, the deep green of the oak leaves going pale, an uneven yellowing of the slumping tussocks of salt hay in the sea marsh, a blackish red blush surfacing in the leaves on the horizontal outflung branches of the pepperidge tree at the end of my road, and a nose-tickling fragrance from the upright brushes of tall, gone-to-seed timothy grass.

And still, with summer slipping away, the heat like a hammer.

The withering was obvious everywhere—in the burst milkweed pods that looked like small brittle taco shells spilling out silken-haired parachuting seeds, the droop of the leggy wildflowers, the sag of the morning glory vines, and the slant of headless daylily stems with the rotted petals beneath them: "Lilies that fester smell far worse than weeds."

The tomato plants in the vegetable garden were mildewed, blotchy, blighted-looking, even as their fruit was at its plumpest and most pickable, the fist-sized Brandywines yanking the weakened plants sideways and fracturing the skinny stems with their weight. The tawny patches of parched grass in the lawn were widening by the week, and the hydrangea blooms, discolored and stiff, were a frizz of brown, the leaves—and the leaves of most shrubs—dirtied by risen dust, the woody annuals with dead blossoms looking stricken and strangled.

I loved this heat. But the warmth of the day was temporary, like a gust of expelled and humid breath, the dog days of mid-August giving way to cooler nights and unpredictable shifts—an occasional storm or a day of chill—like a reminder of what was to come, the clammy hand of fall and the loss of summer's freshness. In the last gasp of vegetation, there was no point in watering or fertilizing or planting anything, since it was a season on the wane, an annual diminishment, the shortening days like an intimation of theft, leaving the impression that you're being cheated of light.

The best time to lock the house and head south, where the heat would linger for months more; to hit the road, to live again for lingering blossoms and green grass and dusty lanes; to recapture good weather and revisit familiar routes and friends, maybe find some new places, chasing summer, with the heightened alertness you feel when you're in a place you don't belong.

Tunneling South

Driving from the high Northeast, through the cruel ugliness of places like Bridgeport and the Bronx under a low grainy sky, was like a rarefied form of tunneling—with bridges and ramps, a route of snakes and ladders—enduring the dense traffic and the stifling and stinking and overheated air of foul particles to find open space, holding my nose to bore through it and find better air in the South.

This image of a tunnel is not fanciful. The potholed chute of I-95 is hectic, unpredictable, dangerous and bleak, cavern-like and confining, at times like shuttling through a sooty culvert. All the way from my home to Washington there are actual tunnels, lengthy ones dug under railway tracks and rivers and harbors, and I sluiced through them in ghastly orange glare as idiot cars raced past. The drive is something to endure: five hundred miles devoid of any loveliness, not even trees (though perhaps New York City will have some symmetry and beauty when, at some distant date, construction ceases and it is finally finished), a journey like a trip through a mine shaft where the air is so thickened by the murk of pollution that even the open road is like a tunnel.

Eleven hours of driving got me to Virginia, and when I awoke the next day and checked my map, I decided to take a different road and head to Georgia, where I had someone to meet in Elberton.

Almost without noticing, I was out of the tunnel and could breathe again, and the back roads of the South had the summer tang and licorice fragrance of softened, sun-heated tar.

"They Took Mah Teeth"

Some drivers were looking for a pit stop or lunch at the diner on the side road near Henderson, North Carolina, and one of them was Rob Birmingham, whom I sat with for a while. He was my age, and our lives had been parallel, black and white, his one of struggle, service, and ill health, mine one of indoor scribbling and disappearances.

"I was in the military. I sure been through it. I could tell you stories."

I was reminded that the South is full of army vets from small towns and humble homes, the military their escape, sometimes their salvation, often their burden, and now and then their punishment.

Rob Birmingham was a heavyset man with an earnest and kindly face, wearing a Washington Redskins cap and thick-lensed glasses. He walked with difficulty, in an odd toppling way, and had trouble with stairs. He was calm in repose—listening—his manner subdued, but when he spoke he became agitated, as though the act of speaking excited him and made him remember. He said he had been wronged.

"Please tell me what happened," I said.

"I was in the 82nd Airborne in Vietnam, 1968 and '69, ask anyone, the worst time. We lost sixty-five percent of our soldiers there. I was in an airmobile unit." He put his hands over his face and sighed, and resumed. "First there was the Agent Orange. We used to drink bomb crater water. We put pills in it to make it drinkable. But the pills were no good. It wasn't fit for a cow."

"It made you sick?"

"As a dog," he said. "I had problems from the moment I was discharged. Later on I went up to Walter Reed, for treatment and everything—for my PTSD and my sickness from Agent Orange. Sometimes it would take the nurse five or six hours to come and change you. They'd take your medication and sell it back to you. Also your shoes and socks—they'd take 'em and sell 'em back to you."

"What was the point of that?"

"It was a numbers game," he said with a grim smile, but I had no idea what that meant.

"It sounds like punishment."

"And mah teeth. They took mah teeth, so's I couldn't eat. I haven't the faintest idea why they did it, but it always caused a fight, and then I was in lockdown. They did a lot of things just to irritate you."

"You mentioned Agent Orange."

"Agent Orange affected my hip, my shoulder. It affected my kids too. My son Maurice had to go to Tucson, Arizona, to live. And my grandkids are affected too—I haven't the faintest idea why. I had my hip done, and back surgery, and both my knees done because of it."

He got up from the bench and sighed.

"They used us as guinea pigs and let us die."

We sat in silence for a while, the word *dah* still in the air, swelling, like a lengthening shadow. As though to break the mood, he asked me where I was going. I told him Georgia.

"You want to be particular careful," he said.

I said it was a pleasure driving the back roads of the Deep South. And I added that he'd been through a great deal, that he was a hero for having endured it. We swapped cell phone numbers.

Four hours later—I was entering South Carolina—my cell phone rang.

"It's Rob. You all right, man? You still on the road? You call me if you need anything."

Last Days

Another indication that I was in the South was the chorus of radio preachers across the whole dial, from frequency to frequency, shouting sermons of denunciation that proved we were in the Last Days.

"As Paul told Timothy—Second Timothy," they said, one after another. "'But know this, that in the Last Days grievous times shall come. For men shall be lovers of self, lovers of money, boastful, haughty, railers, disobedient to parents, unthankful, unholy, without natural affection, implacable, slanderers, without self-control, fierce, not lovers of good, traitors, headstrong, puffed up, lovers of pleasure rather than lovers of God, holding a form of godliness but having denied the power therefore. From these also turn away. For of these are they that creep into houses, and take captive silly women laden with sins, led away by divers lusts, ever learning and never able to come to the knowledge of the truth . . .'"

I went on listening, so I wouldn't miss the preacher asking for money, for good works, for outreach, and to keep the program on the air.

Some music played, and I thought: This doom and gloom is the way of the world, a description as applicable today as in the time it was written, in the first century, probably not by Paul but by a close disciple — the eternal truths of human weakness, greed, insincerity, and self-deception true in any age.

Last Days? Don't they know? These traits are the traits of all days, every day, everywhere.

Massoud: "I Make Curbstones"

In northeast Georgia, not far from the state line of South Carolina, I found the quarry town of Elberton and an unlikely Southerner named Massoud Besharat, who had arrived in Elberton from Tehran via Austria, France, and England. He had been recommended to me as an outsider who had succeeded in the South, where outsiders could claim so few successes.

"What do you do?" I asked.

He said, "I make curbstones." Then he laughed, but it wasn't a joke.

Mounted on the kitchen wall of Massoud's large house, on a side street in the small town, was a Yugoslavian-made AK-47 with a high-capacity curved magazine jammed into it. I remarked on this, saying I could not remember ever seeing a fully automatic assault rifle on display in a cozy kitchen, and what about the magazine, was it loaded?

"Of course is loaded! What use if not loaded?"

He lifted it from the wall and fiddled with the charging mechanism and laughed again, a mirthless mocking Iranian laugh, whinnying in his nose. A foreigner might learn to speak perfect English, but a foreigner laughs in his own native way, often an ancient and menacing noise.

Massoud owned several expensive motorcycles, including a Harley-Davidson Duo-Glide, which he rode throughout Georgia wearing a chic Louis Vuitton helmet. On the sloping man-made cliff of ornamental stones behind his house he had installed a waterfall that you could switch on and off. When it was on, and tumbling and gushing, I could barely hear what Massoud was saying, though this was not a hardship for me.

He put me in his attic spare room, and I got to know him over the next three days. That he was wealthy, boastful, hard-bargaining, nihilistic, art-loving, overbearing, stylish, scheming, wily, generous, calculating, and suspicious he freely admitted, putting these qualities down to his Iranian charm and upbringing. But he was quick to add, "I hate Iran. I hate Iranians. I ran away. I ran to London and I was very happy there working in a fish-and-chips shop."

He claimed to be a dropout, but somehow he had acquired a fortune, a mastery of stonecutting and the science of diamond saws, a connoisseurship of modern American and nineteenth-century French painting, a taste for interior decoration, a skill at selling high-end real estate, and a genuine though exhausting bonhomie. He seemed to me another example of an alien — like the inevitable Mr. Patel — spotting an opportunity in the South and seizing it. But Massoud was more colorful than most, and more enterprising.

Although he was swarthy and hawk-nosed and conspicuously exotic, and loud with opinions, he had many friends and well-wishers in this rural Deep South town of five thousand people. Far from being shunned or badgered, he'd been welcomed, probably because he had an egomaniacal confidence, a sense of humor, and lots of money, and undoubtedly because he was a part of Elberton's success in employing hundreds of local people. He also owned a busy art gallery in Atlanta, about one hundred miles away. Showing me a brochure that pictured the sculptures of the shapely women exhibited in his gallery, he said, "My ex-wives and girlfriends!"

I complimented him on the paintings in his house.

"These are nothing. You must visit me in Paris," he said. "I am finishing a hotel in Barbizon. There is nothing like it in all of France. Just twelve suites, luxury ones, and each suite is filled with paintings of the Barbizon

School. You know Barbizon?" Then he began to yell. "Beautiful painters! Millet! Corot! Félix Ziem! My hotel will be like a *musée* — is already like a *musée!* I have exhibitions now in the salon!"

He happened to be holding a vintage German Luger as he was talking to me. He said, "Guns. I love guns," and pressed the pistol to his face, like a child caressing his cheek with a binkie. Adding to the effect were Massoud's eyeglasses, which were orange-rimmed. He claimed to own fifty pairs of glasses — different colors, but all of them the same goggle shape.

THE TOWN OF Elberton, known mainly for its quarries, sits on a three-mile-thick, thirty-mile-long, solid subterranean bed of blue granite. The first quarry was dug in 1882, and quarrying started in earnest in 1889, flourishing when an Italian stonecutter named Peter Bertoni came to Elberton, bought a quarry, and began cutting and sculpting granite monuments. Elberton claims to monopolize the granite gravestone business in the United States, and it also fashions cobblestones and paving blocks and countertops and obelisks and tall pillars. There were now forty quarries in and around the town and more than two hundred stone companies. Massoud owned Blue Sky, one of the biggest quarries in the area, and was sawing the foundation and underparts of Elberton into chunks, dividing those chunks into curbstones, and shipping them all over the country.

Though he tended to clown and to tease, he was an ingenious man with a nose for profit, alert for ways to augment and improve his businesses. He had hundreds of employees, black and white and Mexican migrants too, laboring in his quarries. The technique of stonecutting was slow and tedious, accomplished with complex and specialized machinery, large steel cranes, flywheel contraptions that drew a continuous diamond-wire loop through the granite wall of the quarry, cooling the wire with a jet of water, and freeing twenty-foot-high blocks, a whole Stonehenge of slabs rolling out every day.

"Can you imagine how much diamond wire we use for this?" Massoud said. "And it's expensive. We used to buy it from China."

"You don't buy it anymore?"

He laughed, giggly mirth, which, with the red-rimmed glasses he had on today, made him seem silly. But he was no fool.

"I make the diamond wire! I have factory in Elberton! I sell diamond wire! I make business."

Later he showed me Imex, his factory on a back street, which was half assembly line and half high-tech laboratory, where thirty or so employees were electroplating diamond chips or beads to a strong but flexible quarter-inch wire. This work of making coils of diamond wire was slow, and there were many fiddly stages in the process, requiring technical skill, expensive machinery, and great patience from the fabricators, given the monotony and exactitude at each stage. In another factory nearby, a team of men and women made rotary saws with diamond teeth — ten feet in diameter — giant discs used for cutting the granite.

"This is eco-friendly. I'm not like the other guys — they use jet-piercing method, flames that heat the rock and make channels. I cut it with diamond wire. Less waste, no fire."

This small town in rural Georgia was noted for its quarries but not for its technical schools or training colleges or manufacturing. So, seeing the many workers in white smocks and goggles, bent over the workbenches, among the fat jars of sparkly diamond chips, and others annealing the diamonds in white-hot ovens, I asked, "Where did these people learn how to do this?"

"Me — I teach!" Massoud said. "And Bijan."

Bijan Amini was his cousin, also a refugee from Iran, and an engineer and chemist, the supervisor of both the quarry work and the production of diamond wire.

"Best for slabbing large surfaces," Bijan said. "Extracting big blocks of stone. Faster. No waste."

"He is genius!" Massoud said. "Now I must go. I have a French lesson tonight. I have business in France. I want to speak this language. But how can I help you? What do you want to see? My butler — you can meet him. He is a redneck! He loves guns! What do you want to do?"

I said I wanted to talk to some of his employees at the quarry, who looked so tiny and well organized in the deep, squared holes in the earth, laboring like Egyptians, as though cutting vast blocks for pyramids, swinging them on tripods and pulleys.

Jesse: "Everyone Knows That Tingly Feeling Goes Away"

In the steamy rain and mass of puddles, the granite quarry looked like botched surgery on a grand scale, the green earth and the woods laid open and the stone innards exposed and carved up and hoisted. Ten different pits had been dug across eighty acres — systematically, the machines whirring, the diamond wire gnawing, but it was all oddly brutal, this removal of solid stone, making a deep, square-sided hole where the surface had once been a curvaceous set of hills. It sounds fanciful to say that the quarrymen were doing violence to the earth, but that was how it seemed to me — like plunder, like violation, disemboweling Elberton. Yet I could not deny the ingenuity of it, the scrambling men, the howling machines, the enormous blocks sawed out of solid rock, the open pits in the ground with smooth rock walls.

At the entrance to the quarry were open-sided, high-roofed sheds where granite slabs were sized and cut with rotary saws into curbstones, and others hacked apart by massive, wide-bladed guillotines. None of this was simple: each slab weighed ten tons and had to be maneuvered, chained to a block and tackle. It was tedious work, and the challenge of cutting and shifting the heavy granite impressed me as much as the sight of the technicians in goggles making long coils of diamond wire in the factory the day before.

In one of the stonecutting sheds a young man with a hammer and chisel chopped at the edge of a granite slab that was acquiring the look of a curbstone.

As I walked past, the man turned away, but just as he did I saw his aggrieved expression and pained eyes. I kept walking, but later, when the rain grew heavier, I used the storm as an excuse to duck into his work shed and talk to him.

"Mind if I join you?"

"Go ahead, plenty of room."

He put down his chisel, picked up a sledgehammer, and began slowly slamming chunks off the block. He was a man of medium height, well muscled, with tattoos all over his shoulders and up and down his fore-arms, decorative ones, none of the boasts or messages that tattooed men sometimes had; many were grinning human skulls. He had sandy hair, blue eyes, and an air of wounded innocence. He seemed uneasy—fidgety, oblique—the demeanor of someone who worked alone and was not quite sure how to deal with a sudden stranger, especially one scribbling in a notebook.

His name was Jesse Minor. He was thirty-five and was born less than forty miles away in the much bigger town of Athens. He'd graduated from Oconee High School in Watkinsville. "It was a mostly white school," he explained. "The town's real small, and it's mostly white too."

"You have a lot of ink, Jesse."

"I got these tattoos in Arizona, from a friend who's a tattoo artist. I said, 'Cover my arms with skulls'—skulls are cool and badass. This here one on my neck says 'Reba.' That's my daughter. That's a story."

He had not slackened; he hammered as he spoke, chunks of granite flying.

"I never worked in a quarry before," he said, swinging. "I was in con-struction, in Arizona for eight years. Prescott, a really nice place with lots of work. But the economy went bad, so I come home." He paused and sized up the block. "Here I am, been here eighteen months. I use this here sledgehammer to clean up the blocks, get them straight. Call it quality control, I guess."

"How's the pay?" I asked.

"I started at nine dollars an hour and now I earn eleven. I work six days a week—fifty hours a week. I don't mind the work, but I'm having a hard time at home."

"You mind if I make notes? I'm kind of interested."

"That's okay." And he put his hammer down. "Thing is, I'm going through a separation. It's like this. Brandy—my wife—says she's going through a midlife crisis, which is really strange, because she's younger than me."

"How would you describe her midlife crisis?"

"She decided she wanted to date a younger guy, that kind of crisis. And she got really weird. She says to me, 'I love you, but I'm not in love with you.' The hell's that mean?"

"I don't know. Did you ask her?"

"Kind of." He began to pace in the shed as the rain came down. "Everyone knows that tingly feeling goes away after a few months, don't it? Anyway, I figured I'd give her some space. So I moved out." Seeing a block of granite moving past on the lift, he snatched his hammer and heaved it and chopped at the block, still talking. "Soon as I moved out, he moved in—the young dude, this guy she was dating."

"That doesn't sound good."

"He don't have a car!" He swung the hammer again and a dislodged wedge of stone flew into a gurney with a bang. "I says to her, 'It ain't going to be how you want it!'"

"What did she say to that?"

But he wasn't listening. He was in full cry. "I says, 'We was a team back in Arizona!' We went through hard times and was doing pretty good. *We was a team!*"

He threw his sledgehammer aside and sat down on a bench by the slab of granite that was being buzz-sawed into a pair of curbstones. He lit a cigarette, wagged the match out, and blew smoke.

"When we come back, we ended up in a real slummy area—Sherwood, for Sherwood Forest, near Danielsville, in Madison County. It's mainly white, a drug-infested trailer community, five or six hundred people. Our trailer was back of the neighborhood."

"How bad was it there?"

"Real bad. Next-door neighbor's girlfriend died and he went crazy. He moved a woman with kids into his trailer. She was a meth-head and always fighting. It was a crazy drama because of the weed and the meth. All this time he's trying to kick her out. She's a druggie. She has five kids and all of them do drugs together, mom and the kids."

"That was your home?"

"Until I left," he said. "That's where Brandy's living now, with the dude." He sat quietly for a long while, smoking. "I worry about Reba. She's everything to me, but I only see her once a week. I want to protect her, but my wife is being real hard. She says to me, 'Someone stole your tools'—power saw and the other stuff. Why would anyone steal my tools and nothing else? The dude sold them, I know. Then it was 'Someone stole the wedding ring'—it was my mother's ring. I know what happened to it, and it makes me mad."

"Jesse, mind my asking — did you ever do drugs?"

"I done drugs, but I gave up when I realized I didn't want my daughter to see me the way I saw my father. She would see me as stupid. I know that because I started doing drugs with my father when I was twelve — weed, cocaine."

The image in my mind, like the one provoked by *She has five kids and all of them do drugs together, mom and the kids,* was of a ghoulish tribe gathered in a ritual of drug taking; but it was more likely a miserable family quarreling and smoking in the confines of a house trailer.

"It was when he got divorced," Jesse was saying. "He snorted coke at night. Thinking of Reba, I remembered what my dad did — smoked weed in the car when he was driving. Me, I usually smoked a joint in the morning before I went to school."

"How old would you have been then?"

"Twelve or thirteen. And I kept doing it." He nodded, seeming to guess that I wanted more details. He said, "I got some felonies. For growing weed. Just a few plants. They were trying to get me twenty years. I wound up doing sixteen months. I was twenty years old. My dad died of cancer when he was fifty-three."

"That's tough."

"This separation is worse. I said, 'I'll kill you, Brandy' — I didn't mean it. But that's why I don't have a gun in the house, and I always had a gun before. She got me a TRO. From her and the dude. Incredible."

I said, "My only advice would be, try to suppress the urge to kill her."

"Oh, yeah. I don't want to do something that's going to wreck my life," he said. "And I still love her. I love my daughter. I want to go back to the way it was." He thought a moment, and his face creased in pain. "When we was a team."

"Where do you live now?"

"I'm back with my mother in Athens. It's awful. All my stuff's in the trailer. I went there for my tools. Brandy says, 'They got stole.' I asked for the wedding ring back, 'cause she warn't wearing it. She says, 'It got stole.' Just those three things got stole — my power drill, my power saw, and the ring. No money, nothing else got stole. It's all fishy."

He picked up the sledgehammer.

"And the dude is living there, in my trailer, with my wife, with my daughter."

He raised the heavy hammer and turned away from me.

"All I care about is my daughter. I live for her, that's why I'm trying to do the right thing and not kill the dude or Brandy. I don't want her to look at me the way I looked at my father, who gave me drugs."

And he brought the hammer down on the edge of the granite, smashing off an irregular corner and sending it flying.

Buddy Case: "You Couldn't Say Nothing"

Buddy, the man Massoud called his redneck butler, was a lanky, friendly, soft-spoken man who called himself a country boy. He was in his early sixties and had fought in Vietnam. "Butler" was typical Massoud hyperbole. Mainly Buddy was an arranger, driver, handyman, and errand runner. He had Massoud's back, and he had certain interests in common with Massoud — guns, for example.

Soon after I was introduced to him, I mentioned Massoud's AK-47, hung on the kitchen wall with the pots and pans and the spice rack. I'd said something like, "I suppose you've got a gun."

"'A gun,'" Buddy said satirically, mimicking me. "I got me forty-five guns."

Later we talked about Vietnam. He'd fought there in 1969, the longest period he'd spent out of Elberton. He was still friendly with the guys in his unit. He said, "We have a reunion every two years in Pigeon Forge."

Pigeon Forge was over the Great Smokies near Knoxville, Tennessee. Recognizing that the South had produced so many army vets, the town put on a celebration every August, Celebrate Freedom Month. The weekend was themed "Pigeon Forge Celebrates Freedom — A Welcome Home from Vietnam." One of the events was "The Parade They Never Got," with motorcycles, marching bands, and the flypast of a UH-1, the Huey helicopter gunship, emblematic of battles and evacuations in Vietnam. There were concerts too, including Smoky Mountain Opry's special Salute to Patriots.

"This show is about Remembering the Sacrifice of those who gave all," in the words of the prospectus. "This event was created to honor our Vietnam Veterans; to hail them as the heroes they are. It is an opportunity for families, friends and citizens to salute them with pride; a chance for a grateful nation to say 'Thank You.'"

Buddy told me about this, saying how he looked forward to it. He described the parades, the music, the fanfare, and the reunion, the Southern food and friendship.

"Must be good to see the guys again."

"It's great." He nodded and lit a cigarette. "Sit around. Have some beers. Then we look at a Google map of our air base, on a hill in 'Nam. Try to figure out what happened to it."

"So you must have been a high school student in Elberton in the sixties?" I asked. "Was the school integrated then?"

"They tried to integrate it in '67," he said. "I was a sophomore at the time. Four black students showed up — two boys, two girls."

"How did that turn out?"

He squinted, as though at a grim memory, and said, "One particular thing I remember. We had assembly in the gym every morning. But there were hundreds of students, so there weren't enough bleacher seats for everyone. Lots of kids had to sit on the floor. You know the way kids sit on the floor?"

Buddy placed his cigarette in a saucer and showed me how, leaning back, his hands splayed out behind him.

"You prop yourself up like this — hands back, sort of resting on your hands."

"I get it."

"The four black students was on the floor, and they hands got stepped on, all of them, by the students walking behind them."

I could see it, the white students looming over them, treading on their outstretched fingers.

"No one said nothing," Buddy said. "I'm sure some felt sorry for them. You couldn't say nothing, though. They couldn't take it, nor the harassment neither. All of them finally left. In '68, more came. More harassment. And more in '69. But by then I was in Vietnam."

Later that night, in a bar in Elberton, I met Ivy, a local woman about Buddy's age, and asked her the same question.

"I didn't go to the high school," she said. "I went to Samuel Elbert Academy. It was a private school, all white. It started in the sixties, when the stuff happened."

I thought hard about Buddy's remark "You couldn't say nothing." He meant: It was impossible to defy the school and take a moral stand on racism. This was what many people said in the South, of the moral dilemma. They said it of Strom Thurmond: Not really a racist—after all, he slept with his black servant and he sent money to his black child. Give him a break, he was merely espousing racist views in order to win votes. It was an echo of what Bill Clinton said of Senator Robert Byrd's membership in the Ku Klux Klan: "He was a country boy from the hills and hollows of West Virginia. He was trying to get elected."

You think I'm burning this cross and forbidding you to go to school here and covering up this lynching, but hey, I'm not a racist, really. I'm just trying to get elected.

Buddy had a sense of the wrongness of it all when he was trying to fit in with his friends all those years ago; he still remembered the racial abuse and the hurt. I was struck by his retelling of the painful day, thirty-seven years before, when the four black students got their fingers stepped on at the school, and how he had been silent. "I could a stayed if I wanted to," Huck Finn says when Colonel Sherburn denounces the lynch mob, "but I didn't want to."

Bill Clinton had more to answer for. He was still repeating the twisted Southern political logic: because taking a moral stand, defying the racists, was an obstacle to electability, you had to pretend to be a racist. He was saying: We had to step on their fingers. We had to claim it was the right thing to do. We needed the votes. You have to get elected no matter the moral cost.

Telling the truth and being ethical often keeps people from political power, but doing the right thing, always, without exception, is all that matters in the long run, and is ultimately powerful. That's why the true heroes of the civil rights struggle were never politicians. They were humble folk on a mission, enduring sit-ins and organizing marches and debates. When they began to succeed, the politicians, seeing an opportunity, followed them.

And that was the reason why, in the end, Rosa Parks was elevated to the status of a heroine, and why she is celebrated today by people who seem to be atoning for doing so little, seeking forgiveness from a woman who was far braver than they were. Her stubborn courage, refusing to give up her seat to a white man, was a gesture of ethical belief, a clinging to truth, that no politician in the South had dared to demonstrate, because — as Clinton said in his shameless apology for Byrd — of the risk of being defeated in an election.

For many white Southerners, pretending to be racist was permissible, perhaps necessary, in a political campaign, and forgivable. You had to be a Southerner to understand this reasoning; it was a cultural thing, a way forward for Southern politicians, who believed, like Buddy, "You couldn't say nothing" or your friends wouldn't like you. They had that belief in common with many awkward adolescents, morally muddled, who crave to be popular.

Alabama Traditions: The Segregated Sororities

Crossing Georgia after Atlanta and the state line, I repeated my previous trip along the back roads of Alabama, staying off the superslab of the interstate, to Talladega and Childersburg, Columbiana and Calera, Montevallo to West Blocton to Cottondale. I did not drive fast — no one could on these country roads. That was part of the enjoyment, and the other part was the plowed fields and the woods and most of all the odor of the hot roads, like industrial damnation, bright black tar blisters and tar bubbles, especially in the new smears and patches on the sun-heated surfaces, an aroma like the tang of hot pitch and the smell of my childhood summers.

Finally Tuscaloosa again, and the university, which was at war with itself over a contentious issue. Fifty years into the civil rights movement, the white sororities were in the news for refusing to admit black women students who had indicated they wished to join.

"This isn't new," Cynthia Burton told me when I visited her the next day.

Seeing her again was a pleasure, but she was ailing: she'd been in a car crash two months before and was in a routine of physical therapy. Added to this were her other ailments: diabetes, high blood pressure, and bad knees. She still used a walker. Yet she did a full day's work, finding housing for the poor of the Black Belt and overseeing the many people who showed up at her office and, under *Reason for Visit*, wrote "Food" or "Utilities."

"You should look up the name Melody Twilley," she said, and told me what I needed to know. "It was ten or twelve years ago . . ."

Melody Twilley was from the small Black Belt Alabama town of Camden, in Wilcox County. "Wilcox is the poorest county in Alabama," Cynthia added, and Camden was about thirty miles south of Selma. Melody's father was a successful businessman in the timber trade. Melody had shown such early promise that she was sent to Mobile to attend the Alabama School of Math and Science, a high school with a predominantly white student body, where she graduated with honors.

She was admitted to the University of Alabama in 2001. She excelled in science, she sang in the choir, her grades were high. She was eager to join a sorority, not to make a political point — though there were no black women in any of the University of Alabama sororities — but because she said she wanted to have the complete university experience. And asked about this ambition, she explained to an inquiring journalist, "My feeling was, if they got to know me, they'd like me."

With its traditionally all-white fraternities and sororities, from which black students were excluded, the University of Alabama was one of a kind, the last university in the South where this exclusion was the case. Melody visited — rushed — a dozen sororities, but only one, Alpha Delta Pi, invited her back for a final interview.

Melody was hopeful, but in the end she was rejected. Race had not been a factor, the sorority said. She simply wasn't chosen by the sisters. She graduated from the university without any sorority connection; she could have joined a black one, but didn't.

"There's something at the university called the Machine," Cynthia said.

"A secret group of people that keeps things as they always were, and that means some stuff is still segregated. Poor Melody Twilley. She tried — Lord, she tried."

This situation of racially segregated sororities existed until, by coincidence, the month I was in Alabama, when eleven African-American women attempted to join sororities, in much the same way as Melody Twilley in 2001 — rushing the houses, hoping to be accepted. This was now mid-September, and the student newspaper, the *Crimson White*, had just published a piece saying that the fraternities and sororities (fifty-six altogether) were almost completely divided along racial lines, and that the Greek system was the "last bastion of segregation on campus."

Though two black women had succeeded in gaining initial acceptance to white sororities, they were, in the end, rejected. This time there was an outcry. Pressured by indignant students, including many women from the sororities, the president of the university, Dr. Judy Bonner, held an emergency meeting behind closed doors with her board of trustees and sorority advisers. The following day the president stated that "our Greek systems remain segregated," and she pleaded for tolerance.

To their credit, a few days later, several hundred students and faculty, including Dr. Bonner, gathered at the university's Gorgas Library and marched to the Rose Administration Building, carrying signs.

Some of the signs alluded to the confrontation, fifty years before, when Governor George Wallace went to the campus and positioned himself before the auditorium door to prevent two black students from entering and joining the student body.

"It was a staged event, more or less," Charles Portis said of Wallace's defiance, in an interview in 2001. Portis was a reporter in Tuscaloosa at the time of the event. He continued, "The outcome wasn't in doubt. Those black students were going to be admitted to the University of Alabama. Wallace had been meeting with Robert Kennedy and Nicholas Katzenbach, and he wanted a big show of federal force there, a lot of marshals, when he made his defiant speech — which reminds me of Leander Perez, that segregationist boss down in Plaquemines Parish, Louisiana. Earl Long said to him, 'What you gonna do now, Leander? Da Feds have got da H-bomb.'" Of the Alabama confrontation, Portis commented wryly, "Some of it was the Civil War being replayed as farce."

In contrast to Wallace's obstinacy (or grandstanding), the present Alabama governor, Robert Bentley (an alumnus of the university), in response to the sororities' segregation, published a statement urging tolerance. Yet his was a cry in the wilderness, and a weak message of "Can't we just get along?" None of the university administrators, nor any Alabama politicians, took a moral stand. The force for change came from the students, who organized protests, wrote letters, and marched carrying signs. It was clear that the majority of the students were not racists and wanted to see more fairness. Though Jesse Jackson showed up and gave a pompous speech, the students were driving the issue and explaining its importance. In a university with one of the top law schools and business schools in the country, it seemed weirdly backward and unjust that some important aspects of university life were still blatantly segregated.

"You should see this for yourself," Cynthia said. "Go on over there."

So I went to the campus and walked around and talked to students. Some kind of sorority ritual was taking place near the stadium. Hundreds of sorority sisters were gathered in groups and running and laughing—and, as part of the game, which had the look of a scavenger hunt, they took turns climbing onto the fifteen-foot bronze statue of Alabama's football coach, Nick Saban. This phase of the game seemed to be a competition to see how many could cling to the statue at one time—eight or nine seemed to be the limit. They clung to Saban's head, sat on his neck and shoulders, swung from his arms, hugged his legs, sat on the pedestal—shrieking, frolicking girls with dimpled knees and faces reddened and damp with exertion, all of them white girls.

They were happy to talk to me, and the dozen or so I spoke to said they were in favor of integrating the sororities. They had black friends, they said; they wanted them as sisters; they hated the bad publicity.

"I'm in a sorority, but that's not why I chose Alabama. I came here because of the football," one of them said.

"Football brings out the camaraderie," her sorority sister said.

"And maybe the drinking and the mayhem?" I said.

"Oh, yeah, all of that!"

"We don't have a problem with black girls joining our sorority," another said in response to my direct question.

"Then why are they still segregated?"

"The alumni don't want it," several said, calling out, competing with one another to convince me.

"The alumni are against it, and they're pressuring us," one girl said. "They're the ones giving money to the university—and to us—so they have a lot of power."

"What about the Machine?"

"That's all secret stuff," one said, laughing.

That week, the *Crimson White* published a reflective piece, "In Sororities Integration Is Still Elusive"—not elusive, but absent. Yet there was a laudable determination among the students to change, to defy the alumni, when they cited a "chapter's letter of recommendation requirements as a reason for the potential new member's removal." In one case, at a meeting at Alpha Gamma Delta, "active sorority members . . . began standing up to voice support for the [black] recruit and challenge alumnae decisions."

"The entire house wanted this girl to be in Alpha Gam," one of the sisters at Alpha Gamma Delta said. "We were just powerless over the alums."

The issue was challenged, and discussed, but not solved. The old Southern black-white division remained, yet I could see that the students wanted to make up their own minds and recruit anyone they wanted, including black students. They were embarrassed by the headlines and agitated by my questions. To the obvious question, Why would any student wish to join a sorority where she was not wanted?, the answer was, They *were* wanted.

But to me there was something inherently farcical in it all. The joining of a sorority or a fraternity, with all its fatuous airs and protocols, seemed to me a ridiculous way of measuring tolerance, since the so-called Greek system was notoriously snobbish and dissolute, a test of clubbability, mingling circus-clown ethics with the secret-society mumbo jumbo of licensed foolery and, very often, *Animal House* values and hazing worthy of a CIA black site. In an annual poll called Greek Rank, all sororities in the United States were evaluated in the categories of looks, popularity, classiness, involvement, social life, and sisterhood. It was a leering, bottom-sniffing world in which academic achievement was apparently not worth mentioning.

Nevertheless, as a gesture, even as a Byzantine charade, joining a sorority had a meaning on an Alabama campus. Tuscaloosa's history was a catalog of racial obstinacy and defiant bigotry. Bishop Earnest Palmer had shown me the hangout of the Klan on Union Boulevard on one of my previous visits, and the Klan in Alabama was a recent memory if not a present fact, along with many active hate groups.

Here was a university that needed the National Guard to protect black students when it was integrated under federal orders fifty years ago. A sensible person could not be blamed for thinking that the alumni would be eager to disavow this racist past and promote the idea that a lesson in tolerance had been learned, even in the corny to-and-fro of sorority politics. But the opposite was the case. The alumni went out of their way to demonstrate how they clung to their spiteful stupidity, beneath the gaze of the entire country, under the pretense of tradition.

Sandra Fair: "It's Getting Worse"

"My son's friends are black and white," Sandra Fair told me. "It was so different from when I was growing up. I graduated from high school in 1968, and we had but one black student. I felt real sad for her."

Sandra was a cheerful, candid, business-minded woman who lived in the small country town of Gordo, in Pickens County, about fifteen miles west of Tuscaloosa. Her husband was a dairy farmer. She was the chief financial officer of the Community Service Programs (CSP) of West Alabama, the nonprofit community action agency in which Cynthia Burton was executive director.

I was seeing Sandra Fair because I had asked Cynthia Burton about CSP's finances. I was used to traveling in Africa and Asia, where hundreds of millions of dollars were given to aid projects to improve or promote education, create energy sources, offer medical care, even help the tourism industry ($700 million to Tanzania and $350 million to Zambia, for example). I was curious to know the budget for this Alabama organization, which provided services in eight counties in this western part of the Black Belt.

"Our operating budget is about fifteen million," Sandra Fair said. She went on to say that around half of that went toward salaries for teachers, advisers, construction workers, repairmen, and clerical staff. "And folks apply for loans or grants, or they need money for heat, for utility bills. They need food, they need advice. That costs us around three million."

"You give the people money to pay their heating bills?"

"No. If they qualify, we make direct payments to the utility company. It's all income-based. There are poverty guidelines."

The income criteria seemed severe. Under the "Poverty Guidelines," a one-person household qualified if the annual income was less than $11,490, a two-person household $15,510, and so forth—not even subsistence incomes. The poverty threshold for a family of four was $19,000. These were very low figures, yet more than twenty percent of this part of the Black Belt—the submerged twentieth—lived below the poverty line and qualified for assistance (the figure was twenty-five percent for Mississippi).

The CSP budget was small by community development standards, but the programs were ambitious. The organization financed programs in housing, education, and "Support Services"—this last included energy assistance and emergency food and shelter. The Juvenile Justice Intervention Project was a program that offered "regularly scheduled sessions to youth who have a first encounter with the Tuscaloosa County Juvenile Court." The program imparted guidance to first offenders on how to avoid violence, and helped keep juveniles out of trouble by offering them educational alternatives and skills.

For educational assistance, CSP provided "Early Intervention": Head Start and Early Start programs for poor parents with small children and little access to preschool. Along with this was a recognition that a two-parent family was an objective to encourage. To this end, CSP offered a "Fatherhood Initiative." "The notion that fathers of children from low-income and high-risk backgrounds always absent themselves from child rearing is erroneous," in the words of the prospectus. "Head Start's Fatherhood Initiative promotes concepts and activities that nurture the children's relationships with their fathers. The Fatherhood Initiative supports and strengthens the roles of fathers in families."

That cost money too, and Sandra Fair said the results were encouraging: more and more fathers were joining the program.

"We also provide housing opportunities for families," she said. This was done by building new single-family houses, rehabbing existing ones, and putting up and maintaining multifamily houses and apartment complexes.

"A big chunk of our budget goes to low-income housing," Sandra said. "Multifamily housing and rentals, and others in lease-purchase arrangements."

"Is any of this working?"

She smiled ruefully. "The problems are growing. There's more poor people, more people in crisis. It seems to me it's getting worse. Every year we see clients we've never seen before. New people show up every day in all our offices. We're helping, we're doing our best, but it's not getting better."

Randall Curb: "My Wings Are Clipped"

The way to Greensboro, into the countryside south of Tuscaloosa, had ceased to be for me the landscape of *Let Us Now Praise Famous Men* or that book's gloss on it. The book and its fossilized families had been replaced in my mind with the reality of my travel and the people I now knew, many of whom had become my friends. Cynthia Burton's organization was building or fixing up houses for the poor in Hale County, and so was Pam Dorr's HERO Project, which in addition had six businesses to fund the housing: pecans, bike making from bamboo, the Pie Lab café, a thrift shop, a day-care center, and Whispers, a line of necklaces made of Italian yarn. ("Exquisite ribbon necklaces and scarves," advertised one retailer, "that are proudly made in Greensboro, Alabama by women, especially for women and to help women in Alabama's Black Belt Region combat the rural poverty of the area.")

Johnnie B. Washington was still mayor and still hoping for a big-box store like Kmart to come to town, Janet May was still poaching eggs for her bed-and-breakfast guests out at Blue Shadows, and Luis was serving tamales at El Tenampa at the edge of town. Reverend Lyles was still cutting hair and preaching. I sat with him for a few hours of reminiscence, and when I left, he said, "Paul, you come from up north. You must know some people with deep pockets. If you do, tell them about Greensboro — send them down here. What we need is investment."

Reverend Lyles said he was proud of what had been done at the old Rosenwald school, how it had been fixed up and was now a well-attended community center. The Auburn Rural Studio was still building ingenious low-cost houses. It was not the town of Agee and Evans anymore. It was still struggling, but it was improving, and hopeful.

On a single visit I would not have seen this, but over the course of a year, in four seasons, the true condition of the town had become apparent. This was not a trip about my having had a good meal or a bad meal, or my laboring toward a destination in the old travel-book manner. It may have seemed to some people I met that I was headed somewhere, but I was still traveling in widening circles, happily, on back roads, meeting people, and revisiting friends.

The last time I'd seen Randall Curb in Greensboro, he'd revealed to me that he suffered from clinical depression. This was not a casual remark but a considered declaration of a profound medical condition. We had last met at lunch with Mary Ward Brown, a delightful memory with a sad aftermath: soon after, Randall had relayed to me the news of her death.

I met him for lunch at the Pie Lab. Though legally blind, he had all the impressive alertness of his other senses, his whole being radiating attention and understanding. Seeing me, he smiled, he reached, we hugged, and then we talked about Mary T.

"I had an email from her about writing, about her plans," I said. "Less than two weeks later she was dead. I'm so grateful to you for introducing me to her. I felt an instant liking for her."

"She liked you too. But then she got ill really fast. She didn't want to suffer or linger," Randall said. "I think she realized how badly she was doing, and she refused to struggle. She didn't eat. She simply lay in her bed and willed herself to death."

"Remember how she mentioned the book about people who lived to a hundred? She said, 'I don't think I want to live that long.'"

"She almost made it to ninety-six," he said. "That's pretty good going."

"When my father died, a friend of mine said, 'The average life span isn't really very long.' And it's true. What's seventy, or even eighty or ninety years?"

Randall grew reflective. He was a big, fleshy man with an impressive head, and his contemplation, his lack of response, was all the more emphatic for his conspicuous presence, his bulk at the table, and not a word or a murmur from him.

"I keep thinking how Mary T said of the blacks in Marion, 'They look at me with hatred,'" I said. "I wanted to ask her more about that. I hardly knew her, and yet I really miss her. She was someone I'd counted on seeing again."

Randall nodded but didn't speak. This talk of death over lunch and his silence brought to mind his melancholia. It was too obvious to change the subject abruptly, so I risked the question: How was he doing?

"Not good," he said. "I was in London earlier in the summer, and then I came back here and I fell into a depression. It was Greensboro, I guess, being back home, this place and its memories."

"'Home is so sad,' as Larkin says. 'It stays as it was left.'"

Randall nodded. "But it's not just that. I feel immobilized here after my travel. I feel my wings are clipped."

"But it seems to me there's so much happening in Greensboro that's positive."

"People come here and like the town and want to make it better," he said with doubt in his voice.

"Is that a problem?"

Randall was holding his head in reflection, his hair damp and tousled, his face pink in the heat. He had told me a number of times of how he hated the Alabama summer, the months of heat that kept people indoors, the cloak of humidity. I didn't mind it, but then I was just moving through the South, a bird of passage.

"I grew up in the civil rights era," he said at last. "Greensboro was incendiary."

"So doesn't it give you hope to see that the town, and maybe the South in general, is improving?" I wasn't sure how much it was changing, but anyone could see that some improvements were being made.

"In that era, people came from the North to promote civil rights. They were called agitators. And that's how outsiders are seen, even today. People who are stirring things up."

This was not entirely news to me. Pam Dorr had told me how she ran into opposition and abuse. "They call me names." And she had laughed, saying, "Now and then someone walks past and spits on me."

"I don't know," Randall said when I asked him whether Pam was seen as an agitator. "But the whole racial issue has been turned upside down. There's a more hostile racial divide now, because blacks are in power."

"Wasn't that the whole point?" I said. "After all, blacks are the majority in this part of Alabama."

"Whites feel disenfranchised," he said. "We have a black mayor, black councilors, black judges. And more. Whites believe they've been left out. They want to regain political control."

"Is that likely?"

"Paul, you've got to understand," he said, somewhat exasperated. "The white Democrats have died out. Ninety percent of the people vote on racial lines. Blacks for blacks. Whites for whites. That's the way it is."

"Maybe if the right candidate comes along?"

"It isn't going to happen any time soon."

After lunch, we walked slowly in the clinging summer heat down Main Street, past derelict shops, and shops and buildings being fixed up, and some doing business. I drove him to his house. "Come back soon," he said, and we hugged, and he stood in the shade of his porch, waving goodbye, then went inside, to his solitude and his thousands of books.

Brookhaven—A Homeseeker's Paradise

Headed to the Delta again, I rose early the following morning, sped over the state line to Meridian, in Mississippi, then south to Laurel, and took back roads west through the pinewoods. I stopped at Collins for the night, and the next morning—getting a tire fixed—I met motor mechanics and construction workers, Big William, Little William, and Ray. They said they had been as far north as Pennsylvania. "We was building a Walmart." Then I drove west on Highway 84, past Prentiss and Monticello, to Brookhaven, another time-warp town, with a weathered sign over Main Street: BROOKHAVEN — A HOMESEEKER'S PARADISE.

Perhaps Brookhaven had been a home seeker's paradise once, as the

Brookhaven-born writer Jimmie Meese Moomaw claims in her memoir, *Southern Fried Child:* "I'll never know for sure who or what I might have been or would have been if I had been born in Connecticut or Detroit, but I am now sure that I am who I am in large measure because I was born in 'Home Seeker's Paradise' and lived a Southern fried childhood, complete with horses and healers and heathens and whores and flawed parents who loved me both too much and not enough."

It seemed to me that few home seekers turned up these days in Brookhaven—even Jimmie Meese Moomaw had departed and now lived in Georgia. The town had been an important railway junction since the 1870s, on the Illinois Central main line from Chicago to New Orleans. The Amtrak express *City of New Orleans* still rolls through twice a day, the southbound train at noon, the northbound train at four in the afternoon, the route of familiar names, Kankakee, Centralia, Memphis, and Jackson. The atmospheric old railway station is in the middle of town, straddling Main Street, the unadorned new one just a few blocks north.

Once, not even that long ago, I would have hankered to buy a ticket and take those trains anywhere—ditched my car and swung myself aboard the noon express to head south to McComb and the Big Easy, or wait for the afternoon train north to Yazoo City and Greenwood. In either direction, for me a true joy ride. But I would have missed so much, and I had become habituated to the spontaneity of my car, the ease of finding any open road, inserting myself into the life of the land by steering myself wherever I wished and stopping often.

What I was doing was so different from being an alien spectator on a train, the traveler I had been in many other countries. But in general those countries (China, India, Russia, Vietnam, Egypt, Argentina, Britain) had been well served by trains and were not road-friendly; the American South had good roads, but train travel was patchy. Once, the South had been crisscrossed by railways lines. Traditionally, these Southern trains provided an inexpensive means, and a route, for blacks to flee the South, in particular in the great black migration of the 1920s, and its terminals gave them specific destinations too, notably Chicago and New York. As a consequence, the trains, and the stations along the way, provided lyrics to the blues and the many tunes that spoke of these northbound trains, a whole songbook of place names and railway journeys out of the South.

So I stopped at the railway station, just to look, and then I walked the streets of Brookhaven. I found the courthouse where, in May 1955, a Brookhaven resident, Lamar Smith, sixty-three, a World War Two veteran and "voting rights advocate," was gunned down while other Brookhavenites, including the town's sheriff, stood and watched, did nothing to help. Smith, who was black, had offended local customs and sensibilities by casting his vote in a local election.

I ate lunch at a diner and resumed walking. I lingered at Liz-Beth Pageants, a store devoted to rentals of evening gowns, one of the busiest shops in Brookhaven and a Southern institution.

"Two hundred to rent, five hundred to buy," Kim, one of the clerks, told me, and in answer to my next question, "Business is real good."

"Who rents these dresses?"

"Everyone. On account of the proms and the parties. Homecoming courts. Beauty pageants."

A "homecoming court," a new term to me, involved the election of a king and queen at a school, another tradition in a region besotted with hierarchies and pretensions. As for beauty pageants, just that month alone, there were ten in Mississippi. These included Miss Dogwood County, Miss Rankin County, Miss Ebony Sweetheart, Miss Southwest Sweetheart, Miss Dixie Sweetheart, Miss Meridian, Miss Tri-County, and Miss Deep South, among others. "Ages 0 to 11" and "ages 12 and up" were specific categories that had me wondering.

Cheap sparkly jewelry was included in the rental fee, as well as appropriate shoes. "Little-girl" pageant dresses were popular, and a display of photographs showed winners in Liz-Beth dresses — six- and eight-year-olds, precocious painted ten-year-olds, coquettish twelve-year-olds in sequins and mascara, in come-hither postures. They had the knowing eroticized gaze you associated with older women, and some of them did not look like children at all but like dwarf versions of beauty queens, meretricious bum-wagging munchkins. The oddity was that the child pageants did not emphasize the extreme youth of the entrants but instead sexualized them, presented them in adult clothes and thick makeup, giving them the heavy-lidded, big-doll look of hardened, pimped-out women rather than the freshness and simplicity and innocence of their age.

Your little girl will steal the show in our custom-designed pageant swim-

wear — a sign, with pictures of lipsticked nymphets posing (hands on hips) in pink bathing suits, elaborately coiffed, and wearing tiaras on their up-swept hairdos, and some — incredibly — had big hair that added ten inches to their height. Little-girl beauty pageants were a feature of the rural South, and *Toddlers and Tiaras* was a successful reality TV show. I am aware that I sound disapproving in describing this cultural weirdness, but never mind my moralizing; I had the strong suspicion that if an older man downloaded any of those promotional photographs and they were found on his hard drive by the typical snitch at the computer repair shop, he'd risk arrest, or at least serious interrogation, and perhaps his house would be searched for possession of lurid images of underage girls.

A few doors down, I stopped at Brookhaven Billiards and talked to some of the fellows idling by the pool tables. No one was playing, though, and Billy Temple, the owner, was contemplating the removal of some tables.

"I thought I was on to a good thing, a billiard place in a small town where people could meet and play games," he said. "But business is terrible. I'm closing this place and moving on. I sometimes think that we're coming to a time in this country when no one's going to have a job. I took over this billiard parlor two years ago. It was a real mess. I cleaned it up, put in some new tables and equipment. You can buy a cue. You can have a soda or a candy bar. No liquor. Should have worked."

"Seems a natural business for a town like this — a place to meet," I said.

"We did fine for a while. Some of the old-timers would come here at five and sit and wait for someone to play with. There was always someone playing, mainly white folks. Every now and then sixty black guys would show up. At first I'd say, 'Oh, boy, here we go,' but we never had a problem. They were fine — just liked to come in large groups."

"Maybe they felt safer in a big group."

"Maybe so, but they didn't come often enough. Business went bad. No one's playing. See all the empty tables?"

Billy was a man of about forty, muscular, in a black T-shirt and jeans, and as we talked he began maneuvering a wheeled cart under one of the tables and hoisting the table onto it. He did this without any help, man-handling the billiard table. I hovered and questioned him.

"What's your plan?"

"I'm giving up," he said, grunting under the weight of the table. "Maybe find another town and open a pool room. Not to give anyone competition but just to make a living."

"Is this your main business?"

"No. I'm a fireman, but being a fireman in this town is tough. The pay's no good. Hey, it's a young man's game. You're sound asleep at the station and the alarm goes off, and you have to go from zero to hero."

"Firefighting is risky too, isn't it? Your life on the line," I asked.

He was still jogging the table over the handcart, grunting, yet he answered, calling out over his shoulder, "Imagine what it's like to carry a two-hundred-fifty-pound person over your shoulder. Heck, even fifty isn't easy — a fifty-pound sack is something heavy. But multiply that by five and you see the problem. Plus, there's smoke and heat and fumes. You're wearing seventy-five pounds of gear. A man of forty like me isn't up to it, and I'm in good shape!"

I said, "Brookhaven seems a friendly enough place."

"Friendly, but the town is dying. The politicians sold us out — everything shut down. Stuff is made in China and India. We sent jobs there. And the Indians came here. They're running the gas stations and motels. What do you make of that?"

"The inevitable Mr. Patel," I said.

"I hear that name all the time. It's some kind of big damn-old family and they're all over the place."

I followed him out of the shop and helped him push the billiard table up a ramp he'd improvised, then onto the bed of his pickup truck.

"Bless you for helping me with this thing," he said. "Where are you headed?"

"The Delta. But I want to go on the scenic route."

"Head up a few blocks, hang a left, stay on Five-fifty. It's real pretty."

"Life Is a Highway"

Yes, it was pretty, another beautiful back road in the Deep South — a narrow road past pinewoods and swamps, the hanks of long grass in the sloping meadows yellowy green in the summer heat. Some orderly farms — a few — were set back from the road, but most of the dwellings were small houses or bungalows surrounded by a perimeter fence, a sleepy dog inside it, and some scattered house trailers detached and becalmed under the gum trees — and shacks too, the collapsing kind that I saw only on roads like these. Every few miles there was a church, no bigger than a one-room schoolhouse and with a similar look, a cross on the roof peak, sometimes the stump of a steeple, and a signboard on the lawn promoting the text for this week's sermon.

> "LIFE IS A HIGHWAY"
> ISAIAH 35:8
> LORD JESUS HAS THE ROADMAP FOR YOUR JOURNEY
> LUKE 24:13–24

A large school loomed ahead, in a compound of flat-roofed brick buildings, with a tall flagpole out front, a Confederate flag slightly lifted by the breeze. Or at least that was my perception, traveling at forty miles an hour. It was of course the state flag, which incorporates the Confederate battle flag saltire (or tipped-over cross), the only Southern state that has retained this image on its flag, and somehow fitting on a country road in the depths of southern Mississippi that seemed to be bearing me backward in time, to the 1890s when that flag design was adopted. (A new design with stars instead of the Confederate imagery was put to a referendum in 2001 and heavily defeated.)

I was driving in full sun on this rolling road and as happy as I had ever been driving in the South. There is a sense of purification that seems to take place in sunshine on a country road, the winking glare in the boughs passing overhead, the dappled light on the hot tar, the glimpses of sky and the stands of trees, wall-like pines in some hollows, enormous white oaks and columns of junipers in others, and a fragrance in the air of heated and slightly decayed leaf litter that has the aroma of buttered toast. Oaks and pine trees lined the road for some miles, which narrowed the road and helped give the impression of this as an enchanted byway in a children's story, one that tempted the traveler onward into milder light and greater joy. I was loving this ride.

It was at about this point that the ominous signs began to appear, nailed to the roadside trees. Large lettered signs fastened to the thick trunks, big threatening signs, their messages in black and red letters on a bright white background.

"PREPARE TO MEET THY GOD"— AMOS 4:12

"THE EYES OF THE LORD ARE IN EVERY PLACE BEHOLDING
THE EVIL AND THE GOOD"— PROVERBS 13:3

"FAITH WITHOUT WORKS IS DEAD"— JAMES 2:26

"STRIVE TO ENTER AT THE STRAIT GATE"— LUKE 13:24

"HE WHO ENDURES TO THE END SHALL BE SAVED"
— MARK 13:13

"REPENT"— MARK 6:12

In a church of believers, these sentiments, spoken by a pastor in a tone of benign understanding, could be a consolation, but painted in big black and red letters on signs nailed to trees in the shack-haunted backwoods of Mississippi, they seemed like death threats.

Delta Summer

I had begun my trip from the North in this season by saying I was chasing summer, seeking the reassurance of sunshine, extending the good mood of fine weather. And through Georgia and Alabama the days had been pleasant and mild, the fruit trees mostly picked clean, the cotton blown open in a mass of tufts awaiting the harvester, some farm laborers in fields mowing hay and bundling it in big folded rolls and bulky bales. But the stifling heat in Mississippi was another story, tasting of dust, with a human odor in it, or a sun-browned meadow of hungry tormented cattle swishing their tails against the clouds of buzzing blowflies.

The Delta was supine and severe and mournful. I was now and then warned that it was dangerous, but that warning gave it a drama it did not deserve. I never found danger in the Delta; it was troubled and poor. Far-ther up the Delta, I met a Mississippi man who had a cousin who lived in Natchez and made a monthly trip to Memphis. He had bettered himself, ran a successful business, but remembered his poor upbringing in the black neighborhoods of Jackson.

"He feels so bad about what he sees, he goes to grocery stores and fills boxes with food in Memphis. On his way home, down Highway 61, he stops now and then, wherever he sees poor people, and he drops off the boxes." It was the sort of impulsive charity you might hear of in Africa or India.

Not all the dead flat fields on either side of the straight road that ran through the Delta had cotton in them, and those that didn't looked ex-hausted, an effect of the occasional pools and creeks of standing water, overtopped by backlit masses of gnats — golden veils of them — and the pools green and thick with stagnation.

Like Africa, I scribbled in my notebook when I stopped to piss against a tree. The tourist imagines Africa to be a wonderland of light and big game and wooded hills, but in the savannah, where the animals are found near the water holes, the air is thick with biting flies and a mud-stink just like that rising from the Delta swamp. In contrast to the immensity of the plains, the habitations of humans — the clusters of huts — are mean, shonky, and improvisational.

Down the dusty roads heading west were the bottomlands, tall trees in the distance and low thickets, and I could see where there was water because of the dazzle of the sunlight skidding against it, the blinding glare amid patches of darkness at the bases of the tree trunks.

The summer that I had been chasing, I found here, but it was not what I had imagined or wanted, not this heat rising from the bubbling decay of the bayous, not the sunshine on the poor shacks and abandoned houses of the squatter settlements on the roadside between the hard-up towns. Yet I was not deluded by what I'd read — not looking for the Delta of Faulkner, nor the Yazoo City of Willie Morris, nor even the Delta of the great blues-men. I might take my cues from books and music, but I knew better than to believe that they still applied. Faulkner's last word on the Delta seemed to be reflected in Ike McCaslin's judgment in old age, that the whole of it was shrinking, vanishing, giving way to modernity and the money-minded.

Yes, it was still shrinking, and it was decaying and losing its people; the modern world was nowhere in sight, and no one I saw had any money. The Delta looked abandoned, and worse in the killing heat of buggy summer than it had in the bleakness of the raw winter of empty roads and cold, scoured fields. A dead, defeated depression hung over the whole strip of farmland, and a green haze rose from the river that lay out of sight, and beyond the swamps and bayous.

And yet, and yet: its very emptiness was an attraction and a liberation, the dead flat land under a dome of sky, the straight road that was so calming to drive, and the knowledge that I'd gained from previous visits that Delta people were not just approachable but unpretentious and friendly to strangers, glad to talk, and especially to talk about the past because they were so uncertain of the future. There was freedom for me in these open spaces. It was only when a town or settlement or roadside trailer camp or a street of houses came into view that the mood drastically altered.

I say houses—though houses is the wrong word. I had seen them before, but hoped that they were an illusion, not representative of what else was there, that there might be more, something salubrious and hopeful, an example to the rest. It was another reason I'd come back. I drove through Redwood and Rolling Fork and Anguilla, and they were the same as in the other seasons of my visits, melancholy and fallen on hard times, and the houses were only approximations of houses, the house trailers dented, their edges bumped and rusted, the shacks woebegone—though here and there an attempt at gentility, an old wreath on the door, a chipped birdbath, a plastic wishing well planted in the stony yard.

Chasing summer, I had left the impartial dazzle of the sun of late summer in a landscape exhausted by heat, yellowing and fading, the tickling odors of plants gone to seed, the seed pods emptying, a ripeness and hardening of berries and a dusty blush on the melon vines—a withering was obvious everywhere. And that was what I had found here too. It was always late summer in the Delta.

The Blues in Hollandale

Just as I was beginning to think all hope was lost, I swung through Hollandale, which was just as bleak and boarded up as the other settlements on and off the highway, but I heard music, which got louder as I entered the town. It was late afternoon and hot, dust rising in the sunlight slanting out of Arkansas, the broken street full of jostling people, and somewhere nearby, a man, out of sight but audible, wailing, and a guitar twanging, and the thrashing of a drum kit and the shiver of a saxophone: the blues, on the Blues Highway.

When I hesitated, a big khaki-clad policeman waved me off the road where other cars were parked. I got out and walked toward a stage that had been set up against a stand of trees. This was the limit of the town, and a powerful growly man was singing, backed by a good-sized band.

"That's Bobby Rush," the policeman said to me as I passed him.

A banner over the stage was lettered HOLLANDALE BLUES FESTI-VAL IN HONOR OF SAM CHATMON, and stalls nearby were selling fried chicken and corn, ice cream and soft drinks, and blues festival T-shirts. Bobby Rush was screaming now, but slowly, finishing his last set, one of his signature songs, "Chicken Heads": "Love that gal / Love them chicken heads too."

And then the clatter and smash from the band, and he took a deep bow and waved — a startling sight on a back street of the old town, with the low sun blazing through the tall trees behind him. As Bobby Rush left the stage, to great applause from the people — about two hundred of them — standing in the dust, another group took the stage and began wailing.

"He got kinfolk here," a man next to me said.

A black biker gang in leather stood in a group and clapped. Old women in folding chairs applauded and sang. Children ran through the crowd of spectators. Youths dressed as rappers, with low-slung trousers and hats turned back to front — they clapped too. And so did little skinny sixteen-year-old Shuquita Drakes — half her head shaved, purple braids on the other half, a sweet face, hardly five feet tall — holding her little boy, a swaddled one-month-old infant she had named D'Vohta Knight. And

Robin McCrae, a willowy dancer from Atlanta who had family in Hollandale, said, "This is just amazing."

But the music was so loud, so powerful, splitting the air, making the ground tremble, conversation was impossible, so I stepped to the back of the crowd, and as I was walking, I felt a hand on my arm.

It was an old man in a sun-faded shirt and baseball cap.

"Welcome to Hollandale," he said. That was the sort of thing that seldom happened to me in a lifetime of travel in the wider world, but it was like a blessing in the Deep South — a stranger approaching me and putting me at ease.

"Thank you, sir," I said. "I'm Paul, from up north."

"I'm the mayor of this town," he said. "Melvin L. Willis. How can I help you?"

And then, of course, I realized that though there were half a dozen whites in the audience, I must have looked like someone from outside the Delta. Or it might have been the fact that I had my notebook open and was writing fast, and also trying to decipher the name "D'Vohta" in Shuquita's scrawl. Or maybe he was just a mayor trying to do the right thing and working the crowd. Whatever the reason, there and then I felt that Hollandale was a place I wanted to know better.

Melvin Willis had been born in Hollandale in 1948 and had grown up in segregated Delta schools. But he had persevered, gone to college, and gotten a job teaching in York, Alabama, a small Black Belt town in Sumter County, near the Mississippi state line — I'd passed through it driving from Demopolis to Meridian. He had risen in the ranks and become the high school principal in York.

"I worked down there in York for forty years, then retired and came back home to Hollandale in 2005," he said. "I had a feeling I could do something here to better this town. I ran for mayor in 2009 and won. I just got my second term. This festival is an example of the spirit of this town."

I asked about Sam Chatmon's relation to Hollandale.

"Chatmon wasn't born here, but he spent most of his life here, playing music in his string band and working at the plantation," Mayor Willis said. "Everybody knows him now. You see we got Bobby Rush? It's been a wonderful day. This is a great town, Hollandale, a great place to live."

One of Sam Chatmon's songs, which he played with his group the Mississippi Sheiks, was "Hollandale Blues" ("My woman says, 'Come home, Sam'"). Others were "God Don't Like Ugly," "Sitting on Top of the World," "You Shall Be Free (When the Good Lord Sets You Free)," and "Nigger Be a Nigger." My favorite (recorded by folk musicologist Alan Lomax in 1978) was "Make Me Down a Pallet on Your Floor," which Chatmon claimed he heard when he was four years old and remembered his whole life.

From old photographs, Sam Chatmon was a slightly built but heavily bearded man, the son of Henderson Chatmon, a former slave from Terry, Mississippi, who had lived to the age of 105. Sam had died in 1983, age 86, in Hollandale. He was buried in the local cemetery.

The music, the crowds, the many cars parked under the trees, the food stalls, and the festive air—none of it could mask the fact that, like the Delta towns of Rolling Fork and Anguilla and Arcola, the place was boarded up and looked bankrupt. I mentioned this with as much tact as I could to Mayor Willis, asking about the hard times in the Delta.

"We're poor," he said. "I don't deny it. Our tax base is so low."

"How low?"

"It's $300,000."

"To run the whole town?"

"The whole town, yes," he said. "We survive on grants. We just got a federal grant of $450,000. Sounds like a lot, but it isn't."

Given the hundreds of millions in aid, both government and private, dumped into Africa, it did not sound like a lot of money. It was the price of one above-average house where I lived in Massachusetts.

"Out of that we have to pay teachers, the firemen, the police, the town hall workers, and so much else. Infrastructure needs tending to, and that costs money. We're said to have a population of 2,700, but it's actually more like 3,500. No one has money, no one in this town. We got so little tax revenue, yet we got to keep going." He sighed and lifted his baseball cap and scratched his head.

"Not easy," I said.

"Lord, it's not easy at all. The cotton doesn't employ many people. The catfish plant was here. It closed. The seed-and-grain closed. The hospital closed twenty years ago. We got Delta Pine, they process seeds. That's about it. There's no work hereabouts."

A white man approached us, put his arm around Mayor Willis, and hugged him with affection. "Hi. I'm Ray Schilling. See this man? He used to work for my daddy at the grocery."

The grocery was Sunflower Food Store, in the middle of Hollandale, one of the few stores still in business. And I'd seen the other Sunflower store in Rolling Fork. Ray, like Mayor Willis, was an exuberant booster of Hollandale, and still lived nearby.

Ray said, "Over there where the music is playing? That was Simmons Street, known as the Blue Front, every kind of club, all sorts of blues. I tell you, it was one lively place on a Saturday night."

"One of the great places," Mayor Willis said.

"Bootleg liquor and fights," Ray said.

But the Blue Front had quieted down in the late sixties, and the music stopped in the early seventies.

"People left. Mechanization. The jobs dried up. We're still in business, though," Ray said.

More people joined us, and it was beautiful in the setting sun, the risen dust, the overhanging trees, the children playing, the music, the thump and moan of the blues from the musicians onstage.

"My father had a pharmacy over there, City Drug Store," a man said. This was Kim Grubbs, brother of Delise Grubbs Menotti, who had sung earlier at the festival. Both Kim and Delise had been raised in Hollandale.

Delise was a petite blonde with a strong voice, and she'd held her own among the gravelly voiced bluesmen. One of her songs, which she'd written herself, was "The Mississippi Delta": "Oh, the Mississippi Delta, the flatland is my home . . ."

"We had a movie theater," Kim said. "We had music. Yes, it was very segregated when I was growing up in the sixties, but we were still friendly, black and white. We knew everyone."

Mayor Willis was nodding, "Yes, that's true."

"It was a kind of paradise," Kim said. "How can we bring it back? What can we do?"

Gesturing to the music and the food stalls and the dancing children, all of it awhirl in the dazzle of the setting sun, I said, "This is a good start."

Mayor Willis put his hand on my shoulder and said to me earnestly, "We can do it again. You come on back. You'll see."*

Doe's Eat Place

Up the road in Greenville, looking for a place to have dinner, someone suggested Doe's Eat Place. I knew the odd name from a satirical piece that Hunter Thompson had written for *Rolling Stone* in 1992, during the presidential election, when he had interviewed Bill Clinton, who had suggested meeting at "a diner called Doe's Eat Place."

"I nodded meekly," Thompson wrote with his customary mockery, "and sat down in a tin chair at what was either the Head or the Foot of the table, thinking that the Candidate [Clinton] would naturally sit at the Other End, far out of reach of me. But no. The creepy bastard quickly sat down right next to me, about two feet away, and fixed me with a sleepy-looking stare that made me very uneasy. His eyes had narrowed to slits, and at first I thought he was dozing off."

As Thompson sighed with exasperation, Clinton explained that there was a Doe's in downtown Little Rock, that it was "a knockoff, of sorts, of a steak-and-seafood shack in the Mississippi Delta." Though it was part of the franchise, it bore no resemblance to the original in Greenville, Mississippi.

Doe's was not a café, not a diner, not any sort of restaurant, really. It was an enormous old kitchen with greasy walls and a much greasier ceiling and yellowing newspaper clippings praising it and smeared photos clapped to the wall. This kitchen and some side rooms were in a plain wood-frame house on a back street in a dense residential neighborhood of darkened homes. For that reason, the place was hard to find—there

---

* I was eager to return and see this friendly and optimistic man again. But one month later, Mayor Melvin Willis, on a routine visit to the doctor, was diagnosed with cancer. He died shortly afterward, in November 2013, at the age of sixty-five.

were no landmarks, no other stores or places to eat. I drove from the center of Greenville, followed detailed directions from street to street, and there on a corner at last was Doe's.

The evolution of this place was odd even by Southern standards. The small building had begun in 1903 as a family grocery, Papa's Store, run by the Signa family (apparently immigrant Italians; Signa is a municipality in Tuscany, about half the size of Greenville); among the founding Signa clan were Dominick ("Big Doe"), his wife Mamie, and brother Frank ("Jughead"). But the grocery business failed because of the Mississippi flood of 1927. This flood—one of the worst natural disasters in US history—destroyed the levee, put Greenville and many other towns in the Delta underwater, killed a thousand people, and wrecked the Delta economy for years.

Moonshining, another Southern tradition, then became the Signa family business, according to Doe's Eat Place's website: "Big Doe Signa went into bootlegging to help the family get back on its feet. After several years he sold his 40 barrel still for $300 and a Model-T Ford."

Reinventing himself as an impresario, Big Doe turned the front part of the store into a honky-tonk ("strictly for blacks") in 1941, and in the meantime, Mamie Signa had perfected a recipe for tamales, which were sold in the honky-tonk. (Greenville calls itself the "Tamale Capital of the USA.") Whites in Greenville heard about the food, and, craving tamales and steaks but unable to enter by the front (black) door, they found their way to the back door of Doe's, and the rear of the building became the (whites only) "eat place," as opposed to the (blacks-only) honky-tonk "music place" out front. The website helpfully explains, "Like segregation in reverse."

Big Doe "eventually closed the honky-tonk and focused on the eat place." He retired in the 1970s, and his sons, Charles and Little Doe, run the restaurant now (with occasional visits from Jughead's wife, Florence), along with a team of hurrying women and perspiring fry cooks in the hot kitchen and adjoining rooms, serving plump steaks and platters of fries in one of the most chaotic and most accommodating eating places I found in the South.

After a dozen broiled shrimp, a side of chili, a platter of fries, and three beers, I swayed in the darkness outside Doe's, much mellower town.

Sunday Morning in Monticello:
Church, Catfish, Football

Hearing that the juke joint Po' Monkeys, in nearby Merigold, was closed for the next few nights – I'd wanted to stop there for the music – I drove west out of Greenville, across the new bridge over the Mississippi, into the flat fields of Arkansas. I followed the far bank of the river for a while, ducked inland, and went through the pinewoods to Monticello. There, I spent the day, first at Shady Grove African Methodist Episcopal Church – a "Pack the Pews Sunday" was planned by the pastor, Reverend Thelma Hampton – and then I walked around town and, following the suggestion of a man from the Shady Grove congregation, went to Ray's Catfish and Barbeque, "A Monticello Tradition Since 1964."

Monticello was a small gray town in green southeastern Arkansas, woods and farming country, nowhere near an interstate. It had once been a busy place of light industry – boat building and weaving – but that was mostly gone. Like many such towns in the rural South, the old shops in the venerable and well-planned town center – the drugstore, the grocery store, the traditional bank, and the dry goods store – had become thrift shops and secondhand dealers. Several well-stocked pawnshops thrived on the outskirts.

The Sunday ritual for Monticello citizens was to go to church – Calvary Baptist, First United Methodist, Pauline Baptist, Faith Baptist, Zion Hill, Rose Hill Free Will, Shady Grove AME, and there were six more within walking distance of the town's main square – and after church to go out to eat lunch, at Cowboy's or Mazzio's or the busiest place on Sundays, Ray's, for the catfish.

Every table was taken, and many were shoved together so that a large extended family could sit in one place, from grandparents down to

...ildren and all the others in between, a dozen or more at some

...

...hough the man who advised me to go there was black—and he ...imed he was headed there himself—all the diners at Ray's were white, a ...undred or more of them.

Pausing over a plate of catfish at a crowded table, Grandpa held up his fork and said in a fat, assertive voice, "I think everyone over the age of eighteen ought to strap on an iron when he leaves the house. Yes, I do."

"Hear that, Daddy?" a woman said, apparently to her husband, a man in a blue denim blazer and wearing a John Deere cap.

"Shoot anyone you want to," Grandpa said.

No one challenged him, though not everyone was listening—most were eating. Satisfied with the silence, Grandpa raised his elbows and worked his knife and fork into his mess of catfish.

"If you has a reason," Grandpa concluded in his drawl.

At the window under the sign ORDER HERE—no wait staff, Ray's was self-service—Hannah, the cashier, said, "Now and then a black person comes in, but not very often. They get takeout mostly. Blacks kinda live on one side of town, and whites on the other."

The patrons in Ray's were wearing their churchgoing clothes, bright shirts and polyester pants and some of them white shoes or boots. They were eating hungrily and shouting back and forth in the facetiously aggrieved way of Southern whites in public places. The only reason I could hear Grandpa clearly ("And there's a big ammo shortage coming, I tell ya") was because his family table was next to mine. Small children ran among the tables, chasing each other through the restaurant; single mothers and daughters sat at some tables; and from across the room I saw a solitary biracial boy sitting with a big white family, and chipping in on the conversation.

As he had promised, the man from Shady Grove entered Ray's by the side entrance, a single black man in a sea of whites. I wandered over to talk to him as he was saying, "To go."

He was Marvin Hobson. Marvin had been born in the small town of Wilmar, about ten miles west of Monticello. Wilmar's population was mostly black and poor, and even now a third of the town lived below the poverty line.

"It was very hard when I was growing up," Marvin said. "I mean, the civil rights thing. There was fighting — mean, bad fighting — people getting hurt and some dying."

"How did your family manage?"

"My father was a farmer, and when I say he was a farmer, I mean he had a horse and plow, on rented land." He laughed in admiration at the memory. "That man worked! Our family picked two hundred acres of cotton, two rows at a time, a nine-foot bag dragging along behind, all day at harvest time."

He was another older Southerner — he was sixty-two — with a memory of picking cotton, someone who could distinguish between "picking" (pinching off the loose cotton) and "pulling" (yanking at the tight boll), describing the long, narrow muslin "picksack," and lying on the soft sack at lunchtime, marveling at the achievement of "tall cotton" — six feet high sometimes — and then the tally of the sacks at sundown, the end of the workday. I met many men and women like him, and I was to meet more of them, black and white, and very few of them ever spoke about cotton picking as misery or forced labor. What I heard — and it was distinct in Marvin Hobson's voice — was how they could pick two or three hundred pounds in a day, and how they looked back on it with nostalgia and pride.

"My father planted cotton, corn, peanuts, and watermelon," Marvin said. "He had that horse and plow for years. Finally he got himself a small tractor, an old Ford 8N. That's the only one he ever had."

Marvin's route out of Wilmar, in the Southern tradition of self-liberation from segregated schools and substandard hospitals and general exclusion, was to enlist in the US Army, making a career of it.

"I retired after twenty-six years — 82nd Airborne out of Fort Campbell, Kentucky," Marvin said. "The last action I saw was the first Gulf War. I'm back home now — and glad to be back."

"But business doesn't seem to be thriving."

"This was a busy town once," Marvin said. "We had three carpet mills. Burlington carpets was big. Muffler plant, boats, some others. They all left — probably went to Mexico or China. All we got now is the wood chip factory over on Midway."

Burlington Industries, maker of rugs and carpets ("tufted bath and accent rugs"), had a manufacturing plant in Monticello of a million square feet. It closed, and its 200 employees were laid off in 2005. Arvin Industries, a maker of car exhaust systems, shut its local factory. The boat maker SeaArk, once a Monticello employer of 220 people, discontinued its plant operations in 2011 after fifty-two years, though its competitor, War Eagle Boats, maker of duck-hunting and fishing aluminum skiffs, was still in business.

Marvin was probably right about Burlington taking its rugmaking to China. As for Arvin Industries, it too was in China, supplying mufflers these days to Chinese carmakers.

At this point in our conversation, standing at the takeout line at Ray's, Marvin was handed his mess of catfish in a Styrofoam container and we were bidding each other goodbye.

"Sure enough, this is a Sunday tradition in Monticello," he said. "Church. Catfish. Then watch football."

"Is that everybody, black and white?"

"No, sir. White folks eat out on Sunday," he said. "Most black folks cook on Sunday."

That was another tradition, based on the fact that the black cook in the white household had Sunday off, to go to church and cook for her own family, while the white family went to a restaurant like Ray's.

Hot Springs—Pleasures and Miseries

My afternoon drive from Monticello to Hot Springs was a long panning shot of sad towns and beat-up villages, Warren to Edinburg, which was poor and small and lifeless, and Fordyce, which I'd heard about in Alabama as the birthplace of the beloved coach "Bear" Bryant, a town where every store was shut or abandoned or turned into a thrift shop. At the crossroads on Fordyce's Main Street, the faded signs and empty premises were a testament that there was no call for Benton Hardware, Farm Implements, a dress shop, or a soda fountain in the Walmart era. Then tiny Tulip, and Malvern, which had some vitality that radiated from Hot Springs, farther along the road.

In a sudden, rocky, high-sided vale of the Ouachita Mountains, with two tall Soviet-looking buildings, one the VA hospital, the other the Arlington Hotel, Hot Springs was a surprise, a spa town with a claim to architectural splendor and the gamy smell of an old circus. The thermal-spa buildings that lined Bath Row were Art Deco marvels well restored, and narrow buildings lined steeply sloping streets on the cliffsides. Half the place was painted, decked out, yet with a residue of its vicious past existence; the other half was blandly residential. The town looked carved from rock in the mountain gap, one of the most dramatic physical settings in any Southern town.

Many signs on the main streets extolled its raffish atmosphere, its criminal history—allusions to the visits of gangsters, gloating mentions of crime, brothels, and sensational murders. "It's hard to imagine the city as a hotbed for organized crime, such as gambling, prostitution and bootlegging," said the Hot Springs promotional brochure, piling it on (it was subtitled "The Past Is Where the Fun Is"). "But from the late-1800s through the mid-1900s, especially in the 1930s, Hot Springs was a popular hangout for Al Capone, Frank Costello, Bugs Moran, Lucky Luciano, and other infamous mobsters. The safe, secluded scenic location of Hot Springs made it the ideal hideout."

Of the many houses of prostitution, the busiest was "The Mansion," owned by the celebrated Hot Springs madam Maxine Temple Jones, who catered to the rich and powerful, criminals and politicians. For decades resisting the mob, whom she ratted on in return for a pardon, she stayed in business into the mid-1960s and later wrote a book about her life and times.

"Honey, I like an old-fashioned whorehouse that has respect and dignity," she told the *Arkansas Times* in 1982. "And my girls were always very proper. I always taught them what my daddy taught me: to walk tall and always remember that it's not what you do, but how you do it."

The gangster era came to an end in the late 1960s and is luridly depicted in the Gangster Museum of America on Central Avenue ("where you won't be gambling on a good time, but betting on a sure thing!"). Because of its pleasant climate and sleaze, the town had been a destination for spring training for Northern baseball teams from the 1880s to 1940—a wild era too, when players routinely binged and whored.

That was Hot Springs's colorful past, but it was the recent past. No place to raise a child, is what you'd say—dangerous, wild, full of malign influences, opportunists, career criminals, tarts, cheats, trimmers, and schemers. Yet that's what the newly married Virginia Clinton did, accompanying her second husband, Roger, there, her seven-year-old Billy in tow.

Bill Clinton was born in the small, sweetly named town of Hope, in southwestern Arkansas, in 1946, as the often-told story has it in the mythology of the man. But the banal truth is that he grew up—was formed, educated, became a man—in raw, reckless Hot Springs, a hundred miles north, amid its miseries and splendors. His father, William Blythe, was killed in a car crash before he was born. His mother studied nursing, so that she could provide for the boy. In 1950, his mother met and married Roger Clinton, and three years later they moved from Hope to Hot Springs, Roger's hometown.

"While Bill Clinton's writings about his boyhood in Hope in the late 1940s acknowledge the racial separation of the town of 7,500 people, his memories are mostly sepia-toned and nostalgic, like those of his Pawpaw's grocery store," the Arkansas writer Jay Jennings explains in *Carry the Rock* (2010). "But in the first two decades of the twentieth century, when cotton was king and Jim Crow was unwritten law, Hope was the site of enough racial murder that it was sometimes called the lynching capital of the South."

In Hot Springs, Roger Clinton was known as a shiftless drunk. In a town of degenerates, being a boozer was no shame, but Roger proved to be a wife-beater as well as a demented alcoholic, and when young Bill was old enough (he says he was fifteen), he defied his stepfather's wrath and defended his mother. The marriage ended. Virginia continued working as a nurse anesthetist, but in an expression of hope over experience, she remarried the same pathetic man a year later.

Meanwhile, young Bill studied, learned to play the tenor saxophone, excelled academically at Hot Springs High School, attended church at Park Place Baptist, bought chili cheeseburgers at the Polar Bar (now Baily's Dairy Treat), ribs at McClard's Bar-B-Q, apple pie at Club Café, and ice cream at Cook's Dairy, and went to movies (Elvis movies, biblical epics) at the Paramount and Malco theaters. He tells us this in his autobiography, *My Life,* displaying great affection for the town and an extraordinary memory for detail.

But he does not say that the theaters' balconies and back entrances were for blacks, that the motels and restaurants were segregated, and that the black part of Hot Springs was miserably poor and decrepit. Speaking of the time of Governor Orval Faubus's racist intransigence and of the federal marshals forcing the integration of Little Rock's Central High, all he says is "Most of my friends were either against integration or unconcerned. I didn't say too much about it, probably because my family was not especially political, but I hated what Faubus did." He is equally disengaged when describing segregation in Hot Springs: "It bothered me that Hot Springs' schools weren't integrated. The black kids still went to Langston High School."

One afternoon in Hot Springs, I made a point of driving over to Langston, the neighborhood on the opposite side of town from where Clinton lived. I found broken streets, run-down houses, a wholly black area around the school, Southern impoverishment, the other side of the tracks. Still a disgrace fifty years after Clinton lived in town, still poor and obviously neglected, Langston looked like a black "location" in South Africa, ripe for uplift from an NGO (though none was in sight), the very sort of place that should have been a target for improvement by the Clinton Global Initiative, but wasn't.

While Clinton was a teenager (and from his account he roamed freely in Hot Springs), gambling was rife, murders were common, gangsters were part of the scene, Maxine Jones's brothel and many others were thriving, and the town, run by a crooked political machine, was alight with roisterers, whores, and high rollers. You're bound to wonder what effect that ingrained culture of vice might have had on an impressionable schoolboy.

Contemplating Hot Springs, it is difficult to imagine a more unpromising origin for a president, one so likely to warp a mind or corrupt a soul. Yet the defining characteristics of a president are worldliness and guile. The world in all its bizarre forms had come to Hot Springs, and Clinton was buoyant in it; the town was clearly the making of the man. In *My Life*, Clinton repeats the tedious Hot Springs boast of larger-than-life visitors—"outlaws, mobsters, military heroes, actors, and a host of baseball greats"—and describes his upbringing: the abusive stepfather, the hardworking and loving mother (who was also a drinker, gambler, chain smoker, and harmless flirt—an Auntie Mame type, adored by her son), his love of the tenor sax, his visits to relatives, his after-school job at the small grocery, his classes as a math whiz, his dabbling in student politics, his earnest posturing that successfully masked a troubled home life.

The pain of being hard-up and frugal in such a flashy, freewheeling place; the necessity to succeed, to achieve something and get out, to prove himself worthy of his mother, and to redeem her belief in him — these aspects formed him. It's an American story, but in Hot Springs it is gaudier than most. Clinton was transformed by his upbringing, yet he was, like many white Southerners, a late convert to vocally demanding integration. In *My Life* he extols the diversity of the Hot Springs population — Jews, Greeks, Arabs, Italians — but the black side of town, the Langston neighborhood, is not mentioned; black life does not exist for him; he apparently has no black friends.

In his autobiography, Clinton continually makes the point that he was a keeper of secrets, leading a double life, never letting on in school of the turmoil at home. The succession of houses he grew up in (now all privately owned and unwelcoming) were in modest but respectable white neighborhoods. But a visit to Hot Springs is convincing proof that throughout his early life, as a young boy, as an older student, Clinton was performing a balancing act, keeping his head up while tiptoeing through a mud-puddle sludge of human weakness and greed, crookedness and carnality (the survival strategy of many politicians).

His relief at leaving Hot Springs is palpable in his telling. He had chosen Georgetown University because "I wanted to be in Washington." Yet after Georgetown, a Rhodes scholarship to Oxford, and Yale Law School, he did what many might regard as the unthinkable: he returned to Arkansas. It was a calculated move. He was still in his twenties, it was a state he knew well, and he was implausible anywhere else. Perhaps he had a long-term plan — he doesn't say in his book, but you can see he is driven: the desperate, do-anything-to-win drive of the man from nowhere, who seems to be hiding something (wounds, fantasies, transgressions, family secrets). He taught law for a year at Fayetteville, then ran for Congress in 1974, and lost. He became state attorney general in 1976 and governor in 1978, at the age of thirty-two — "the boy governor," as he was known.

To his supporters, Bill Clinton was a man of immense charm who improved health care and education in Arkansas, at the same time mastering the art of consensus building, while retaining his amorous disposition. To his enemies, he was the fiddler and liar who turned the governor's mansion into a fornicarium. He served multiple terms, totaling almost twelve years, and, still only forty-six, became president.

It was a breathless run, and he kept on running, for a second term, and afterward — he has never lived away from the public eye, has an obvious, perhaps pathological aversion to solitude, has always sought attention — for the role of world statesman, global humanist, and reformer; but also plotter in the shadows, conniver in schemes, and double-talker, in a mold described by Thoreau in a skeptical essay, "Now, if anything ail a man so that he does not perform his functions . . . if he has committed some heinous sin and partially repents, what does he do? He sets about reforming the world."

Hot Springs had two distinct sides, so did the Clinton household, so evidently does Clinton himself. This conflict could have made him a criminal, or disillusioned him, turned him cynical; instead it made him ambitious, adaptable, eager to please, charming, charismatic, sympathetic, and hardworking. But it also made him covert, adept at role-playing and posturing, with a hint of the huckster in everything he proposed, a teller of half-truths, and a master of secrets. Clinton's drive to succeed was unstoppable, and it continues: his passion to lead, to be in charge, to relieve the planet's ills, to be an explainer, a crowd pleaser, friend to the great and good (Nelson Mandela, the Dalai Lama), emotionally immature, and hungry for the world's affection. "He seemed like the hungriest man I'd ever met," a writer friend told me after accompanying the candidate on the campaign in 1992. In his autobiography, Clinton continually interrupts the narrative of his early life by flashing forward and describing how he learned a lesson or atoned for one lapse or another. America knows him as the great atoner, the fixer, the compromiser. The bird-dogger of chicks is also, inevitably, the most fervent sermonizer at the prayer breakfast.

Hot Springs has tried to reinvent itself as a family-friendly holiday town and destination for conventioneers. It has a look of solidity and criminal elegance, a big-city gloom and density, rare in a Southern town — the shadowy aura of a place in which many dramas have occurred, the rub of history, where a great deal of money has been spent to tempt the visitor to linger.

Horse racing and some low-level gaming persisted, as moronic pastimes rather than vices, but the present was simply seedy, college kids barhopping and late-summer tourists traipsing the streets, darting in and out of the gift shops and bars, shabbily dressed, pushing baby carriages, screaming at their children, hunting for fun in a place that seemed chilly and bleak. The barbecue joints and the occasional pageant or festival could not compete with the shootouts and the orgies of the past.

Now Hot Springs is a place wholly itself: the decaying abandoned buildings and vacant hotels on the main drag, funky motels, tacky shops, a whiff of damp motor courts on the outskirts—Southern neglect combined with Southern casualness and vulgarity, and redeemed by hospitality and self-parody. Part of the town's good fortune is that it is just a gap in rocky cliffs, minutes from the deep woods and lovely hills.

There is something joyless in a place advertising itself as joyful, a note of desperation in the hype. Faded glory, faded hope, faded hilarity, the weird junk shops, the air of desperation, the stink like an alcoholic's breath or a carnival sideshow, the shallowness and obvious scheming that is part of every gambling town on earth. And, like every other boomtown, doomed to failure.

But Hot Springs had once been a vortex of energy, and it is a characteristic of the power of such libidinized places to make their residents morally blind—you could say the same about the White House. Hot Springs, destination of murderers, cheaters, and whores, produced a president, a peculiar one, morally blind on many occasions—as in 1992 when Governor Clinton rushed back to Arkansas to sign the death sentence of drooling, brain-damaged Ricky Ray Rector, sending him gaga to the electric chair, so that candidate Clinton would win votes as a crime fighter. Complex and contradictory, the public man seeking redemption, mock humble in manner but lusting for glory, perpetually enlisting big companies to help him expand his brand, Clinton is the quintessential Southern huckster who does not know when to stop, and Hot Springs, the corrupted town, which advertised its waywardness, was itself Clintonesque.

Road Candy at the Dixie Café

"Poverty is a great educator. Those who have never known it lack something," the Anglo-Irish writer Gerald Brenan observed in *Thoughts in a Dry Season*. Brenan spent most of his life among peasants in Spain, but this wise saying was a great epitaph to the Southern lives that were themselves peasant existences. To travel through the South is to see this insight proven over and over; Southerners, especially the older folk, black and white, often reflected with pride on the pleasure they took in their austerities.

I thought of Brenan's words as I made my way on a lovely summer afternoon drive from Hot Springs northward, along simple Route 7, through farmland and forest, past Jessieville and Ola and Dardanelle, and across the Arkansas River, dark brown in spate, to Russellville.

There, at the Dixie Café, I met Patricia Atkinson, who had grown up in poverty in a family of fifteen children, ten boys and five girls. She was number twelve, and now in her late fifties. Her eldest brother had recently died at the age of eighty-nine. The family home had been near Hughes, in northeastern Arkansas, in the Delta; her father, Jim Short, had done sharecropping, cotton mainly. An enormous, poor white family farming outside a country town, but they had struggled and succeeded and stayed together. Later, Pat went to college, got a job as a secretary in a housing development organization, learned the ropes, stuck with it through a transition — "It's self-help housing" — and was now executive director.

We sat among the remains of catfish, chicken stew and dumplings, fried tomatoes, fried onions, fried corn on the cob — the cobs dipped in egg, battered in flour, and deep-fried.

"My father used to cut off the corn kernels and fry them up," Pat said, poking at her corncob. "Very good eating. But we ate everything. Imagine, fifteen of us kids. Only five of us graduated from high school. If you're farming, you can't go to school. One of my brothers never set foot in a classroom — my father wouldn't let him."

"Because he needed him on the farm?" I asked.

"No. Thought he'd be bullied. My father was protective of Hopper," she said. "Short for Clodhopper. He was always running around the fields."

"Fifteen children — how big was your house?"

"Put it this way, there was two or three beds in every room. Privacy was unknown. We shared the room, we shared the bed."

The three beds had always held all the Lesters, Erskine Caldwell writes in *Tobacco Road, even when there were sometimes as many as eight or nine of them there.*

"I guess you all had to cooperate."

"We had hard times," she said. "I started picking cotton when I was six or seven, using a pillowcase. Later on, I had a tow sack, about the size of a feed bag. Then I got a proper cotton sack — nine foot long. The boys used to step on the end of it so I couldn't pull it. They thought that was real funny."

"But you were still in school all this time?"

"Oh, yes. The cotton we picked on Saturdays we got to keep for ourselves — kept the money, I mean."

"What sort of money?"

"In the 1960s we got a dollar-fifty for a hundred pounds. My brothers could pick three hundred pounds apiece, easy."

"Doesn't seem like much money," I said.

"It wasn't, but we had to do it. Imagine trying to feed fifteen children in one house. It was always a problem. We always worked, and we helped each other. We raised our own meat — pork and chicken — and we hunted deer and squirrels. We trapped raccoons, mink, bobcat, and sold the hides. Catch a good coon and you could sell the hide and eat the rest."

"Raccoons — I've trapped them," I said, "when they were being a nuisance, crawling down the chimney, clawing the shingles off the roof. They're so smelly, scavenging in the garbage."

"Baked coon is some good eating," Pat said. "A lot of people around here eat it. Baked raccoon and sweet potatoes. Skin it, cut it up, salt and pepper, then bake it some. Chunk up some sweet potatoes and put them around it and bake it some more."

"They can sleep through a freezing winter," I said, "so they must have a lot of fat."

"Lot of fat on a coon. It bakes off, adds to the taste."

"You mentioned squirrel?"

"Squirrel's big," she said. "Squirrel season's coming."

"How do you cook them?"

"Squirrel for breakfast—smother-fried," she said. "Gut the front shoulders and back legs and rib cage. You can cook the head too. Roll all of them in flour and shove them in the skillet. Squirrel cooks real fast. Then put water into the skillet with the browned squirrel. The flour turns into gravy. Cover it, let it simmer awhile. It's delicious first thing in the morning."

"I guess you had chores to do on the farm, before you went to school?"

"For many years we didn't have water in the house, we had a well. Jerked water out with a pump. It's sometimes real cold in the winter in Hughes. I remember going out to get water one winter morning when I was a girl. The snow was up to my waist." Pat had shoved her chair back and was looking into the middle distance, reflecting on this scene in her girlhood. "Course, you had to prime the pump, so we always kept some water back for that. That day we had to dig a lot of snow out from around the pump before we got any water."

"I think of the Delta as warm," I said. "It wasn't that cold when I was there in the winter."

"The summers are very hot, but summertime was fun for us. We'd fill a sixty-five-gallon barrel of water, leave it in the sun to heat up, and play in it. If you don't have money, you make your own fun. We made toys out of corncobs. Soak 'em in water, get 'em soft, and throw them at each other. We were barefoot most of the time, wore hand-me-downs, just like everyone else."

"By 'everyone else,' you mean black people?"

"Blacks were our neighbors. We worked in the fields with them, side by side."

"But the Delta in the fifties and sixties was segregated."

"We worked together. I didn't feel any prejudice." She thought a moment. "My dad was from Tupelo, and he was old-fashioned. He thought blacks had their place." She shook her head and added, "He had a sad life. His parents died in 1915, when he was twelve. He was deemed 'too old' to go to the orphanage with his two brothers and two sisters, who were younger. So he was separated from them and was sent to a woman he called his grandma—only she wasn't. She was some distant relation, Aunt Jones."

"Did he reconnect with his brothers and sisters?"

"He wanted to. He tried to find them later, but never did," Pat said.

"Then I tried—tried everything, all the databases, all the connections. But I failed. It was a sadness to him his whole life."

"Your upbringing was amazing," I said.

"Growing up that way is the reason I'm doing what I'm doing now."

What she was doing now was improving housing for the poor in nine counties in west-central Arkansas. Her stories of growing up poor in the Delta, offered modestly, were wonderful examples of the full life she had led. The stories were like road candy to me, the happiest aspect of my seasons in the South.

"There's Some People Who Never Hit a Lick at a Snake and They Expect Help"

Over the next few days in Russellville, I got to know Pat Atkinson better. She introduced me to her staff—organizers and contractors and clerks—and some of her clients. And she told me how she had become part of this housing program.

After graduating from business college in 1981, Pat had joined a self-help housing organization called ARVAC, working as a secretary and then moving up, taking on more and more responsibility. Her long apprenticeship in housing development resulted in her present post, more than thirty years later, as executive director of the Universal Housing Development Corporation of Russellville, rehabbing homes, building houses, making repairs. As she said at the Dixie Café, growing up in a large, hard-pressed sharecropping family in the Delta was good training for this.

Anyone who was approved for housing help was expected to work on the house—"sweat equity." Her organization's budget was $2.5 million, much of it from federal grants and most of it going to programs rather than salaries. We were sitting in Pope County, one of the nine served by Universal Housing, a county that was mostly white (ninety-two percent) and very poor (home to a submerged twentieth). The Delta and urban areas—Little Rock, for example—had a greater percentage of black residents and about the same or higher poverty levels. Universal Housing built, on average, about thirty new homes a year and rehabbed about fifty. It was the largest self-help housing program in Arkansas, and the most successful, though still a modest-sized organization with a relatively small budget.

"Our clients are the working poor," Pat said. "Around here that works out as about thirty-two thousand dollars for a family of four."

"The price of a car," I said.

"A good car," Pat said. "If they're earning more than that, they don't qualify. On that kind of income all they're doing is surviving. We have a long waiting list, mainly white. That's the demographic here."

"Many Hispanics?"

"Hispanics are classified as white," she said. "Some of them show up and ask for help. We say we need to see documents — IDs, Social Security cards, tax bills, whatever. Now and then they say, 'Do they have to be my documents? Can they be someone else's?' You know? They're serious!"

"How long is the waiting list?"

"About four hundred at the moment. Some of them are on the list so long they don't make it — they pass away before they get a house. We've got people who've been waiting ten years or more."

In Arkansas, insurance companies made regular inspections of policyholders' houses. In many cases, the houses of clients had deteriorated so badly that the companies canceled their policies. The owners were left uninsured, with leaky roofs and broken windows and no means to fix them.

"You can see sunlight through those roofs," Pat said. "The people call us so we can help them with a roof or a repair. But we expect people to work and help. We give advice, we help with plans and with ordering materials, and the house owners do most of the work themselves. They involve family, friends, neighbors, anyone who's willing."

"Do people usually pitch in?"

"There's some people who never hit a lick at a snake and they expect help," Pat said. "There's all sorts of issues. I don't understand people who expect you to help them without their thinking they could help themselves. And then there's people who don't ask for much. They don't want to admit they're poor."

"Proud, I guess."

"Little old woman, Dolores Malton, up on Crow Mountain. Tiny lady, a hundred pounds or less, a little biddy, she came to us for help. She wanted us to put in a water line."

"She had no water?"

"No running water. She lived in a little old storage building, just an eight-by-ten shack. No plumbing — she used a chamber pot. She said she was getting too old to carry water. Probably in her eighties."

"Did you put in the water line?"

"We wound up building her a house," Pat said. "Another client, mother and daughter and the daughter's two children living in two small storage buildings. No plumbing. Terrible conditions. We built them a house."

"I'd like to meet some of these people you've helped."

"I'll see if I can arrange something," she said. "I need to get their permission for you to visit. I'll make some calls."

"How about Bill Gates, and Clinton, and the other charities — get any help from them?"

"We never see them, we get nothing — they want to help Africa," she said. "It really bothers me that Clinton does so little here. I wish he'd help us. He's in Africa and India, and other people are helping in the Third World and those countries. We don't see that money. Don't they realize our people need help?"

The Cabin on Quickerstill Lane

Dover, a small, pretty town at the edge of the green bumpkin hills of the Ozarks, about twelve miles north of Russellville, sunny today in smiling summer heat, was notorious for a massacre. In 1987 Ronald Gene Simmons murdered his entire family, fourteen people — his children, their spouses, and their children — one of the saddest victims a seven-year-old girl he had fathered through an incestuous relationship with his daughter. And afterward, still in a fury, he drove to Russellville and killed two more people. Then, unshaven, grubby Ronald Gene Simmons meekly surrendered.

"But he was from Chicago," Dover people told me. That was true. Simmons had served twenty-two years in the air force, fought in Vietnam, and retired to New Mexico. When a charge of incest was filed by his daughter, he fled to Arkansas. There he lived north of Dover on five fenced-in acres, with many of his family members, in a pair of jammed-together house trailers with no running water. Heavily bearded and bald and swivel-eyed, he seemed in the beginning to fit in.

A drinker and a loner, with no friends, he had attempted to work at clerking jobs in Russellville, but ultimately was shunned as a weirdo and a woman-pesterer. One woman in particular who had resisted his advances became a nonfamily victim of the massacre. Simmons chose the days just before Christmas for the murders, which he carried out with calculation, shooting some with a .22 pistol he'd bought at Walmart, strangling others with his bare hands, and drowning the smallest children by holding them underwater in a rain barrel. All this mayhem was carried out in and around the trailers, which were strewn with unopened Christmas presents.

He apparently said to the children, "Come in here, I got a present for you," and killed them one by one. Others had shown up for their holiday visit and were shot. After spending a night with the corpses, Simmons drove the next day into Russellville, drank a beer at a bar, and shot two more people, whom he considered unfriendly to him, and wounded five others. When he surrendered, he said to a bystander, "It's all over now. I've gotten everybody who wanted to hurt me," and demanded the death penalty. His wish was granted: he was executed less than three years later.

Apart from that killing spree, Dover's history is mild; it is a tiny, quiet town, mostly white families and rather poor, even by Arkansas standards. Ten miles outside Dover, not far from the site of the massacre, at the end of a dirt road called Quickerstill Lane, in lumpy, wooded hill country where the Ozarks begin to rise, I was met by Fannie DeAlba, a small, cranky-voiced woman of sixty-six, who greeted me sourly by complaining, "I don't get many visitors."

"I wonder why," I said, meaning to be ironic.

She answered me sharply: "I don't get visitors 'cause I'm hateful and mouthy."

"You seem very pleasant," I said.

"That's bull," she said, and smiled, seeming to test me with her bad temper.

She was small and smooth-faced and stout, with an impish smirk, and later, when she stopped being vexatious and became friendlier and took out her rifle and challenged me to a shooting match—knocking down a beer can—I noticed that she had a way of cradling the weapon on the paunch of her bulky body, both resting it and keeping it handy. With the rifle vertical and the butt on the ground, Fannie DeAlba wasn't much taller than the muzzle.

"Also, this here is country poor," she said, meaning *Why would anyone bother?*, and canted her grizzled head at the dirt road, the trash pile, the heap of discarded car tires, the piles of lumber and a few flower beds, and the dense woods that continued for sixty miles north, the deep green and mostly trackless heart of the Ozarks.

She'd been born Fannie Campbell to a sharecropping family in Dumas, and saying the name, she added, "Bet you don't know where that is."

"It's near Monticello," I said.

"Think you're so smart," she said in a teasing tone. "We were raised old-fashioned. Cotton, soybeans. No indoor plumbing. I never had a steak growing up. When you're on a farm and poor, you eat pork and chicken. I had shrimp for the first time in California—my second marriage. I'm looking at the shrimp and thinking, The hell's that?"

That second husband was DeAlba, and though Fannie married a third time, and divorced him too, she kept the name DeAlba. "His family was all Spanish. They explored California. Some of them was royalty."

How she had come to this small cabin on Quickerstill Lane—"Named either for Mr. Quicker or maybe his still, no one knows"—was a long story, she said, and hardly worth knowing. But I encouraged her to elaborate. The salient fact was that she had for many years lived in a trailer in the woods off Morgan Road, a long, dead-straight country road south of Dover. "The trailer was junk. It caught fire four or five times. It belonged to my ex." That was her third ex. About twelve years ago she moved out and bought a trailer on Quickerstill Lane. Then it caught fire. "The whole thing was burned out from a gas fire. We couldn't move on."

That was when she got in touch with Universal Housing. Pat Atkinson sent a contracting adviser, Shawn, to see her, and he assessed what it would take to repair. In effect, the burned-out shell was turned into a cabin, the materials costing $4,674. Fannie signed a contract and a deed, and she got a loan, vowing to pay it off after the work was done: new metal roof, new bathroom, new porch, plasterboard walls inside, new floor tiles.

"It was a self-help deal. Different friends helped. And Shawn from the agency told us what to do and how to do it. And I paid it off, every penny."

Shooing cats — she had eleven of them, she said — she showed me inside, a kitchen and living room arrangement, and behind the rear wall, the bathroom, which she insisted I see.

"I fixed this up myself. See that angel?" It was a sweet-faced winged creature. "I painted that. I mess with painting and drawing all the time."

It was a simple flat-roofed cabin, and it was cluttered, but it was secure — and a far cry from her old junk trailer on Morgan Road, or the burned-out shell that it had been before Universal Housing had helped her.

"After deer season we'll get the rest of the porch put on," she said. "You can't get anyone to work. They're all hunting. And if it's not bow season, then it's black powder season, or modern rifle. They close school the first day of hunting season. No one would show up anyway."

"You do any hunting, Fannie?"

"Not as such," she said. "I hate possums and raccoons. My dog trees 'em and I shoot 'em. They kill my chickens. I killed a seven-foot chicken snake a while ago. They like eggs. They can smell 'em. Them snakes are all over, or in the weeds. They got into my horse trough. I couldn't shoot into the horse trough and make holes, so I got me a shovel and chopped it into pieces." She looked at me, gave me a naughty child's smile and wink. "I ain't real partial to snakes."

"I take it you're a good shot."

"Middling. Probably better than you."

That was when she got her rifle out of a closet, and a box of ammo, and told me to follow her. She hugged the rifle against her belly, then set up a beer can about thirty feet away on a tree stump.

"You first," she said.

"Go ahead. You've got the gun."

She raised it, fired, and sent the beer can flying. And then she laughed — the first time I'd heard that witchy cackle — and it was my turn. I fired, missed, fired again, hit the stump, and swore.

"You're pulling it down, mister."

After a few more shots I managed to knock the can over, but with far less panache than Fannie had.

"You need to know how to protect yourself," she said. "Take my new stepgranddaughter. She's from Wisconsin. Never been around guns. She had anxiety attacks when she come down here. I fixed that right away. I don't think anyone should be intimidated. No one intimidates me. I think you should be able to do and say what you want."

"You told her that?"

"Yep. She was kind of scared, though."

"What's the answer?"

"Taught her how to shoot is the answer. First my thirty-eight, then my twenty-two. We hung up targets and I showed her. There was a buzzard flew over. I can't hit no damn buzzard, but we tried! We shot up the trash barrels, we shot up the targets and the cans. Now, guess what?" Her face tightened in an imp-smirk and she wagged her head. "She don't have no anxiety attacks."

"Everybody's got a gun."

"Everybody's got a *lot* of guns," Fannie said. "And for a reason. I remember a time I had kids in my car — small kids. And some other kids come chasing after me, some doing harassment. I pulled out my gun. They left! I woulda shot 'em. I had kids in the car!"

"I guess they learned a lesson."

Fannie was now perspiring heavily, excited by telling this story of a close call. She was breathing hard, too, and said, "I also got me a crossbow. Any stupid son of a bitch comes into my house will get an arrow in him." She was panting, and then with an effort she shouted, "I will nail you to the wall!"

She put her rifle down and sat on a low bench to get her breath, leaning over and gasping.

"I been in fourteen wrecks," she said. "People kinda run into me."

Still she kept her head down, forearms resting on her knees, recovering her wind. It was late afternoon, and a coolness was settling into the Quickerstill hollow, the sun tangled in the trees.

"I'm part Choctaw and part Cherokee. My dad was an Indian. My great-grandma claimed to be Black Dutch — her name was Snow Flower."

The term "Black Dutch" has complex roots and many conflicting definitions, depending on the region where it was used. In Arkansas it im-plied a Native American passing for white in order to own land and resist being forcibly removed to a reservation. This talk seemed to upset Fannie, who was fighting to breathe.

"You feeling okay, Fannie?"

"Out of breath. I got high blood pressure. 'Cause I'm hateful, and I get mad."

"What makes you mad?"

"This was the Cherokee reservation. Then they split — Trail of Tears. Dardanelle was a reservation too." She was speaking in an aggrieved voice, a tone of indignation. "An Indian could not vote, could not own land."

"Terrible."

"You said it. Blacks complain, but what I get pissed off about is that. Blacks complaining. Get a job. Get over it."

"Your house looks nice from here," I said, to change the subject, hop-ing calm her, because she was breathing hard and her face was pink with a glow of sweat.

"I'm happy with what we done," she said, lifting her head, picking up her rifle, surveying the small cabin that sat under the trees, among the small flower beds and the slowly moving cats high-stepping through the piles of discarded tires. She dabbed at her damp face. "It's only got to last twenty years."

"Really — why?"

"Because I don't want to live longer than that," she said.

The Back Road to God's Country

Sticking to narrow back roads, driving cross-country northwest of Dover, toward Lamar, I was thinking how many of these numbered county roads in Arkansas, gravel and dirt, were Third World thoroughfares irregularly lined by Third World shacks. "Don't they realize our people need help?" Pat Atkinson had said to me a few days before, speaking of the billionaire donors to Africa. It was she who had directed me here, to this area of considerable poverty in a landscape of outstanding beauty, to meet some of her clients, among them Chester Skaggs and his wife, Rose, whom Pat always referred to, in the delicately formal Southern way, as Miss Rose.

"This is God's country. It's beautiful out here," said Chester Skaggs, leading me through the heat, up the long rutted drive to his small, rebuilt cabin, his dog nipping at my shoes. "There's a dozen families"—none were visible, just open country in the foreground, the Ozarks rising behind it—"Holman Community, some call it. Or Hickey. The voting polls are in Lutherville."

I looked north beyond the pastures toward the mountains, where I could see the promise of a lovely valley like a nick on the rim of the horizon.

"Most of this community is lower class," he said, stating it as a fact, not a complaint. If the word had occurred to him, he might have said, We're peasants. And he gazed with me at what could have been the rusted roof of a distant barn, adding, "All poverty level."

Chester Skaggs was fifty-five but looked much older, from a life of hard labor begun in childhood on his father's farm and sawmill, and ultimately curtailed by a back injury on an oil rig. Forty-five years or more of work. He had never entered a schoolhouse or faced a teacher. Rose was about the same age but also looked older: white-haired, plump, a bit frail. Chester was skinny, ironic, a chain smoker with a smoker's wheeze and a fruity cough. He wore a baseball hat with *Cherry* stitched over the visor.

Driving to the Skaggses' house was another time-warp experience for me of entering an earlier age in America, a simpler era, serious poverty relieved by the misleadingly picturesque. I agreed with Chester Skaggs, it was beautiful, meadows bordered by enormous trees, the undulant foothills of the Ozarks, all of it deep green in the summer noontime.

"I don't see any other farms. Didn't see any on the way in."

"There's some. All sorts. A black family too—Tyrone Williams. We get along fine." He laughed and lit another cigarette. "Fact is, Johnson County's getting crowded."

"You from around here?"

"I was born near here, on the family farm. There was only eleven of us kids, five boys and six girls. Besides the farm, my father had a sawmill. We had cattle and chickens and a lot of lumber."

He noticed his dog nipping at my foot and gently pushed it away. When the dog toppled, I saw a scabby patch on its underside.

"That there's Speedy. She's hurtin'. A copperhead bit her on one of her mammaries and rotted the skin out."

"I keep hearing snake stories in Arkansas," I said, thinking of Fannie DeAlba's finding a chicken snake in her horse trough and hacking it to pieces with a shovel.

"We got snakes. Some poisonous, some not," Chester said. "Speedy found that copperhead and was boogerin' at it and got bit. After that she was lyin' down with her tongue hanging out. She was the nearest thing to dyin' I ever seen, rotted off her mammary."

"She doesn't look too bad." The dog was yapping and jumping.

"I give her some medicine and squirted some of that stuff you squirt on cows to keep the flies off. She's better — runnin' around."

We were still walking up the drive, which was more a back road than a driveway, and in about the same condition as the unpaved county road beyond the thicket.

"I'm the one hurtin' now," Chester said. "Worked at the farm and at my father's sawmill, then when I was younger at the shoe factory in Wynne. Later on, I worked in the oil fields in Oklahoma. I got into pipelining."

"Travel much?"

"We done a coupla jobs down in Texas, years ago. My back got so bad I couldn't lift nothin' and in the end I couldn't stand up."

We had come to the house now, which was less a house than a cabin or a primitive farm building, a low structure under a vast overhanging sycamore tree.

"This house used to be called the old Metzger place," he said. "It's a hundred and fifty years old."

"Looks like you did plenty of rehab on it."

"Got a lot of help and advice from Pat Atkinson over at Universal Housing," he said. "The shingles was old on account of the trees. That walnut and that sycamore and that oak. Universal supplied the roofing." It was a metal roof, heavy panels, 24-gauge, laid over the frame where the shingles had been. "No leaks now."

"Must have been a lot of work."

"Windows and doors too. This place was a wreck before. We did the fixin' ourselves, with friends and volunteers. They was good people, and hardworkin'. I couldn't afford to pay anyone."

Rose Skaggs had been listening. She said, "When my stepdaughter Rachel was about twelve, her friends from Lamar come over. School friends. Afterwards—" Rose had started to laugh, and needed to calm herself before she could continue. "Afterwards, they said, 'Rachel lives in a barn!'"

Chester laughed too. "It was in rough shape," he said, seeming to agree with the mocking schoolgirls.

Now the roof was new, the doors and windows were new, the outside trim had been painted white, and new siding fastened on. It was a small house but it had been restored, and, set in the grove of trees, it looked idyllic from a distance. Up close it was the humble home of two people in poor health, living on—what? I didn't dare ask. Perhaps disability.

When I remarked on the good workmanship, Chester took that as a cue to say that all he had learned in his life had been practical, on the job, no schooling.

"School isn't nothin'," he said, volunteering the observation. "It's only a guideline to learning. It's not learning anything, really. They can teach you pronouns, but so what? You got to educate yourself. That's everyone's responsibility. You got to learn your skills outside school."

"I agree with you," I said, thinking, The tigers of wrath are wiser than the horses of instruction.

"I worked making shoes in Clarksville," Rose said. "That was back in '78. I believe they're still making shoes, some. But they may be shutting down, going overseas, like everyone else."

With Rose following us, Chester led me into the house. Every house has its own peculiar odor. This one smelled of cold soup and damp bedding and Speedy. Two horizontal rifles rested on a gun rack on the bedroom wall, a .30-30 and a .22—you could reach either of them from the bed. And there were more, upright in Chester's gun case. I remarked on them.

"Antigun people are buying up ammo, and the government is too," Chester said. "I know where they're stockpiling it. The Pine Bluff Arsenal."

"Really?" I said. "I know there's an ammo shortage, but I didn't realize it was a conspiracy."

"Yep. I got that from a friend of mine."

I looked outside at the sunshine, Speedy still nipping at my heels, the wind ruffling the sycamore boughs. Life here had seemed so simple: chickens in a coop, a goat tethered to a post, the yappy dog, and Chester puffing on a cigarette and talking about the jobs he'd had and how he and the friends and volunteers had rehabbed his house, turning it from a shack to a weather-tight bungalow.

Inside the house, Chester seemed to become more furtive, whispering, as though under siege, someone in need of rifles, believing that dark agencies were eliminating the availability of ammo. The interior had the clutter I'd seen elsewhere—stuffed toys, souvenirs, biblical mottoes framed on the wall, several chunky clocks, an old TV set propped across from a sofa. In the small parlor the sofa and chairs were draped in throw rugs printed with tiger stripes, zebra stripes, or leopard spots, with gold fringes and tassels.

All this time, Rose had been shadowing us.

"We done the bedroom too," she said, beckoning me in while Chester ducked outside to smoke. The bedcover was another bright, animal-skin print, wide stripes.

"I pity the guy who tries to break in," I said, patting the rifles above the bedside table. "Are you a good shot?"

"That's a story," Rose said, lowering her voice. "I come back from church one day and Chester and his friends are here trying to shoot some walnuts out of the tree. They're not hitting nothing, just missing. But still shooting. I watched for a while, then I says, 'Let me try.' Chester says, 'You won't hit nothin', Rose.'"

Then she nodded. She leaned sideways and saw that Chester was out of earshot.

"I picked up the gun," she said. "I aimed it. The Lord then told me, 'Don't think about it, just you pull the trigger.' And I shot."

She began to laugh, as she had outside when talking about Rachel's school friends—so full of laughter she couldn't speak.

"So what happened?"

"Them ole nuts went flying!" she said at last. "Chester wouldn't speak to me for a week, 'cause I outshot him in front of his friends, with the help of the Lord!"

Being in the house put her in a more confiding mood, as it had Chester. I saw a Bible on the bedside table, open to the book of Revelation.

"You're reading Revelation, I see."

"I'm studying Mystery Babylon," Rose said with a tone of innocent pedantry, and lifted her Bible. She smacked her lips and in a steady cautioning voice she read: "'I saw a woman sit upon a scarlet colored beast, full of names of blasphemy, having seven heads and ten horns. And the woman was arrayed in purple and scarlet color, and decked with gold and precious stones and pearls, having a golden cup in her hand full of abominations and filthiness of her fornication. And upon her forehead was a name written, Mystery, Babylon the Great, The Mother of Harlots and Abominations of the Earth. And I saw the woman drunken with the blood of the saints, and with the blood of the martyrs of Jesus: and when I saw her, I wondered with great admiration.'"

She placed the book, still open, on the bedside table, under the rifles.

"Powerful stuff," I said lamely, at a loss for words but thinking of what Chester had said, "God's country"—and it had a new meaning.

"I'd like to write a book about it," Rose said. "We're like Sodom and Gomorrah, which God destroyed. Homosexuals are taking over. They're in the government. They're getting married. But they weren't meant to. It's in the Bible. They can't have children. It's all a sign."

"So, what do you think—sign of what?" But I knew what was coming.

"We're in the End Times," Rose Skaggs said. "I believe that's one of the main signs."

"Paul's Epistle to Timothy," I said.

"You know your Bible."

"I heard it on the radio a few weeks ago," I said. *But know this, that in the last days grievous times shall come . . .*

I craved to get out of the house, with its low ceiling and its stifling doggy air and the strange biblical confidences of its owners. And when I did, and the sun was shining on my head again, Chester and I sat under the walnut tree and just chatted. He scratched Speedy's head with one hand and smoked with the other.

The sight of the fixed-up house calmed him, and I had the impression from the casual remarks he made that he loved this place, where he had been born and still lived, up this dirt road, and wanted no other; that he loved Rose and looked after her; that he loved his dog Speedy — adored the dog, really; and that with this fixed-up house and having figured out a frugal way of living, humble though they were — "all poverty level," his words — they were not afraid of growing old.

Deep-Fried Chocolate Pie

Avoiding Little Rock — I would go there later — I drove across Arkansas to Brinkley, arriving late, thinking that the town was simply shut down for the night. But the next day, in sunlight, I could see that it was shut down pretty much for good, the main street desolate, the stores boardedup, the houses shabby, and this was not deep country but a sizable town just off the interstate.

I looked for a place to eat and found half a dozen small mom-and-pop places, soul food diners, Brinkley Country Kitchen, and at Market and Sporting Goods, with a LUNCH SPECIALS sign, I walked in. At one long table were fourteen big white men in overalls sitting at their noontime meal. Hearing the tinkle of the doorbell, they lifted their querying, somewhat disapproving faces from their plates of chicken-fried steaks and mashed potatoes and stared at me, twenty-eight scrutinizing eyes, no hello — very odd for the South, where I had gotten used to a greeting — and a shadow of serious suspicion, and a fork in one hand and a knife in the other.

"Just a soda, please," I said to a woman in an apron, and squeezed to the cooler in the back, picked out a can, paid for it, and retreated, feeling cowed, as if I'd blundered into a private party, which in a way I had.

Another eatery in Brinkley was Mom's Diner, a small, one-room cottage at the roadside, calling to mind the caution of Nelson Algren in the three rules he articulates in his novel *A Walk on the Wild Side*: "Never play cards with a man called Doc. Never eat at a place called Mom's. Never sleep with a woman whose troubles are worse than your own."

I drove back to Gene's Barbeque, had a pile of fried catfish and black-eyed peas, and then was offered dessert.

"Want some deep-fried pie?"

"Never had it."

"You'll love it. Chocolate pie. We wrap it in pastry and deep-fry it crispy. Why are you smiling, sir?"

A Serious Row to Hoe

Brinkley, Arkansas, experienced a brief boom in visitors when it was reported that an ivory-billed woodpecker, believed to have been extinct, was sighted in the swampy wooded bottomlands outside the town in 2005. Bird watchers from all over came to verify this unexpected news, but no one saw the large, yellow-eyed bird with the thirty-inch wingspan again, and the luckless town went silent. For three years after the alleged sighting, the place had been hopeful, but now it was like many towns in the South: the decaying main street, the thrift shops, the shut-down factories.

I was in Brinkley to see Dr. Calvin King, from Aubrey (pop. 221), in Lee County in the Delta, Arkansas born and bred, educated locally, and committed — as he put it — to reversing the land loss among blacks in this part of the state. A great number of blacks in the Delta had been farmers. They had lost their land for various reasons, and so had lost their livelihood. Dr. King wanted to see black farmers back on the land.

From a farming family himself, Dr. King was one of many admirable people I met who, having grown up poor, were committed to using their experience of overcoming hard times to help others. Like Pat Atkinson, Dr. King had come from a large, hard-pressed family.

"I'm number eleven of eleven children," he said in his office, in a brick building up the road from Brinkley, a hamlet called Fargo. He was sixty years old, scholarly-looking, and formal in a coat and tie, mustached, with confidence and a quiet intensity. "That many kids — you got a serious row to hoe. Four boys and seven girls. Nine of us went to college, and now they're schoolteachers, nurses, college professors."

"All that education is impressive," I said.

"My dad had a real serious thing about getting an education," he said. "When my older siblings were coming along, it was like going to school, learning from them."

"What were the schools like in Aubrey?"

"Not good enough," he said. "In order to go to schools, the good schools, you had to move a little. I went to high school in Marianna, thirteen miles away. I lived with a relative—this was the 1950s and '60s. We didn't get integration until 1971. Little Rock integration was earlier."

"Segregated schools?"

"Racially speaking, it was straight-line segregation."

"How did you manage in that environment?"

"'Fear no man,' my father said. 'Fear only God.' He had a high confidence level and that helped us."

"He had to feed eleven children," I said.

"Food!" The idea made him laugh. "We had everything to eat. I meet with my brothers and sisters and we talk about how lucky we were. We didn't know we were poor. We didn't realize it."

"How big was the farm?"

"My father rented land at first, then he finally bought land, ending up with about a hundred acres in the 1970s and '80s. But the first market was our family. We always had plenty."

Considering that Dr. Calvin King had been born in 1953, and his ten other siblings earlier than that, it seemed a long time that his father, Sterling King, had rented land and worked it before finally buying some. On his rented land he had grown cash crops and cotton and soybeans, and vegetables for the family, but his savings were meager.

"We had cattle, pigs, geese, guineas, and what we called a truck patch—a field, really. We grew everything there, all our vegetables, beans, corn, peas, beets, watermelons."

"Your mother was part of the whole operation, I take it."

"Mom was an outstanding homemaker," he said with a note of pride. "She was always preserving, canning—peaches, pears, apples, you name it. And my father had a smokehouse. We had all our own processing. He smoke-cured slab meat and ham. We always had plenty of meat."

"How did you manage to study and work on the farm?"

"Each of us had a task," he said. "You have some people doing it now in the Delta, maybe not many. I never had to look for a summer job. There was always something to do on the farm. We had our own molasses. We would strip the sorghum and make the syrup from it. It wasn't just our family—lots of other people did it."

"Did you sell the produce and molasses, and get money that way?"

"We created a sort of barter system. My mother would say to someone, 'I sure would like a quilt for me,' and then after a bit, 'I've got a hog.' When we killed a hog, other people in the community would come and help, and for that help we'd give them a portion."

Reverend Lyles in Greensboro had told me the same story of his upbringing in Alabama, bringing a chicken or some eggs to the doctor as payment for a visit. And Floyd Taylor's family had made molasses. The common culture of the peasant South.

"What about hunting?" I asked. "I keep meeting people who still hunt for the pot."

"My father used to hunt rabbits and squirrels. Smother-fry squirrel we'd have for supper, with gravy and potatoes. Supper was 'long about seven. Sometimes we'd have guinea."

"How was that prepared?"

"Guinea with dressing," he said, swallowing, as people do when talking about a favorite dish. "The way I remember it, you boil a guinea to make the broth. Make your cornbread. Take the guinea, stuff it, and bake it with the dressing. Guinea with dressing is very tasty."

"Raccoon—did you eat them?"

"We had coon sometimes," he said. "My father liked squirrel a lot. But they're small. You need three or four squirrels for a meal. Squirrel dumplings, same as chicken dumplings to make."

"I hear this story all over Arkansas—baked raccoon, smother-fried squirrel. It's like a menu from another age."

"People hereabouts still eat them," he said. "But we had plenty of other food. We had cows, so of course we had plenty of butter. My sisters and I reminisce about how we used to come home from school and there'd be chicken or ham for supper."

"Please tell me about your mother," I said.

"My mother's name was Jessie Hill, born in Phillips County in the Delta. She was part Cherokee." His mother's features were visible on Dr. King's face, his sharp jaw, his hooded eyes. "She was raised over in Coffee

Creek. And my mother made the best lunches — all my friends used to remark on them. She had kinfolk in Chicago. We used to send them food, preserved and canned fruit, smoked ham."

Memories of a whole, congenial, hardworking, self-sufficient family; memories of good food, of food sent to hungry, homesick relatives in Chicago.

And as with others I'd met, Dr. King's upbringing had determined his path in life. After graduating from Arkansas State University in Jonesboro and earning an advanced degree at Philander Smith College in Little Rock, he conceived a plan to uplift the farmers, and in 1980 he founded the Arkansas Land and Farm Development Corporation in Brinkley. He had grown up on a farm and been taught his parents' solid values, had eaten well and learned dignity and a work ethic. His mission was deeply personal.

"This organization was designed to reverse land loss and the decline of the family farm," he said. "Housing is another of our concerns. And youth services."

"What sort of clients do you have?"

"The working poor. Some of our people have two jobs and still no money, no stability, no home ownership."

The waiting list for rentals was long, and more than two hundred people needed their houses renovated or rebuilt.

"We've built what we call Safe Communities," he said. "You have to qualify. We have regulations and requirements, we do background checks before you can be accepted. It's just like the process of buying a house or getting a credit card."

Brinkley was dying, he said. Unemployment was twice the national average. All the "support assets" were in place — roads, water, rail, the infrastructure of the past — yet there were no job opportunities. Sanyo had been there, making old-style cathode-ray television sets since 1977, but it had shut down, and manufacturing was now ended. Instead of upgrading the nearby Forrest City plant to make newer-model flat-screen TVs, they had outsourced production to Tijuana, just over the Mexican border — cheap labor, no taxes, no unions, easy importation into the United States.

"People from up your way come down here to teach," Dr. King said. "They say, 'I can't believe the way things still are here!'"

"A lot of what I see here is Third World," I said. "But I also meet good people, many of them doing what you're doing. Making progress — small steps, maybe, but life-changing ones."

"To have growth you need a shared vision, a collective sense," Dr. King said. "We need to sit down and talk together. To be frank, there's whites who say, 'What's the problem? We have a school — private school. Lee Academy in Marianna. Marvel Academy in Phillips County.' They don't realize what the rest of us are up against. It's not all the whites. It's the wealthy whites. No shared vision."

"The Clinton Foundation has billions and spreads it all over the world," I said to him, as I had said to Pat Atkinson in Russellville. It seemed an obvious question. The foundation was immensely wealthy, and from time to time — if you looked at its website — you'd read of the former president promising money to people with projects in Africa or India, or this: "Chelsea Clinton took time out of her 10-day humanitarian trip in Africa to meet some of the kids that her AIDS work is benefiting . . ." I asked, "Do you see any of that money?"

"No," Dr. King said solemnly. "We have not received any funding support from the Clinton Foundation or the Global Initiative."

"Would you like to get some?"

"Yes," and he was nodding, "we would more than welcome such support." He added, "We have lots of people working hard. Family farms. All over the Delta."

"I'd like to meet some," I said.

"I was hoping you'd say that."

Working Poor

Arkansas was a place of outstanding natural beauty: the rumpled hills and granite cliff faces, the damp willow-haunted riversides, the meadows and plowed fields bordered by tumbled stone walls. But it was a poor, hungry, ill-thought-out, and badly housed state, and the rural areas were notoriously hard-up. In some counties, almost thirty percent of the people were living below the poverty line, and one in four of Arkansas's children were classified as hungry—"food deprived."

The overall figure for "food insecurity" in the state was unusually high. According to a 2013 Department of Agriculture report I'd read about at Arkansasmatters.com, "19.7 percent, or roughly one in five Arkansans, do not know where their next meal is coming from." This was the sort of statistic you might encounter in Sri Lanka. And when I checked, the figure for food insecurity in Arkansas was exactly the same as that for Sri Lanka, an island that was struggling to overcome the effects of a recent and long-lasting ethnic war.

Many of Arkansas's unemployment problems, and its hunger, were related to its decline in manufacturing. With time to kill until I met Dr. King's Delta farmers, I sought out people who'd lost their jobs to outsourcing. One was a cheerful woman who called herself Dee. ("It's not really Dee. I changed it because the Japanese couldn't pronounce Odelia.") She was sixty-nine and had worked at the electronics plant in Forrest City, not far from Brinkley, for forty-two years. Like most of the working poor in Arkansas I met, she was uncomplaining but clear-sighted.

"Wasn't Sanyo in the beginning," she said. "It was Warwick Electronics, owned by Sears. That was years ago. We made TVs mostly, but the company was going broke. That was the late seventies. Sanyo bought the plant, put a lot of money into it, and turned it around. It was real big."

Sanyo's moving into Forrest City, their taking over the TV manufacturing and creating employment for four thousand people, was one of the important stories in the business pages of national newspapers in the early 1980s. "Japanese Turn Arkansas Plant into a Success" was a headline in the *New York Times* in 1983. A deal was struck with the union, $14.4 million was invested in upgrading the plant , the new sets were an improved design, quality control was introduced—under Sears's management ten percent of the TV sets had been lemons. The majority of the new workforce was black, though Dee was white.

"People care about you," one of Dee's coworkers had told the *New York Times* in 1983. "There is more effort on quality, better follow-through. There is a lot of sensitivity to the feelings of the workers. Management goes out of its way to obtain views of workers, to see how they can make the work more productive, more conducive to doing a better job, to see how they can make the job easier for the workers."

The economy of Forrest City was saved, and the Japanese managers became members of the local golf club—though there were still no black members. Everything was rosy for about ten years. Then, in 1994, with advances in TV technology, and more investment and retooling needed, the North American Free Trade Agreement was approved and implemented. "We have the opportunity to remake the world," President Clinton said at the signing of NAFTA in December 1994. "In a few moments, I will sign the North American free trade act into law. NAFTA will tear down trade barriers between our three nations. It will create the world's largest trade zone and create 200,000 jobs in this country by 1995 alone."

It was the beginning of the end for Forrest City. From that day, in Clinton's home state, Sanyo began to shrink its plant and move its manufacturing to Mexico. And Forrest City became another haunted-looking, not to say spectral, town of high unemployment and boarded-up shops, with a Walmart and fast food outlets and little else.

"My manager got curious and went down there to Tijuana," Dee told me. "It's tax-free now. No union. He said the workers are real young. They got little hands. They can handle the parts good. They're real hungry. And they don't get paid much."

Dee was now working at a motel part time. So was Julie, whom I met around the same time in a town farther west. Julie was thin, sixty-something, a motel clerk, a chain smoker, toothless, with an alarming croupy cough, cheerful enough but battered and ill kept, like the motel, Patel-owned. My room stank so bad—dirty bed, decayed carpet—the humming pong of rug rot kept me awake. Even the lobby, where Julie sneaked a crafty butt at the back door, was malodorous.

"There's no work here except for six or seven Mexicans living in one room and not paying taxes," Julie said. She told me her story, but warned me in advance that it was one of failure. "Worked in a shirt factory for years. We made flannel shirts, outfits for state troopers, quality clothes. It all went overseas—China, Dominican Republic, God knows where."

"What sort of work were you doing?"

"That's the thing. Come to what I was doing was I was taking out labels saying 'Made in Honduras' and sewing in labels saying 'Made in the USA.' That was late eighties, early nineties. I said, 'This is not right,' and I quit. Not too long after that the whole factory closed. Now there's nothing. Four red lights and a Walmart, like most other places."

"And you came here to the motel?"

"No," she said, and took a pull at her cigarette. "Got a job at Burris, making oak drawers and cabinet doors." Julie took another long puff and blew the smoke out the door, dispersing it with slaps of her bony hand. "They was bought out. Then we'd get the real cheap swamp oak with lots of knots and couldn't do nothing with it. I was laid off in 2000, and I was supposed to have a pension, but they didn't give it to me." She sucked on her cigarette again. "Under arbitration, they say. So here I am." And she flipped the butt, twirling sparks into the parking lot.

In the silence—I didn't know what to say—she became reflective.

"All I do is drive to the next exit. I go home, put the dog out, put on my robe, and watch TV." She shrugged and tapped another cigarette out of her wrinkled pack. "I got divorced a couple of years ago. The kids are gone, my ex is gone. I work here, if you want to call it work. That's about it."

Roadkill

In Arkansas, the poorest towns, the most beaten-down people, could be found in the prettiest hollows and river valleys, the small, mean, ugly houses and scabby trailers set in magnificent landscapes—soft, green, thickly wooded, rolling hills and murky, crawling rivers. Avoiding Little Rock, I had drifted west off the interstate to the hamlets of Altus and Ozark and Mulberry, each as attractive as its name, in "Arkansas Wine Country," some of it settled by Germans and Swiss, who planted the vines 130 years ago. The wineries and restaurants got mixed, not to say hostile, reviews, but the winding road was so pleasant and wooded, bounded by pastures where horses and cattle grazed, it was a relief simply to slow down and enjoy the scenery, to contemplate the clouds of gnats stirring in the golden slant of sunset.

"Hear about the storms?" a motorcyclist asked me at a gas station near

Altus. He had just come from Memphis; he was riding up and down the whole country. "Tornadoes are coming. I'm heading to Fort Smith to hunker down until it passes."

Perhaps it was the sharply winding road, the proximity to dens and warrens and the brakes and nests of nocturnal animals, but I saw more roadkill in forty miles of this country road than I'd seen in hundreds of miles of highway.

What caught my eye at the exhausted-looking river town of Ozark was its tranquil square surrounded by a hospitable-looking jail and a forbidding courthouse, and at the edge of town, Rivertowne BBQ, surrounded by a fragrant vapor of scorched meat. Like most of the towns in this part of the state, the population was overwhelmingly white. I'd seen a sign advertising Butterball turkeys outside of town. Ozark's primary source of income, its Butterball turkey-processing plant — ninety turkey farms in the vicinity provided the birds — had been in the news a few years before when People for the Ethical Treatment of Animals (PETA) released an undercover investigation with the headline "Butterball's House of Horrors." The report detailed the company's cruelty in the slaughterhouse, some of it intentional and thrill-seeking, the rest of it the industrial methodology of slaughtering and bagging the birds — fifty thousand a day, more nearer Thanksgiving, millions in a season. The USDA investigated, the abuses were corrected, and Ozark does not prosper but it survives, to the gobbling of desperate, doomed Butterball turkeys.

Outside Rivertowne BBQ, I said to a biker, "I hear there's a storm coming."

"Tornadoes," he said. "Just sit tight. It'll pass."

He recommended the ribs, the breaded and fried pickle spears, and the fried green tomatoes. Possum dumplings in coon fat gravy and creamed possum were also on the Rivertowne menu, along with the celebrated spice rubs. I had the chicken salad with a side of fried okra and then continued west on the lovely road.

In the desolate, dirt-poor, rustic town of Mulberry, boys and men, black and white, were diving into rusted dumpsters to retrieve usable junk, and near them on the road, as if in mimicry, a hopping clutch of ravens were pecking at the rubbed-red hash of roadkill.

Jack-Jawin': "Little Bitty Ole Meth Lab"

The next day, outside the town of Alma, I had intended to spend the whole day at two of the Sunday activities in the South, a church service and a widely advertised gun show — always friendly folks and strong opinions and plenty of food — but in both cases they'd been canceled. It was the dire weather report.

"Got some twisters coming out of Oklahoma," a weather-wise woman told me in the parking lot of a convenience store. And she was in a hurry. "I'm heading home."

The day was dusk-dark but there was still no sign of a storm. I drove off the main road, Highway 71, and took a dirt road up a steep slope into the woods, past shacks and trailers. At the summit, where the road became a muddy track, I came to a ramshackle house — a spectacular ruin at the edge of a field littered with cast-off shoes, rags of clothes, old rubber tires, hubcaps embedded in the earth, children's faded toys twisted apart, plastic bags tangled on bushes, areas strewn with bottles and jugs, and shards of broken glass — a hovel with junk heaped against it.

It was a damp Deep South day in the mountains, of gray lowered clouds, yet the young man in the yard was barefoot, in rubber flip-flops, scuffing through the broken glass, and the woman behind him wore torn shorts and a hoodie and cowboy boots — Ozark work clothes. Bending and grasping, with the concentration of scavengers, they were rooting around the tall grass, filling a plastic oil drum with bottles and beer cans that had been discarded. A barefoot child and a dog followed them, impeding them in their work.

They did not look up when I pulled off the road to examine their house, its tin roof partly torn off, the porch knocked sideways, the windows gaping. In the yard fossicking amid the rubble, they were like strangers who'd found this abandoned house and were taking possession of it by scooping up its junk, and when that was accomplished they would penetrate the house itself.

But they lived there, this mean place on the mountain was their home, and that was their own barefoot child and their own drooling dog. They were both in their early thirties. They laughed when I said I was lost and needed directions, which was simply my ploy to disarm them.

They too mentioned the oncoming storm, that it was one more thing to worry about, like the terrible economy and lack of work, which became the topics of our conversation.

"But I've got me some work putting up garage doors," the young man said. He added with glee, "I worked fifty-two hours last week, and I'm still hoping."

The garage door workshop was at the edge of the town of Mountainburg, down on the highway.

"The town is nothing, and never was nothing," he said. "Never had no work here. We're all struggling to get by."

His wife kept tossing beer cans and plastic bottles into the oil drum, and it seemed from the force of her actions that she was attempting to make a point, which was: I am working and you are standing in your flip-flops talking. But I was thinking: This family is the very definition of the working poor — putting in the hours, hoisting the garage doors, and living in this wreck of a house with their barefoot child.

How lucky I was, fetching up here as a stranger on this back road in the Ozarks and being welcomed by this cheery young man, who was happy to answer my intrusive questions. This friendliness was one of the pleasures of Arkansas, and the green glory of the landscape was another.

"Any black families around here?" I asked.

He laughed, in the same way that a white person in Bar Harbor, Maine, or on Nantucket Island would have laughed at the same question, finding it preposterous.

"There are no black people here, none at all," he said. "No black person ever lived in Mountainburg, and I doubt they ever will."

"But half of Arkansas is black," I said.

"Nothing like that," he said. "Not even twenty percent."

He was right: the figure is fifteen percent.

"You won't find any blacks until you get across the state — say, around Conway," he said. "It's all white up here and black down here. That's the way it is."

"I haven't looked closely at Conway."

"I get down there on a regular basis," he said, and laughed hard, rocking in the wet grass on his flip-flops. "Visiting my father in prison. He's in Harrison now—Boone County Jail. Not too bad of a place, but man, he did plenty of years in a regular old prison."

"A lot of years?" I asked.

"He was sentenced to twenty, but he's doing eleven. I guess that's a lot," the young man said, and nodding, he added, "He'll be out in a month."

"And you've been visiting him in prison all that time?"

"Almost every week," he said. "I was twenty-one when he was convicted. I'm thirty-two now. I still visit on a regular basis."

"Mind if I ask what he's in for?"

"It was drugs," he said. "He was cooking meth over here," and he pointed to a shack that was even more ramshackle than the nearby house. "Hey, he wasn't no dealer. It was just for himself and his own purposes."

"But a meth lab," I said.

"A little bitty ole meth lab, a couple of jars in a room! It was nothing. But someone turned him in—someone who had a grudge against him, probably who wanted some of the product." He shook his head and gave another ready smile. "It was his first offense! Eleven years for that!"

Seeing his wife glare at him, the young man picked up some cans and pitched them into the drum, where they rattled and clanked, but he was still talking.

"He was a skinny dude with long hair when he went in. Now he's a big fat old guy, from sitting all that time. With short hair."

"What'll happen when he gets out?"

"Not much. He can help me fix up the house, but that's about all. He won't be able to get much of a job. With a prison record you ain't got prospects."

"It seems a very long sentence for cooking meth for himself in that old shack."

"Oh, yeah. All those years, and a wasted life. It don't seem fair." He kicked at the grass and guardedly looked around at his wife, stooping and snatching at cans. "But he had to pay the price."

I wanted to talk more, I wanted to know more, yet I felt fortunate in this young man's candor and good humor and forbearance. I was a stranger who had driven out of the damp low clouds and parked at the edge of his property, and within fifteen minutes or so he had told me these details of his life.

"My wife thinks I'm jack-jawin' here," he said. "I got to get back to work. You take care."

I headed back to the highway that is mentioned in Derek Walcott's evocative long poem, one of his best, about race and history in the South, "The Arkansas Testament":

> The dusk was
> yielding in flashes of metal
> from a slowly surrendering sun
> on the billboards, storefronts, and signs
> along Highway 71 . . .

Old Testament Weather:
"Baseball-Sized Hail"

The storm that had been talked about for days came as a "severe storm warning" news flash at six in the morning, as I woke in a grim motel outside the town of Alma in the west of Arkansas, near the Oklahoma border, the far western corner of the Deep South. Storms are frequent here, twisters especially, barreling across the region of the plains known as Tornado Alley, unimpeded by any mountain range, gathering speed, flattening the grass, battering the corn stalks, whirling into splinters any dwelling in its path, crushing the house trailers, felling the trees. Multiple tornadoes were forecast, with high winds and heavy rain, and the words that caught my attention: "baseball- and golf-ball-sized hail."

"I think the trouble is that America just happens to have hyperbolic weather," my friend Jonathan Raban wrote to me when I spoke of the weather mentioned in the hyperbolic mock ordeals of travel writers in the United States. And he went on: "I'd never seen such biblical thunderstorms as I saw in Montana—they seemed to be straight out of the Old

Testament. Tornado alley. Great droughts. The Mississippi floods of 1993. Or the New Madrid earthquake in around 1820, when the Mississippi was said to flow backwards for a week."

Maybe the biblical thunderstorms inspired the preaching and the Last Days themes of sermons in the South, the weather matching the Doomsday mood, all of it portending that the end is nigh.

A "tornado watch" was issued. "Baseball-sized hail" sounded deadly, like a shower of white rocks hammering down from the angry skies, bursting through the roof, smashing windows, breaking your skull, fracturing your bones. Another example of Old Testament weather and seemingly the judgment of an angry God, hurling ice down upon your head.

I had been surprised, and sometimes shocked, by the emphatic weather in the South—the extremes of temperature, the strong storms—but even so, the warnings seemed overdramatic. Then, in Alma, surprised in my skepticism, a few hours later the first rain came down, loud and blinding, bringing forth sudden floods. The rain had started when I was in my car, and it was as though I was being soused and isolated in a car wash. I couldn't see ahead of me, the road was awash, the wind picked up and was thrashing the trees, bending some saplings sideways so sharply I expected them to snap in half, but they wagged and sprang upright and then kowtowed again to the puddled earth, nodding furiously.

Unable to negotiate the road, I pulled off and sat for an hour, the rain cascading down the windows, flashes of lightning giving the nearer shacks a sickly hue, explosive thunder shivering their old planks. I was now isolated by the heavy rain, by the way it shrouded me, by the noise of it clattering on my car roof, by the novelty of a tumbling creek where moments before there had been a gutter of red earth and a footpath. The thunder cracked, erupting in big swelling syllables like a long, booming, and gabbling word shouted by a giant, just after the dazzle of the lightning flash that was green and gold. My goodness, after all this time on the road, an ordeal!

But it was a mock ordeal. The rain passed, leaving pools of water and sodden grass and drooping tree branches—and vapor, like the expelled breath of the storm. And a silence, almost peacefulness, overtook the little roadside settlement where I'd sheltered. I thought it was over, the storm having moved on.

The air was still heavy, the sky dark, an overhanging oppression of stillness and humidity. I had gotten out of my car and, standing in the wet grass, was wondering where to go, or whether I should go at all.

"How you doin'?"

A striding man in a plastic poncho, tugging a dog behind him, waved to me.

"He's freakin' out," the man said. "Got stuck up the road. Headin' home."

"Bad storm," I said.

"This ain't the storm. This is just the rain. Somethin' comin'."

"You mean the tornado watch?"

"Tornado warnin'."

"What's the difference?"

"One's been sighted. Probably more than one. Comin' this way. Supposed to hit tonight."

So this was only a prelude. I drove farther up Highway 71, then back to the interstate, and the rain came again, more softly. I drove in and out of Conway, but because of the storm warnings, most of the businesses were shut and people were off the streets. I bought a sandwich and ate it in the car. Beyond Little Rock, the rain was heavier, the wind picked up, and, deciding that I should stay off the road, I found a motel.

"I got to tell you we're under a tornado watch here," the woman at the front desk said. She was solemn and smooth-faced, twirling a lock of dark hair with a busy finger as she spoke. Her badge gave her name as Jamie. "Take this."

She handed me a printed page from a stack of them on the counter. It was headed "Tornado Procedures," with an itemized list of explanations ("A 'tornado watch' means that weather conditions are favorable for a tornado to form") and directions for sheltering and evacuation.

"I'll call your room if we're under threat," Jamie said. "You can shelter under the stairs with the other guests, or get into your bathtub."

This sort of dire warning, with specific orders ("get into your bathtub"), suggests to the wanderer a promise that by morning there will be something important and timely to chronicle. Bad news for the civilian is often welcome to the travel writer looking for a tale to tell. Wild weather sounded dramatic, and the worst weather had the effect of tormenting a landscape and putting it in sharp relief, giving it a face and a mood.

Driving the rain-doused roads had tired me. I went to bed and slept soundly. The phone did not ring. When I went downstairs at seven the next morning, I found three agitated youths, a man and two women, heaving a tangle of paraphernalia into the back of a vehicle — not conventional luggage but black cases, the sort that holds technical equipment.

"Anything happen?" I asked.

"You didn't hear the news?"

"I was asleep."

"We was up all night. It was awesome," the young man said, swinging a microphone on a long rod into the car. "Eight twisters."

The tornadoes had blown through during the night, taking with them two of the suburbs of Little Rock I'd passed through, looking for — but not finding — a place to stay; the towns of Vilonia and Mayflower had received direct hits.

"We came to within two miles of the tornadoes at Mayflower, where all the destruction is," the young man said, his voice rising in excitement.

He sounded strangely happy, even somewhat delirious. I remarked on his mood.

"We're storm chasers!" he cried.

His name was Stephen Jones, a student at the School of Meteorology at the University of Oklahoma in Norman. Following the tornadoes, he had entered Arkansas, crisscrossing the high winds and rain, taking pictures of the storm cones and the whirling debris, recording the howl of wind. Photographing lightning bolts was one of Jones's specialties, and since thunderstorms help create tornadoes, he had taken many such pictures of blazing, sky-cracking light.

"I guess we're crazy," he said, but he didn't mean that; he meant they were passionate. He was still hurriedly loading his car. "We're heading to Mississippi, maybe get more footage. The twisters are hitting there today."

"What should I do if I'm in my car and there's a tornado?"

"Never pull under an underpass or a low bridge. The wind funnels through — it'll kill you. Safest place? Believe it or not, a car wash."

And then they drove away, the storm chasers, toward Mississippi and the twisters.

In the aftermath that day, the main headline in Little Rock's *Arkansas Democrat-Gazette* was "Tornado Deaths Reach 15," and the article described "the 40-mile-long path of destruction" through north Little Rock and three counties of central Arkansas — where I had happened to be, but I'd been bypassed by the fickle, slithering storm — "before moving back into the clouds." All the warnings had been accurate: the storm had been as lethal as it had been predicted to be, perhaps more so. It had snaked northeast, springing across the interstate, "mangling recreational vehicles and flipping over 80,000-pound tractor trailers."

It had bypassed Conway, but nearer Little Rock it had flattened Vilonia and Mayflower, where there was now a 7 p.m. curfew, and heaps of debris, fallen trees, houses reduced to splinters and planks. The newspaper was filled with tales of unlucky people trapped in basements, flung out of windows, dying under collapsed walls. Hundreds of people had taken refuge in shelters, where they remained.

"Twister's Path: 3000 Dwellings" was the headline two days after the storm. The affected areas were declared a "major-disaster zone." This storm had been one of the most powerful in Arkansas history, and in some parts of central Arkansas almost eight inches of rain had fallen in three hours. Flooding was general, roads turned into rivers, houses submerged, people drowned. Witnesses spoke of "the rumbling freight train sound" of the twister moving past their houses while they hunkered in basements and safe rooms. This storm that I had slept through a few miles away had now claimed thirty-five lives, including people in Alabama and in Mississippi, where it had been particularly destructive in Tupelo. Swathes of trees in the path of the storm had been scoured from the earth, and ones on the periphery had been debarked.

A greater factuality, and a summing-up, appeared in the Little Rock newspaper on the third day. On the Enhanced Fujita Scale — the scientific measure of tornadoes — the storm was designated a category EF4, with winds up to two hundred miles per hour. The force of such winds can derail a train, demolish an entire house, and uproot trees, sending the trunks flying like battering rams. This was the worst storm in Arkansas since a category EF5 hit in 1929, killing twenty-three people and wiping out the town of Sneed: the place was abandoned and never rebuilt.

Days after the strange selective storm, the local hospitals were still unable to cope with all the injured and dying, and people kept arriving with severe trauma, broken bones, pierced flesh, collapsed lungs—150 victims at one hospital. An accompanying story in this locally well-reported tragedy was a lengthy account of "storm-tossed pets," such as the Labrador retriever found hanging in a tree—and rescued.

I had slept through it all. That was the oddness for me in this punishing and dramatic weather event that had gripped three states. I had gotten wet feet, but otherwise the storm had not touched me and had hardly inconvenienced my travel. It was a day or two of alarm, of reports, of voices off. The terrible wind came and went, a singular Arkansas drama, and though it was reported throughout one news cycle, it was not headline news anywhere else in the United States.

"This is a weather state," a man said to me later in Little Rock. "People are crazy about the weather—always discussing it. Maybe it's because we're agricultural and need to know. And we do have amazing weather."

One church took advantage of the tornado to put up a billboard:

DOESN'T THE UNUSUAL WEATHER TELL US THAT JESUS
IS COMING BACK VERY SOON?

Citing Luke 21: "And there shall be signs in the sun, and in the moon, and in the stars; and upon the earth distress of nations, with perplexity; the sea and the waves roaring; Men's hearts failing them for fear, and for looking after those things which are coming on the earth: for the powers of heaven shall be shaken. And then shall they see the Son of man coming in a cloud with power and great glory."

But if you weren't directly in its path, it was no more than a wet day in the Ozarks, unremarkable except for the sounds of distant thunder. For those who were buffeted by the power of the whirling wind, it was devastating, the commencement of days of funerals and laborious cleanups and sad stories of sudden homelessness.

But it was a remote episode; it was local. It was just more misery in the South, and for most of the United States the storm, with its disruption and death, was so far beneath notice it could have happened in a foreign country.

The Arkansas Literary Festival

During these stormy days, while I drove through the rain around central Arkansas, I happened upon a literary festival in Little Rock, four days of talks and book-related events. Many authors were featured, most of them Arkansans. The Arkansas novelist Charles Portis lived in Little Rock, and I hoped — because I was one of his readers — he might be speaking. But Portis's name was not on the list of eighty authors who would be appearing at the festival.

Most literary festivals, featuring self-promoting authors with tangled beards and strange hats, eager publicists, and the hoopla of signings and free T-shirts, amount to little more than a frenzied harlequinade. But the mission of this festival was, so its advertising stated, "to encourage the development of a more literate populace." In a state in which some rural counties had a twenty-five percent adult illiteracy rate, where statewide more than fourteen percent could not read or write, and almost twenty percent of Arkansans did not have a high school diploma, a more literate populace was a worthy aim. Whenever such dire statistics were trotted out, the response was usually, "But in Mississippi it's worse," which was the melancholy truth. Yet the intellectual sterility in Arkansas was palpable and made more obvious by the strenuous attempts to deny it.

The Arkansan writer Ellen Gilchrist was advertised as a featured speaker at the literary festival. I had read several of her collections of stories and hoped to hear her. Her short stories, many of them sequential, with a recurring cast of characters, concerned the tribulations of educated, middle-class, white Southern women. The stories were not to my taste, but that wasn't important: the drawling, sprawling prose of Gilchrist was revealing, such chattiness often more revelatory and helpful to an outsider like me than a virtuoso display of literary technique. Gilchrist never failed to describe women's clothes, every color and style, the shoes too — the shoes especially — and the women's makeup and coiffures. These were descriptive details to which the male writer was usually blind or oblivious. From the literary point of view, her fiction had no weight — at least for me — but the stories I'd read clearly reflected the love, work, mating habits, and marriages of Southern women, which she portrayed with conviction.

The issue of race was seldom raised in Gilchrist's fiction, though one set of connected stories was narrated by Traceleen, a black housemaid working in the home of one of Gilchrist's characters from other stories, a dizzy, much-married drunken Southern belle named Crystal Manning Mallison Weiss. Traceleen is sober, reliable, and hardworking, and in one episode, trying to be helpful, she takes over the driving of an expensive Mercedes and unavoidably crashes it, causing its (male) owner to remark, "Holy Christ, Crystal. You let the nigger maid drive my car?"

I longed for the privilege to ask Ellen Gilchrist about this story, included in her prize-winning collection *Victory over Japan*. Why the sustained and unruffled tone of the black narrator? Whence the farcical situation that develops from the crash? And why does Traceleen seem to accept the word of abuse, or at least why does she evince no reaction at all to this language in what seemed to me a charged situation? And did Gilchrist receive any flack or umbrage for using the word?

But the storm had kept Ellen Gilchrist in Fayetteville, and her talk was canceled, as I discovered when I visited the Main Library on Second Street, not far from the odd, intrusive library and museum in the form of a cantilevered upswung big-rig trailer, the William Jefferson Clinton Presidential Center, on the south bank of the muddy Arkansas River.

The woman in the more conventional Little Rock Main Library, sitting at a wide desk at the top of an elegant staircase at the entrance, sat like the captain on the bridge of a ship, fielding questions, directing people to books and rooms and festival activities.

"Very impressive," I said, paging through the program she'd handed me and remarking on the many events and numerous writers participating in the festival. "I'd love to meet the organizer."

"That would be Brad. But he's pretty busy with the writers."

"Perhaps I might leave him a note?"

I wrote my name and contact number on a torn-off square from a pad of Little Rock Library stationery.

"And what would this be in reference to, um, Mr. Thorax?"

"About writing in Arkansas," I said, and when she snatched at her blond hair and kept her blue eyes on me, hoping for more detail, I added, "I'm a writer myself."

"Do you write under your own name?"

"Generally."

"What sort of things do you write, Mr. Thorax?"

Though I made a tactful attempt, I felt it was like describing the color green to a blind person.

"You're going to love the festival," she said, and that was when, hearing that I was looking forward to hearing Ellen Gilchrist, she told me her talk had been canceled owing to the bad weather.

I saw that, within the hour, Congressman John Lewis was going to speak about a new book he'd written, and would be appearing at this free event at the Mosaic Templars Cultural Center on Ninth Street, across town. I got into my car and drove there to hear him.

John Lewis, a long-serving politician from Georgia, was one of the stalwarts of the civil rights movement. Inspired as a youth by the speeches of Martin Luther King, he had met Dr. King when he was eighteen, and before long became an effective speaker himself. That was the beginning of his life as an activist at sit-ins and protests and voter registration campaigns throughout the 1960s. For his nonviolent, somewhat sacrificial efforts, Lewis had been violently beaten on many occasions, and on the Selma march on Bloody Sunday in 1965, his skull had been fractured by a state trooper's truncheon.

Born to a sharecropper family outside tiny Troy, Alabama, about forty-five miles southeast of Montgomery, Lewis was educated in the segregated schools of Pike County and later at Fisk University, graduating with a degree in religion and philosophy, with a further degree in theology. This academic background in Scripture amplified his role as a preacher, and he developed a sonorous rather than a hectoring tone in his speeches, which generally took the form of sermonizing. His pronounced Pike County accent made his pastoral homilies more persuasive.

Elected to Congress in 1986 to represent Georgia's 5th District (most of Atlanta), Lewis still held this safe seat twenty-eight years later. Along with listing his numerous medals and awards and his fifty honorary degrees, his official congressional website described him in these terms: "Often called 'one of the most courageous persons the Civil Rights Movement ever produced,' John Lewis has dedicated his life to protecting human rights, securing civil liberties, and building what he calls 'The Beloved Community' in America."

This taxpayer-funded gush bordering on ardent hagiography is perhaps forgivable in a man who had put his life on the line. He had suffered throughout the civil rights struggle, served as a rational voice in the movement, become an able legislator, was a living witness to history, and remained a conscience in government. He had distinguished himself by his insistence on ethical behavior in Congress — an uphill task, given the number of crooks, sneaks, junketers, opportunists, liars, tax cheats, adulterers, sexual stalkers, senders of selfies of their private parts to perfect strangers, and unembarrassed villains in that tainted assembly.

Congressman Lewis was just one year older than me. I was drawn to him in order to reflect on the parallel lives we'd led — his so busy and political in the Deep South, as a constant speaker and campaigner; mine one of a lifelong immersion in writing, of travel, of unexplained absences and phantom appearances as "Mr. Thorax." Lewis had been an activist and legislator; I had been a bystander and eavesdropper. While I'd been teaching in obscure schools in Africa and Southeast Asia, he'd been taking his stand in the Deep South against segregation. He was a public man, a role I avoided.

Lewis was a luminary now, garlanded with honors, with a battered sagacious face and a noticeable limp, and was regarded as a statesman, an icon, a man of courage in a pinstripe suit. Now we were face to face, and I was — what? A wanderer in a wanderer's rumpled clothes, sitting among a mainly black congregation, for that was how the attentive and pious audience seemed to me. But we were both writers. Lewis's book, *March: Book One*, had just appeared, and he was promoting this work at the festival.

The work, his book, was not a proper book but a comic book. Nor, I discovered, was it written by him. The stories were John Lewis's, but the writing had been done by his congressional aide Andrew Aydin, the illustrations by an accomplished comic book artist (*Swallow Me Whole, Tiny Giants*, and many other titles), Nate Powell. This effort was, to use the dignifying expression, a graphic novel. As a boy, I had clutched at such comic books and reveled in their simplicity. The thought of the large Mosaic Templars auditorium full of literary festival people gathered to hear John Lewis's peroration about a comic book made me wonder.

But it was more than a comic book, and it had a serious history and a significant precedent.

In his talk, Lewis spoke about a comic book he'd read as a teenager, *Martin Luther King and the Montgomery Story,* which was a mere sixteen pages and sold for ten cents. It described the events leading up to and causing the 1955 Montgomery Bus Boycott. The theme was the success that Rosa Parks, Dr. King, and fifty thousand others had had using the power of nonviolence to end segregation on city buses.

"It became like our Bible," Lewis said to the audience, who knew a thing or two about Bibles.

That comic book had not been written by Martin Luther King. It was the idea, in 1956, of a pacifist reporter named Alfred Hassler, who had been prompted to write it after seeing how effective nonviolent action had been in Montgomery. His idea was to produce an account of the protest that would be accessible to potential activists throughout the South. Dr. King dictated passages and related dialogue to Hassler, and afterward, seeing the comic book in print, praised the work. Dr. King wrote, "You have done a marvelous job of grasping the underlying truth and philosophy of the movement. I am sure that this comic book will be welcomed by the American public."

Almost a quarter of a million copies of *Martin Luther King and the Montgomery Story* were printed and distributed in 1957 by the Fellowship of Reconciliation, an organization dedicated to resolving conflict in the world. Dr. King's portrait—brooding, portentous at age twenty-eight—was on the cover, over the words *How 50,000 Negroes found a new way to end racial discrimination.* The book was whispered about, shared, and praised, and the whole printing sold out—a success. In some parts of the South this comic book explaining the concept of nonviolent protest was regarded as seditious and had to be circulated covertly.

One copy fell into the hands of seventeen-year-old John Lewis in Troy, Alabama, and inspired in the boy a sense of mission. Many years later, he remembered how this story, simply told, had affected his life. Hearing this, his aide Andrew Aydin researched it and made it the subject of his master's thesis at Georgetown University. And Aydin decided to do something similar, to create a graphic novel about John Lewis's life, depicting his upbringing and the culture of segregation and the march on Selma. Aydin found the illustrator Nate Powell, and so the effort was collaborative, the three men making the book, *March: Book One,* the first installment of what would become an autobiographical trilogy.

Aydin and Powell shared the literary festival stage with Lewis, who spoke of how he'd been influenced by the earlier comic book. He praised Nate Powell's pictures as having reality and simplicity.

Lewis didn't say anything about Alfred Hassler, the moving force behind Dr. King's comic book. I later learned that Hassler (1910–1991) was a quietly courageous man. A conscientious objector during World War Two, he was jailed for nine months in 1944 for refusing to fight, and later wrote a book about it, *Diary of a Self-Made Convict.* After joining the Fellowship of Reconciliation, he edited its magazine, and among other campaigns he urged food to be sent to China during its catastrophic Mao-induced famine in the mid-1950s. Hassler became an antiwar activist, visited Vietnam on a peace delegation in 1966, and, persuaded by a growing belief in Buddhism, befriended an influential monk, the Venerable Thich Nhat Hanh, and brought him to the United States, where he lived in exile for thirty-nine years, founding monasteries and teaching. It was Hassler who persuaded Dr. King to take a stand and denounce the Vietnam War, for which defiance he was vilified by many and harassed by the FBI.

(Looking into the life of Thich Nhat Hanh, known by the honorific *Thay* — Master — I found a nice story. A wealthy American socialite invited him to her grand house and offered a large donation to further his work, providing he could assure her of the truth of reincarnation — that she had nothing to fear of death, that after her demise she would be reborn. *Thay* said, "If there is no self, who is going to be reborn?" and went away empty-handed.)

In the packed Mosaic Templars hall, Lewis gave a rousing speech, noting that this was the fiftieth anniversary of the civil rights movement, and nearing the sixtieth of the bus boycott. And, flanked by his collaborators, he spoke about the graphic novel.

"It's much stronger and much better than just simple words," he said, elaborating on the effectiveness of the imagery of a pictorial work. "They say music is a universal language, but when the eyes behold something, a figure, somebody moving, it's real, and it cannot be denied. When you see or hear a word or a phrase here and there, it can be interpreted one way or the other, but when you see the actual drawing, it says more than anything else."

The audience was almost all black and mainly older, more women than men, well dressed, some of them extravagantly so — wide-brimmed hats trimmed with flowers, satin blouses with frilly sleeves, purple gowns, bombazine and bonnets, many breasts and collars bejeweled: churchgoing clothes. And that was suitable attire, because Lewis's tone was a preacher's, and his message one of forgiveness. He was aware of his being a historical figure, a living witness — the word "icon" was often attached to his name. What a perfect delight to find oneself an icon! But Lewis was a portly and ailing and battle-scarred and patient one.

In an atmosphere that was thick with sentimental adulation, Lewis acknowledged the emotion directed at him — not basking or gloating but in a mood of bland acceptance, like a prince responding to a mob's acclaim, with a modest glance and casual hand gestures. Something regal about his head, a little too big for his body, commanded attention, and showed the effects of the war in which he was a much-decorated veteran. His was a trampled face, slack-jawed but otherwise featureless, and lopsided like that of a fat beaten boy. Inexpressive in the best of times, his face did not register much emotion today, as he waited for the applause to die down, seemingly aware of his symbolic value, the benign imagery of a lifelong campaigner, who now and then reached out, a hug for some older women, a laying on of hands, but nothing for me.

After his talk came the signing, the three men sitting side by side at a long table on the stage, Lewis, Aydin, and Powell. A line formed to the right — one hundred people, because the entire shipment of one hundred copies of *March: Book One* had been sold at the information desk on the ground floor. Powell signed first, then Aydin, finally Lewis, and each time Lewis scribbled his name on the cover with a felt-tip pen, the buyer of the book joined him behind the table and was photographed with the congressman. One hundred books, one hundred photos. Skinny, seventy-year-old Willie Jones and his wife, Mildred, had made the 208-mile round trip from the town of Wynne for a copy of *March* and a souvenir photo.

Mildred wore a purple top hat and lavender blouse with ruffles. "She mah queen," Willie said to me as he watched her pose for her picture with John Lewis. The congressman looked exhausted, but he was game, and stayed till the last comic book was defaced with signatures.

I watched it all from beneath the stage, where a group of people – the congressman's entourage, and friends and supporters – stood beaming at the man and at one another. They were stylishly dressed – no bonnets, no bombazine, no frills for them – in dark well-cut suits and chic designer dresses, one man with a lacquered coif of stiff, crenellated hair. These were the black elite.

"Hello," I said.

They were startled by my greeting, like a shoal of leathery sharks jerked to attention by the sight of a pale snorkeler, and then their response was muted. But I persevered. I introduced myself as a stranger from the North and a well-wisher. I received wan smiles or pitying stares in return. Some of them were excessively polite in a deflecting stance, the way elaborate manners can be indistinguishable from rudeness; others were offhand, with measuring glances. Far from welcoming, they seemed somewhat wary of me.

"I see you've got extra copies of the congressman's book," I said.

Twelve copies were stacked on the chair next to a woman in an elegant dress.

"They're sold out downstairs," I said. "May I buy one from you?"

"You may not," she said, and turned away. "These are for some people."

This disapproving group were the urban blacks I'd hardly encountered on this Deep South trip, compounded by the Arkansas instinctual query – suspicious, chilly, with a suggestion of hauteur in their greeting, as if they were still learning how to deal with whites. And who was I, in plain clothes, rumpled by travel, my shoes still wet from the storm?

Never mind what John Lewis had described up there on the stage – his parents cowed by segregation, his confrontations with the cops and the Klan, his wounds, his cracked skull, the march that had ended in a bloody battle. For Lewis it was the distant past, no bitterness, much sanctimony; for his entourage it was just yesterday – or today.

"Who might you be?" they seemed to imply, squinting at me and smiling anxiously, almost in mockery. Perhaps I seemed a bit presumptuous. I took them to be the Little Rock power set, gleaming with privilege, inhospitable to any approach from me. They still lingered in a tight and glittering posse below the stage, under the congressman's benign glow. Handsome, well turned out, chatting among themselves, posturing, they were a different sort of group from the poorly dressed or overdressed blacks in churchgoing clothes, shuffling in the long line to mount the stage for a signature and a picture: the older bumpkins in broken shoes, the poor, the peasantry.

My pitch to the well-dressed power set was: I'm traveling the Deep South, I'm a writer, I'm a stranger. What did they think of *March: Book One?* Hello?

In their mingled skepticism and confusion and unease, during which I could not get an answer, I felt a sense of rejection, as though their talking to me might end badly, because, after all, I was white, and they were not sure what response they wanted or would get. They were distrustful, probably with reason, because this was Little Rock and they were black. And rejection and exclusion, I supposed, were reactions they knew well, especially when meeting a confident and casual white man.

But I was dressed badly, therefore I was implausible. In that crowd, looming like an intruder, I might have been an assassin. This was a city where appearances mattered, and it occurred to me that, dressed as I was—baseball cap, sun-faded cotton jacket, blue jeans, wet shoes from the rainy street—I could only be a cracker. I was an older man too. Of course, I had to be a peckerwood.

"But this is what a writer looks like," I wanted to say. "Not the pinstripes of politics! We have no entourage! None of us is an icon! We look dangerous and unbalanced! Yes, I suppose some of us look like peckerwoods, but we are harmless."

For a few minutes, in the presence of disapproving and powerful blacks, I had a little glimpse, as if through a knothole in a splintery board, of what it was to be an old and indigent white guy in Arkansas—a living annoyance, the creepy Mr. Thorax.

Perhaps this was all paranoia on my part and I was wrong about their hauteur. Perhaps they were merely indifferent, or busy, or tired—it was the end of the day. Perhaps, being city dwellers—or so they seemed from their stylish clothes—they were more skeptical of strangers, less inclined to appease them with a smile, avoiding the fellowship of the rural areas, the routine greetings that I'd been accustomed to.

Anyway, they turned away from me and, smiling, held out their arms. On flapping feet, loose-armed, fatigued, Congressman Lewis was descending the stairs from the stage. They closed ranks and gathered around him and escorted him out of the hall in a slow and dignified procession, seemingly protecting him from me while I watched.

Buddy: "Be Careful"

Unexpectedly, as a happy accident, the way things shook out or converged if you lingered the way Southerners did instead of hurrying away, I bumped into Charles Portis in Little Rock. I had hoped to meet him. He was one of the few living writers whose work I admired, thought exemplary, not only for *True Grit,* the book that everyone knew because of the two popular movies, but for his four other novels. *Norwood* and *The Dog of the South* particularly resonated with me, for being quests in the form of road trips, and his occasional pieces, written over almost sixty years and collected in his book *Escape Velocity,* show him to have spent a lifetime as a dedicated observer of human foibles. One of his essays is the best piece I have ever read anatomizing cheap motels. On the evidence of his reports from the road, it seemed we were kindred spirits in resorting often to, and sometimes celebrating, seedy lodgings.

As a traveler, as a portrayer of American misfits and obsessive quests, Portis is casually brilliant, and not simply fluent and funny but a comic master at deadpan deflation. Portis is a strange creature, but genius is always strange — to paraphrase the description of Nikolai Gogol by Nabokov, who adds, "Great literature skirts the irrational." Portis much resembles Gogol in his "irrational insight," and the "message" of his books (which is no message at all) is similar to Gogol's in Nabokov's summary: "Something is very wrong and all men are mild lunatics engaged in petty pursuits that seem to them very important, while an absurdly logical force keeps them at their futile jobs."

By reputation Portis is reclusive, yet any number of Little Rock friends and restaurateurs could testify to his sociability and wit. He had reported on the civil rights movement and the war in Cyprus, lived in London, and rambled all over Mexico, and can quote Sir Thomas Browne's *Urn Burial* — my kind of drinking pal.

Yet in all his literary utterances he shows himself to be the least vain of men, once telling an awestruck fan who praised him as a great writer in a Little Rock bar named the Faded Rose, "I'm not even the best writer in this bar."

His friends and family, who call him Buddy or Charlie, speak of how he lives his life exactly as he pleases. Once, having applied for a job at a New York magazine, he was summoned to a preliminary interview and across his desk a senior editor asked, "Why do you want this job?" Pondering this question, and the implications of it, for a minute or so, smoking a cigarette, Portis replied, "Actually, I don't want this job," and left the room without another word. He is known as a listener, not a raconteur, a man of few words, eloquent and expansive on the page.

He happened to be ruminating in a rocker the morning our paths crossed in Little Rock. He looked content but a bit wary when he glanced up. In old age, as some men do, he'd acquired the features of a sly child, the same smooth features and suggestion of enigma that arise from watchfulness and perhaps justifiable self-protection.

I said hello.

In an accommodating gesture he tipped himself forward out of the rocker and stood up, slim, rangy, upright, as physically fit, it seemed, as when he was a marine, but with an ex-smoker's sallowness — he'd given up smoking ten years before, when he turned seventy. He led me through the door to a terrace facing a garden. It was a lovely Arkansas morning of blue sky and sugary, blown-open blossoms. The hot gravel gave off a dusty fragrance like a whiff of pollen, and the freshly mown grass had a sharp, healthy-salad aroma.

Well aware of his hatred of interviews, I simply told him how much I admired his work — the apparent ease of his writing, the wisdom of his offhand remarks, his great ear for the cadences of Southern speech, his absorption and seeming delight in the mishaps of the road.

He smiled his crooked, small boy's smile and said thanks, but even at eighty he resisted praise and anyone fussing over him. He clawed at his shirt cuff as I was speaking and sneaked a look at his wristwatch. Then he waved away someone attempting to take his picture and, spooked, checked his watch again. He had something to do—I knew the feeling—and was impatient to be away.

I knew I'd interrupted him. I thanked him for sparing me a few minutes and said, "I'm heading out—the Ozarks, the Buffalo River, then maybe down to El Dorado and Smackover, swinging by Brinkley."

Nodding, he hooked his thumbs into his belt, leaned back to size me up, and said, in the tones of a blessing, "Be careful."

Old Folks

On a warm, rainy afternoon, two heavy white women, late sixties or early seventies, their plump arms on the table, reading newspapers and eating barbecue at Gene's in Brinkley, dropped their heads and muttered as an older man approached their booth.

"How you doin', ladies?"

"Jest fahn," one said, straightening, as the other woman turned away.

"Rain," the older man said. He was stout, wearing suspenders and a baseball hat.

"It'll clear," the same woman said; the other had not spoken but looked serene. "Ah don't mind. How's Shelby?"

"Still hurtin'." Then he turned and, speaking to himself in a hungry, reassuring tone, said, "Get me some pah."

He shuffle-scuffed away on old shoes, approaching the pastry counter, and was out of earshot. The old woman who had not spoken said, "When I was in the second grade and he was in the third, he called me Fatty."

They returned to their newspapers and their plates of barbecue.

As I was writing this down, astonished by the recollection of a snub, a grievance perhaps sixty years old, another Deep South incident occurred.

A tall, very old—mid-eighties—formally dressed white man entered Gene's. He wore a blazer with a gold badge on the breast pocket and a necktie. He leaned on a cane with one hand, and his other hand rested on the shoulder of an almost as old, gray-haired black man in bib overalls who was nearly as feeble in his movements. They inched to a table, the black man serving to support the white man, and seated themselves across from each other.

"Still raining," the white man said.

"Yep."

They ordered catfish from the waiter, a young man who at the same time wiped their table clean with a rag. While they waited for their catfish to arrive, they spoke of their grandparents.

"My granddaddy," the white man said, and spoke of a fond memory.

"My old grandmama," the black man said, and offered his memory.

They swapped stories of their grandparents, laughing at the particularities. "Old folks," one said, I was not sure which one.

"They had money," the old white man said. "They had land. They had two barns. Rode on horses."

"Ain't that something. Mm."

"Always wore a suit when he came to town."

Their meal was served and they ate, still talking about old times, speaking in low, peaceful voices, each appreciating the other.

Farmers on a Rainy Day

On a wet day in Fargo, just north of Brinkley, I made my way under a gray sky along muddy fields — some of them silvery with puddles and others lightly flooded — past the turnoff to the derelict town of Cotton Plant, to meet Dr. Calvin King again. As he promised, Dr. King had invited some black farmers to meet me — early risers, they had arrived before me, and some had come many miles for this meeting. We gathered around a table in a room at Dr. King's Arkansas Land and Farm Development Corporation, a low brick building on a Fargo dirt road. Black Angus cattle grazed where the road abruptly ended at a fenced field; they were stock from the experimental ranch, chewing at bales of damp, darkened straw.

The farmers were men in overalls and feed caps, the oldest in his late seventies, the youngest twenty-three. A woman sat at a side table, appearing to take notes. Two other women, both of them farmers, had been invited, but at the last minute had other obligations. They were silent, watchful, patient men, somewhat ill at ease among the bare tables and many spare chairs in the conference room. Farmers are not a sedentary lot, and these men seemed restless and out of place.

"I'm a stranger," I said, to introduce myself. "I've traveled and written about many foreign countries, but I realized I hadn't spent much time in the Southern states, where many of the problems are the same as in the so-called Third World."

I went on in this vein, explaining that I was traveling through the Deep South, trying to understand what I saw. I thanked Dr. King for arranging this session and said I was grateful to these workingmen for meeting me on a weekday morning, a helpful turnout.

"It's the weather," one of them said. "It's too wet to do anything on the farm. If this had been a sunny day, you wouldn't have seen any of us. Our fields is flooded."

"And we already done our chores this morning," another said, and laughed with the others.

They were resigned to the realities of Mother Nature and human nature, but they were anything but passive and fatalistic. As I was to find, their willingness to work, to plant, to harvest, to repay loans, made them self-sufficient and gave them dignity.

They laughed again and introduced themselves. The first man who had spoken was Andre Peer, who was forty-two and had been farming for twelve years. He now had four thousand acres under cultivation, near where he lived, about forty miles away, outside Lexa, in Phillips County. He was a stocky, well-built man of medium height, forthright in gesture and word, who looked me in the eye and spoke his mind. The best educated of this group, Andre had earned a degree in agriculture in 1995 from the University of Arkansas at Pine Bluff. He grew wheat, corn, grain sorghum, and soybeans. I later learned that he had made such a success of his farm, he and his wife and son had been named Phillips County Young Farming Family of the Year in 2013, with a profile in the *Helena World*.

"But it's always a struggle," Andre said, and placed his muscular farmer's hands against his head and squeezed hard. "You got to hear about the banking."

"That's a mighty big subject," Ernest Cox said. He was a slender, mild-

mannered, and sinewy man in his late sixties, weather-beaten from a life
of farming—he'd worked in the fields since boyhood, on his father's acres.
He had an attractive and disarming habit of smiling and nodding even
when he was speaking about something unpleasant, such as debt or financial obstacles or the hurdles at the loan office. He ran a large third-
generation farming business with his brothers, Herschel and Earmer, on
five thousand acres. This family farm—soybeans, wheat, and the grain
sorghum known as milo—was just outside the small town of Marvell, also
in Phillips County.

All these men—family farmers—lived and raised their crops in the
Arkansas Delta, in communities ten miles or less from the Mississippi
River, and near the river town of Helena, where their crops were loaded,
to be barged downriver. Talking to them, I remembered Reverend Lyles in
Alabama telling me how his father had been advised by a white man not
to sell any of his land to a white person. "Sell to blacks," he'd said, because
that was the only way a black man could get a foothold in a rural area.

"I've got views on the banking," Samuel Ross said. In his late seventies,
he was the oldest of the group. "But I'm retired. I'll let the others speak."
And that was all he said for an hour, though he was an attentive listener.

"Me, I've just started, sort of," Roger Smith said. He was twenty-three,
yet was in his fourth season farming. He'd begun as a smallholder at the
age of nineteen, leased a few hundred more acres each succeeding year,
and now had seven hundred acres in rice and milo. He was soft-spoken
and shy, with a drawl so heavy and such a sideways reflex of talking that
many times I had to ask him to repeat himself, and even then had to mentally translate what he said.

"And that's Rickey Bone," Dr. King said, introducing another older
man. "He's the only one here not planting row crops."

"My wife and I are growing produce," Rickey Bone said. "She's really
the one who should be here. Mary's a ball of fire."

"For these men the problem is access to capital," Dr. King said. He was
a farmer too, as he had told me before. And although he had an authoritative, almost scholarly way of speaking, he was fluent in enumerating the
issues. He ran the Arkansas Land and Farm organization, so he was used
to conferences and workshops and committees. "It's imbalance," he went
on, "and it's the problem of expanding impoverishment. Listen, I had a

friend said she was going to South Africa. I asked why. She told me about the need. I said to her, 'You don't have to go to South Africa to find the need.' She was from Little Rock. I said, 'What about *our* need?' She said, 'I don't think it's the same. In South Africa it's water quality issues.' I said, 'I can tell you about water quality issues right here!'"

I said, "I started traveling in the South for that very reason, because I saw so many outsiders committed to solving Africa's problems. They were the same problems that exist here — poor housing, poor access to health care and education. Child hunger. Illiteracy."

"And the banking," Andre Peer said, tapping his thick fingers on the table. His tapping was insistent, but he also had a way of widening his eyes to express impatience.

"Banking is a white monopoly in Arkansas — it's white controlled," Dr. King said. "Traditional banks lend on the basis of a hundred and twenty percent credit security. Think of that. And there are serious problems of imbalance at the USDA."

"We need operating loans," Ernest Cox said. "Every year we have to go to the bank. We're doing all right — I'm farming with my brothers. But we're at the mercy of the merchants."

"Thing you got to understand," Andre said, and thought a moment before he proceeded. "Bankers give other farmers more."

"What other farmers?" I asked.

Andre widened his eyes and blew out his cheeks but said nothing.

"You can speak plainly to Mr. Paul," Dr. King said.

"By 'other' I mean white," Andre said. He told a story about a loan he had sought.

It was then that I realized what these men were up against, because the loans — for machinery, for seed, for infrastructure — were considerable, in the many hundreds of thousands.

"She let me have $442,000," Andre was saying. "It was a bad, disastrous year — 2006 into 2007 — drought and excessive heat. My harvest was poor. I asked her not to turn me in to the USDA to file a loss claim. I didn't want to be in default. I knew I could make good on it. I know how to work. I wanted to pay what I owed. I needed time. And I did pay — every dollar." He thought a moment, then said, "White folks say we lazy. All we want is opportunity. We willing to work."

"These guys are surviving against the odds," Dr. King said.

"If you're in a bind, in serious default, white farmers want to buy your land," Andre said. "They're just waiting for you to fail. They're on one side, bankers on the other. My bankers are all right, but I have to explain a lot to them to get them to understand my situation. There are no black loan officers. It's not talked about, it's not written about. There's none."

"Loan officers," Ernest Cox said in a knowing voice, smiling, nodding, adjusting his cap.

"Another loan officer," Andre said. "We just talking, talking about people. I said, 'Would you give that man a loan?' He says, 'No.' I say, 'But you don't know him.' He says, 'How can he buy all that equipment? Must be selling drugs.' He thinking, 'How he able to do that, 'cause black people don't do that.' The same ones talking like that are the ones sitting on the banking boards."

"Arkansas is not like other places," Roger Smith said in his drawl, and turned aside, as though he'd surprised himself by offering an opinion. He was shy and oblique, but he was not timid.

"The Klan don't wear sheets," Andre said, and looked around at his fellow farmers. "They sitting behind the desks in the banks. Uh-huh!"

"The South gives indications of being afraid of the Negro. I do not mean physical fear," Frank Tannenbaum wrote ninety years ago in *Darker Phases of the South*. "It is not a matter of cowardice or bravery; it is something deeper and more fundamental. It is a fear of losing grip upon the world. It is an unconscious fear of changing status."

Roger said, "Harrison. That town—it's a Klan hotbed."

It was not by chance that this remark was dropped into the conversation. Allusions to the Klan, to the past, to the insecurity that Southern blacks face especially in rural areas, I found to be common, for the Klan was the historical nightmare, the arch-destroyer, relentless and reckless, with connections in high places. Harrison is an Ozark community, the seat of Boone County, in the center of the northern edge of the state, where it lies flat against Missouri. Its decent citizens, of whom there were presumably many, hadn't made any headlines, but its cranks were infamous.

Roger said, "Harrison has a big billboard advertising the Klan."

"Oh, God, Harrison" was a murmur in the room.

The farmers talked generally about the miseries and abuses of Harrison, and then Ernest said, "You don't have to go all the way to Harrison to find this business. Moro does not have a black family."

Moro was a crossroads in nearby Lee County, with fewer than three hundred people.

"A black family moved in some years ago," Andre said. "But they bought him out."

"So many inequities here." The speaker was the woman taking notes, Ramona Anderson, whom I had taken to be a recorder of the remarks in the meeting. But she was a staff member of the Arkansas Land and Farm Development Corporation, and up to now had been sitting quietly over her notebook.

She told a story about the strange history of Cotton Plant, a town just north of Brinkley. "A man came in the 1960s and saw a bird — not the ivory-bill woodpecker that everyone talks about, but another rare one. He was the only man who saw it. The result was that town authorities set aside many acres for that bird. They used eminent domain to get black farmers off the land around Cotton Plant."

"This was done maliciously," Dr. King said. "No one wants to talk about inequities in race around here. Brinkley has a majority black population but has never had a black mayor. This is not talked about."

"Cotton Plant was once an important town," Ramona said. "It's now small and poor."

"The big landowners don't want schools and hospitals," Dr. King said. "Marianna Hospital closed in 1980. It has never reopened. DeWitt is just the same size, but it has a hospital. DeWitt is majority white. They don't want educated blacks, they want blacks driving their tractors."

This again put me in mind of the white farmer James Agee mentioned in his survey *Cotton Tenants* in 1937: "I don't object to nigrah education, not up through foath a fift grade maybe, but not furdern dat." Rural Lee County, where Dr. King lived and farmed, had one of the highest rates of illiteracy in Arkansas (and the nation).

"Public education continues to deteriorate," Dr. King said.

"Economic development has no color," Ramona Anderson said. "But they manipulated the minorities. Instead of a Delta-wide initiative, they control each portion by dividing them. A true community development plan would benefit the poor, and that's not something they want."

"Who's 'they'?" I asked.

"The powers that be," she said. "Instead of a big hospital, they put in a clinic. You think that's all right? But in a true community development plan it would be a big hospital rather than a clinic here and a clinic there."

"People have forgotten about the farmer," Andre said. "We are producing food for people to eat. We are creating exports. How about rice? Our rice is exported. It's seven dollars a bushel — the price is up. Our production is increasing." All true, I found. The National Farmers Union reported a massive increase in rice growing in the United States, and that exports were going to China, Africa, and the Middle East. Andre went on, "But all the while it's a struggle. We're fighting the good ole boy." He clutched his head again and said, "Keep Pigford in mind and class action."

"Pigford" was a word I heard from other black farmers. It was shorthand for a court case that related to some of what these men were telling me about the racial inequities in the farming business. *Pigford vs. Glickman* was a class action lawsuit brought in 1997 by Timothy Pigford, a black farmer from North Carolina, and four hundred others, against the Department of Agriculture (and its secretary, Dan Glickman), seeking redress for the routine denial of loans to black farmers, whom the USDA had discriminated against, thus leading to a sharp reduction in their numbers.

Although a settlement was approved in 1999, and more than a billion dollars had been paid so far by the government (under both the Bush and Obama administrations), serious allegations of fraudulent claims have been made, and there was proof of connivance by profiteering lawyers and politicians, scammers and "race hustlers." If you look into the details of this tangled case, it is obvious that a trough was provided for the benefit of many worthy farmers (successful claimants got $50,000 apiece) as well as for the snouts of many opportunists. Yet black land loss was reversed, and after years of decline, the number of black farmers and black landowners had grown in the South and elsewhere.

"But we're still struggling with the banks," Andre said. "We're still struggling with the good ole boys. After all these years we still have to prove ourselves."

I said, "Bill Clinton spends a lot of time in Africa and India. Couldn't he do something here to help?"

"If Clinton came here," Andre said, "the good ole boys would say, 'Why you coming here? Why you want to change things?'" He looked around the room for approval, and got the nods he expected. "That's why he doesn't do it."

All this time, in all this talk, I could sense the men were restless. As farmers, habituated to digging, to fetching and carrying, loading trucks, repairing machines, tramping the margins of their fields, they were un-used to sitting indoors for such a length of time. They were too polite to object but still seemed uncomfortable, hitching forward, clasping their hands, squirming on the plastic chair seats.

I went on asking them about their farming operations, until finally, one of them—probably Andre, because he was the most frank of the group—stood up and said, "You won't learn much here from us talking. We have to show you, if you have the time."

I said, "I have all the time in the world. I'd love to see your farms."

"I was hoping you'd say that," Dr. King said, as he'd said to me before. Then he took me aside and said, "When you look at the Delta, do you see businesses owned by blacks, operated by blacks? In manufacturing? In retail?" He smiled, because the obvious answer was: very few. He went on, "Compare that to the black farmers here, who are part of a multibillion-dollar business."

"Food Deserts"

The newest farmer, with the smallest amount of acreage, was Rickey Bone, who with his wife, Mary—Mary A, as she was known—had been growing vegetables on land adjacent to where the Arkansas Land and Farm Development Corporation sat in Fargo. The Bones planted about ten acres, a truck farm. They grew what would sell, what people wanted fresh: okra, squash, watermelons, purple peas, and pumpkins.

"Last year, we had okra plants that was six feet high," Rickey Bone said on the side road leading to his fields.

Ricky was sixty, born and raised in Little Rock, a graduate of Central High School, the scene of the racial confrontation in 1957 when federal troops protected nine black students from an angry white mob and the defiance of Governor Orval Faubus. The Little Rock Nine slipped in through a side entrance, integrating the school and making history.

"I'm sure you heard the stories about it," Rickey Bone said. "I was just a little kid then."

"I was in high school in Massachusetts. It was big news," I said. The shocking, enduring image was of the fifteen-year-old black girl, Elizabeth Eckford, being screamed at by whites. These scenes of persecution—and bravery—were vivid to me because the students being abused were exactly my age at the time. And now, almost fifty years later, Central High was no longer a battleground but a monument.

"Man, there's things a lot better about Little Rock than Central High School," he said. "But I remember how tough it was." He smiled, as though to signal an absurdity. "The black schools inherited textbooks from the white schools."

He had a clear memory of his first integrated school, his seventh-grade class in Little Rock.

"I heard how awful whites were," he said. "My mother—she was Creole, from North Carolina—she told me I was as good as anyone. First day I was thinking, They don't all look alike. I found that was all bullshit. I thought, They're not evil, they're all different, they don't look alike at all. We played football together. The kids didn't have the hatred of their parents."

We were walking along the margin of one of his fields, a narrow path, because there was deep mud on either side and the path itself was goopy.

"Teachers, though." He clucked at the memory. "They put me in a remedial class, with clowns."

"How did you deal with that?"

"I thought, This is not working. I talked to my English teacher. He listened. They moved me out." Rickey reflected some more, treading the wet path. "Thinking different don't make you different." He seemed to be summoning up the sage advice of his mother. "Give me a chance and I can accomplish anything." We were still walking. Suddenly smiling, he said, "You know? I've had everything I've ever wanted."

After graduation, he'd been a butcher in the meat department of a supermarket in the city. Then, two years in the US Army — Fort Dix, New Jersey, and a taste of the North. On his return to Arkansas and civilian life, he joined the Little Rock Fire Department and spent thirty years dousing flames. And now retirement, but not a conventional one, instead more work, inspired by his wife, Mary A.

Mary A. Valentine Bone had been born in Lakeview, in the Ozarks. Lakeview was only thirty or so miles from Harrison, with its racial cranks and blasphemers — and decent citizens. Lakeview was just as white, proportionately, but it was more salubrious, tucked in a southern corner of Bull Shoals Lake. Mary A had had a career as a teacher in Little Rock, but now, newly in retirement, wanted to return to the farming life she'd known as a girl on her parents' few acres. She'd had a lifelong dream of running a farm — not bossing field workers, but planting seeds, weeding crops, harvesting with her own hands, growing food.

"Mary A wanted a tractor," Rickey said. "She had a passion for it."

The farm, he said, was all Mary A's; she was in charge, he was a junior partner. For two retired people with grown children — four girls — it seemed to me an ambitious operation, even with the help of Rickey's brother Donald.

"Where do you sell the vegetables?"

"A lot of it at produce stands in Little Rock, where there are — ever hear the term 'food deserts'?" Dr. King explained it to me: "Poor area, no grocery stores, no fresh produce, no stores at all — closed because of violence. Gangs."

That was perhaps true. The deprivation in central Little Rock and some of the nearer suburbs was visible: the boarded-up shops, the tumbledown houses on the joyless grid of numbered streets, especially south of I-630, the Wilbur D. Mills Freeway, a dividing line that bisects the city, "a boundary . . . a part of the geography as real as a river or a ravine," in the words of Little Rock writer Jay Jennings. Even the riverside neighborhood just off I-30, around the Clinton Presidential Library, was bleak, except for the revived River Market. But there is more to the city, and it is surprising if you have a car and a half hour to observe the difference.

Leave the Clinton Library on East Markham, hang a right at Gus's Fried Chicken, and continue on La Harpe Boulevard, which is Route 10, and follow it until it becomes Cantrell Road and widens, heading west. Past the districts known as the Heights and Hillcrest, and for ten miles — you're still within the city limits of Little Rock — the houses are stately, set amid flowering trees and the hilltop towers of Rivercliff. The mansions of Edge Hill are imposing, many of them newly built and triumphant on their large lawns, and in the malls and shopping centers there is no hint of gang activity or a food desert. I mentioned the modernity, the beauty, and the obvious wealth of this part of Little Rock to a man born and bred in the city, and he defined it in two words: white flight.

RICKEY AND MARY A still lived in the humbler part of Little Rock. But out at Fargo, an hour east, where they farmed, they had a new John Deere 85-horsepower tractor, a planter, a refrigerated truck, a hoop house for winter growing, and more. All of it they had bought with their retirement savings and by borrowing from the bank and from the USDA. They faced the small-farmer's obstacles that I heard about often in the South, all the discouragements.

"The woman at the USDA in Hazen said, 'You need a hundred and fifty percent collateral to get the loan,'" Rickey said. "That bothered me. Why not a hundred? We had to mortgage some land to get the loan of $137,000. But anyway, we got the loan. We pay it back once a year, after harvesting."

"What about the foundations? The charities? The do-good organizations?" I asked. "Ever get any money from them? The Clinton people?"

"I heard back there yesterday you talking about him," Rickey said.

"He was governor. He was president. His philanthropic charity is worth a couple of billion. I don't see him spending any of it in Arkansas."

Rickey Bone was smiling at me again. We entered his hoop house through a flap to see the strawberries he was growing.

"Clinton's complicated," I said.

"Aren't we all," Rickey said, and smiled, and offered me a strawberry.

These three soft words pierced my heart to such an extent that, traveling on, I never mentioned Clinton again.

"Sundown Town"

All the talk of Harrison and the Klan provoked me to take a sudden detour. Such was the size of Arkansas that it was a mere half day's drive from the Delta to the heart of the Ozarks. Harrison promoted itself as a great retirement town, on the list of "The Best Small Towns in America." It was a white town and had been known in its Jim Crow past as a "sundown town." ("Boy, don't let the sun go down on you.") I got there by a two-day roundabout route, skirting the northwest of the state to look at the urban disfigurement of Bentonville, home of Walmart; Springdale, home of Tyson Foods; and the salubrious university at Fayetteville that is surrounded by a blight of strip malls. Then I was in the boonies, crossing War Eagle Creek and Onion Creek, Dry Fork and the tiny hamlet of Old Alabam, where the Ozarks begin to bulge from woods and pastures.

The Ozarks are mountains in the Deep South sense of the word, not pyramidal peaks or potential ski slopes or alpine crags, but irregular elevations, a succession of low, deep green ridges, a sea of long, lumpy hills to the horizon in a dramatic panorama. That there is an identifiable and sundown-framed horizon in their midst gives the Ozarks their uniqueness: mountains that allow a great, gaudy, and effulgent sunset. No single Ozarkian topographical feature is apparent, but the whole of it—the broad shifting vista of elongated hills—appears like flattened and thickly forested mesas. And the view is especially moving because it seems unpeopled, the isolated communities hidden in hollows and behind the slopes, some of which are bunchy with old-growth trees, still remote and beautiful.

"And thinly visited," as I mentioned to an old-timer in a junk shop in the hard-up town of Leslie, which was once prosperous making oak barrels. He replied, "I hope it stays that way."

This man, in his overalls and boots and faded hat, had the beaky country profile that occurs frequently in Thomas Hart Benton's sketches of the 1920s Ozarks, some of this portraiture transferred to the "Deep South" and "Mid-West" panels of his mural *America Today*. On any given morning in the small-town diners of the Ozarks—Harrison, Marshall, St. Joe, Bellefonte, and Yellville come to mind—the older men are Bentonesque. In this place of enduring backwoods, the forms of work and pastimes, which Benton recorded, are unchanged: family farms, hog raising, turkey rearing, the hoeing of cabbage patches, the spitting of tobacco juice.

"Welcome to Hillbillyville," a man said to me on a side street in Alpena, with the self-deprecation that is common in Arkansas. He later said, "People are poor here, but that's a good thing for them. The economy don't affect them. Up or down, they live just the same."

This man also mentioned that when he first moved to town from not far away, he had a visit from the Grand Wizard of the Ku Klux Klan, who had driven over from Harrison, encouraging him to join.

I asked the man what his reply was to this dubious invitation.

"I said, 'You and me don't have enough in common for that to happen.'" He hoicked a gob of tobacco juice into the street, punctuating his dry reply, then added, "He took it pretty good and went away."

Driving around Harrison, which was a prosperous-seeming farming community of about twelve thousand people—busy this weekend because of the Northwest Arkansas District Fair—I didn't see the Klan billboard the men in the Delta had mentioned. I found another billboard that had become news, because this was a state that was trying to shake off its racist history. In large letters the yellow sign said, ANTI-RACIST IS A CODE WORD FOR ANTI-WHITE.

There had been local protests and demands to remove the offensive sign. One man who lived near Harrison said to me later, "I've read that sign twenty times and I still have no idea what it means."

It was true that the Klan existed in Harrison, though how many Klansmen were active no one knew except the secretive Klan itself. As Andre Peer had told me, they didn't wear sheets anymore. The tiny hamlet of Zinc (pop. 103), a few miles from Harrison, was home to Thomas Robb, who used to be a Grand Wizard but now styled himself National Director of his Klan splinter group, the Knights of the Ku Klux Klan. At Klan rallies, Robb (Michigan born, raised in Arizona) customarily denounced blacks and Jews.

Jew hating was also an article of faith and a spiritual practice at another organization in Harrison, the Kingdom Identity Ministries. A transplant from California, Mike Hallimore, the head of this bizarre Christian sect, called his mission a "politically incorrect Christian Identity outreach ministry to God's chosen race, true Israel, the White, European peoples." Another article of faith was that idolaters, homosexuals, blasphemers, and abortionists should be put to death.

Racism and anti-Semitism were encouraged by Kingdom Identity Ministries, because, as they helpfully explained, "race-mixing is an abomination in the sight of Almighty God, a satanic attempt meant to destroy the chosen seedline." Jews were the descendants of Eve's having sex with "the Devil or Satan and called the Serpent," and the "seedline" was "commonly called Jews today." All of Christian Identity's assertions were backed up by Scripture, to which they provided chapter and verse, which proved yet again, as I had seen in many lands, that the Bible was often the happy hunting ground of an unbalanced mind.

Consider this text from 1 Corinthians 11:6: "For if a woman does not cover her head, she might as well have her hair cut off; but if it is a disgrace for a woman to have her hair cut off or her head shaved, then she should cover her head."

A reasonable person might question the stark biblical choice between a headscarf and a baldy, but in a tent at the Northwest Arkansas District Fair just outside of town, at the Harrison fairgrounds, two young women dispensing hot popcorn to stimulate interest in their husbands' businesses — roofing and repairs — were modestly dressed in long-sleeved old-fashioned cotton frocks, and each wore a light headscarf, an abbreviated hijab. They were, they said, Mennonites.

"We call it 'veiling,'" one of them explained. "We never take it off, outside or inside."

Rather than allude to the Bible, I asked if the head covering had a special significance.

The taller of the two, scooping popcorn, said, "It means that we submit to our faith and to our husbands."

I said, "So you pretty much do what your husbands tell you to do?"

"Pretty much."

Which proved to me yet again that traveling in the hinterland of the United States now and then resembled traveling in the wider world, listening to pious and irrational simplicities from credulous folks.

All this time, the two women were filling bags of popcorn and handing them to passersby, not an ideal situation for my delving into the subject of Harrison's racial politics.

When I persevered obliquely, the smaller, younger of the two said, "It used to be much worse. It's getting better."

"The old people, they still believe the racism," the tall one said, and smoothed her veil.

There were no black faces at the district fair, for which the whole town, it seemed, had turned out, for the carnival rides and the rodeo. Much more than a family-friendly weekend, though, it was a serious competition among cattle raisers in three categories, American, English, and Exotic. Some of the creatures weighed half a ton, with lovely eyes and long lashes, moaning in iron stanchions, awaiting the judges. Breeders vied for blue ribbons for their chickens, ducks, goats, hogs, and sheep. There were competitions for preservers of fruit, jelly makers, and honey gatherers; for quilters, carvers, and weavers — all the classic country passions, artisans and ranchers, the salt of the earth (Matthew 5:13).

But that night, at a motel outside Harrison, a woman said to me, "If a black person came here, they'd hurt him. They'd burn his house."

In Silver Hill, I met a man who was pausing here with his wife, on their way from Harrison, to marvel at the beauty of the Buffalo River nearby.

"No one has a good word for Harrison," I said. "Is that fair?"

"Great place, but we still have" — and he made a face — "those people."

"The Klan," his wife half whispered, half mouthed, with widened eyes.

"I'm a doctor," the man said. "I treated one of them that lives around here, over in Marshall." He casually pointed down the road. "Lots of them there."

I decided to have lunch in Marshall, where a waitress — middle-aged, friendly — said, "There's no blacks here. The older folks don't accept them."

Marshall was an old expiring town with a main square, still with an impressive and cavernous hardware store and a drugstore. The drugstore, in addition to filling prescriptions and retailing shampoo and aspirin, sold rifles and handguns and displayed shelves of ammunition, all calibers.

Behind the drugstore, a three-story squarish building made of fitted sandstone blocks, with heavily barred windows, had been the county jail. It was vacant now but possessed a gloomy majesty on the back street. Dating from 1902, it was said to have been designed in a style known as Romanesque Revival, oddly pompous for this small town. Seeing me sizing it up, a man wandered over and said hello.

"How you doing?" I said.

"Gooder'n taters, better'n snuff," he said and winked. "Not near as dusty. Ha!"

It was a local expression, he said, much appreciated by people passing through.

"As a boy, I used to go by this here jail," he said, "and the prisoners would put a string out of the upper windows, hang it down, and throw us a nickel. We'd go to the drugstore yonder, buy a candy bar, and tie it to the string. They'd haul it up. That was in the fifties."

For all the talk of racism in and around the town, the only place to stay, and the best home cooking in Marshall, was at the Marshall Motel and Restaurant, owned and operated by a Chinese family, the Phungs, An Chay and Gay, who were well liked and content in Marshall, where they'd lived for twenty-eight years. Mrs. Gay Lee Phung was highly praised for her catfish dinners.

"Whites here in the Ozarks got no opinion of blacks, really," a crusty old man in overalls in a junk shop in a small town west of Marshall said to me. "Want to know whah?"

"Yes, please."

"People here never grew up around blacks," he said. "Never knew 'em. And they never leave here. You're born in St. Joe, you stay in St. Joe, and everywhere else is the same. So all they know is what they see on the teevy."

"That's enough, isn't it?" I said.

"Nowhere near," he said. "All you ever see on the teevy is a smart black guy and a dumb white guy."

He was sorting soda bottles, caked with dirt, that had the look of having been recently dug up, disinterred like ancient amphorae.

"It's all gone to hell, the world, and it's getting worse," he said. "But it don't matter what's going to happen. I'm seventy-seven. I reckon I got another ten years. Let someone else figure it out." He was still handling the clinking bottles. "Mind, they's some sorry whites here."

"What sort of thing do the sorry whites do?"

"Wait for the next check," he said, holding a bottle up to the light to examine its markings. "The whole country thinks we're eejits here. Fine with me. They can stay away."

Now he was examining the lettering on the bottom of another bottle.

"Why is it," he said, "that you never pick up something — anything — and read the words 'Made in Africa'? Just never happens, that experience, does it?"

I said, "That depends," and wondered where this was leading.

"Don't get me started on the damned niggers," he said.

I cleared my throat and said, "Some people object to that word."

"Not around here they don't," he said joyfully, and chuckled. He put a dirty bottle down and leaned into my face. "Now me, I'm real conservative."

"I'm old school," a middle-aged man said to me in Heber Springs. "What I mean is, I call 'em niggers to their face. They don't mind. They call me a redneck."

"They don't object?"

He looked at me pityingly, as though I was new to the language. "Nigger's not racial, you can look it up. Nigger just means you're sorry. They's white niggers and yella niggers too, all of them sorry. Some of them white trash are worse than any niggers. They on drugs — meth, you name it. They scare me."

Buffalo River

As a break from this spirited but pointless to-and-fro, one day I rented a canoe and paddled for a whole day down the Buffalo River. The Buffalo — gloriously undammed — which crosses the state, flowing from west to east, is the central artery of Arkansas, splashing through the heart of the Ozarks. A whole, old-style travel book could be written about boating and camping down Arkansas's wilderness rivers: wet feet, wildlife, intimations of danger, and observations such as "just ahead, the diabolical chatter of the rapids sounded like an invitation to disaster."

I had other plans on this warm morning in early September. I found a boat at an outfitter near Silver Hill and paddled all that day, from Baker Ford to Gilbert, stopping at intervals to inhale the fragrant air, to watch the sun flashing on the rapids and the insects stirring on the surface of the shallows. The river was greeny gold in the stiller pools, as two deer upwind, a doe and her fawn, picked their way across the river ahead of me, occasionally pausing to nibble or sip. I saw herons and a cormorant, and the drumming of a woodpecker echoed from the cliffs and sheer rock faces, which made it seem that some parts of the river were coursing through a canyon. In this silence and solitude I had the reassuring sense — because of the visible slope of the river — that I was sliding downhill, on a tongue of the rapids in some places, on a wide washboard of water-tumbled stones in others.

A lovely day of serenity in the Ozarks: no mention of race, of conflict, of poverty; no sign of the outside world; no other people, only the gurgle and gulp of the river bubbling along, unimpeded, and my solitary picnic on a big warm boulder, watching cooter turtles that had crawled, like me, onto other boulders, sunning themselves with their jaws open.

Then I handed over my boat and drove south and east to the Delta again, stopping at a gun show in Jacksonville, a town about ten miles from Little Rock. Like other gun shows I'd been to, it had the usual stalls and stands, sellers of new guns, old guns, knives, Tasers, Mace, ornery bumper stickers, Nazi memorabilia, Civil War relics, and ammo. But this being Arkansas, I saw that one visiting family — five of them — were barefoot ("We're just down from Letona," the patriarch told me), and the gun show food area offered deep-fried pie.

"I'm In Too Deep to Quit"

Garrett Grove, where the young farmer Roger Smith had directed me, was not a town or a village. It was a few houses and, in one portion, an austere all-black graveyard, St. Paul's, with about forty small headstones, many showing birth dates from the nineteenth century and first names such as Parthenia and Pankie. Four of the stones were nameless blanks — unknown or unremembered.

The three houses, small white wood-frame bungalows facing plowed fields, sat under tall pecan trees on a dirt road, a turnoff from a narrow state highway and a gutter of tadpole-stirred water called Little Piney Creek. One of the houses belonged to Ocie Trice, a man of seventy-four, with teasing ways, who had left this dirt road as a young man to live in Chicago for fifty-one years. He returned in the year 2000 when he and his brother inherited the family's property, four hundred acres. Some of this land they leased to Roger Smith. Ocie's older brother was named Eoies Oree Trice. Ocie laughed, saying he could not explain the names — maybe they were biblical. Yet the fattest concordance to the Bible is innocent of those names. Ocie began teasing Roger, who was single, about the possibility of his getting married to the wrong woman.

"She start out good but maybe she break bad in the middle of the stream," Ocie said. He was sitting under a tree at the back of his house, resting from tinkering with his car's rusty engine. In his small house, with his inherited land, yet without much status, he struck me as a rich peasant, the sort known in Russia as a kulak, the word for fist.

"Got no time to get married," Roger said. "Don't even have me a girl-friend."

"Git one," Ocie said, and laughed again.

Roger drove me in his pickup truck to one of his milo fields. He had begun to farm at the age of nineteen, having studied and served in Future Farmers of America. He had also attended the community college in nearby Forrest City. He farmed seven hundred acres altogether, all of it rented land. He was helped by his uncle Larry Terry, an older man, roughly bearded, teeth missing but unexpectedly fluent on farming issues and philosophical on other subjects. Larry joined us in the truck.

Roger and Larry plowed and planted, sprayed for weeds, fertilized the sorghum and milo. Milo had qualities similar to corn and was sold as feed for cows, chickens, and pigs.

"You can grind it and make flour," Roger said.

Roger was proud of the machinery he'd accumulated — his tractor, his harvester, his levee hog "for pulling levees," creating the low walls of rice fields — angular, imposing, big-wheeled vehicles, and very expensive, bought with loans.

"I borrowed $200,000 this year. I could have used more. I really needed $240,000."

"You got it from the bank?" I asked.

"I go to the Farm Service Agency and beg."

"What's your profit?"

"Weather-wise, I haven't seen a good year," he said. "And the first year I farmed it was terrible hot. Last year I had $28,000 in my pocket after harvest and paying off my loan. But any profit I make I put back into the farm. I have to pay people. I have to hire a semi to take the crop to Helena."

"Why Helena?"

"The river. Truck it down to the river, put it on a barge."

I wanted to see his rice fields. I had often seen rice growing, pullulating in exquisite terraces and ponds, in Uganda, Malaysia, India, China, and the Philippines. The peculiar contours of the fields were aesthetically pleasing, and the rice planter was an emblematic figure, laboring under a wide-brimmed woven hat, shin-deep in water, shoving slips of rice into the mud beneath to take root. When rice was half grown it was the most attractive crop imaginable, a watery field of luminous green grass. At harvest it lost its color, went brown, and drooped gracefully, the head of each stalk heavy with tassels of rice grains.

After a few flat miles of straight Delta roads abutting fields, Roger swung his truck onto the road's shoulder and drove across a bumpy verge to the edge of a rice field, a lovely sight for the oddity of the enclosing foot-high levees, none of them straight but all containing a walled-in section of rice shoots.

"This is Roy J rice," Roger said. It was a new high-yield variety, developed at the University of Arkansas just a few years before. It was sturdy — "straw strength" was important when the wind came up, he explained.

"All those walls," I said. "Looks like a lot of work."

"Easy with a levee hog," he said. "After we pull the levees and get some rain, we plant twenty foot at a time with a drill" — a seed drill instead of the fingers of a peasant bent over in the mud.

"You take this crop to the river too?"

"Down the river it goes. Export."

"Profitable?"

"If it all goes right. If we get a hundred fifty bushels an acre. That's two or three hundred dollars an acre. Not bad."

For the eighty-four acres he had under rice cultivation it was not a lot, and from that he had to deduct the cost of seed, fertilizer, labor, and truck rental, as well as service the farm loan. Roger had mentioned that the previous year his profit had been $28,000 on his entire harvest. He worked every day. He not only had to deal with his farm — which was very small by Delta standards compared with the vast corporate farms, but still demanding — he also had to manage the business side, the sales, the negotiations with Ocie Trice. He also had to maintain and repair the machinery, all of which he'd bought secondhand. And there was the weather, dramatic in Arkansas and often destructive.

In the pickup on the way back to Garrett Grove, three of us abreast, Larry Terry in the middle, I said, "A lot of people might say that it isn't worth all this work to make $28,000."

"It's worth it," Roger said, his voice flat with conviction. "When I get squared up I'll do all right. Four or five years maybe. I'm in too deep to quit."

We passed in silence through Moro, known, as they'd said, for being a community of all white families — the crossroads, the church, the school, the depots and sheds, farm machinery parked side by side, the small tidy bungalows.

"Moro," I said, reading the road sign.

"Some things meant to be," Larry said without looking to the left or right.

"You Need a Tough Skin"

I was in Andre Peer's home, a renovated one-story ranch house, not grand but solid and well maintained, the kind a local attorney or an insurance agent might own, at the end of a country lane in the Delta town of Lexa, population less than 300, and of that about 100 blacks. Andre pointed out his window to a nearby field. "That's a story."

"Tell me."

Andre had a white neighbor who had not shown him any friendliness, and who had planted a vegetable garden on an adjoining field that he did not own, some of the garden dug up and overlapping on Andre's own property. It annoyed Andre that the man had done so, digging the land without asking permission or saying a word, nor had the man offered any of the vegetables to him as compensation. So Andre went to the owner of this in-between plot that was being presumptuously planted by the neighbor and offered to buy it. The owner, who lived in another state, agreed to a price. At the appropriate time, Andre called the neighbor and told him that he now owned the field and that the man would have to cease gardening there.

The neighbor then became friendly for the first time, and offered Andre a bag of vegetables from his garden.

"I don't want any of your vegetables," Andre said. "What I want is you to stop growing them on my land."

I thought this a nice illustrative small-scale narrative of power and land, of country people living at close quarters, the sort of story people call Chekhovian.

Though Andre was forty-two, he had the experience and the maturity—and the capacity for risk-taking—of someone much older. He farmed four thousand acres, most of it on rented land, but his ambition was to buy more land of his own. He had impressed me with his work ethic, his frankness, and his refusal to be deterred by anyone in his pursuit of farming—by the bank, the USDA (with its much-hated bureaucracy, red tape, and fickle ways), or the white farmers, many of whom, he suggested, did not wish him well.

We had left his house and were driving beside one of his cornfields with its neat, symmetrical rows of stalks, and farther along, beside one of his wheat fields. Andre, like the others, was also impressive for his pride in his work.

"People get discouraged," he said. "A lot of black farmers left to go north, to get away from the fields. They didn't want nothing to do with farming. But it's a good life if you work at it. Other people waiting for you to fail. They say 'You messin' up' and all that." He sighed and added, "You need a tough skin."

"My feeling is that you have a tough skin, Andre," I said. "I think I'd probably get discouraged. You're up against the big corporate farms that want to encroach."

"Ain't going to encroach none on me," he said. "But it's funny. My wife was in Jonesboro. A woman asked her, 'What does your husband do?'"

"April said, 'Farming.'"

"Woman says, 'Is he white?'"

"April says, 'No.'"

"Woman says, 'Never heard of no black man farming for a living.'" Andre turned to me and stared with his wide-open ironical eyes. "True!"

That was the difference between Jonesboro, a large, mainly white university city in the northeast of the state, and the tiny farming communities down here in the Delta. The woman, who was white, had lived her whole life in Jonesboro. A black farmer was improbable, a novelty.

"A lot of those people think we don't know how to do this," he said. "But, you know"—he widened his eyes again and nodded—"I can read!"

"If You Can Tell a White Farm from a Black Farm, You in Trouble"

Ernest Cox, who was sixty-nine, was sitting on the axle tree of a tractor in his open-sided work shed on his family farm in Marvell, talking slowly. Andre had driven me here because the farm was so far outside town and hard to find. We all sat together, out of the sun, in the cool, high-roofed shed. Just a mile from here, at the crossroads of Turkey Scratch, the drummer, singer, and icon of country rock Levon Helm was raised, which perhaps was the reason he could sing with such feeling, "Poor old dirt farmer / He lost all his corn . . ."

"We're originally from Parkin," Ernest was saying. He had grown up outside that tiny town, in Cross County, an hour or more north of here and nearer to Memphis than to Little Rock, too high up to be regarded as the Delta. His father, Earmer Senior, had abruptly moved the whole family to Marvell, in the Delta, in 1950.

"Reason he left, he was living on a plantation," Ernest said. Parkin, another flyspeck, was a modest grid of streets, with nearly all white-owned houses, on the St. Francis River and surrounded by fields. "The owner was a white man, name of Hauser. Came about this way. My brother Herschel and a neighbor was watching over some cows. And the cows wandered over to where they wasn't supposed to be. Hauser roughed them up. Well, he didn't mess much with Herschel, but my father saw what happened and said, 'Time to go.' We moved here to Marvell. He rented some land and bought some mules and farmed ninety acres."

Ninety acres, a family smallholding, with a mule-drawn plow and mule-drawn wagons — it was the 1950s, but in terms of equipment, it was a glimpse into the distant past. And the era was archaic in Arkansas terms. Any sort of racial conflict in 1950, especially in a small white town, could turn into serious trouble. Earmer Senior, proud and premonitory, had had a bad feeling in Parkin and acted upon it.

"It was all cotton then," Ernest said. "We young kids was choppin' cotton." He explained that chopping is weeding the cotton plants, hacking around them, clearing them with a hoe. "After that, picking cotton by hand. That was some hard work. First time I chopped cotton I was nine years old. I chopped all day for my neighbor. He was a black man. He said to me, 'I like what you do. You come back tomorrow and I'll pay you.' Huh!"

Ernest grew, the farm grew, his brothers each built a house on the property, and they farmed together, their sons now too, a classic family farm — an extended family, living together in their own small community of one-story brick houses and high sheds, with a million dollars' worth of green and yellow tractors and harvesters. The family had stopped growing cotton twenty years ago and now concentrated on sorghum and milo and rice, like the other farmers.

"I believe farmers got to stop telling their sons to leave," Ernest said. "We know why our parents told us to leave. Because it was so difficult."

Seeing us, Ernest's older brother, Earmer Junior, had walked over as Ernest was speaking. He said hello and took a seat. He wore a battered wide-brimmed hat and faded work clothes. He was in his mid-seventies, but heavy work had clearly taken its toll on his body, and his hands were knotted and arthritic. He eased himself onto a stool, then sighed and said, "Sure was."

"But we don't suffer physical abuse no more," Ernest said. "Now it's more mental and financial."

Earmer Junior nodded and looked at his shoes, which were battered and dusty, like his hands when he leaned to tighten the laces of one.

"But there are benefits," Ernest said. "You can make a good living. Anything worthwhile is worth fighting for. We're still trying to prove ourselves. Years back, we'd look for finance. It was hard. The loan officers in the Farm Service Agency in the 1970s used to say, 'I'm not going to give you the loan. Y'all won't to be able to farm next year.'"

"What was your reaction to that?" I asked.

"We didn't give up," Ernest said.

Earmer Junior said in a gruff, downright tone, "Man said to me, 'Blacks got no business farming.'"

"In the 1970s?"

"Last year."

"Dumb as a box of rocks," Andre said, and blew out his cheeks in frustration. "The black farmer has to put up with more resistance than the others. It's not on paper, but it's true. We can feel the opposition."

With the sun lower and a slight breeze ruffling the leaves of the oak trees that shaded the houses, we walked around the sheds and barns, among the machinery, and then I got into Ernest's pickup truck and we toured some of his fields.

"A lot of white people have helped us," Ernest said. "But if you can tell a white farm from a black farm, you in trouble."

An Agitator at Cypress Corner

Sometime during those days in the Delta, driving again, this time with Roger Smith and Larry Terry, we stopped for lunch at Cypress Corner Bar-B-Q, on Highway 1 outside Marianna. The diner was popular with farmers, set in what had been an old corner store at a crossroads in the middle of plowed fields, no other structure around it. Near a stern sign forbidding the use of cell phones at the order desk was the menu: pork and beef barbecue, catfish and hamburgers, with the usual sides of beans, hush puppies, coleslaw, and fries.

I had the sense, entering, the screen door loudly slapping behind me on the twang of its spring, the place full of white farmers, that I was intruding on a men's club, a roomful of muscular outdoorsmen and portly, like-minded members sitting together and conferring. They dropped their voices when Roger and Larry and I — just as farmer-looking in our old clothes — took the only empty table in the middle of the room. We got no greeting, but neither was there any hostility. Something else occurred, a soundless vibe — averted faces, the odd glance, one from a man in a feed cap with a jaw like a ham. Conspicuous at our table, we were conspicuously ignored in a room otherwise full of cordiality.

When you're strange, I was thinking. In Little Rock, at the John Lewis event in the Mosaic Templars Cultural Center, a hall full of attentive blacks, I had attempted to hold a conversation with the well-dressed members of Lewis's entourage and local greeters. I had failed, got what I took to be an unmistakable rebuff, something rare for me in my Southern travels. I had a flicker of insight, that they regarded me disapprovingly as a peckerwood or a cracka.

Here at Cypress Corner I was strange again, in a new context, not peckerwood enough, sitting among thirty white farmers, picking at my barbecue with two black farmers, the only blacks in the place. And the silent message I felt was that I was that much more dangerous an outsider, probably a Yankee, undoubtedly a subversive, definitely an agitator.

Harvest

Standing at the edge of a field bursting with tassels of medium-grain rice — "We call it Jupiter rice; we export it to those countries that like to eat medium grain, like China and Japan" — Andre Peer pronounced his harvest a success. He plucked a stalk, and in a flourish swept the air with its heavy tassel of rice grains as though in benediction. He hoped to have

30,000 bushels, at roughly $6.50 a bushel, and would harvest the rice in a few days with the same combine he used to harvest his soybeans.

"What's driving the price up here is the floods in California this year," Andre said. "They couldn't get their rice planted. But even so, I'm still a small farmer. My neighbor has thirty-five hundred acres of rice." He plucked one of the tassels and handed it to me. "I didn't inherit any land like he did. He's on his forty-third crop."

I mentioned how I'd heard, from Dr. Calvin King and others, that a great number of African Americans owned land that they didn't farm, that even some large landowners showed up at food pantries, and that many had sold their inheritance.

"A lot of African Americans don't want to use their land," Andre said. "That's also called being lazy."

"Mind if I quote you?"

He raised his hands and shouted, "You go right ahead! Hey, they ain't makin' no more land. But who wants to get up at four in the morning and rassle with this?"

The complexities of farming were daunting. His farm loan was almost half a million dollars. His equipment and labor costs were very high—his used combine harvester cost $270,000. He had seed to buy, land to rent, and two huge grain bins (recently built for $212,000) to pay off—another note at the bank. "They don't want black people to own these," he said, "because this makes us independent." Each bin held 32,000 bushels, and one was almost full, with $128,000 worth of yellow corn kernels. All this detail made my head spin, and it was easy for me to understand someone who was unable to face the complexities of farming.

"This is like money in a bank," Andre said as we stood on a ladder at the top of a grain bin, looking down at the brimming yellow kernels. "If I need money, I can sell some of it."

But, he insisted, he was a small farmer, and from a year of working every day, of struggling to get loans, of worrying about fickle weather, of planting and weeding and fertilizing, of finding workers and keeping machinery in good repair, he hoped to make a profit of $100,000.

"Maybe more, depending on prices."

Roger Smith reported a good harvest, and so did the Cox brothers.

Rickey Bone had bad news: although he was only thirty miles north, he had experienced heavy rains, flooded fields, and—except for pumpkins—a failed crop.

Lunch Under the Pecan Tree

Samuel Ross, whom I had last seen at a table in Fargo, was climbing down from Andre's combine harvester when I approached, walking across a stubbly, just-cut field of straw-like soybean chaff on a very hot Delta day. This was in the flat, dusty land outside the town of Marianna.

"I own this field. I rent it to Andre," Samuel Ross said, laughing. "By running the combine and getting these soybeans in the truck, I'll be sure to get my money from him."

But he was less a landlord than a good neighbor, helping out in this frantically busy time. The truck, shaped like a tanker, was nearly full with a thousand bushels of soybeans, harvested that morning; ten thousand dollars' worth of beans would be taken to Helena later today to be weighed and loaded onto a river barge.

Two other men, Vaughn and Roy, were headed across the field to the yard of a deserted shack and the shade of a pecan tree and a nearby garden. The dusty, thumb-sized nuts were scattered on the ground. Staked tomato vines and bushes of snap beans filled the garden, and one edge of it was untidy with a tangle of yellowing watermelon vines and some plump watermelons that had straggled into the tall grass. A young man whose name I did not hear hugged a watermelon to his chest. He placed it on the back gate of Andre's pickup truck and slashed it open with a hacker, offering pieces to the rest of us.

To thank this helpful crew, I had just come from Marianna with the lunch they'd suggested, two buckets of fried chicken and containers of mashed potatoes and gravy. It was midday, the temperature in the nineties, all of us gathered in the shade of the pecan tree. These men had been up since before dawn, and this was their first meal of the day. Their shirts were soaked with sweat, their boots dusty. Samuel Ross, who out of respect for his age they called Mr. Ross, wore a straw hat that was sweat-stained too.

We ate in silence for a while, and then I asked Vaughn where he'd been born.

"Around here, nothing interesting," he said, a piece of chicken in his fist. "Ask Mr. Ross—he got the stories."

"Mr. Ross?"

"I was born in Indianola, Mississippi," Mr. Ross said. "Nineteen forty-six. My father was sharecropping for a white man—cotton, about twelve acres, maybe less. Small place."

"What sort of life was that?"

"Sharecroppers are always in debt," he said. "You plant, you work, and all that time you're getting credit at the store. But at the end of the picking you don't make enough to pay off your debt at the store, or your rent to the owner. So that debt is added to the next season, and what you owe gets more and more. You're always owing. Gets so you never able to pay it off."

He was describing the situation known as peonage, or debt slavery, the sharecropper tied to the landowner in a never-ending and impossible trap of owing.

"There were five of us kids, and my mother and father," Mr. Ross said. "We all worked. We picked by hand, we chopped. I was just a little kid, but I worked in the fields too."

He was still eating, mopping his brow, taking his time, in the lacework shade of the pecan tree boughs.

"So what happened?"

"We come to Marianna—Aubrey, in fact, which is nearby, where my mother had an auntie." He chewed slowly.

"I see," I said, but it seemed anticlimactic, the sudden shift from Indianola in Mississippi to this small town across the river in Arkansas.

"That's the story," Mr. Ross said. "It was dangerous."

"What was dangerous?"

He tossed his chicken bone into the trash bag and wiped his mouth with his handkerchief. He took a drink of soda, then said, "Dangerous leaving at night. Dangerous because we owed money. Seven of us in the car. We had to be right careful. We's sharecroppers with no rights. If they catch you, no telling what they do."

"You had to escape?" I said.

"That's right. At night. Seven of us in the car. Maybe two in the morning my daddy woke us up. We didn't know he was fixin' to run. We had to get out so fast we left everything behind—pots and pans, chairs, clothes, everything. All we had was the clothes we was wearing."

"That's dramatic—scary too."

"Very scary," Mr. Ross said. "We got in the car in the dark. It was a Chevrolet. This was 1953. My father was worried he'd get caught and dragged back. We drove all the way to the Mississippi and waited for the ferry to Helena."

Afterward, looking at their risky, desperate flight on a map, I saw that they would have driven a long way, probably on back roads, north to Drew or Cleveland, and then to Clarksdale, over seventy miles in the dark, in an old car, and another thirty miles to the ferry landing, more than a hundred miles altogether, all the time fearing that they were being followed by the angry landowner, threatening capture and punishment. They were leaving a county in Mississippi that was near Leflore County, where, one year later, Emmett Till was lynched for being insolent—"biggity"—to a white woman.

"They were no bridges then, just the ferry," Mr. Ross said. "I was six-seven years old, but I remember it all. Crossed over through Helena, came to Aubrey, and we were taken in by the auntie. And then things changed. We sharecropped cotton, but we made money here, because the owner of the land was black. Robert McCoy. He had a one-hundred-percent different attitude from the man in Mississippi. We raised sorghum, cotton, and our own hogs. I drove a tractor when I was thirteen. This was '58, '59. I got five dollars a day."

"No more debt," I said.

"We were never in debt after that."

With the money he'd saved, Mr. Ross's father bought some land, and later Mr. Ross himself added to it. He was now a large enough landowner to rent some acreage to Andre and, at this time of year, to help with the harvest.

We were still standing under the tree, eating. Then Vaughn and Roy went back to loading the soybeans, leaving Andre and Mr. Ross and me in the shade.

"Mr. Ross has the stories," Andre said.

"That was a good one," I said. "I've got another question, a personal one."

"Go ahead," Andre said.

"I'm just wondering, did anyone ever use the n-word with you?"

"No one ever used that word on me," he said. "I have never encountered it."

"I'm a little surprised."

"It doesn't mean black person, you know," Andre said. "It means abuse. Look it up in the dictionary."

"I've looked it up," I said. "It means black person."

"But it also means abuse," he said, and as he talked, he tidied up the chicken bones and soda cans and watermelon rinds, filling a trash bag. "Funny thing. We were over at the garage in Marianna, and there's two white guys in the back working on an engine. They didn't see us, but we could hear them. One says, 'You're getting on my nerves, you damned nigger'—to a white guy!"

"What did you say?"

"Nothing to say. We're just standing around the corner, out of sight. But then the guy who said it came out and saw us. He said, 'I apologize for that. I didn't know you was here.'"

"You weren't offended?"

Andre sighed, bugging out his eyes, as he often did when he took me to be obtuse or slow to understand. "He was saying it to a white guy!"

Mr. Ross said, "No one ever used that word against me. Maybe they said it about me some other place, behind my back, but I didn't hear it."

He stretched and yawned, preparing to walk back to the combine and finish the day's harvesting. He saw me writing in my pocket notebook, recording the details of Andre's story about the garage.

"Ask the older folks," Mr. Ross said. "They probably got a different story."

"The Whole World Is a Family"

In circulating around the Arkansas Delta, I kept moving and seldom stayed in the same motel two nights in a row. One afternoon, at a motel near Forrest City, a man dragging a suitcase out of his car in the parking lot saw me and said, "You're going to like this place."

I didn't know what to say, so I smiled.

"It's clean, not like the others." He leaned closer. "No Indians."

He was referring, without saying the name, to the inevitable Mr. Patel.

The motel was fine, clean, well swept, with the customary complimentary breakfast of orange Kool-Aid, brown-spotted bananas, and Froot Loops in a Styrofoam bowl. The clerks were older white women, the cleaners Hispanic.

Passing through the lobby, I was greeted by a smiling Indian, who introduced himself as the owner and manager.

"You can call me Bee," he said. "Kind of a nickname."

"Bee for what?"

"Bert," he said. "Bert Patel."

That made me smile. I said, "I think your birth name is more exotic."

Now he smiled. "Bhakti," he said. Bee and Bert were unremarkable names, but Bhakti, in Hindi, means devotion.

His was the old story: Born in Ahmedabad, in Gujarat, he had come to America as a student decades ago. Engineering. He had stayed. His marriage had been arranged in India. And like the thousands of other Patels, former students, recent arrivals, he had become a motel owner in the South.

"Warm weather is a factor," he explained, for his choice of region. As for the motel business: "Indians can't run restaurants, because we are Hindu, and the selling of meat would be a problem."

"Why a problem?" I asked, baiting him.

"How can you run a restaurant and not taste dishes?"

"No meat for you."

"No meat."

"What about life here in Arkansas?"

"Life is good."

I phrased the next question delicately, saying, "And the *hubshis*?"

Hubshi (sometimes *habshi*), the Hindi word for a black person, has an interesting etymology, deriving from "Abyssinian" (in Arabic, *Habashi*). It is the politer term. The Gujaratis I knew in East Africa, Patels and Desais and Shahs, would sometimes refer to Africans as *karia* — blacks (and I was a *dorio*, a white). Bhakti Patel understood what I meant by *hubshis*.

"I know *hubshis*. We have *hubshis* in Ahmedabad. They're Muslim."

"You mean Siddis?" These were Afro-Indians, the descendants of African slaves who had been brought to India, still living in various parts of the subcontinent, unassimilated, surviving on the margins, still visibly African.

"Siddi, *hubshi*, is same. I have no complications with the *hubshis* in Arkansas. Live and let live." He then became expansive. "To those *hubshis*, and others, and you, my friend, I say *vasudhaiva kutumbakaam!*"

He spoke it again loudly, like a battle cry, startling some other people in the lobby and causing the older women at the desk to wince. He was quoting the Sanskrit of an ancient Vedic astrological text, the *Mahopanishad*.

"The whole world is a family!" he cried, and grasped my hand and shook it.

"No problems, then? You're happy?"

He smiled and pointed through the front door to a new and slightly larger motel than his, across the road.

"Only that." His smile was grim.

"Who owns it?"

"Patels," he said. "Patels from Little Rock. My main competition."

Chain Gang

In Hood's Chapel, Georgia, in 1936, Erskine Caldwell and Margaret Bourke-White, in their old Ford, came across a chain gang — fifteen or twenty black men in black-and-white-striped prison clothes, legs chained together in shackles, digging a ditch, supervised by a fat white man in overalls with a shotgun resting on his shoulder.

"The gang goes out in the morning and the gang comes back at night," runs the caption in *You Have Seen Their Faces*. "And in the meanwhile a lot of sweat is shed."

Another caption to a photo of the same men, at rest under a tree: "It don't make no difference where you come from or where you're going, because when you're on the gang you're here for a long time to come."

Those words and poignant photographs stayed in my mind, and so driving through the Arkansas Delta town of Marianna, seeing five obvious convicts in orange jumpsuits sweeping South Liberty Street and hacking at weeds, I parked in the main square — Court Square — and walked over to them.

These black men were supervised by a black policewoman, of intimidating size and weight, whose name badge was lettered WILLIAMS. Though she carried a pistol, a truncheon, and a canister of Mace in holsters on her belt, she merely stood calmly watching the men. Her eyebrows were tinted gold. In her tight-fitting uniform, blue shirt, black pants, feet apart, hands on her hips, she was like a big blue barrel swaying on a pair of black posts.

"How you doing?"

"Jess fahn," she said. "How you doing?"

The men kept busy, didn't look at me, scraped and swept, and one shoveled the debris into a barrel.

"I'm passing through," I said. "Are these men from the prison?"

"Yes, 'deed, they are, but they good workers," Officer Williams said. And lest I take them to be violent offenders, she added, "They misdemeanors, they not felonies."

Drunks, disorderlies, trespassers, vandals, pickpockets, petty villains, mildly desperate or luckless men.

"You're keeping them in line?"

"It's all about respect," she said, looming over them.

They made their way, in the heat and bright sunlight of Marianna, from Liberty Street to Court Street, Officer Williams and the so-called misdemeanants in bright orange, pushing brooms, still desperate and luckless but almost dainty compared to the oppressed convicts in stripes that Caldwell had described and Bourke-White had photographed.

The Valiant Woman in Palestine

One of the women who had been unable to meet me a few weeks earlier was raising livestock some miles north of the small Delta town of Palestine. She was Dolores Walker Robinson, forty-two, a single mother of three boys: Mack, twenty-two, Malcolm, eighteen, and Franklin, twelve. After more than twenty years of travel with her serviceman husband, and work, and child rearing, and a sudden divorce, Dolores had returned to the place where she'd been born and educated, to make a life for herself and her boys. I thought of her as the Valiant Woman.

"I didn't want my sons to live the harsh life of the city," Dolores told me as we walked through her cow pasture. Most of the places she'd lived as the wife of a soldier had been urban, or at army posts near big cities. "I felt I would lose them to the city—to the crimes and problems that you can't escape."

Soft-spoken, she had a gentle manner, an unlined face, and a vaguely Asiatic cast to her hooded eyes, but when she moved—carrying a bucket or feeding her animals or unhooking and swinging a farm gate—she showed strength and purpose. She seemed to have great health, and though she was dressed in her farming clothes she had style as well, yellow boots, leather gloves, a red kerchief knotted on her head. The dominant quality she possessed was maternal, not just a reflection of what she had told me about moving back to Palestine and wishing to keep her children safe, but her whole approach to farming and to raising livestock, her instinct for nurturing.

Her small house and half her land were on high ground, and I thought of the lines in *Ulysses*: "The movements which work revolutions in the world are born out of the dreams and visions in a peasant's heart on the hillside. For them the earth is not an exploitable ground but the living mother."

With her savings as a certified nursing assistant, she had bought forty-two acres of neglected Palestine land. The shack on it was uninhabitable and falling to pieces. With volunteer help from friends and her boys, she fenced the land, built a small house, and began raising goats. Four years passed. She heard of an organization based in Little Rock called Heifer International, a charity devoted to ending hunger and alleviating poverty, with a simple but effective program called Passing on the Gift: "This means families share the training they receive [the mission statement said] and pass on the first female offspring of their livestock to another family. This extends the impact of the original gift."

Dolores enrolled in the program, and after attending meetings and training sessions, she received two heifers to fatten. She now had a herd of ten cows — and, keeping to the rules of the charity, she had passed along some cows to other farmers in need.

"I wanted something I could own," she said. She'd been raised on a farm near here. "I wanted to get my sons involved in the life I knew."

Apart from the herd of cows and goats, she had sheep, geese, ducks, and chickens. She encouraged the birds to sit on nests of eggs, sold some of the fowl, sold and ate the eggs. She grew corn to feed the cows. Because the cash flow from the animals was still at a break-even point, she worked six days a week at the East Arkansas Area Agency on Aging as a caregiver and nursing assistant. Her two younger children were in school, and the eldest was in college. Money was always a problem.

Early in the morning and after her day job at the agency, she went about the farm chores, feeding and watering the animals, repairing fences, collecting eggs. Some days she attended livestock management classes — she'd recently been to one in Greenville, Mississippi. "I made a lot of friends there. We're all trying to accomplish the same things."

Easygoing, uncomplaining, yet tenacious, Dolores Walker Robinson had all the qualities that made a successful farmer: a great work ethic, a strong will, a love of the land, a way with animals, a fearlessness at the bank, a vision of the future, a gift for taking the long view, a desire for self-sufficiency.

"I'm looking ten years down the road," she said as we tramped the sloping lane. "I want to build up the herd and do this full time."

Never mind that she was on a relatively small piece of land with a modest number of animals; being with her I was heartened, hopeful, happy, admiring her valiant spirit.

Many Southerners I met asserted — with grim pride, or with sorrow, or quoting Faulkner — that the South doesn't change. That's not true. In many places, the cities most of all, the South has been turned upside down; in the rural areas the change has come slowly, in small but definite ways. Delores Robinson was someone who had shaken herself loose from another life to come home with her family, and she seemed brave on her farm, making her life, looking after her children.

It goes without saying that the vitality of the South lies in the self-awareness of its deeply rooted people. What made the South an enlightenment for a traveler like me, more interested in conversation than sightseeing, was the heart and soul of its family narratives — its human wealth.

Old Man

Traveling alone in eccentric circles these last Delta days, passing from farm to farm, observing lives being led, I'd somehow been tracing the course of the big river. But even when I was far away from its flow, earlier in my trip, the river was on my mind, as a symbol of the South and a solace.

Some days in the Delta the river was the only vivid feature in a landscape that seemed otherwise lifeless — no leaves stirring, no people in motion, cattle like paper cutouts, hawks as black as marks of punctuation in the sky; the monumental stillness of the rural South in a hot noontime, all of it like a foxed and sun-faded masterpiece of flat paint, an old picture of itself.

Yet the river poured through the land, endlessly sliding between levees and low banks of trees and the throats of backwaters and bayous. The onrush was unfailing, the one constant in a region in mild flux, the unappreciated South, resigned to neglect and disappointment. No wonder so much romance and promise was attached to the river's muscly current, its course still a thoroughfare for goods and crops, bearing them away. As the

Delta farmers I'd met had said, "Take 'em to the river," because the river led to the world.

The Mississippi, the "Old Man" of Southern folklore, is the central image and the plot mover of the Faulkner story of the same name. Contrapuntal (as Faulkner grandly described it) to "The Wild Palms," in that book of the two tales, it is one of his most powerful fictions, the drama of a nameless convict in a rowboat who has been charged with rescuing victims of the great flood of 1927. Setting out from camp near the levee, the convict hears an unfamiliar and continuous sound. He has never seen the river before and is perplexed by the "profound deep whisper" in the air.

> "What's that?" the convict said. A negro man squatting before
> the nearest fire answered him:
> "Dat's him. Dat's de Ole Man."
> "The old man?" the convict said.

Later, in a small boat on the river, the convict rescues a pregnant woman from a tree and takes her aboard. The progress of the story is their bobbing up and down the Mississippi, the convict hating what he sees, disgusted by the strange woman, and yearning to be back on the prison farm, probably Parchman. The truth in the Faulkner line about the South, that the past is never dead, never past, is that his fictional convict's Parchman endures as a prison today. The Mississippi State Penitentiary was a bit south of Clarksdale, on the opposite bank, quite near to where I was now in Helena, Arkansas; it is still referred to as Parchman, from the old plantation it displaced. Parchman is also the subject of a number of blues songs, notably one by Mose Allison (who was born in nearby Tippo), which closes with the lines "Well I'm gonna be here for the rest of my life / And all I did was shoot my wife."

On a previous trip at Natchez, I'd thought how the Mississippi River is one of the gorgeous and unalterable metaphors for the South, oldfangled, its eddies flickering in sunlight, much of it undredged, with seasonal moods, thickening and slowing, or else brimming and breaching the levees, drowning and spreading fertile muck over the floodplain. As the river traffic has declined and riverside business has slackened, the river towns and villages have struggled. Floating casinos represent a last reckless gasp of commerce, the gambling on riverboats with fake smokestacks and fanciful stern wheels at Natchez and Vicksburg and elsewhere. The boats are as unseaworthy as chamber pots, moored in the mud, noisy with the jangle of slot machines, the embodiment of the Delta diminished, its past revived as fluvial kitsch as ephemeral as flotsam.

But Helena still mattered. In my last days, I crossed and recrossed the river, from Lexa and Marvell and Lick Creek and over the bridge to Lula and Moon Lake, towns or villages tucked into bends and bayous. I lingered at the depot at hollowed-out Helena. In *Life on the Mississippi,* Mark Twain wrote, "Helena occupies one of the prettiest situations on the Mississippi. Her perch is the last, the southernmost group of hills which one sees on that side of the river." The moribund Main Street now was an architectural heirloom deserving of preservation, like many other Main Streets in the South: ornate and ambitious shop fronts, dry goods stores and banks and theater marquees, cast-iron columns and the skeletal Cleburne Hotel, all from the late nineteenth and early twentieth centuries, when Helena was booming. "This was a great town once" is a repeated lamentation in the South. In Helena the river was a presence, opaque with mud, swirling with risen silt, wide and empty of boats, a brown serpent sliding south past Helena Reach, snaking through a wilderness of bayous, canebrakes, and swamps.

What I had seen of the rural South, with few exceptions, were level landscapes, deforested and flattened farmland, tufty, snow-like expanses of cotton fields, low hills at best, thin parched woods, their dead leaves crackling under the strutting claws of wild turkeys, meadows blinded by rows of hickories and black gums at the margin of stony roads that looked as if they led all the way to the nineteenth century, and many did: an exhausted countryside, circumscribed and spoken for.

But in the great hot sadness of a land that looked gnawed and hacked at and dug out and trampled, the river counted as a thing of beauty, a singular example of grandeur. It was no wonder that Southern writers, singers, and poets celebrated it. The central artery of the South, most of the lesser creeks and streams drained into it, fattening the thing and enlivening it. I smiled when I remembered its traditional nickname.

Often, talking with someone in the South — a young farmer, a fifteen-year-old mother, a perspiring and potbellied policeman, an indignant gun nut, a toothy preacher, an idle college student, a genteel bank clerk, a harassed community volunteer, or an insulted citizen—I gathered from their response that I was speaking a different language, one that caused them to open their mouths in incomprehension and squint at me. At first I took it to be my Yankee manner, the affronted wanderer, the unlikely stranger with unexpected questions, someone to be appeased or placated.

No, it was something else. It dawned on me slowly over months that to them I was an old man, who didn't really count for much but who needed to be humored or grudgingly respected. This response made me mutter and shake my head, because I didn't feel old. I felt—still feel—I am in the prime of life. But it's wrong to say that aloud or to object; protestation is a grim old coot's standard reflex. The hardest thing for anyone healthy to accept is increasing age. Yet why should you feel old if you're not infirm? I was fit enough to drive all day, hundreds of miles, and to manage this trip; to be lost and to find my bearings; to endure abuse at times; to take the knocks and reverses of the road and a degree of skepticism or hostility from folks en route. Possibly some of them cupped their young hands and whispered behind my back, "De ole man."

A news story I heard on my car radio gave me a clue. The announcer said, "An elderly man and a child were struck by a car late yesterday afternoon as they crossed Mabry Road near Highway 49 in Tutwiler," the sort of details that resolved themselves into the jerky afterimage of an unlucky man holding a child's hand at dusk, on the road, on foot in the heat—because the man was old and poor. Then more facts: "Warren G. Beaver, seventy-two, and his granddaughter . . ."

I laughed out loud and punched the radio off. Elderly!

THE OLD MAN twisted and flowed, ancient but ageless and unstoppable. Take it for granted and it may fool you, dam it and it will flood you, ride it and beware of its fickle flotation, study it wisely and don't make the mistake of believing that its surface—whether placid or turbulent—reveals the depths of its inner state. After a certain year, old is just old, indefinable. But oldness is also a sort of psychic weight, the accumulation of experience, which is why for the old nothing is shocking except the obvious repetition of human stupidity, and very little is new. All your electronics are toys. But it is not only the young who contrive to make you feel elderly, boasting of their toys, how cleverly they manipulate them; some older people connive at it too, as though in resignation, surrendering to bafflement, to expiate some fear or deficiency in themselves.

Travel has always been my way of defeating this sinking feeling, partly because travel is a form of escape, and travel itself—the elemental farewell—becomes the fugitive fantasy of a new life, travel inspiring a sense of hope. I began my real life, my life of intensity and solitude and discovery, as a twenty-two-year-old traveler in Africa, then elsewhere, everywhere, and that formed me as a writer, alert to every sound and smell and to the pulses of the air. At last, in old age, I came back.

I sometimes wondered what I was seeing in the South, and what I missed. So much of what we see is unknowable. You don't have to be young to have a keen awareness of sensuality. In the rural South I never recognized a beckoning of the sensual, though a certain sluttishness was the unmistakable trope here and there. The land bereft of temptations, of dreams deferred, was overwhelmed by reality, the presence of decline and death; a world where people are struggling to survive offers no occasion for the sensual, which if it existed there would look like another dead end. It was odd never to be in the presence of temptation, no flirting, no romance, no promise of another life. The valiant woman Dolores Robinson's sweet anticipating smile represented release and freedom, not passion, and her life, like many I encountered in the South, was a wounded one, with questions to which I did not have any answers.

Perhaps that is an old man's response to a long trip, but so what? This trip was not about me, not a journey to There and Back, overcoming obstacles on bad roads, an autobiographical diversion about my moods and petty successes. No one ever got to know me well, and few people asked anything of me. "What sort of things do you write, Mr. Thorax?" I took to be my triumph of anonymity. Only two out of the hundreds of people I met had read anything I'd written. Fine with me. It's better to be a stranger, without a past; it is a bore and an encumbrance to be conspicuous. Fame is a nuisance, and anonymity is bliss. (*Bene qui latuit bene dixit,* wrote Ovid. To live well is to live unnoticed.) I did not really mind being singled out by blacks as a cracker, or by whites as an agitator, in either case a controversialist, since those misidentifications helped me understand the mind of the person who saw me that way, and it helped me become, if only briefly, part of the scene.

But in the travel narrative of struggle, I was not the struggler. I was the bystander or the eavesdropper, recording other people's pain or pleasure. I knew very little discomfort, never sensed I was in any danger. No ordeals, few dramas. I nearly always felt I was in the presence of friends.

From state to state, county to county, I breezed along, and this progress was a way of understanding how lucky I was, because the confinement that Southerners feel, their keen awareness of themselves as stereotypes — provincials and yokels, in literature, in life — is something palpable. No wonder, given the obliqueness of Southern fiction (and one way to know a place is through its writing) — the evasions, the jokes, the showy literary metaphors. No wonder the grotesque preponderance of the gothic and the freaks — the reality was too brutal to state baldly, unbearably so.

Critics and academics extol the South for the abundant wealth of its literature, the region encouraging a storytelling tradition. This praise seemed to me a crock and self-serving. The opposite was the case: there was not enough writing, and what existed, with a few exceptions, was insufficient. Missing was a coherent introduction for the outsider to the South that exists, the South that I saw. Most of the South's fiction suggests that it's a broken place, but that's not news. Anyone who strikes up a conversation there or wanders a little can sense the crack that runs through the South from one end to the other, a crack that began as a hairline fracture in the distant past and widened through its history to an abyss. The broken culture, perhaps unmendable, that Southerners were still trying to reckon with bewildered some people into intransigence and made many others gentler, and needed more chroniclers.

"Read the books," people say. "Study Southern gothic and the evocative poems."

I say ignore the books and go there. The Deep South today is not in its books, it's in its people, and the people are hospitable, they are talkers, and if they take to you, they'll tell you their stories. The Deep South made me feel like a fortunate traveler in an overlooked land.

Catastrophically passive, as though fatally wounded by the Civil War, the South has been held back from prosperity and has little power to exert influence on the country at large, so it remains immured in its region, especially in its rural areas, walled off from the world. I had not realized until I spent some time there how cruel it was that so many American companies had fled the South for other countries and taken the jobs with them; that the American philanthropists and charities, benevolently concerned with poverty and deficiencies elsewhere, had traveled halfway around the world — was it for the acclaim? for the picturesque? for the tax benefit, for the photo op? for an escape from reality? — to bring teachers to Africa and food to India and medicine elsewhere; they had allowed the poor in the South, a growing peasant class, to die for lack of health care, and many to remain uneducated and illiterate and poorly housed, and some to starve. Though America in its greatness is singular, it resembles the rest of the world in its failures.

An old man gabbling another language, I was the quintessential stranger, but a welcome one. I made friends. With rare and farcical exceptions, I was treated with kindness by people I met by chance. "Kin Ah he'p you . . . in inny way?" was the rule. I cherished these experiences. In my life they will be fewer and fewer, because I am moving across the earth like the Old Man, to end my days in the sea, my dust to dissolve into undifferentiated mud.

Lingering, driving slowly and stopping often, procrastinating, I didn't want this trip to end. The land matched so many images I'd had in my imagination, and I understood what Rebecca West had written in the 1930s of Macedonia, how it was like a vision in the midst of muddled slumber. That was the Deep South for me: a dream, with all a dream's distortions and satisfactions, "the country I have always seen between sleeping and waking."

In a long traveling life, I had always depended on public transport: the clattering train, the slow boat, the tuk-tuk or scooter rickshaw, the overcrowded chicken bus, the careering East African minibus known as a *matatu*, the shuttling ferry, the trolley, the tram. For the first time I was driving myself the whole way in my own car. What made the experience a continuing pleasure was that, in my car, I never knew the finality of a flight, being wrangled and ordered around at an airport, the stomach-turning gulp of liftoff or the jolt of a train, but only the hum of tires, the telephone poles or trees whipping past, the easy escape, the gradual re-lease of the long road unrolling like a river, like the Old Man itself.

Except for the fart and flutter-blast of a johnboat below, skidding side-ways in the current like a soap dish in a murky sink, I saw no river traffic today from my parking place on Walden's Landing, on the Arkansas side of Helena Bridge. Beneath the bridge, a truck parked next to a conveyor belt had opened its hopper onto the belt, which was emptying into a moored barge the soybeans of Andre Peer and his fellow farmers, $600,000 worth of beans. In sharp contrast to the geometry of plowed fields on the nearer banks was the curvaceous Mississippi, slipping southerly in languid liq-uefaction, so brown it was like the solid earth made fluid. A "reminder / of what men choose to forget," the poet from St. Louis had written of the Old Man rolling along, pulling at the banks that were in places as soft and crumbly as cake, touching lives, stirring the edges of the land in inquir-ing eddies, squirming through backwaters, fetching up at bungalows and whispering at the fringes of cotton fields, then moving on. I was the river.

When had I ever felt this way, reluctant to go back to my desk, not wanting the trip to end, this procrastinating sense that, even after a year and a half of being on the road, between the Southern salutations of Lu-cille's "Be blessed" at the start and Charles Portis's "Be careful" at the end, I wished to keep going? That same St. Louis poet had also written, "Old men ought to be explorers." I could have kept on, easily, on this rare trip that was a cure for homesickness. Because the paradox of it all was that though I had come so far—miles more than I ever had in Africa or China—I had never left home.